PRECISION SHOOTING

The Trapshooter's Bible

For The Advanced Trapshooter

Those Who Strive To Be.

IT TAKES YEARS
FOR MOST SHOOTERS TO WIN MAJOR TOURNAMENTS.

FOR YOU IT COULD BE
THIS YEAR!

SPECIAL THANKS
To all who share their knowledge to the benefit of others.

IN RECOGNITION TO
All gun club volunteers who dedicated time and resources to further the great sport of trapshooting. For their unrelenting labor we truly owe appreciation.

PLUS
The A.T.A., P.I.T.A, and Olympic TEAM U.S.A. for taking trapshooting where it is today for future generations to enjoy.

AND
All the trapshooters who have given myself, and others, shooting advice and tips freely to enhance the quality of our sport.

DEDICATED TO
I Am; Father, Son and Holy Spirit

A THOUGHT TO PONDER
I believe I can.

A SPECIAL DEDICATION OF THANKS
For the Ten-Commandments; the Word of God and his infinite promises to come to the aid of all those who call upon Him. He is faithful and trustworthy beyond measure for he is the God of Miracles.

THANK YOU TO
Shotgun Sports Magazines and all the writers who sweat and strain to write articles for you to enjoy.

BEST WISHES
To you!

"PRECISION SHOOTING - THE TRAPSHOOTER'S BIBLE"

"Precision Shooting - The Trapshooter's Bible"
Printed in the United States of America.
Published by James Russell Publishing
780 Diogenes Dr, Reno, NV 89512

"Precision Shooting- The Trapshooter's Bible"
Written by James Russell
First Printed Edition © November 1997
Second Printed Edition © March 1998
Third Printed Edition © December 1999
Fourth Printed Edition January 2000 (no ISBN change)
ISBN No. 0-916367-10-X

THIS BOOK CAN BE PURCHASED FROM:

Any major bookstore via special order and on the Internet World Wide Web. Or you may order direct from the following:

➢ **Pinnell's Competitive Components**, Inc., P.O. Box 3703, Central Point, OR 97502 (541)-664-4994.
➢ **Shotgun Sports Magazine**, P.O. Box 6810, Auburn, CA 95604 (800)-676-8920, (916)-889-9106.
➢ **Clay Shooting Magazine**, Thruxton Down House, Thruxton Down, Andover, Hampshire, England SP11 8PR Phone: (01264-889533).
➢ **Scribani Rossi Olympic Shooting School**, GPO Box 1390, Sydney, Australia NSW-1043
➢ Phone: +61(0)295552728.
➢ Amazon.com, Barnes & Noble, Borders Books, Waldens Books, Books-A-Million, Chapters (Canada), Varsity Books, your local bookstore.
➢ Check our ad in the **ATA** - Amateur Trapshooting Association's **Trap & Field Magazine** P.O. Box 567 Indianapolis, Indiana 46206. Look us up on the Internet. Search via book titles or by James Russell Publishing or use search word; trap shooting. We are also linked on the major trap shooting sites.
➢ Visit our Website: http://www.powernet.net/~scrnplay for free trapshooting lessons and where to find professionals who give lessons (some are listed in this book).

TABLE OF CONTENTS

CHAPTER 1

"Faith is the most powerful force in the universe. Just believe it."

INTRODUCTION

"Those who know don't tell; those who tell don't know."

Trapshooting is a demanding sport requiring precise accuracy. One target lost and you may likely lose! Few sports have such extreme odds with absolute punishment for error. You simply don't get a second chance to come back with a winning play, not today. Tomorrow is another day, thank Heavens, but will it be a repeat performance? Apparently so. If targets are slipping by and the score keeper is yelling, "*Lost*" all too often, it's time to tighten up your sight pictures. Easy as it may sound, this is not a physical accomplishment as many believe but a mental technique. "*Precision Shooting*" will take you on an interesting journey into the mind, where you will discover yourself in ways you never thought possible. And when you are finished with the practice tips, you will be shooting with so much precision you'll wonder how you ever got any wins prior to reading this book! You will learn powerful techniques, many that may appear awkward and mysterious, some familiar, but all so potent you'll be seeing 'dustballs' floating in the air with dead-on hits greatly reducing the odds of losing a target.

The journey to success can be formidable, the path laden with challenge and heartache, and finding your way requires precise knowledge. You are now holding the road map in your hands. Most of the practice tips you will read I developed over a period of years from trial and error associated with scientifically proven technique based on research. I found most scientific studies, though valid in essence, fail to work for the trapshooter without significant measures of blending, alteration and reconfiguration of technique... it's a forgotten sport! What was needed is a technical book specifically for trapshooters. I couldn't find any true-to-form, down-to-earth practical instructional books on the market, so I wrote the first book "*Trap Shooting Secrets*" to fill the need. Then another black hole surfaced, trapshooting didn't end, but continued on to deeper levels. Shooters -- experienced and accomplished trapshooters -- needed a book to advance towards greater precision and enhanced accuracy. This book, "*Precision Shooting*" fills this vacuum. Many sports books tell you what not to do and are of little practical help to the shooter. We all know what not to do... show me how to do it right! This book tells you what to do, so you'll easily learn what you're not supposed to be doing. As a writer, it is a self-inflicted responsibility to share learned knowledge. Based upon truth and reality, the tips within have worked for me, for others, and will work for you. This information could prove to be of greater value to you than you may yet realize. The skills you learn here will not go unrewarded. The final authority is the reader, the trapshooter who desires results, and may the results speak for themselves. For the greatest authority is he who wins!

OLYMPIC TRAP, UT, DTL, WOBBLE TRAP, DOUBLE RISE, ETC.

Keep in mind we are discussing lead shot, not steel in this book. And this lead shot must obtain high-quality competition grade 5% antimony rating. Also, we are talking about handicap shooting, not singles or double-trap unless otherwise noted. If you shoot **DTL** (Down The Line) many of these tips apply to you with some obvious modifications related to taking the second shot. See the **Double Trap** section for assistance. This also applies to **Continental/Wobble Trap, Universal Trench** and **Olympic Trap**. There are many tips in this book that apply to these disciplines!

A NOTE FROM THE AUTHOR
"Start slowly, but do start."

It takes years for shooters to build precision, but for you it may only be a few weeks away. You won't learn gimmicks and mysteries, however, you will discover how to annihilate targets with superior consistency and accuracy with quick and easy suggestions and practice tips to resolve complex problems. Consider *"Precision Shooting"* a trouble-shooting manual to add to your library of knowledge. There are no shortcuts to success. It takes an innovative approach to take your game to a higher level. It is not necessary to agree with my logic, only to try it -- and in the course of implementation a deeper insight can be discovered, an invention to fit your form. The results are undeniable. I have included a Question and Answer chapter to help dissolve the innumerable misconceptions floating aimlessly about in search for an eager listener. It wouldn't be a mistake to read this chapter first, then proceed to Chapter 1. Scan and read the illustrations first, okay? It will help you. Upon request from readers, I have included in this edition more "double trap" tips in the illustrations section of this book and have done so in the *Trap Shooting Secrets* book.

Ultimately, people have to be successful. For if failure occurs too often interest fades and the trapshooter may abandon the sport. *Precision Shooting* can give you the accuracy you need to be successful and preserve trapshooting as a challenging, yet winnable, sport after all.

FAIR WARNING!
"Only two things are infinite, the universe and human stupidity, and I'm not sure about the former." Albert Einstein

This book alone may or may not be of much use to you without first reading *"Trap Shooting Secrets."* If you are still a short-yardage handicap shooter, odds are you are not ready for this book; not to say it couldn't help you, but you can't put the cart before the horse, or at least you should not do so. You'll need to polish up on basic physical techniques before you can move into the "invisible world" of mind exploration and fine-tuning eye and gun hold points, etc. After you have read *"Trap Shooting Secrets"* you will be much better prepared to step into *"Precision Shooting"* without score-busting mass confusion. The techniques herein are not for the novice but for the highly accomplished trapshooter who needs to 'fine-tune' technique, increasing ability to annihilate the infernal target, targets that unceasingly exhibit a scheme to slip by unscathed, resulting in the shooter losing the tournament. One more point, this book is written for short, mid, long-yardage handicap event shooters. Singles and doubles need not apply, although, I have included some double trap tips in the illustration section. You can order *Trap Shooting Secrets* book where you purchased this book. Or see title page of this book for addresses.

SPECIAL INSTRUCTIONS
"I believe I can... so I will."

Keep this book in your car. It will do you no good sitting at home when you need it at a registered shoot! When the day arrives that your shooting tumbles into a dark hole, you'll wish you had this book on hand so you can refer to it when necessary. Often, when you are shooting, something goes wrong and you can't seem to put your finger on what it is... if this book is in your car it will save you from disaster on the next event and quite well help you to solve the problem and win the shoot. So don't trust your shooting to memory alone, bring the book with you and keep it accessible at all times and you will shoot respectable scores no matter where you go.

DOUBLE-RISE DOUBLE-TRAP

"Double-Trouble - Twice The Fun!"

Double rise (double-trap) shooting instruction is included in *Trapshooting Secrets* and *Precision Shooting - The Trapshooter's Bible*. Do not confuse the subject matter as only in the double-trap sections will advice be given for this unique discipline. Unless otherwise noted the material herein relates to single barrel target shooting.

IN THE BEGINNING

"Prepare for the worst. Expect the best."

We won't spend much time on gun fit, foot position, stance, and point of impact, although I've supplied some drawings and text as a reminder of their importance. See Fig. 1, 2 and 3.

Adjusting point of impact (POI, also known as vertical lead) is almost like cheating, it's an edge. First, it's important to know that adjusting the POI is not patterning. It is the aim point where the shot hits the pattern board. Patterning reveals a subjective density and diameter of the pattern. Many trapshooters do not understand the importance of having a properly fitted gun that shoots where you look and having a high POI to make the job of breaking targets easier. These are all rudimentary though routinely ignored by more and more shooters entering competition. It is no wonder so many become frustrated with low scores and hardly ever being in the money. Do yourself a favor: **1,)** Visit a stock-fitter and make sure the gun fits you. **2)** Ensure the gun's POI is adjusted to at least 80/20 at 35 to 40 yards or wherever yardage is the zone you shoot in. Some shooters like a flatter pattern of 70/30 while some like a higher 90/10 impact. See Fig. 57 and 58 on POI. **3)** See a shooting coach so you can learn the right stance and rapidly gain tried and true techniques. **4)** Practice with an extra-full choke and shoot the events with a snug full or light-full choke or accuracy will always evade you. **5)** Wear a shooting vest. **6)** Use 3-dram 1 1/8 handicap loads with 8 or 7 ½ shot. **7)** Insure eye-prescription lenses are current. The money you spend here will be returned to you many times over. Consider it an investment... for it is!

TRIGGER WORDS AND WHEN TO USE THEM

"There is no one right way to accomplish something."

Trapshooting can be summed up as vivid images and feel, not complex technicalities. One simple thought or "trigger word" can set in motion complicated series of moves to translate into image and feel. Memorization is not an efficient means to recall what you have learned because you will certainly forget. We memorize automatically, it's all packed away somewhere in the gray matter, but it's the recollection of memorized knowledge that is key to excellent shooting. We memorize most efficiently through "association" and "visualization." When you read, you are storing knowledge in a weak file in the brain. When you do you invigorate this file of knowledge. Looking at a picture, you don't have to think to close your eyes to recall the photo. When you "link" words to a learned subject it's like recalling the photograph, but in this case you'll be recalling a mind-set. You may even forget to recall the "trigger word" on the trap line when targets are lost. This takes training to do as a habit, so let's do it. See Fig. 23 & 24 and *"Compressing & Expanding The Zone."*

1. Shoot a round of trap. Don't be so meticulously accurate, just make sure you are sloppy enough to miss a few targets. When a target does fly away unburned, invoke the trigger word *"Fixation"*. This is all you need to do. Easy, isn't it? But will you remember to recall this <u>before</u> you miss a target? Try this.

2. When you insert the shell and close the breach, invoke the trigger word until it becomes habitual. Once you are in the habit of fixating concentration, then you don't have to remind yourself because you will be doing it, and if fixation doesn't exist you will certainly feel something missing. Dismount the gun and start over.

3. Another trigger word: *"Put the bead on the target."* This will help you to stop shooting with your eyes only and get you back on track with using the gun sights for reference (back-sighting). You will learn that precision shooting is more than just seeing and looking at the target because you have to know when to pull the trigger! It can be done subconsciously, but first you must learn how to do it consciously. More on this later.

4. *"Positive Pressure"* to keep your head down on the stock!

5. *"Smooth Precision"* to swing smooth and see an accurate sight picture before pulling the trigger.

Depending on the conditions you are facing, the trigger word can be related to other techniques you need to recall. Clearly, if concentration is not the problem, perhaps the timing of your swing to the target is causing you to overshoot and miss, as on a breezy day. In this case you would use the trigger word *"Smooth and Slow."* Understand that trigger words are helpful aids, but the goal is to eventually not have to self-communicate these phrases. In time, with practice, all of these triggers will become automatic without need to recall. You don't want to constantly be reminding yourself what to do when shooting. But you do want to remember trigger words, for they can be invaluable, especially when that first target flies into the sky undamaged or you chip it, a clear warning a correction is required. Trigger words will help you get back into the groove when you derail. Throughout the text, trigger words will be given as examples for your use. You may develop your own, but do use them.

I was faced with a problem of shooting over the top of suppressed targets. Simply saying *"Stay under the target"* on each gun mount before calling did the trick. The moment I did not perform this reminder I shot over the top again. When shooting conditions change we have to force ourselves to conform to shooting properly, not naturally. To shoot where the target is, not where we think it will be. You see this all the time when breezes or traps set improperly upset normal target settings, shooters get onto the trap and drop targets. Then a pro steps on line and runs them all. So, when you recognize a problem, knowing how to compensate for it will rescue you from an otherwise damaging score. But simply recognizing something is wrong is never enough. We know something is wrong the moment the first target slips away. But what are you going to do about it?

RECOVERING FROM A DAMAGING SCORE
"If winning isn't everything, why do they keep score?"

Most shooters are creatures of habit and shoot the target the same way, the same timing, the same way again and again. This repetition *is* trapshooting, but there are times habits become damaging. This is why it is so important to stop for a moment to examine the targets before shooting the trap, not just looking at one target after you step on line. When the first target is dropped there will be a chain reaction and more will be lost. No matter if the problem is target suppression or excessive rise, trap or station misalignment, corrective action must be taken and that means you have to change something. The problem is we all tend to change the wrong thing and more targets slide away. Here are the common errors and what to do about them.

1. Target is lost, other shooters are losing them too, a chain reaction sets in. Extra concentration is required, but not excessive, strained concentration that induces extremely aggressive emotion. This stiffens up the swing and makes pulling the trigger a chore and often untimely. Are you watching the other shooter's targets after you reload? Do you know why you missed? It was likely you shot over the top and/or behind... the most common errors trapshooters make.

2. If the target is suppressed, you have to slow down your swing. If the targets are rising rapidly? You have to slow down your swing. Easy to remember. When you miss targets, you are shooting too fast, even if it feels right! Slow down, even if it feels wrong! Speed is a killer. Until you know how to adjust the zone, you simply have to slow down and break the target a little bit further away from the trap. But this is not being *cautious* where you begin to feel fear of missing, it's taking that extra time to see the target and smooth out the shot. You are extending the zone's depth a smidgen. Once you find the sweet spot where the target can be acquired and broken, then you adjust your eye and gun hold to compensate so your timing is reestablished. This is called zone shifting and you will be learning all about it in this book.

3. So far we have applying extra concentration to see the target and to slow down. Now it's time to stop worrying about the targets slipping away, even if they still are. This is a trick you must learn. Fear or concern of missing is a thought that will produce what you believe. This is all you need to do: concentrate, slow down, and stop focusing on missing. Now you should be able to see what the targets are really doing and you can then track them. But how?

4. Lower your gun hold an inch or two from normal if you shoot a high gun. The main problem handicap shooters have is not seeing the target properly and seeing the target too late, which causes a mad dash reaction to chase the target. And if the hold is too high -- which most high gun shooters are holding the gun too high -- you'll be swinging the muzzle left or right and that is absolutely damaging to precision shooting. You must ride the track of the target and that means vertical muzzle movement so the muzzle can pass through the target's true flight path. Most high gun shooters employ a spot shooting form where they call for the target, see it rise under the barrel and shift the muzzle left or right with a tad of vertical muzzle rise. This is called intersection shooting and you have to be an incredible marksman to pull it off because the shot string is really traveling left or right of the target like a car passing through a right angle intersection. By dropping the gun hold, you can see the target better and sooner, catch a ride on the target's true flight path and the shotstring will be aligned where room for error is in your favor. Just drive *through* the target and pull the trigger. Are you driving through the targets?

5. This brings us to swing. You have likely abandoned your swing thinking because you shoot long yardage there is no time or need for it. Watch the pros and you will see a swing. Yes, it is blink-of-the-eye fast and it takes a skilful eye to see it, but there it is. Pros who shoot a high gun do ride the target's flight path. They don't just swing left to right, they flow with the target to align the shotstring to their utmost advantage. So, you can see that by simply lowering your gun hold it forces you, naturally, to stop pushing the gun's muzzle around and start inducing a swing to the target.

6. Once a target is lost, shooters tend to get upset and try harder the next time. This is a mistake. You don't try harder, you try *smoother*! Slow down! The harder you try to hit targets the more you will tend to stab at them, spot shoot, snap shoot, cross-shoot the intersections, etc. You'll begin to *experiment* to correct the problem, often shooting faster or slower and dancing with various leads. Now you're in trouble. The next time you fall apart on a trap you'll see I am right about this. This will sound confusing to you, but shooting slower is not shooting slower, it is actually shooting faster. In reality, when you slow down your swing to a smooth motion, the target will be broken a bit deeper and higher in the zone. To you it feels agonizingly slow, and it *is* slow. But by simply lowering your gun hold and raising your eye hold, the zone compresses on all sides like tunnel vision. Now, with that slow swing your timing *increases* due to the zone shift and suddenly you are shooting fast and more accurately than you thought possible. Then when you add a smidgen of eye pre-focus, the targets slow down and you speed up (so it seems to you) but the truth is, people are watching saying, "*Wow, that shooter shoots fast and hits them hard.*" It's a slow-motion mode of shooting. By slowing down you begin to open the door to this mode of shooting. So all you back-fence shooters pay attention here. You don't shoot faster, you shoot "*slow and smooth*" and that's a trigger word you should be using.

7. When you are wildly missing targets, having a horrible day on the trap line, what are you doing wrong? Could be a ton of things. But this we know. You are pulling the trigger at the wrong time! The sight picture is wrong. If you are shooting with your eyes only, it will be hit-and-miss time. Now you can certainly relate to that, right? Pulling the trigger, missing, and not knowing why? What is happening is you are shooting on *time* alone. That internal time clock in your head is telling you, "*Shoot now,*" and you do and hit some and miss some. It's like roulette, gambling on a target, relying on luck. But five things are out of phase. **A)** You are shooting too fast as the subconscious mind is telling you to do so. **B)** You don't have your swing dynamics in tune with the subconscious mind's timing. **C)** Your eyes are not acquiring and following the target. **D)** You have lost the zone, shooting in a zone you can't shoot. This is called "*Out of Phase*" shooting. You'll recognize it when you find yourself pulling the trigger and the target doesn't burn and you wonder why. Trigger control is lost. Remember, the subconscious mind controls the trigger, not you. As much as you try to deny this fact, thinking you have full control of the moment you pull that trigger, you will only continue to drop more targets. However, it is not a 100% subconscious event in which you have no control. So what triggers the subconscious to pull the trigger? The sight picture. **E)** I bet squad influence is causing you to shoot too quickly. Keep with your own timing, play your own game. Be very aware of this and maintain control. Let no one influence you whatsoever.

8. When targets are being lost the sight picture is off. Certainly, that is a simple equation as other factors are also involved, but to simplify matters pertaining to this instruction lesson... you have to learn to see sight pictures and see them clear and precisely. If you are shooting fast, faster than your abilities, the sight picture will *flash* in an instant and that causes you to pull the trigger *fast*. Now, you should pull the trigger fast and crisply, but only when you see the perfect alignment of the sight beads (or end of muzzle) coming up onto the target. If you don't see this clearly you are not shooting with precision. Back-sighting is seeing the sight picture, beads/muzzle and target alignment, and if you are shooting in slow-motion mode this sight picture will not suddenly flash, but will be smooth and prolonged. If you want to stop missing targets, then learn to back-sight. If you want to stop pulling the trigger and missing, learn to back-sight. See the subchapter *"Seeing the Sight Picture."*

9. Shooting off the end of the muzzle is an advanced trapshooting technique. When we first learn to shoot our shotguns we are taught to mount the gun and check the sight beads for proper figure-8 stacking to insure the gun mount is correct. This is fine, but we tend to forget to lift our eyes up and away from the gun's rib so it is not seen when the target exits. What happens here is the eye is too close to the gun and that creates a very strong temptation to look back at the sight beads, which freezes the muzzle when we pull the trigger. We then shoot behind the target. Shooting the end of the muzzle is seeing the muzzle tip or sight bead only approach the target, not the gun's rib. This is difficult to explain or even make a drawing of it, but if you go to practice and just try using the end of the muzzle to point at the target instead of employing the entire length of the gun, you will see what it is. The advantage of this method is it allows you to get onto the target very quickly, as it doesn't feel like you are swinging a broad stroke, but a quick glide path right to the target. It allows for precise pointing control and flexibility. It makes the gun come alive. Give it a try and see how accurate it really is. Just remember to slow down because you will be able to come on to the target much faster due to its dynamic fulcrum effect. The gun acts as a seesaw where the muzzle rises and moves horizontally much higher, wider and faster, than a traditional swing would allow. But you still must see a solid sight picture.

10. Did you read, *"Trap Shooting Secrets"* on missing targets? If not, you need to buy the book. If you purchased the book, it's time to go back and read it again. Most missed targets are due to an improper setup.

11. Always look back at your setup when you drop a target, something has changed. The trick is to find it right away. If you can't find it, just slow down your shooting, but don't be cautious, just slow down the swing. By lowering your gun and eye hold, you can expand the zone so you won't upset timing and you'll naturally swing slower to the target. This will give you more time to really see and look at the target and better enable you to ride the target's flight path. This technique will work for you more than any other I know.

EXPANDING & COMPRESSING THE ZONE
"You can do everything right and still have it come out wrong."

This expanding & compressing the zone can be a bit confusing. See Fig. 23, 24, 34, 35, 77 and 78. The zone is simply a bubble-like view of where the targets will be shot. It's like cupping your hands by your eyes to obtain a confined area of view... which is why you should be using "blinders," for it helps establish a consistent zone and removes physical distraction and light refraction from the view. The zone, or bubble, can be entirely raised or lowered simply by adjusting your gun hold up or down. Raise gun hold and the zone naturally rises.

The zone, or bubble, can be expanded or compressed. It works in reverse here... raise eye hold and the zone collapses, seeing less target area. Lower eye hold and the zone expands... to see more of the target area. Generally, you want to see *less* of the target area so you can focus tightly on the target, so most shooters should *raise* eye holds to *compress* the zone.

Here's a better way to understand it. When you shoot double-trap, you are likely seeing a very compressed zone on the first target as you spot-shoot. The eye and gun hold is normally dropped closer down to the house. Since the gun is low, the zone has dropped and you see the target quickly. Since the eye is lowered, the zone has increased in total size so you can see the second target's flight location. If you hold your eye and gun hold too high on double-trap, the first target is shot too late, allowing the second to also escape the zone. There are more double trap tips, see the *"Illustrations"* section in this book and *Trap Shooting Secrets* book.

Go to the practice trap and find the zone, then practice shifting this zone up, down, left, or right simply by moving your gun hold point. You do this when you mount the gun with your eye looking straight down the rib as you check the figure-8 pattern of the sight beads. Look straight out and you'll see the zone is dead-straight ahead not up in the sky. Remember the three basic target angles on each post? Now you can shift the entire zone to take full advantage of these limited target angles you receive on each station.

Now take it one step further by compressing or expanding the zone by shifting your eye hold point. Raise your eye hold higher over the gun and the zone compresses. You will now see the area where the targets will be broken at some distance above the traphouse. The traphouse will be visible peripherally, but the central focal point of the eye is higher, exactly where you will break the targets. This is exactly where you will see the arcing of the targets in good detail as they bend in flight.

Combine both methods... and now when you see the target the gun will be in the proper position to acquire the target's true flight path, and your eye will be in the ideal position to see the target. Talk about precision shooting... it's hard to beat a shooter who uses the zone to his/her advantage!

You can see there is a gun/eye divergence taking place here. The eye is lifted up away from the gun prior to calling for the target. This is the best method to use for most trap shooters. Yet for others a gun/eye convergence of keeping the eye along the sight rib may work better. Everyone is different, but most are going to benefit with divergence. Why? Because it's the only way to shoot off the end of your barrel, unless you know how to make the muzzle-tip rise during the swing. You can blend both forms, too. You may want to employ gun/eye convergence when shooting shallow angle targets on post #3. Why? This will ensure you do not lift your head and sight-in tightly on those so-called 'easy' targets that often seem to slip away. Experiment with zones and find the formula you can use on each post that works for you. Once you find them, you will really be smashing targets with much more ease and precision. But let's remember one thing... it's still hard work to break them all. The moment you think it's easy you will drop a target. Don't become complacent. Work hard on each target and expect it to be a difficult shot and you will be mentally prepared to put the energy required into the task at hand. Remember: *"There are no easy targets!"*

COMBINING TRIGGER WORDS
"It's kind of fun to do the impossible." Walt Disney

Once you learn to break down each phase of the setup and attack the target with small trigger words you can later develop one trigger word to enable all of them, so your mind isn't trying to memorize ten or fifty of them. But first, use individual trigger words for intense training. To combine all of the elements, associate them with the word "*Power.*" This will, if you will it to be, combine all trigger words you have learned. It's like a computer program macro, automatically executing individual commands at the push of one button. You may use any trigger word of your choosing to do this. Just remember, it won't work unless you have developed a series of individual trigger words and associated each with a specific purpose.

You may have used the following at practice sessions: Smooth Mount, Positive Pressure, Focus Eyes, Drop Gun, Slow & Smooth, and others. When you have perfected each phase, then practice mentally combining them all at practice sessions. It is simply a mental command, "*Combined Power*" or something similar to associate all trigger words you have learned into one trigger. This will take time, maybe years to polish the method, but it will begin to pay off the moment you begin using it... just as individual trigger words paid off as you used them.

PRACTICE
"It's not that winning is so exhilarating... losing is just too damn painful."

Too many shooters over-practice. They practice so much at the range they become fatigued and lose their swing and most all of what they learned. You can't reliably learn ten things at once, but you can solidly embed one learned technique to remain with you forever. Believe me, if you only shot once per week and deeply learned just one thing each week for a year, you'd be a tiger to contend with on the trapfield. Here's a shooter who has 52 solidly built techniques blended into form. The problem is, most shooters don't know how to learn or how to practice! It's not a matter of how much you shoot, it's quality over quantity. The proper way to practice is to shoot just enough until you get what you want, then leave. Get what you want? Yes, it means you must have had a plan, with a reason to attend a practice session, something you want to improve upon. The plan is simple, each week learn a new thing. It may be getting in touch with your timing, tempo, sight picture, concentration, stance, swing speed, etc. Nothing complicated here at all, just one thing at a time. Look around you at practice. How many shooters have a true plan? Not many, they are just having fun shooting... hoping a revelation will materialize out of thin air, yet their form and technique are horribly flawed. No thought whatsoever is given to the setup... the most critical technique overlooked! Eye focus, call tone, visualization are never mentioned at practice sessions, yet how important they are! There is more talk about reloads, patterns, guns and excuses for missed targets than how to practice properly. Certainly it's fun, but it won't help anyone to ignore the true rules of the game. So we practice the same mistakes over and over again until the errors become technique! Having a good coach will separate you from the pack, so consider it if you wish to be a tournament shooter, or get down hard on the gun and practice with a clear-cut plan. Be serious and strive to learn. Be willing and ready to experiment, a lot! Use all of your might to develop self-control with dead seriousness to make each shot count for something. This mind-set will also slow down your swing, increasing accuracy and speed up your shot timing. Begin to get the feel for the game, for trapshooting is all feeling, not thinking. When you feel the game you are not reasoning and certainly never shooting on blind luck. You can't memorize shooting, you have to feel it. When you do, the gate to concentration swings wide open.

PAYING ATTENTION
"Here is the place; today is the time; this is the moment."

At the heart of trapshooting one must pay attention to the situation at hand. Many shooters don't pay enough attention, because they are concerned only with the target and hitting it. They are not fully aware of their situation and the events taking place around them, like observing the wind direction to get a read on target behavior or watching the trap target angles and speed prior to shooting. If you're too wrapped up in yourself, you're overdressed. Once you have given the proper attention to field conditions and developed a plan to compensate, you are well ahead of other shooters who fail to perform these evaluations. They go out on line and discover "strange things" happening then battle the quirks during the event, often with miserable scores to show for their efforts. When confusion like this sets in, it's awfully hard to pay attention to shooting! Now you can concentrate on paying attention without any surprise disruptions to your game. This phase is not easy to control. The mind has a tendency to wander, even when you are focused. You have to really convince yourself to look at the target with true dedication. This is often easy to do on the first two traps, but then concentration wanes on the next traps, or in your case it may be in the opposite order. If you practice eye fixation exercises, this attentive focus can be learned and maintained. You can also learn it through trial and error shooting 50,000 shells per year but that is not the most economical or easiest way to learn.

For this reason I recommend not shooting all the events at a registered shoot until a measure of stamina can be built. Ease into the events, slowly adding them as you develop concentration control. It does the novice little good, as well as the experienced shooter, to run out of steam half-way through a shoot and prominently blunder the handicap event where the big money is at stake. When concentration falls, stress rises, and when that happens the targets suddenly make you feel like you're facing a train. Then the timing goes haywire and scores plummet. I know you've experienced a loss of concentration. You ran the first two or three traps and whammo! You dropped targets on trap four. Have you ever considered that you may not have the stamina to sustain concentration for two events? I ran into this problem myself shooting the singles and falling apart on the handicap, or dumping badly in singles and winning the handicap. It was an up-and-down roller coaster never knowing which way the day would end. Focus takes concentration and not everyone has the endurance to tackle multiple events. The solution, for me, was to stop shooting three events and focus on the handicap. Once stamina was built, I could shoot the singles and handicap and later doubles. Concentration can't be forced or the mind will shut down. When you consider the big shoots are over 5 days of shooting, you can burn out quickly without even knowing it. You don't have to feel tired to be mentally exhausted. Consider backing off from over-shooting so you can play one event with all the talent you have. It's not the number of events you shoot that counts, it's the number of times you win. And you can only win if concentration is sharp, fresh and ready for action.

ONE-EYE & TWO-EYE SHOOTING TECHNIQUES
"Ambition, talent and the right equipment drives success."

One-eye vs. two-eye. Which is better? Both work fine. I'm not going to explain all of the nuances between the techniques that have already been hashed over in magazine articles and other books of the benefits of one-eye vs. two-eye shooting. Both techniques work absolutely fine in trapshooting, for depth perception is not a factor in trap as it would be for sporting clay shooting. Let's just get to the shooting tips.

Two-eye shooting has the advantage of holding a higher gun so there is less gun movement to get to the target. It is the most natural form of shooting but, believe it or not, requires the most skill to master. The problems arise with eye-crossover, holding too high of a gun so the swing is at a right-angle to the target, throwing a shot charge horizontally instead of semi-vertically. So, rule number one is to lower your gun hold so you can see the target better and gain that extra split second to get on track to ride the target's true flight path. This will now reduce crossing the gun horizontally at right angles and align your shotstring for a proper follow-through shot. See Fig. 82 and 85. Eye-crossover is a common problem and many high-gun shooters miss because of it. When the opposite eye takes visual control from the gun's eye along the rib, that is crossover. You can try patches on shooting glasses, but your better solution is to slow your swing. It is likely too fast as all high-gun shooters shoot way too fast and post low scores because of it. Also, eye pre-focus is improper along with gun and eye hold points. Work on these areas and you will find the solution. Another major problem you must resolve is to insure you still have a swing in your move to the target. Too many back-fence shooters have *abandoned* the swinging body pivot to *pushing* the gun's muzzle to the target. What is even worse, many of these shooters refuse to admit they have abandoned the swing! You'll forever have poor scores if you do this. If you are in a prolonged slump? You are likely *pushing* that gun. The first step to a cure is to admit you are doing it. Watch the pros, they don't push the gun, they use body English. It's often hard to detect, depending on the shooting style, but you *will* see the swing. See the *Questions & Answers* section for more details on this.

One-eye shooting is often rated as being a disadvantage. That is not true. It's a *different* technique and whenever you try to measure one form to a dissimilar style, arguments arise that should not even be discussed. It's like saying a Ford truck is better than a Chevy truck. It's all subjective, as both get the job done. Let's not split hairs and simply accept the fact the two systems differ. One-eye shooter will always see the target sooner due to the low gun hold on the house. Yes, there is a longer swing angle to the target. This can give rise to errors, but so will a high-gun shooter have the disadvantage of crossing over to align muzzle to target. So, the bottom line is both techniques have inherent faults and benefits. A one-eye shooter has the opportunity to clearly see the target's true flight path sooner. You must be aware that in the time you acquire this target and angle there is a large gaping distance between the target and the gun's muzzle. The tendency is to close this gap quickly, but that is where you get into trouble… swinging too fast to play catch-up. It looks like the target is escaping fast and you'll never catch it. The one-eye shooter needs a different setup procedure than the two-eye shooter. Primarily, adjust your foot position so you can make the swing with ease. Adjust your left foot (right hand shooter) to point where you will break the target and the swing will be unimpeded, especially on the extreme angles on post one and five. Experiment with differing gun and eye hold points to take maximum advantage of acquiring and swinging to the target smoothly. Swing speed does not need to be fast on a low gun hold if your eye catches the target properly, and that includes back-fence shooters. One-eye shooters always have a longer swing and that can cause problems because the swing dynamics in many cases are all wrong. You have to be extra careful to insure when you do pivot the muzzle is not rising. You want the muzzle to *drop* on the extreme angles. That's right, drop, not tracking a straight horizontal line, because the target is dropping not rising even though it appears to you it is running straight, it is not. This is why you'll shoot over the top of these hard angles. See the *Questions & Answers* section for more details on this phenomenon.

The conflict - Should I switch modes? This will raise a storm of criticism, but here it is in black and white. Many shooters who are holding a high gun and experiencing an *eternal* slump, and have tried everything, including coaching, and still can't shoot to win should consider reverting to a low gun hold. And then, even consider one-eye shooting. Reason? Why stay in slump misery forever? What if it works? You will never know until you try. Same is true with one-eye shooters. Maybe it's time to progress into two-eye shooting? Now, scores will tumble to amateur levels, and that's the price to pay. But it could be the ultimate solution. It could be a disaster. You will learn something new in the process and hopefully revert to your old form and now be a better shooter. It's the ultimate experiment! I would only do this under two conditions: **1)** You are an accomplished one-eye shooter and now trying two-eye. This is less painful. **2)** All other things have failed and this is the last recourse. Keep in mind; all disasters are not permanent. They set you back, but knowledge and a new awareness of the game is gained. That is what you want, more insight. It's better to try this last resort than quit the sport.

CHAPTER 2
"Indifference? I have no opinion to give."

THE SETUP
"Change your thinking and you'll change your life."

The setup is not a chain reaction event to be taken for granted. It is not to be taken lightly because it is here where the shot is made or lost, long before you track the target and pull the trigger. The setup is a logical procession of correct foundational processes each standing alone to perform a montage of smooth preparation procedures to enhance the odds of addressing the target. A well-executed setup results in a precise shot. If the setup is faulty, everything suffers as the swing can never be well-timed. You must concentrate on good posture, geometrically correct body alignment to produce accurate swings and good aim. The setup is 95% of making good scores. Practice your setup so it will become second nature. This is easier said than done. How can I remember all the things I need to do? You can't memorize for if you do you'll surely forget and revert to old bad habits. So, you need to *"feel the game."*

FEELING THE GAME
"It's a great thing to do a little thing well."

Trapshooting is not placing a gun to shoulder, calling for the target and chasing it down for fun and games. It's a demanding challenge and a daunting task full of uncertain variables. It's a feeling, a mood, an attitude of inner seriousness and momentous aggression that must be developed to see high scores consistently. You must feel the game! Let's take a stroll to the practice trap. Perform the following:

1. The feel begins in the setup. You're on station, close your eyes, feel your feet on the pavement. Do you feel steady, rock-solid and comfortable? Beware! If you are too comfortable, fluid or relaxed, your foot position and stance may be totally incorrect! You should feel a sense of power in your feet and body. A sense of absolute control. Open your eyes. Do you still feel the same way? If not, adjust your feet and stance until you do. I recommend you begin at the full side-on foot stance to structurally align your body to a rigid form. This will iron out many posture and swing defects. Once you have the "feel" you can revert to the traditional 5-past-3 foot stance position. Use 5-to-9 if left-hand shooter. Beware, changing foot position and altering body stance alters geometry of the swing and requires a steep learning curve to remaster.
2. Close your eyes and shoulder the gun, slowly. You should feel every muscle in the movement and, most importantly, feel shoulder pressure! Open your eyes. Your eye should be centered down the sight rib and the beads stacked in a figure-8. The muzzle should not be canted. It must be level and true. If not, you are not mounting the gun properly. If you still can't get it right, the gun does not fit you. Stop here! Go to the stockfitter immediately. Continuing on will only create more frustration every day you shoot. The gun must fit to shoot well! Mount the gun. What did you feel? Are you hugging the gun? Do you feel cheek pressure? Grip pressure? Gun balance and weight direction on swing? You need to feel these things so you can identify when you are doing something right or wrong.
3. Focus your eyes in the proper area. You should feel when it is right, along with seeing it is right. If it doesn't feel right, dismount the gun. Now call for the target and chances are you will miss too many. What went wrong? Think! Here's the answer:
4. You didn't develop a plan. Know which station you are on and what angle targets you will receive, and visualize where you plan to break them. Visualize the target breaking. This too is a 'feel' not to be disregarded. Be prepared with a plan. You should be ready to pounce on the most severely angled target emerging from the trap. Expect it without anticipating it. You don't want to be surprised, but absolutely ready for it and confident you will attack the target with unrelenting authority... this too is a 'feeling' you must develop.
5. Call for another target. You should feel your body moving to the target, not just your arm! Practice swinging the gun at home, smoothly, with eyes closed. Feel that gun in your arms. Feel the cheek pressure. When you shoot with <u>feeling</u> it is hard to mismount the gun, swing too fast, or miss targets. You and the gun must feel as one.
6. When the feeling is correct, you will pull the trigger. This feel is developed with sight pictures. You will know when you have it right when you recognize the target is smoked even before you pull the trigger. Do not feel the trigger! You should never feel the trigger. If you do, then it needs adjusting or you're using conscious

thought which distracts concentration. The gun should fire the instant the sight picture is correct, without any deliberation by the shooter. The moment you think of the trigger, your scores will tumble. Slap shooting with the pre-firing mode -- finger entirely out of the cage -- is the most difficult form of trigger control to learn, but it pays money, eliminating flinches and mind-searing trigger hang-ups. It's the technique I use which insures a subconscious trigger pull and deeper entry into the target for true-center hits. Release triggers are useful also to reduce trigger feel, though dangerous if mishandled. Let the subconscious mind handle the trigger and you'll have less trigger / timing problems. Many shooters say, *"Breaking targets is all in the trigger."* Let me reassure you it isn't in a device. It's all in the mind! Many shooters revert to a release trigger to resolve a flinch, but all along the flinch was a timing problem, a problem in setup, chasing targets in panic dashes, shooting without a plan, improper gun fit, flawed concentration, improper visual focus, etc. Recoil flinching, in reality, is a rare event unless the gun does not fit and slams your face unmercifully. In the above examples, switching to a release trigger will not raise your scores. Use a release to take your mind off the trigger if need be, but is better yet to work on the true cause of the problem than search for a quick fix that may never work for you. Many pros use release triggers, and many do not. Actually, breaking targets is all in the eyes! Eye controls trigger!

7. When you are attacking the target, you should "feel" the swing move and feel the sight picture. The latter should feel like, *"I got it!" "It's dead." "Right on."* It feels right and it is right. Learn to feel the game! When you do, it opens an entirely new dimension to annihilating targets with low conscious effort. When you feel the game, confidence and authority rise to incredible levels, along with precision. One more thing: feel the shot. Now you're not being so mechanical and habitual but "in tune" with the game.

GRIP PRESSURE
"What if this weren't a hypothetical question?"

Smoothness can only be accomplished with proper grip pressure. The forearm grip should not be ironclad tight. You already know this, but are you aware grip pressure is consistent when shooting-off in a tense situation? Once tournament anxiety sets in, tension increases and it kills precision. Feeling the game doesn't totally eliminate tension but it does minimize it. The brain, once trained and acclimated to feel, will impel the muscles to relax when the target emerges. The trigger grip should be snug and the angle of the grip should enable you to pull the trigger easily and squarely. If the trigger finger is not square, trigger timing will be upset and inconsistent. As the trigger edge indents the finger in a centrally focused area (finger print area) the nerves in the finger at this point become hypersensitive, sending signals to the brain, indicating possible pain, even though no pain is felt. This causes a shooter to flinch and pull the trigger randomly. A canted trigger can be installed to correct the misalignment. Also, length of pull affects the geometry of the trigger finger; if it's too long or short it can induce flinching and inconsistent trigger pulls. As you can see, everything affects everything. There are complications to this game to be recognized and dealt with. Get the hint that gun fit is critical?

ADDRESSING THE SHOT
"Failure is a temporary state that seems to last forever."

Many shooters fail to understand the importance of the setup and that is why many shooters shoot inadequately. There is also a swing setup to be recognized that is founded upon the foot position, stance and gun mount setup discussed. To determine if your swing setup is properly executed for repeated, solid target breaks, you must examine how you swing the gun. If the primary setup routine is flawed, the swing setup will produce all sorts of swing errors, so keep checking the setup to insure you have it right and it stays right.

1. First, shoulder the gun, close your eyes and feel the weight of the gun on your arm, hand, shoulder, back, legs, and feet. If you feel unusual strain it means: **A)** You're out of shape and muscles need to be toned. **B)** Your foot position and body stance is flawed and you are not standing square to the traphouse. **C)** The gun does

not fit and / or is out of balance. **D)** The way you hold the gun is revealing the gun is not braced snugly with the muzzle weight excessively dragging down on the forearm grip.

2. Now dismount, rest for a spell, shoulder the gun and swing as you would when tracking a straightaway target, a quarter angle, and a hard angle. Swing to both left and right targets. Try it with your eyes closed. Feel every muscle movement. You should not be using your arm to push the gun to the target. Use your upper and center body, pivoting from the hips in a fluid manner. This may not appear to be a dramatic revelation, but it will make the difference between a well-controlled shot and a poorly inconsistent, luck-of-the-draw shot.

3. Check your shoulders to see how tilted they appear when you call for the target and when you track the target. Depending on technique, especially those who cant the muzzle, a slight tilting or bowing of the shoulders is okay as long as one shoulder does not rise and the other fall excessively. If so, the muzzle will likely rise or fall, as you track the target. This again is okay, but only if you know what you are doing and have incorporated muzzle drift into your style... but most shooters don't consciously use gun canting methods in trapshooting.

4. Now hold the gun to the traphouse and instead of calling, cough. Did the gun move? Try it again. Probably won't this time since you snuggled up on the gun and that is good. Memorize the feel. You don't want the gun jiggling when you call for the target as it causes missed targets from eye-hand coordination disassociation.

5. You can track your muzzle along a wall-to-ceiling joint on a straight line to test the stability of your swing. You should also track curved lines. Why? Precise control. Those medium left and right targets do not travel in straight lines and the moment you try to track a bending target your face will lift from the stock. So try this; shoulder the gun and with your cheek down tight, trace a large one-foot diameter figure eight with the muzzle. Don't use your forearm to guide the muzzle, use your cheek and your body! Your forearm should only be holding the gun upward, not pushing the muzzle around. This exercise is a good habit to build body English into the control of your gun. It's easy to keep your head down snug to the comb when you use your cheek to manipulate the gun's swing. Trace slowly. You don't want to whip the gun around erratically. Feel the smoothness of controlling the gun as the muzzle swings. Feel the precision when you hug that gun and use body English! If it feels as though you have solid control of the gun, it's because you do. The gun and body work together in harmony, not independently. Move forearm and body together.

6. Watch a game of basketball, notice the shooter's eyes are totally transfixed to the target basket when the shot is made. It is important to visually select a precise target for eye-hand coordination to be precise. Your eyes will control all moves as long as your eyes are truly looking at the target. If you do not see the target clearly, coordination becomes tilted and sloppy with a missed target due.

PRACTICE TIPS Phase 1.
"This is the devilish thing about trapshooting: It is hellish as it will not always conform to our whim."

Let's do some practice on the trap line in real time.
1. Call for the target, swing as you normally would. Evaluate if the swing was excessive. Now try using your cheek and upper body to move the gun to the target. Be fluid and relaxed if possible. Did you see it? Go ahead, try it again. Now did you see it? You may be asking, "*See what?*" Did you see how easy it was to keep the sight bead locked onto the target? If you did it right, you would have used many muscles to track the target, primarily the neck, shoulder, back and hips. You would find that you are no longer chasing a target trying to get the sight bead to catch up to the target, but truly getting on the target much quicker and tracking it like a heat-seeking missile. Try it a few more times. Notice that you are no longer primarily using the arm to push the muzzle to the target. That's a great accomplishment you have just achieved. You will even notice flinching dissolving, too, because your muscles in your arm are not sending jerky signals to you brain and visa versa. The swing is smooth and since you can catch the target quicker, there is no perceived rush or anxiety the target will escape. Suddenly, shooting becomes more comfortable and controlled. Of course you will need to fire a few thousand shells to adapt to this new form of gun control, but I'm certain you will see the light and pursue

perfecting this highly accurate swing technique. Remember, the muzzle should accelerate gradually to the target building speed constantly, smoothly. Trigger word: *"Be smooth."*

2. Notice how easy it is to cant the gun muzzle so you can: **A)** Attack and reach the target quicker. **B)** Position the sight bead on the target snugly. **C)** Place slight canting forward of the target to bend the shotstring for direct, dead-on hits. **D)** See the trajectory of the target clearly. **E)** Muzzle control is precise and in full control. **D)** Your arm is no longer stabbing at the targets. **E)** Automatic lead is placed on the target. **F)** Accelerates muzzle speed. **G)** Your scores rise! Okay, after a few thousand rounds scores will rise, but rise they will... guaranteed!

3. If scores do not rise, or they rise and suddenly fall when using the cant method, remember to not overly cant the gun. You don't need much. Sometimes, at least I have found, I've had to stop canting the gun so I could cant the gun properly. The problem arises when we "think" of canting the gun. Don't think of it, just let your body make the moves to get the job done without thinking. Make certain your stance is rigid and you bow gently, using the cheek to control muzzle alignment to the target and to apply the cant with your upper body. Never twist the muzzle with your forearm. As you bow, the gun swings to the target, but your cheek pressure puts the sight bead exactly where you want it. Make sure your foot position and stance is rigid otherwise, the muzzles will tend to dramatically rise or fall on the swing.

4. You do not have to use the cant method if you don't want to. You can swing straight to the target as many shooters normally do with a solid on-the-line swing, but you still must flow smoothly to the target using body English. If you don't, you'll resort to erratically pushing the muzzle to the target with your arm. True muzzle control is lost when you "push" or "pull" the gun and your cheek will rise as a bird flies. You know you'll miss clean if your head lifts. You must learn to use your body to move the gun if you want to be a precision shooter.

5. I want you to practice shooting a target, but do not follow through. Freeze the muzzle the moment you pull the trigger. Why? **A)** You don't need follow through on trap targets. You can break them with more precision without follow-though because you will know exactly when to pull the trigger seeing a clean sight picture instead of a blurry sight picture when following through. **B)** I want you to experience looking at the sight picture to see what you did right or wrong. **C)** When you look back at the sight bead or muzzle I want you to understand that when you do this, taking your eye off the target, you'll miss clean, shooting behind the target because the muzzle will stop its swing. You would be surprised to learn that many of the lost targets are due to taking your eye off the target. Once you experience it, you'll know not to do it again. Keep in mind, if you follow through on a trap target, your muzzle is passing the target, which has a tendency to drag your eye off the target to the muzzle. Another missed target! When your timing is right-on and your gun's point of impact is properly set, you will be able to put the sight bead right on the target and puff it... without lead, without follow-through. This, however, requires dedicated practice to speed up your swing to the target and fine POI tuning. The rewards are no less than incredible scores! When you blend and apply the tips in this book... it will happen!

6. Shoulder the gun to a mirror. Insure your shoulders are squared and the muzzle is not canted in any way. The gun muzzle should not dip downward. Close your eyes and mount, then open your eyes. Canting must not take place on the initial gun mount, only after the gun is properly shouldered. If the gun cants when mounted: **A)** The gun does not fit you. **B)** You are mounting the gun wrong. **C)** Your stance posture is incorrect. **D)** Foot position is inadequate. **E)** The gun is too heavy or out of balance. **F)** Sight rib is bent or beads out of alignment or stock has slipped out of adjustment or just plain loose. **G)** Your gun hold grip is too tight or too loose or in the wrong place. See Fig 9. In most cases the gun does not fit. The secondary reason for mismounting is simply not knowing how to mount the gun properly or failing to repeat the correct procedure consistently, usually by rushing the setup. Slow down and be precise. It's important! Slower is better.

7. Examine your mounted gun and your swing with diligence, for if it is wrong the muzzle will swing excessively and tend to twist away from the target's flight path as you move to the target. No wonder so many targets are lost! The muzzle must swing on the target's plane. Shooters who do not cant their guns will have the most problems here, for once the swing commences it is near impossible for the swing angle to be corrected in mid-

flight. This is often the cause of shooters randomly stabbing at the targets. Here's a tip for those who do not cant. Control the gun by rocking the shoulders! Keep both shoulders level and rock by pivoting the shoulders with the waist, using cheek pressure to make fine alignments to the target. The trick is to rock the shoulder ever so slightly, not lift one and drop the other or as shrugging your shoulders. Both shoulders will gently rock simultaneously as a seesaw. Your shoulders will dip, but always on the same plane as a rigid fulcrum. You don't want your shoulders to do the work alone. Use your back muscles and the hips. You'll need to keep the sight bead below the target on the swing to compensate for the tendency to overshoot the flight path.

MIND CONTROL
"Imagination is the one weapon in the war against reality." Jules de Gaultier

Fig. 11 shows how you will be rotating your right index finger in a circle moving toward you while your left index finger will rotate in a circle away from you. Go ahead and try it, you'll have a tough time and may even believe it is impossible to do or sustain, but it really isn't. What is the purpose of this exercise? Separation of hand motion. Your forehand assists in controlling the gun while your opposite finger pulls the trigger. By separating the movements you'll obtain enhanced control of trigger and swing motion. Keep trying the exercise until you can do it with relative ease. It will always remain difficult to do, but it will be easier the more your try. Once you have it down, rotate the fingers in the opposite direction. You will feel terribly uncoordinated and frustrated, but keep on trying you can do it! Here's the trick: do not look at any finger. Focus between the fingers so both remain in peripheral vision. Visualize each finger running inside the race of a metal ring, as this will help guide the fingers into tight concentric circles. Don't move the fingers only, you must rotate the entire hand and arm. When you have satisfied the requirements of this test, you will find that your can keep your visual attention on the target yet feel every body move required to move the gun to the target and pull the trigger. That is the power of separation.

An entire book can be written on mind control techniques, in fact, there have been. Let's just say your thoughts will determine the outcome. If you believe you will shoot poorly and lose the event, you likely will. Negative thoughts, like a law of the universe, will materialize exactly as you think. Shooters who win are not negative thinkers. If you don't believe in yourself, then what chance do you have of performing above your expectations? If you would like to know more about the science of mind and the realities of the mind's power, you can contact: *Science of Mind* magazine, P. O. Box 18087, Anaheim, CA 92817-9942, (800)247-6463. A book you should first read is "*How To Change Your Life*" by Earnest Holmes. It's available from Science of Mind. Very powerful principles you can certainly use in trapshooting. This is not positive thinking, it's understanding reality and the power available to you to live a successful and rewarding life. Give them a call.

HEAD-LIFTING
"The thing that impresses me the most about America is the way parents obey their children." King Edward VIII

No matter how good you are, head-lifting still happens. It is still the primary reason why precision shooting and targets are lost. So here are a few tips to put an end to the scourge.

1. Hug the gun and hold firmly to shoulder with cheek down snuggly. Not too hard or too soft as both can cause the head to lift away. By hugging the gun and feeling it, the gun will follow the eyes.
2. Keep eyes on target, but gun must move with eye and to do this "force" your cheek to be solidly glued to the comb. You must feel this cheek pressure at all times. When you don't feel the pressure the gun will move all right, but it won't be pointing where the target is. Cheek pressure breaks targets!
3. Abolish lazy or comfort shooting. You must hold the gun with a definite purpose and do so snuggly so it feels a part of you. Don't simply mount the gun and call like so many shooters do. Imagine the gun as though it

were an extension of your body. If you and the gun feel as one integral entity, scores will rise and the head stays down.

4. Steer the gun to the target with your cheek. Even if you don't actually steer the gun, due to your technique, at least feel as if you are. Imagine that the muzzle can't move unless your cheek allows it to move. Doing this will force your cheek down as you call and swing, otherwise, your head will rise and scores will fall. Cheek pressure is extremely important to maintain, always. Just try it and see what happens!

5. Increase cheek pressure slightly as the muzzle swings. In the bow technique of canting the gun, the cheek does exactly that so you can never lift your head.

6. Do not shoot beyond your ability. Increasing your timing and tempo will cause head-lifting.

7. Use a louder more aggressive call. If your call is weak, your head will lift in an attempt to see the target when you receive a borderline slow pull. Try applying increased cheek pressure as you call for the target.

8. Never swing hard. The harder you swing, the more the gun will move away from your face. This is one reason why you should never push the muzzle to the target, but use body English. Be smooth.

9. Your eyes and the gun must simultaneously flow smoothly to the target. Don't turn your head to look at a target or snap your eyes quickly. If you evaluate, you may discover yourself doing this, especially when a target takes you by surprise. These are panic reactions, moving the cheek away from your gun, and if your eyes snap quickly, so will the muzzle. Be smooth. Proper eye pre-focus will solve the problem. See Fig. 27, 28, 48, 49, 72, 73, and 74.

MASTER THE MENTAL GAME
"Things are only impossible until they're not." Jean-Luc Picard

I'd like to explore every aspect, but unfortunately, this would require a book in itself to pursue in detail. So, I'll simply probe a few tips listed in mini subchapters. Shotgun Sports sells a book titled "*Mental Training for the Shotgun Sports*" and will be well worth reading. Use the following tips just before you go to shoot.

PRESHOT ROUTINE
"Discovery consists of seeing what everybody has seen and thinking what nobody has thought." Albert von Szent-Gyorgyi

Develop a preshot routine. There are two of them. **1.)** It is important to try to do the same things, almost robotically, when preparing your equipment for the shoot. This routine begins to set up the mind for the shoot. **2.)** The second preshot routine is what you do after you smoked the target. You must be machine-like so you can repeat the process. It also is necessary when you get into a high-pressure shootoff. If your preshot routines are perfected, you'll perform much better than without them. Often, it's the little things that count the most in life. So it is in trapshooting.

CONCENTRATION
"If you shoot at mimes, should you use a silencer?" Stephen Wright

You must *learn* concentration. Concentrating for a half-hour can be tiring. Concentrating in a 100-bird event can take an even greater toll on stamina and is exhausting. So, it is important to limit the amount of concentration you do prior to shooting the event. When the event begins, concentration should be controlled, turned on and off at will. You turn it off after the target is broken and turn it on as the gun is mounted. This will give your brain small, though vitally needed, rest breaks. If you stay keyed up too long, you'll run out of steam and discover scores blown on the last trap due to mental fatigue. This also applies whenever you use the practice trap before an event. Don't over-concentrate when it is not needed. See Fig. 13.

The mind can only concentrate on one thing at time. Concentration requires 100% devotion upon an object. Right now you are "thinking" and your mind is concentrating lightly as you read, yet the radio or some other background noise is present. Concentration is often misunderstood and habitually overlooked, especially with shooters who are addicted to machine-gun squad rhythm. They shoot out of habit, *"It's my turn, got to go!"* They fail to take that extra second to "focus" the eyes or mind, nor is there any substantial visualization taking place. Many inconsistent shooters I've talked to have no understanding of these precision shooting techniques, and admit they don't use them. No wonder they are so inconsistent and often heard to say, *"Handicap is a crapshoot not a trapshoot!"* You can be as accurate on handicap yardage as you are on the 16-yard line. There is no significant difference because accuracy is accuracy, and if you shoot with accuracy the targets will break regardless of your handicap.

I spoke about dustballing targets in my *"Trapshooting Secrets"* book. You do this using tight chokes and intercepting the target in the proper zone of flight. Common knowledge, but still misunderstood by many experienced shooters as they continue to shoot the singles with loose chokes, randomly point at the target and pull the trigger. At such close range, certainly, many targets will break, but accuracy is nonexistent, only to reveal gross errors in aim and precision on the handicap events. If you can't tighten the sight picture on singles, how then can you do so on the handicap? The inverse is also true though to a minor degree.

VISUALIZE
"Drawing on my fine command of the English language, I said nothing." Robert Benchley

Don't over-visualize. Just spend a few moments alone, viewing in your mind's eye targets breaking perfectly. You should see the sight picture and feel the timing too! Once done on each post, that's all you need. Don't keep forcing yourself to visualize more targets because you will likely see a target missed in the visualization process. In other words, your imagination begins to intercept. As the brain tires, it becomes bored and will wander, seeking excitement.

Practice this. Think positive thoughts by visualizing breaking the target. How do you do this? First you learn visualization with your eyes closed. You can think of a funny event that happened one day at a trapshoot, like the time your buddy fell off the barstool. Then you practice doing this with your eyes open. It will help if you look at an opaque background like a blue sky without clouds. Now visualize a traphouse tossing targets in the air. Next, you simply visualize your gun's muzzle swinging to the targets dusting them into oblivion. That's all there is to visualization. Now, try it again, but this time missing the targets. This may be a touch more difficult to do and it is anti-productive, but it is good training to "control" your visualized scene. You can take this to a deeper level, by allowing thoughts to step into your dream. Negative thoughts like, *"Don't miss!"* or *"I'm going to lose."* Once a negative thought materializes you should shut off the trap machine, wipe the mind clear of thought and restart the visualized scene of breaking the targets. As you already know, these or similar negative thoughts do creep into your concentration when you are shooting. And when they do, you want to know how to control the mind to flush these thoughts down the drain. Now think positive thoughts and burn each target in the scene. Learn to switch on and off your newly acquired visualization skill. It will develop perfect concentration, and most of all... the ability to control emotions, the breeding ground for intrusive thoughts. Perfect concentration is a key to high performance as it induces relaxation and instills authority.

AUTHORITY IN THE SHOT
"I thoroughly disapprove of duels. If a man should challenge me, I would take him kindly and forgivingly by the hand and lead him to a quiet place and kill him." Mark Twain

The mind is a constant battle of wits. A duel of what you want and what you believe takes place each time you shoulder that gun. Don't walk out on the line with humility. Step out there with a firm conviction of your authority to break the targets. Act professionally, be professional. It's a mental tune-up, a means of staging up your attitude. You have to have an authoritative attitude towards the targets (not people) otherwise the targets win. You don't *chase* targets; you *attack* them... and you do it with authority. It's easy for the pros to have this authority because they already have the power, but they too had to *learn* how to develop this *before* they actually had the authority. Mind before matter, that's what it is, invoking faith! Faith is believing in what you don't already have. Certainly, you have to have skills to complement authority, but you already have the basic skills, otherwise, you wouldn't be reading this book since you already read *Trap Shooting Secrets* (or you should have before entering advanced *Precision Shooting*). The point is, when will you begin to take charge? When will you begin to believe in yourself? When will you tap into that power source of developing that deep resolve to win? When will you commence enforcement of that *burning desire* to win by invoking all your mental might into annihilating the target? There is no better time than now. Regardless of how bad you have been shooting lately, you must get out of the hell of your own making and believe in yourself. Take charge. When you do this it also opens your mind to *learn* new things. To explore different ways to break targets. That alone helps break slumps. Stop feeling sorry for yourself. The pros have gone through those stages too, we all have. But the time is today to change your life, your attitude, your beliefs. No more negative thinking!

Most shooters step on line *knowing* they will lose. Are you doing that? If you can't drum up that much faith, how about staging it, "*I may not win 1st place, but I sure will score decent today.*" These little affirmations have a huge impact on your shooting performance. The mind is more powerful than you think. One thing about trapshooting is you learn a lot about yourself. Your weaknesses, your incompetence, your disbelief in yourself, your fears are just some of the major emotional conflicts trapshooters deal with. The better shooters have learned to reverse their negative thinking patterns. Now, the reality may be you need more practice or are in an unforgiving slump with no way to turn to escape from it. You're just in a slump and that's that. It's all temporary, but it can become *permanent*. If you believe you are a poor shooter, how will you ever become a good shooter? Practice shooting targets all you want and you'll still be a poor shooter. So, let's stop this vicious circle today and take charge of your authority. It's easy. Just believe. Here's a trigger word: "*I have the authority to break the targets.*" Keep telling yourself this each time you mount the gun, or just before shouldering and you will see positive results. Okay? Got it? Good! You <u>can</u> break the targets. Now when you call for the bird, call with authority. Don't pamper the call and don't scream, just use full authority in your voice. This will amplify your convictions and force faith into action. I know it sounds simplistic, but it works. So who cares? Just do it. You have to use authority, otherwise, you will chase targets and that is not trapshooting, it's crapshooting. So, the first step in gaining good scores is believing you can.

STRESS AND TENSION
"A stitch in time would have confused Einstein."

It's present and it won't go away. It's a distraction and it's here where the negative thoughts begin to play on your mind; "*I may lose or perform badly.*" Don't think of losing or winning, just think of smashing every target to great balls of dust. Slow down your walk, talk, thoughts. Keep a calm mind. If you begin thinking about how you will place your shots and measure your performance you are punishing yourself before the performance. This expectation can and likely will become a self-fulfilling prophesy. Use the stress to your advantage by talking to yourself with positive thoughts; "*I'm ready and I'll do just fine.*" Don't say, "*I'm going to win this shoot.*" That puts too much pressure on you, and when the pressure builds and a target is lost, you'll fall into a deep hole, mentally, and more targets will escape. Try to be neutral in all you do, say, and think. Breathe easy and try to enjoy the day.

AWARENESS
"Truth is more of a stranger than fiction." Mark Twain

Don't try to block out distractions, people laughing, talking, etc. In fact, listen to all things around you, even the chirping birds. The more aware you are of your surroundings, the more intense concentration will be. Many shooters walk around like zombies prior to the shoot and when changing traps, trying to block out everything around them. It's not necessary and it only overloads your senses, inviting fatigue and a mental lapse. Keep a quiet mind but be aware of all things around you. Don't fall into a tunnel-vision mode, blocking out every sight and sound. Concentration is awareness. You can retain intense concentration by practicing triggering concentration at will. When you do, put the fire in the eyes. Simply focus, focus on seeing the target and lining up your back-sighting. The more you try to block out distractions, the more they will disrupt your shooting. You must use the opposite of what most shooters are doing if you want to score well. It is only natural to try to filter out noise, but when you consciously do that, you divert attention away from shooting the target. When concentration is right, you won't even know you're doing it! If you feel that you are concentrating you are only compensating, diverting energy into a strain-like mind-set that serves no purpose but to make you believe you are focused. You know what I'm talking about. You see shooters looking like zombies and when you look at their low scores at day's end they reflect poor concentration. Implementing an attitude of authority will trigger natural concentration. Remember that. Try it sometime. You'll see it works. No strain, no stress, no sweat.

SUBCONSCIOUS AVERSIONS
"As far as the laws of mathematics refer to reality, they are not certain; and as far as they are certain, they do not refer to reality." Albert Einstein

Be aware of your own timing and maintain shooting your own game no matter what happens in the squad. If the squad speeds up, don't change. Slows down, don't change. Squad becomes cautious letting targets out of the zone, don't mimic them. If squad breaks targets faster, shoot your own zone. Be aware of these factors because the squad will certainly induce your subconscious mind to mimic the other shooters. Don't believe it? Watch other shooters when they first start a trap, then see if anything has changed on the last trap. Then look at the score sheet. You have your answer and the proof. Want more? Just watch when someone misses a target and then everyone else misses. Then when one is smoked, everyone starts hitting them again. You don't hear shooters talking about the subconscious mind. You hear lots of complaints, blaming other shooters, conditions, etc. But nobody says, "*Gee, I let my subconscious mind do what it wanted to do today instead of what I was supposed to do.*" But in reality, the subconscious mind is extremely powerful and often your own worst enemy. Why it wants to do the wrong thing I'm not so sure, but it certainly seems to have an adversity towards us. It's like the Devil constantly making you screw up; "*Do the wrong thing, you know it's the right thing to do.*" Still don't believe it? Well, consider this. How is it that every top-gun shooter will tell you they always have to keep reminding themselves to go back to the basics when they start to drop targets? Why do errors keep creeping in? Why do we keep reverting back to elementary mistakes? We don't want to, but we do. That's the subconscious mind taking over. It's a rebellious son of a gun and it wants to ruin your day. But, there is good news. The pros have learned how to control this wild beast. It can be controlled! It can be taught to behave, to conform to *your* will. It will fight you tooth and nail, but you can enslave it. Sounds crazy doesn't it? It is. But that's just the way the cookie crumbles.

So how do you get a handle on this invisible monster? It takes time to beat it into submission, but you begin right now by recognizing its existence. That is step one. Step two is beginning to talk to yourself. (Oh, oh, I knew this writer was nuts!) Use *trigger words* religiously. That's how you wrap the creature in chains. One day, I hope to get a better grasp of this subconscious critter and write a battle plan. For now, the simple approach of using trigger words will work, which is again, faith in action. Shooters who shoot poorly and have done so for years will find every excuse in the book of their life experiences to blame for their scores. If only they understood it was their own subconscious mind taking over, they would crank out better scores. A lot of people simply will not allow themselves to be torn apart with internal conflicts. George Orwell wrote: *"The quickest way to end a war is to lose it."* They will not address the subconscious issue and will continue to shoot on luck alone. They expect to lose and will lose, maybe get lucky here and there, but it's all hit 'n' miss shooting. The more you think about applying precision shooting techniques into your game, the more the subconscious lets go of you and begins to obey your commands. Simplistic explanation but it's true. When you take charge and initiate *authority* you will have mastered that unconscious wretch within who has been destroying your shooting for so many years, keeping you in a perpetual slump.

DISTRACTIONS
"After all is said and done, a lot more will be said than done."

There are no distractions. It's all in your mind how you perceive events taking place around you. Desensitize yourself. It will do you little good to permit the life forces around you to disturb you. If you hear noise or see the shooter near you moving around that is your problem. Managing distractions is a skill to be learned from mastering concentration. If you allow distractions to break concentration, then you are not concentrating properly. You should hear and see everything yet maintain pure focus on the targets. Never say you can't do it, because if you apply yourself you can. Remember, concentration is enhanced awareness, not blocking.

TALK TO YOURSELF
"There used to be a real me, but I had it surgically removed." Peter Sellers

It's okay to talk to yourself despite what psychiatrists and people may tell you. But you should only do this when you are experiencing trouble shooting. If all is going well, there is no need, but a pat on the back for some shooters will go a long way. Humans are weak creatures and have overly sensitive minds. Our mood and scores can be destroyed by one insult or lifted by a compliment. Don't talk yourself out of a good score by thinking of shooting; *"The wind is picking up and I'm going to miss"* or *"I missed again!"* Any thought or self-spoken word must be positive. If you have nothing good to say, then say nothing. This includes excuses, *"I wouldn't have missed if...."*. Here's an example of a good prep talk: *"It's my responsibility to hit the targets and that is exactly what I'll do."* Some shooters talk to themselves and others don't. You'll have to try both routines to see what works best for you. Basically speaking, emotions will arise with thoughts, so if you are plagued with emotions leading you astray, then don't think or talk to yourself.

BE AGGRESSIVE
"It matters not whether you win or lose; what matters is whether I win or lose." Darrin Weinberg

Don't be lazy or rely on luck. Passive minds typically don't think, but they certainly don't excel. Aggression is turned on by desire, not by thought alone. Using trigger words usually won't trigger effective aggression such as *"Kill the target."* or *"Take no survivors."* Aggression comes from intense concentration and immense aspiration to explode the target. Be careful, though, as aggression is an emotion and if it is too intense will cause you to attack the target with excessive force resulting in stabbing at the targets. Timing and swing rhythm is destroyed. A happy medium must be found. You'll know when you have it right when you feel aggressive yet totally relaxed and confident. It's a strange state of being only you can experience. It's a very serious phase of mindset yet body moves are fluid and relaxed. The pros have it down pat. **Example**: You can really see it watching Daro Handy shoot. He's so calm yet so aggressive it radiates in the air. It's called stage presence, that likewise allows feature film actors to perform to perfection on the silver screen. Other pros have this presence, too.

You need to shoot with an attitude. Lazy shooters hardly post high scores. The pros work hard to bust every target and so should you. If you're too cock-sure and overly relaxed, your eyes will be the first to lose focus and a target will slip away. A tinge of inner aggression forces the mind to redirect energy away from nervousness and other damaging thoughts and emotions. To trigger aggression, practice a mean stare at an object as though the object insulted you. After all, that's what unbroken targets do. Focus hard on it and feel your facial muscles droop as you would when expressing an intense stare. Do not think negative thoughts, just feel the aggressiveness. Now try this before calling for the bird and look hard and mean at the target. Give it all the stare you can muster. This is developing inner aggression and will help you take dead aim on every shot. The trick is to keep control of the aggression so it does not spill over into external aggression. You'll know it has when you begin snapping at the targets, pushing the muzzle with force. Losing targets is insulting and the low scores doubly so. By ingraining the relationship between target insults and aggression, a vital link is formed in the mind to channel constructive concentration to the target. This will prevent absent-minded shooting. Try it, it works.

WRIST CONTROL
"Just because something doesn't do what you planned it to do doesn't mean it's useless." Thomas Edison

The forehand holds the gun but it can also control the gun. It's another technique to be used on specific targets. The left-hand shooter could use it on hard lefts and the right-hand shooter for hard rights. It's not easy to learn, as the wrist often refuses to move slowly since it is conditioned to move with speed in daily service. By adding a slight twist via the wrist, muzzle swing is greatly reduced and timing increases. It also has a very strong tendency to twist the comb away from your face, so it must be performed diligently with constant cheek pressure. It's well worth a try to see if it will work for you. Keep in mind, when the muzzle tilts, POI shifts accordingly so a differing sight picture will be required. It's a good technique to catch those fast-angle targets without having to swing your entire upper body to extreme angles. You can use it as a safety play. When I'm swinging to a target and it's getting away, I'll apply body/wrist canting to catch it. It does work. It is so fast, very little lead is required. Just put the bead on the target. Why? The wrist snaps the muzzle forward with incredible speed and the arcing shot-string applies the lead. Try this if the wide-angle targets are giving you trouble.

VIRTUES OF A LOW GUN HOLD
"Talk sense to a fool and he calls you foolish." Euripides

Shooters that hold a high gun are totally sold on the technique and that's fine because it's a good technique that requires less moves to the target. But what about the shooter that keeps dropping targets? Especially on breezy days? Why not learn how to shoot low gun holds? At first thought, the high-gun-hold shooter rebels at the idea of putting the muzzle down on the house. They immediately think of the swing dynamics and that is where the bottom falls out. The shooter will hardly know the difference if it's performed properly. The trick is very simple and easy to do. Put the muzzle on the house but keep your eyes way up, level with your height looking straight out. The moment you look down at the edge of the traphouse swing mechanics become chaotic. By looking high you'll see the same target picture as holding a high gun but better! There is no muzzle obstructing any viewpoint in the field. If you keep your eyes on the target, you will swing to it without thought and even break the target sooner. This occurs because your eyes have locked on faster, which more than compensates for the slight additional swing that may be required. Have you ever noticed on windy days those who hold a low gun score higher? They can see and get to the target faster instead of waiting for the target to rise up to the muzzle. Targets that do not rise are taken with relative ease. The low gun hold is a basic fact of life for European shooters, and the trapshooting targets they shoot are much more challenging than our American version of trap.

The targets are also much faster, yet they still hold a low gun. You don't have to convert if you don't want to, but on windy days at least get that muzzle down as much as a foot or more below your normal gun hold. If you shoot a very tight close-in zone, a few inches in muzzle drop will give you the edge and prevent shooting over the top of the targets. Also see the, "*Muzzle Transition*" subchapter for low gun holds for the high gun shooter.

SUPPRESSED TARGETS
"The future is much like the present, only longer." Don Quisenberry

Tail wind and improper trap settings are troublesome as speed of target increases substantially and they refuse to rise. Trap shotguns POI is too high to reliably hit these critters and four things must happen to do so. **1)** Smoother, yet faster swing, but refrain from stabbing the muzzle. **2)** Low gun hold on house to reduce muscle memory over-swing. **3)** Sight bead aim to bottom of target by looking at the lower portion of the target. **4)** Expect the target not to rise so you can track and place your shot properly. You'll find these conditions in a tail wind and on coastal ranges where the targets are damp and the air is heavy. You'll also find on coastal ranges, including the East coast, targets are slightly harder to see but are thrown much faster out of the house to reach the center field stake. It is this increase of speed, combined with reduced visibility and often heavily forested backgrounds, that makes these targets so challenging. Many optical illusions occur in humid air. The best advice to hit suppressed, fast targets is to slow your shoot timing and swing a smidgen and hard-focus your eyes before calling for the target. Soft focusing just doesn't work in these conditions. Keep telling yourself to shoot where the target is, not where you think it should be. You may want to drop your POI if you have an adjustable rib gun, but it is not necessary. Hold the gun low on the house or lower than you normally do and lower your eye hold.

FAST-RISING TARGETS
"The human mind treats a new idea the same way the body treats a strange protein; it rejects it." P. B. Medawar

Fast-rising wind-blown targets are more than a challenge; they are devilish to hit. More so when the wind causes the targets to alternate between risers and cliff-divers. One just doesn't know which form to use to hit them. Any wind gust that suddenly jinks a target can't be predicted or corrected. But the mindset to shoot in these conditions is simple. You are shooting another game, not trap! Think Sporting Clays, Continental or Automatic Ball Trap (ABT a.k.a. Wobble Trap). Here total eye-hand coordination rules. Keep your eye on the target and don't think zone or timing. That's all out the window now! Shoot some sporting clay or single target Continental Trap (trap throws targets at all angles including vertical oscillations -- also known as ABT in Europe) to get the feel and technique down. Since wind does peculiar things to targets, which totally upsets the shooter and his ability to see what the target is doing, the head always tends to come up off the comb. Here, hugging the gun solidly and pressing down the cheek to the comb when you call will allow you to stay into the gun and break more targets.

Again, a hard-eye focus will help immeasurably to track these wild beasts. Hold the gun low on the house or lower than you normally do or try a higher hold, depending on the degree of target rise. Generally, in the wind, the hold should always be lower. The alternate technique is extremely fast zone shooting, hitting the target long before the wind can cause the target to deviate. This takes great skill to do and most shooters can't break targets 20 feet from the traphouse. And there is another technique some swear by. Don't change anything, just shoot like you always do. This holds water because there is no telling how well a shooter can shoot except by the shooter himself. Here's a good tip: when the wind blows, loosen your death grip on the gun's forearm, as it only tightens your muscles, restricting your swing. Hold the gun tighter in the shoulder if anything, not the forearm. If the wind is not blowing and the targets are simply rising quickly, raise your gun hold and your eye hold.

CHAPTER 3
"Function determines form, results determine technique."

THE FIRST STEP TO DEVELOP PRECISION ACCURACY
"I always wanted to be somebody, but I should have been more specific." _{Lily Tomlin and Jane Wagner}

How often have you heard this phrase, *"It's harder to break the targets when you get punched back in yardage."* If I had $1 for each time I've heard it, I'd be filthy rich. Yes, it is true. Moreover, I'll tell you why yardage punches appear to be troublesome for many shooters. **1)** They believe it is difficult, therefore it will be. **2)** Shooters who use "loose as a goose" chokes will stumble and fall apart. Trapshooters will do almost anything for a high score and will readily resort to using open chokes for a quick fix to increase odds of winning. It is the choke which dooms them the moment they insert a shell into the chamber. Accuracy is nonexistent. This dreadful mistake began the very first day of shooting, and for more shooters than you know. It's a huge error for the competent shooter. Here's the logic most novice shooters, including experienced trapmen and women shooting singles targets, will use a modified choke. They want that big pattern. And why not? Scores do increase, no doubt about it! But all along, bad habits have been deeply entrenched into the shooter's mind for years upon years of shooting -- true accuracy was never learned. Example: Next registered shoot I want you to look at the scoreboard. Notice the top-gun shooters commonly have high scores on the singles and handicap. Most of the other shooters will have a satisfactory singles score and a cussed handicap score. Interesting development isn't it? It's not moods or shooting ability or mind-set doing this, it's a pure and simple lack of precision in aim. For those who solely point a shotgun at handicap targets, getting punched a few yards certainly can be a grueling experience, but it doesn't have to be!

Novice shooters should begin with a modified choke when shooting singles, but the problem becomes serious as the shooter becomes addicted to the choke, rationalizing that everyone else does it and, worse yet, justifying the choke by saying, *"My scores are higher when I use a modified choke!"* Then, the shooter merrily steps on to the 20 yard handicap yardage -- tries a full choke because that's what the pros use on handicap -- and scores tumble downstairs causing frantic searching for the choke wrench again. Now the shooter is happy as scores once again have risen to satisfactory levels. If you ask this shooter, *"Why don't you use a full choke?"* He answers *"I'm not a pro yet!"* Ask the experienced shooter why he uses open chokes on the 16's and you'll hear a barrage of technicalities on pattern dimensions and *"There's no need to use tight chokes, it's a disadvantage!"* I won't argue with that, it can be ruinous to scores, but I'll go one further, *"How then are you to learn how to shoot with razor sharp precision?"* The answer is commonplace, *"Practice makes perfect."* Well, it doesn't make perfect, only perfect practice makes expert practice. You are an experienced shooter so there is no need for you to practice your skill using wide-open chokes, even when shooting singles. The novice needs to advance quickly to a tighter choke as soon as he runs his first trap 25-straight; otherwise, the next run on the trap will be a long time to arrive, and forever when punched to long yardage.

The point made is this: If you are using modified chokes on the 16-yard line then switch to full choke on handicap you will acquire a higher singles score, but you'll likely add your name to that long dreary list of shooters with devastating handicap scores. If you want all of your scores to rise, you need precision in your shooting, not patterns! You can't be satisfied with being close to the target when the hammer falls, you need to be right on the bull's eye. This way when you do miss, you'll likely rip the hind end off the target and still 'X' the score card. If you watch pros shoot, you'll notice something about how their targets break that 'other shooters' don't seem to do so often. The pro dusts the target, takes a tiny sliver, or misses clean. The target usually doesn't break into large multiple fragments. That's what accuracy does! You'll know you're shooting with precision when you find the vast majority of your targets are no longer fractional breaks.

Do this, even on your next registered shoot (except novice shooters). Install a light-full or full choke to shoot the singles. Why? **1)** Singles is nothing but a warm-up to shoot the handicap. If you're warming with sloppy sight pictures you'll dump on the handicap event where accuracy reigns supreme. **2)** The only way you can gain precision is by being precise. A tight choke on singles target's will develop the precision required. **3)** Accuracy can never be achieved through imprecise shooting, for deliberate shooting is required, and a tight choke will certainly cause you lost targets if you are not deliberate. Shoot the singles with a tight choke, as it will increase both your 16 yard and handicap scores by building precision shooting into your game.

Once you have established true sight-picture accuracy, and you're shooting with precision (after much practice), later, you can return to the modified allowing the pattern to ease your job. But don't overlook the fact you will occasionally need a refresher session and return to using the tight choke to reestablish accuracy. You have to do things in reverse. Most shooters use modified on 16's. Do the opposite... use full on 16's. Keep in mind, many pros use tight chokes all of the time and may only change shot size (8's or 8 ½'s on 16's and 8's or 7 ½ shot) on handicap, depending on yardage. Ask a handicap shooter who is having a tough time on score when the last time he used a full choke on the 16's. When was the last time you did? You may not like the cure as you see your scores collapse, along with the embarrassment of being beaten by less-skilled shooters, all so eager to tear your heart out, but if you want the option money and trophy, it's the price you'll have to pay to excel. What if you are using a full choke and dropping targets all too often? Forgive me for being blunt, but you never learned to shoot with precision. If so, you will now! If you are in a slump, then this is an entirely different symptom of the illness. The disease is often, but not always, a progression, where pointing at targets simply no longer works for you. Your mind is rebelling, screaming at you as loud as it can muster by allowing targets to slip away to gain your attention. So many shooters are not in touch with their subconscious and sometimes not even the conscious mind. The brain is telling you, *"I cannot continue to perform at this low level of proficiency. I am bored stiff. I want to progress to the next level."* Chuckle as you may, it is a fact that we humans are always in need of reaching outward to experience new challenges, to visit an interesting place. The mind, too, needs a vacation. When you ignore this outcry for change, you will drop targets.

Here's the resistance factor: *"I've been shooting for 15 years, worked my way to the back fence, won my share of trophies. I know I'll be back on track again."* Don't count on it. I've seen many shooters dive-bomb after the challenge is over. Working your way back to the 27, your mind was hardly idling on neutral, it had an intense goal, a challenge and the desire to win. Then one day, something just isn't right. You go to shoots and repeatedly under-perform. Fact is, you may even go to the shoot expecting to under-perform! Think like that and I promise you will get what you are praying for! As discussed in *"Trapshooting Secrets,"* you'll have to work on pulling yourself out of this boring shoot routine and 'experiment' with new ideas to break targets. You can't rely on past successes or old stale form and technique to increase proficiency. When you are in this dead-end mode of shooting, obviously something has to change. When you drive down a dead-end street, you don't sit there in your car looking at the roadblock, you put the car in reverse! That's right, you go backwards so you can proceed forward to reach your destination. It applies to shooting. For the experienced shooter, going backwards is 'relearning' techniques. Techniques you may not even want to learn, or try, due to personal doubt and reluctance to change. It's your choice. You can sit back and do nothing and watch other people win, or you can take on the challenge to "relearn and undue" past mistakes, break the gridlock on your mindset and step into the whirlwind of the tornado. That's the best way I can explain it. You'll have to dismantle the comfortable home you have built for yourself that is giving you security. For many trapshooters, just some simple, easy-to-apply concentration and accuracy training is all that is needed to zero-in on those targets. A good knife in time dulls. Good shooters remain good shooters because they sharpen their skills.

WHAT IS MENTAL CONCENTRATION AND HOW TO DEVELOP IT
"I was going to buy a copy of 'The Power of Positive Thinking' and then I thought: What the hell good would that do?" Ronnie Shakes

What is concentration? What should it feel like? How do I recall it? This is the most difficult subject to communicate, as concentration is intangible. It is furthermore a highly individualistic phenomenon, unique and unduplicated by anyone else but the person behind the gun. The mind is a complex machine, not fully understood by science or medicine. I can help you with practice exercises to develop and recall concentration, but only you will know what it feels like when it is right. Mental concentration is many things to nothing! Concentration is not thinking. If you were playing chess, and I disturbed you, you would likely say, *"Not now, I'm concentrating on my next move."* But in reality you are not concentrating at all... you are thinking. Perfect concentration is a state of supreme focus. Focus? Yes, a blank stare out into space where there is perfect silence and no intrusion of thought, even though there is ambient noise and physical distraction around you. You can call it a hypnotic trance, because that is exactly what it is. It is almost like daydreaming, placing your mind into shifted dimension, lifting yourself to another environment. You don't have to be a psychologist to learn perfect concentration, but you do need to learn how to concentrate yourself. The subject matter we will be entering into may appear witless; however, trust me... you will swear by it by the time we are done and you'll see a dramatic increase in your shooting ability... more than you ever thought you were capable of. These precision shooting techniques are easy to learn, once you are shown how it is done. Fact is, they are so easy you'll kick yourself wondering, *"Why didn't I think of that?"*

SEEING THE TARGET BRIGHTER WITH CONCENTRATION
"Nothing is too good to be true. Nothing is too wonderful to happen."

1. When concentrated hypnotic focus is right, you will feel an instant drain of muscular tension, especially your jaw and cheek muscles, and a strange fixation of the eyes that gives you a severe tunnel-vision view. There is no eye squinting or strain; it's just a crystal clear intense focus as if your eyes have locked-on to some object and won't let go. How nice to have when looking at a target in flight! You can trigger this concentration through practicing looking, staring, fixating your attention and eyes on a small distant object. This is so simple and you may consider just reading on to the next paragraph, but don't do this. This easy little practice session will boost your visual awareness to incredible levels of expertise. Go ahead, locate a small object on a telephone pole or a tree branch. Stare at it, softly but intensely fixing your eyes so they don't shift or move. Zero in on the object and hold your attention on it for 30 seconds. Now glance away by turning your head to the left, looking down at the ground. Now swing your head and eyes back in the general direction of the object. Did you notice anything? Try it again! Now, did you notice something you have never done before? If not, try it again. I want you to notice what your eyes are doing that you normally don't do when you casually turn your head looking at scenery. Go ahead; do it again.

You are likely doing what I want you to do, but you are not 'aware' of what you are doing right. Awareness is very critical in trapshooting and it must be learned. Then again, maybe you did it wrong. Let's see. When you turned your head back to the object did you notice the car parked in the street, or the neighbor's house, or the cloud in the sky? Or did you fixate back onto the target object? If you looked at the target you did it right. If not, then try it again... you'll get it right this time. This is the practice session. Fixate on an object, take a deep breath to help force concentration and flush thoughts. You should breathe in slowly and deeply while your ears can hear your breath. Make sure you can hear your breath... it's a key to deeper concentration! Fixate as long as you can. It may take some practice to go beyond a minute, but that's okay; we don't need a minute, only a few seconds in trapshooting. Now, turn your head away from the object and swing back to it. Your eyes should instantaneously snap right to the target! Easy to do, isn't it? Now try it without moving your head, using the eyes only to look away and again return to fixation. Now you are developing eye exercises and rapid focus, along with complete, dedicated concentration. If you fixate, it won't feel like you are just seeing the scenery, you'll tunnel-vision as if the only important thing in the world in this moment in time is that object.

You should see the object very clearly; in fact, it looks like it's standing out from all the other background scenery. You may even think it so obvious and wonder why you never looked at it before. Now you can't keep yourself from looking at it every time you turn toward it! There is one more thing you will notice. The object appears brilliant, more brightly lit than other nearby objects. Why? Because you are focusing entirely on your central vision. You have now learned target acquisition. Total, complete focus on the target, and it was performed so rapidly yet with such comfort and ease and without thought. You didn't have to search with the eyes to find it... it's right there! Now try it with a sparrow in flight. And on clay targets every chance you can get. Watch other shooters' shoot targets. I bet you won't see targets flying in the air like you used to; they appear brighter and more lively. Practice fixation multiple times per day. You can do it anywhere, except when driving a vehicle. Put the word "*fixation*" on your "To Do" list for the day. You need to learn how to fixate immediately upon command so you can recall it on the trap line during the setup phase. You may be in the supermarket shopping, come upon the word "fixation" on your list and do it right there for a 5 to 10 second spell. Just don't do it to a blonde or you'll likely get slapped wide-awake! One more word of warning. Be aware of your surroundings whenever you practice fixation, since in this state all peripheral activity is totally oblivious to the conscious mind. Practice visualizing yourself on the trap line in perfect composure, a huge crowd watching and you're dustballing the targets, winning the event. Do this as often as you can daily for one month before your next registered shoot. Do it on the day of the shoot and see for yourself, your performance will increase. The mind will duplicate what it believes!

2. Deep breathing. There are three ways to breathe, but we are only interested in one, the one most shooters never use. **A)** You can breathe through your mouth as if you were running. **B** You can breathe through your nose as you are probably doing now. **C)** You can breathe along your palate, which you may have never heard of before. Palate breathing is an intensely deep form of breathing used to deepen sleep, but can also produce huge volumes of oxygen in the body. With mouth closed, breathe inward through the back portion of your nose, as if breathing from the throat, feeling the palate snore a sliver. Now, breathe in slowly and smoothly without snoring, filling lungs slowly to capacity, then exhale normally through the nostrils not using the palate. You will notice your breathing sounds twice as loud as normal. You'll know when you have it right because you will indeed feel a burst of energy on the third to sixth breath. If you feel light-headed, stop.

In trapshooting, you need only take one or two breaths to produce an energy burst, magnifying concentration and visual acuity. This is hypnotic breathing. For reasons not fully understood by science, yet proven in hypnosis, this form of breathing triggers the subconscious mind into action. Don't debate it, just do it and see it truly works wonders. Remember, how you breathe determines mood. It's a proven fact you cannot breathe the same way when you are calm as when you are angry. Breathing is the key to triggering that ideal mood which makes shooting seem so effortless. The next time you are shooting on the dime, recall how you were breathing at the time. Mimic this breathing and you can recall the mood again and again anytime you desire, in most cases. The trigger word "*breathe*" can be used to launch this high-energy state of mind.

3. Noise isolation is a technique you can use to develop concentration. Locate a noisy place or a quiet place, it doesn't matter. If it is noisy, close your eyes and isolate just one noise source and force all your hearing attention to that one source, blocking out all other noise. If it is quiet, listen to ringing in your ears, or a bird singing in the distance. The next step to try is visual isolation. Locate an optically noisy place, a busy location with much movement and focus your eyes on only one wavering movement. It could be tree leaves fluttering in the wind or ocean waves. Focus only on one object. If your eyes switch to another objective simply force awareness back to the target. Now, listen to the ambient sounds. Select one tonality and while visually fixating, isolate and control both your hearing and eyes to remain completely focused. The objective is to reduce the tendency of the mind and senses to shift attention. In a fast-paced society, our attention spans are drastically intolerant to fixation. We are constantly juggling thoughts and projecting attention onto the next intrusion. You know this also happens on the shooting line. Random thoughts intrude and shooting performance deteriates. You may be of the opinion these exercises could be a complete waste of time. Still, once you do them, you'll ascertain increased mental concentration and control has in fact materialized on the trap line. Concentrating on a sole target becomes natural and effortless. When more targets break, skepticism fades.

So, mental concentration -- as far as trapshooters are concerned is fixation! The ability to focus your undivided attention on an object without thought or distraction. A total immersion of self. Let's try one easy practice session. Wherever you are, find an object no larger than 2" at 7 to 10 feet away. Now just stare at the object. Don't apply any effort, just casually look at it. Notice how the eye wants to shift focus, or drift away from the object. Hold your focus and keep your eye on the target. With your eyes still locked on to the target, and without moving your eye, expand your awareness to peripheral vision. You should still be focused on the target, but all the other items in the room can still be seen quite clearly. You may not be able to read the labels on any peripheral items, but you can recognize what the items are. Now, as you focus on the 2" item, imagine a bright orange clay target racing up from the floor past the object. If you can't actually visualize this target, you can at least see how easy it would be to observe any moving object entering your focal zone. Try waving your hand within the peripheral zone and you'll see how you can focus on one object yet clearly identify a moving object. This is what I describe as 'double vision'. By fixating on a distant object, you will see a moving object with enhanced awareness. Now try it again, but shift your eye to your hand the moment you see the hand enter your peripheral zone. Notice how large your hand looks. It appears larger! That is exactly what will happen with a clay target... it will appear clean, bright and much larger in size. A large target is an easier target to hit! Learn this technique and imagine what it could do to your scores!

HOW TO CONTROL CONCENTRATION
"Some things have to be believed to be seen."

Too many shooters simply don't aim their shotguns and don't play very well in the event. If you don't aim, how can you not miss? How do you point and aim a shotgun? Through concentration! Knowing sight pictures is elementary, but in spite of this awareness it is still difficult to repeat the necessary body mechanics time and time again. You can't do this by thinking as it has to come from the mind via concentration. Concentration should be sharp and direct with a sense of authority, not a fleeting, fuzzy, hopeful feeling. It's a command. With practice you can stimulate concentration at will, especially if you use trigger words to unleash the energy within you. Visualization exercises will perfect it. Then we come to the scourge all trapshooters fear, the loss of concentration through disruption. Shooters become very aware of noise and movement when they are concentrating. If you do, then you are not concentrating properly. You believe you are, but you have developed a 'misleading feel' for what concentration truly is. If you are concentrating properly, you will notice everything around you! Read that again. Yes, you will see the rabbit springing in the field, hear shooters speaking behind you. You'll hear and see it all. True concentration is a heightened awareness, not shunting off events. The more you try to tune out the noise and sights, the more it will ruin your concentration. I've seen shooters stop shooting to scold spectators for speaking too loudly. So have you. But once the silence is restored, the shooter continues to miss targets. Concentration is very flexible and forgiving of events taking place around you, it will focus intently on the job at hand regardless of the noise or visible distractions... if you let it! The moment you "think" extraordinary events are destroying concentration, it is already destroyed by your "thought command." It's like sleeping by a construction site or busy freeway, if you focus on the noise you'll end up an insomniac. If you concentrate on sleeping you'll fall asleep and remain so through the barrage of noise and commotion. Learn to understand the difference between concentration, and thinking you are concentrating. You can do this at a practice session at your local club, feeling the enhanced awareness. Then learn to control your emotions, for emotions will always lead you astray! We are emotional beings. We remember all so well past hurts, yet forget miniscule events. See how the mind can remember past failures? Get the past behind you by telling yourself today is a new day and a new opportunity for advancement... and you will experience it!

THE CONCENTRATION SINE WAVE
"Tradition is what you resort to when you don't have the inclination to do it right."

Before you reach for your gun, sit down, close your eyes and visualize yourself standing on each post seeing the three basic angled targets emerging. Where will you put the sight bead on each target? Where will you break the target? Locate the zone and feel the timing. Observe the gun muzzle smoothly intercepting the target. See Fig. 18, 45, and 48. Now step to the next station and shoot in your mind's-eye the next three basic angles. Continue doing this until you reach station five. You are formulating a plan of attack and instructing your subconscious mind to break the targets. Do this before you step on the trap line and you will see your scores rise to impressive levels. It's that simple. No mystery here. Remember to be very smooth, but quick to the target. You should feel a dream-like state of mind where you just can't miss. It should feel so easy to do. When you do finally step on line to shoot and you think of this exercise and concentrate to recall the feel, you will trigger this dream-like trance. Everything will appear in slowmotion and the target will be larger than life. They will explode just as they did in your mind. This is perfect focus and concentration and it can be learned. You already know the feeling... the day you shot so well it felt as though you were in a dream and couldn't miss even if you tried. With practice you can recall this winning mind-state. At first it may be difficult, but here and there you will feel it materialize then fleetingly vanish. Keep working on it. It will materialize again and soon you'll be able to trigger it at will and maintain this intense concentration throughout the event. This one tip alone will do you wonders.

Right before you shoulder the gun, concentrate by focusing eyes out in the trapfield. You should "feel" the tunnel-vision effect take hold. This will require practice for some folks, for others it may come easy. Wearing blinders will help. Just keep doing it until you find the mood that feels right for you. You should feel all thoughts vanish from your mind as though you are in a slight trance. Now, identify the sine wave of concentration. It is a perceptible rise in concentration intensity that keeps rising then suddenly drops off. When you performed fixation exercises you must have felt this intensity. You want to put this energy to work for you. You'll need it to focus hard on the targets, mentally and visually. Every target requires great effort; otherwise, you will never run the trap 25 straight, and the next, and the next. You'll need to practice tapping into this energy source and turning on the switch when it's your turn to shoot. Try these practice tips:

PRACTICE TIPS Phase 2
"Whenever I'm caught between two evils, I take the one I've never tried." Mae West

1. When you are up to shoot, prior to shouldering the gun, your eyes should already be looking out into the trap field, or at the far edge of the house -- whichever works best for you.
2. Turn on the visual fixation just prior to shouldering the gun. Visualize a target exploding into a cloud of dust. If you can't visualize this, just the act of thinking of a target exploding will do just fine.
3. As the gun is mounted, be aware of this concentration energy. It should still be rising. Some shooters may want to back-focus a tad to insure the sight beads are stacked, if so, do it quickly so visual focus is not overly

disturbed and energy dissipated. Get your eyes back out into the field. Call for the target. Don't move your eyes, don't move anything, just call for the target. This is a good time to see if your call tone is disruptive or in harmony with your concentration level and timing. You'll know if concentration breaks when you call. If so, it is time to change your call routine. Your call should actually give you a burst of concentration! Just calling, "*Pull*" can be so far out of focus and out of tune, though some shooters continue to use the word when a soft vowel sound would enhance concentration and prevent muzzle dancing. For others, calling the word "*Pull*" is just fine. Is it fine for you?

4. Don't move your eyes back down toward the muzzle. Remain fixated on an object out in the field or in a space between the traphouse and the center field stake, but eyes up higher than the field stake, much higher no matter where your eyes are focused. We don't want a soft focus at this time, we want an intense focus, even if it strains your eyes. We want to exercise the eye muscles forcing them to focus and develop the ability to keep the eyes from losing focus or wandering at will. Later, you can return to a soft focus and your eyes will gladly lock onto the target for you with ease.

5. When the target emerges, keep eyes fixated until the target has come near your central vision area. When the target leaves the peripheral vision zone it will enter the central area where you were fixing your gaze. Now is a good time to use the trigger word "*Slow Motion*" and move muzzles slowly and smoothly to the target, never taking your eyes off the target. Your eyes should be so locked onto the target you could literally see if the paint was chipped on it. This will take much practice to gain the enhanced visual acuity to discern target defects or target wobble in flight, but it can be learned with practice. It's actually easy to do once you really concentrate on looking at the target with all your might. It just comes naturally, in time.

6. You should still be aware of the concentration sine wave as you swing to the target. Is the energy intensifying or diminishing? Measure this intensity. Know how long it can be sustained, before it drops off. The energy level should still be rising, right up till the target boils into a cloud of smoke.

7. After the target breaks, relax. You should feel an instant drop in emotional mental energy. It's time to rest and recharge the batteries for the next shot. Each time you shoot you should fully concentrate on developing and managing this sine wave of energy. At first it will exhaust you, then with practice and time it will emerge as second nature with reasonably effortless mental exertion. If you are practicing these exercises and you are too calm you are not "working" at it and definitely not doing it properly. You should feel drained of energy after a round of trap, then you know you're finally discovering how to manage energy. Accuracy requires effort. Little effort harvests low scores!

WHEN TO TURN ON CONCENTRATION
"Imagination is more important than knowledge." Albert Einstein

Everyone can use their own schedule once they have mastered turning on the switch of concentration. Just prior to a shoot, after eating a light breakfast, is a good time to begin exercising the mind to fixate. When on deck waiting to shoot, it is advisable to double-check concentration intensity. If for some reason it doesn't seem to "click-on" don't worry about it whatever you do. It will come once you are ready to shoot on line. If it still doesn't? Don't concentrate or fret about it. If you simply fixate when you step on the firing line, it will trigger deeper concentration with no further effort required. It just happens. Use the trigger word "*Fixate*" and you'll galvanize concentration. It's not a difficult thing to do. If you have to force yourself to concentrate, you are probably using too much effort. Lighten up. Relax. It will arrive. Of course, it will only arrive once you have practiced concentration techniques. Otherwise, you'll be one heck of a relaxed shooter with an embarrassing low score to show for your efforts. Do not turn on concentration for long periods of time prior to a shoot. Remember, concentration dissolves rapidly over time. It rises slowly, peaks and drops in a sine wave just as targets behave. You turn on concentration just prior to mounting the gun as you fixate and visualize breaking the target. When your cheek drops to the comb and your eyes are focused and ready, concentration should be peaking. Call for the target and the energy will be there waiting to reach out and break the target. Now you know why it is critical to dismount the gun if a broken target or an errant pull occurs. You can't keep the gun shouldered and expect to reset this flow of energy with mind control alone. Concentration is triggered by actions. To prove this point, note the day you can't concentrate well, then once you step on the line, shoulder the gun and call, the energy reappears. Muscles and the act of doing, trigger concentration on the task at hand. Likewise, if the gun remains mounted, this action will not release concentration energy and over-activity in the brain commences. As the brain locks up, so will your muscles stiffen and the "*smooth*" motions required for accuracy are taken out of the game.

WHAT IS VISUAL CONCENTRATION?
"Today's vision is tomorrow's performance."

It is really a simple process, as all of trapshooting really is, though developing the skill is often not so informal. Visual concentration is simply not seeing, but looking and looking hard! From the "*Trap Shooting Secrets*" book we already know the difference between seeing and looking, so let's take it a step further. Visual awareness is a learned technique in which your eyes have been trained to evaluate minute objects and the deviations of such objects. The ability to fixate your eyes on a target and see it larger than life is a good definition. As you focus intensely on an object, the target appears larger. This naturally is beneficial to the trapshooter, making it easier to observe the target. No doubt a larger target is easier to hit than a small target. Visual concentration will do this for you and your scores should leap to higher levels. As you read this, you are using visual concentration to comprehend the subject matter, but you are not using visual awareness, which is ever more powerful. Simply concentrating your eye focus on this "*word*" will reveal intricate details of letter shape and form in contrast to the body of the text. Expand this narrow focus to a clay target in flight and details will again stand out on the target in relation to the background scene of the trap field. Many shooters "see" a target exit the traphouse and shoot it, but they should first see the target to determine its true flight trajectory, then "look" at it before pulling the trigger. The eye fixation practice exercises in this book (see Fig. 19, 20, 21, and 22) will develop the visual concentration skill required to raise precision aiming and scores.

WHAT DO THEY MEAN WHEN THEY SAY... FOCUS?
"He who asks is a fool for five minutes, but he who does not ask remains a fool forever." Chinese proverb

Focus mind... focus on target. You need both mental concentration and visual concentration to perfect concentration. The two combined become one intense weapon of war for the trapshooter. Leave out one and the other will fail you. Be alert! Pay attention! Don't get lazy or brain dead! Sustained focus is not an easy technique to learn because two factors must first be not only perfected, but blended into one form; mind and visual fixation focus. And once learned, it then must be integrated with your shooting technique, which again is not an easy task to do. It will require solid conscious effort to blend these three forms into one. Once you do, your focus will be perfect, or as close to perfection as one can hope to achieve.

PRACTICE TIP Phase 3
"The only way to discover the limits of the possible is to go beyond them into the impossible." Arthur C. Clarke

1. Start on station #3 and think of nothing but what you are going to do with your eye hold and eye focus points. As you know, eye focus prior to target call is critical. So are eye focus points. Fig. 27, 28 and 29 reveals an example of a trapfield with a diverse background. Fig. 46 is a field without a background, just flat land and a blue sky. Fig. 59 and 60 reveal a basic rule to determine a starting eye hold point. Further adjustments are made after you learn this basic rule of thumb.

2. It is easy to focus on an object with a background, but what if there is no background to focus on? This is where eye training and imaginary depth perception come in handy, as you can fixate on an imaginary spot in the sky. Let's try it. Look up at the sky. Imagine this clear blue sky has three distinct depths, and you are looking through a blue colored blanket of gas. Close, middle, distant. Focus your gaze deeper into the blue sky until you feel you are seeing the fringe of outer space. Now bring your focus back in to within six feet. Search for the middle and hold fixation as long as possible.

3. If you are focusing your eyes properly, you should not be seeing 'floaters' - tiny black specks dashing about randomly. But now, we want to see them for they can be useful not in the act of trapshooting itself, but for learning how to concentrate on small objects. Gaze into a clear blue sky and you will see tiny black objects zigzagging about appearing as fissile atoms in a chain reaction. The test is over! Simple wasn't it? What did you just learn? You learned to concentrate 100% of your mind and visual focus on a object within yourself. Do it again. Feel the mood. If you look at targets in this same manner of intense concentrated undisturbed focus you will see them more clearly and break them easily. Try this exercise before you shoot the targets and you will see improvement.

4. Let's shoot a round of trap. You must bring this book with you! When it's your turn to shoot, stop! Don't habitually mount the gun just because it is your turn to shoot. We want a deliberate delay, right now. A time to build energy, to mentally prepare the mind to concentrate. It's called pre-focus time. It is here and now you should be turning on your ability to envision breaking the target. Like a race car driver looking ahead seeing the groove he must follow to negotiate the curve, the trapshooter should also envision where the targets will be. If you cannot visualize (some people can't) then flush all thoughts out of your mind by staring at an object (fixation). Sort of like just gazing out into space (soft focus) not seeing anything; "shutting down your brain" is a good description. You will feel energy build. When it peaks, that's when you shoulder the gun. But for now, at this practice session, don't concentrate so hard, because we want to focus on visual fixation prior to the call.

5. Shoulder the gun, insure sight beads are stacked properly, move your eyes way up away from the sight rib. How high? As high as you would standing perfectly erect. See Fig. 36 and 37. Fig. 27, 28, 29, 59, and 60 show a convenient background, a few bushes we will be using as the "visual fixation target" to focus your eye(s). The visual fixation target must be in line with your gun's muzzle, or wherever you normally hold your eye point when calling for the target. You don't want to fixate on an object that is to far off to the left or right, or too high or low to the ground. Maintain a straight eye alignment or a couple feet over the traphouse.

6. With your head down and cheek snug on the comb, your head and neck is suppressed, so you'll have to lift your eyes higher to the 'visual fixation target'. If fixation is correct, you won't see the bush, you'll be seeing the leaves on the bush! You may feel uncomfortable because by now you likely would have already let off your shot. Squad disruption? Yes, it is. Let the practice squad wait... this is practice, not competition.

7. Don't call for the target! Just let the gun hang onto your shoulder with your eyes focusing on the visual fixation target. This is a hard focus, not a soft focus. Focus vigorously! Telescope your vision to see the leaves. Don't worry, your eyes will fall in and out of focus in a blur because you'll need to train your eye muscles just as any other muscle must be trained to behave to the command of the mind. Now, pick not just the leaves, but a single leaf, or clump of leaves if leaves are too small to be seen individually. Focus until you see it clearly. You can use a tree branch or any other distant object. You can use the center field post if there is no background, but be aware the eye hold point may be too low, but it's better than nothing at all!

8. When your eyes are truly focused on the leaf, sharp and clear, call for the target. The target will emerge and should not have a comet tail or streak, it'll be bright and highly defined. Why is this? Your eye focus is much more distant than the target during it's most highly accelerated point of travel. Peripheral vision is not so precise in detail, so the streak will be canceled out. However, you will still see the target's true angle from the traphouse from peripheral vision alone. Once the target rises and gains distance from the traphouse, the target begins to enter your central vision focus. Since the target is now much closer to where your eyes are focused on the visual fixation target, your eyes will pick up the target in a millisecond -- faster, clearly and more accurately than you could ever do so looking down at the traphouse.

9. Amazingly, you will forget a few critical things the next time you shoot and you will revert back to "hit 'n' miss" shooting again. We all forget what we have learned! So this is going to be a real bear of a practice session for you coming up next. Now that I've warned you, it should be fun. Finish shooting the round of trap just as steps 1 through 5 described. Now, start another round, but this time forget about what you have just learned and see what happens. You tell me, I've not the slightest idea what is going to happen. Just shoot as you normally do. If your hits have become more authoritative, something has triggered a positive result and it's likely you have learned to see the target with more clarity. If your scores drop, good for you! Now you know how important it is to have the proper visual fixation before calling for the target.

10. Now, go back and rehearse this over and over again. It's difficult, and you may be saying to yourself, *"I'm learning a bundle of bad habits here. I'm freezing when it's my turn to shoot, my eyes are cruising in and out of focus, I'm losing my instinctive shooting habit."* Rest assured, you are not learning a perpetual bad habit. You will not become forever sloppy or lose instinctiveness. What you are learning is control. When everything is right-on that's when you call for the target, not just because it's your turn to shoot or you "think" you are ready, when in reality you are not even prepared for the target. With practice, things will speed up and you'll do all these steps within the 6 second total setup time. Even if, ever so often, you do take an extra second to focus, you have to learn to play your own game with your own timing. An occasional delay in squad rhythm is acceptable, it happens all the time for other reasons; gun jams, misfires, gun dismounts, etc. Why shouldn't it not happen for you? If you watch the pros shoot, they are doing these things described in steps 4 through 10, it's just that they do it fluidly.

11. Now comes the hard part, where you must combine *mental* concentration and *visual* focus concentration and combine them with technique. There is no easy explanation on how to do this, but you can develop this through consciously practicing with this stated goal in mind. You may find it fairly easy to combine the three, but where the difficulty arises is the timing. All three don't "click on" at the same time. **Example:** discover the moment in your setup when mental and visual concentration arise. Usually, visual will occur first if you are fixating on a object or space in the trapfield. Next, turn on mental concentration as you visualize breaking the target. Maintain both of these at the same time as best as you possibly can while you call and swing to the target. Body motions sometimes can turn off concentration, so you'll have to practice to perfect it, but more often than not concentration increases and is triggered with body actions. This brings us back to the subject of *"body English,"* moving with the gun as one entity and applying motion to the gun with body English. Don't just push the gun with your arm to the target, move your body to move the gun! Pushing will only cause the muzzle to waver or rise, drop or rush the target, and push the sight beads away from your master eye. Consolidating mental, visual and technique appears easy, but it is a bear to get down to repeatable perfection. You really need to practice blending all together and all in proper timing sequence, without any of the three overpowering the other. Each is a force and each must be distributed equally. If any of the three are missing, this advanced phase of the setup is instantaneously demolished. Though difficult to perfect, do not believe it is a complex project. You are simply using three techniques at the same time to break the target. With practice it will materialize. When it does, you will see and "feel" the heightened awareness. The trick is to recall the mode at will on another shooting day. Use the trigger word *"Consolidate"* to help recall the mind-set.

12. Last but not least, jot a note down on a 3 x 5-inch index card the next time you go out to practice. We are going to use a trigger word: *"Visual Target Fixation."* Make certain you remind yourself to fixate each time you mount the gun. Forget and the target may slip away. You have to keep telling yourself to remember lest you'll forget.

Review the illustrations in *Trap Shooting Secrets* and *Precision Shooting*. The more you do, the more you will discover new things to learn. These books will help you for many years to come.

VISUAL AWARENESS TRAINING
"There ain't no rules around here. We're just trying to get things done." Thomas Edison

First, what is visual awareness and how will it benefit the target shooter? When you are watching TV and the movie is captivating your full attention, yet you are perceptually attentive of your surroundings. The cat may amble by, and if a family member asked if you saw Fluffy you would respond, "*She's in the kitchen.*" But this is general surface awareness and will do us little good; in fact, this sort of awareness is a distraction. What we want is profound visual awareness, a keen visual talent for recognizing the unrecognizable. The ability to see things you have never really seen, yet have observed them numerous times. Example: You're driving down Main Street in broad daylight and you begin to notice street light lenses. You see the design, shape, color of metal. Turning the corner you notice the lamps are of a different design. This is the beginning phase of developing visual awareness. You are no longer driving blindly down the street but rather focusing your attention to previously unrecognized items. What does this simple exercise have to do with hitting targets? It opens a new world of consciousness. The ability to lock your eye onto a object despite peripheral motion, noise, and intrusive thoughts. If you can, at will, suddenly devote your entire visual attention to an object, you can initiate true visual awareness leading to fixation and instantaneous concentration. This is exactly what a clay target shooter needs, yet few have the talent. Why? They never learned how! Let's try a few practical "eye-locking" techniques. But first, I want to give thanks where thanks is due.

I remember reading Frank Little's book, "*The Little Trapshooting Book,*" and he mentioned to practice looking at targets. He alluded to explain the difference between *seeing* a target and *looking* at a target, but he stopped just shy of explaining exactly how to do it, and most of all... how do you know when you've got it right? I tried pulling and looking at targets, but it just didn't make much sense to me because I didn't know what to look for. I now understand what Frank was trying to illustrate. I like the part when Frank said to watch the little chips fly when someone on the squad breaks the target... that advice was right on the money. It really does help see targets with more clarity. I use this technique often, and you should read Frank's book, too! *Shotgun Sports* magazine sells it.

1. Go for a walk. Visually discriminate various objects you have never really "looked" at before, things that have escaped your attention in the past. It may be the shape of streetlights, the color of a sign, an odd-shaped tree, plant or a home with a missing brick in the foundation or chimney. Try to locate items that you just never saw before. You are learning to open up your mind to being aware of your surroundings on a deeper level. Note that your eye and mind are searching for the unusual and locking-in on the objects. Really easy isn't it? Doing this often will give your eyes the ability to locate the unusual and tighten focus. You may also realize that you didn't even notice the cars or the traffic noise. Now you're starting to get the feel of concentrated focus. All of your attention is devoted to the task at hand... searching and identifying targets at will.
2. Now it's time to develop color awareness. The next time you are driving (drive with caution of course) train your eye to only search for the color orange. You can use any color that resembles the clay targets you usually shoot. Within minutes you will be able to lock-on to even the tiniest orange colored objects. This practice is quite amazing because it reveals the power of the mind and eye to filter out all other colors and only zero-in on orange. Soon your eyes will zap onto orange targets so fast it will astonish you.

Now exactly what did you learn? Probably not much to speak of. But you did learn something very valuable. You trained your mind to search out and identify objects out of a myriad of other objects. Ordinary items suddenly are no longer blended into a whole. Specific items do stand out because you are now looking for them whereas you never did so before. The brain now knows how to "pick-up" any target you select. This microscopic talent will help you rapidly shift attentive energy directly to the clay target, smoothly and without having to consciously look for the target. It prevents head-lifting because targets are so easy to see, there is no need to take a second look. Now that alone is worth all the effort of performing these simple awareness exercises.

CHAPTER 4
"Bells and whistles are the refuge of the insecure and talentless."

PRECISION SHOOTING
"When you stop worrying about what you do wrong, you'll do what's right."

Few people have natural talent and even those who do eventually arrive at a point where they need to learn precision. The heavenly scores of sixteen and short yardage shooters simply tumble downward in the mid and long handicap distances. You can point at targets at these close ranges and get away with it, but in handicap shooting those who point, miss! The only way to point at targets in handicap is to shoot a narrow zone with fierce, rapid timing, breaking targets in less than ½ second. Not everyone can be so quick. Regardless, sooner or later you will need to come to grips with your shooting performance to increase accuracy and control. For you, it is today. Don't skip a word, for this chapter holds the keys to high scores!

USING THE SIGHT BEADS
"If you aim at nothing you will surely hit it."

Surprise! Surprise! You will now learn how to "rifle shoot" a shotgun. Despite what you have heard, or how you have shot in the past, simply pointing a shotgun randomly is bound to produce a fistful of lost targets. Don't worry, this is just a practice session. Later you will revert to your pointing routine, to a degree. What you are to learn about accuracy could earn you a bunch of money. Accuracy, like voodoo, is rarely discussed among trapshooters, as aiming terminology is for rifles and pistols only, a fallacy to be dismissed. Top guns shoot with precision, incredible accuracy. What we want to do here is deeply implant into your mind what a proper sight picture looks like. I mean a dead-on sight picture, not a random close ringer. To shoot subconsciously you must first learn to shoot consciously. If your subconscious mind learns what a tight sight picture looks like it will always attempt to duplicate what it knows to be correct, even if it's wrong! But what if you have never trained your subconscious to recognize what precision looks like? Targets slip away. Many shooters simply copy other shooters, put the gun up and shoot. Nothing to it. Use pure instinct only. It works too, but not all of the time, and in trapshooting it's got to work every time or your option money will be transferred out of your wallet faster than a sinking shipwreck in stormy seas.

Sight pictures can be deceptive. Each shooter can have differing interpretations of what it should look like. Many of them could be wrong! And I mean as wrong as wrong can be. You have to know where to put that sight bead on the target, not near the target, but right on the target or on its flight path (lead). When shooting singles targets, the bead can be on the target on all targets as long as you are shooting relatively quickly. At handicap distances the sight picture is a different animal (some call it a beast). I'm not going to delve into point of impact variations and timing, you should already know about them as they are explained in the *Trap Shooting Secrets* book. So, when do you use the sight beads? You can use sight beads, if you want to, anytime you need to. There is no law against using sight beads on a shotgun, unless you are blessed with special pointing ability over and above average, you better use them if you wish to rack high scores at mid to long handicap yardage. At these distances from the target, precision must be right on. It's not like shooting close range singles with enormous, dense patterns working in your favor to forgive errors in accuracy. What is the proper sight picture? I don't know! I can't give you a formula, but we can do a simple test.

SEEING THE SIGHT PICTURE
"Ignore people who say it can't be done."

There is much confusion as to what a sight picture looks like. Many shooters can't even describe it. I'll make it easy for you so you'll have absolutely no doubts whatsoever what it looks like. Here goes. Standing in front of a mirror with index finger passing by your nose as your eyes are focused on your eyes, you will see the ghost sight picture. Imagine the fingertip as the muzzle or sight bead of your gun. Now try it without the mirror. If you see a double image of your finger with both eyes open you can practice this to help control and prevent eye cross-over. If you are a left-handed shooter, use right index finger. Right-handers use left finger. Simply wink an eye to verify accuracy. Now you should have a clear understanding of seeing a sight picture and how you can incorporate precision bird / bead relationships to enhance accuracy. Notice you are still pointing the gun, but there is room for manipulation to precisely aim the gun too without looking at the sights! Try it. This is called "back-sighting" and it is *essential* to use in handicap trapshooting. If you're not back-sighting the sight bead to the target you'll never gain precision accuracy and consistency. You'll be shooting with the eyes only, which is shooting on pure hit'n'miss luck. The *"Trap Shooting Secrets"* book explains all this.

This is a hidden secret the pros use. It remains hidden because there are too many shooting articles written on "pointing" a shotgun and telling the shooter not to use the sight beads. Readers are misled to believe seeing the sight bead is "bad technique" so they just keep on pointing the gun. Wrong! Not in trapshooting at long-yardage handicap distances. You may get away with it in singles and double-trap or skeet, but no way in trap. You use the sights just as you saw in the mirror in the above demonstration. That is not rifle shooting, it's back-sighting and seeing the sight picture. Now you're well on your way to precision shooting!

Now the choice is yours. You can continue to point the gun like you may be doing now and live with your scores, or you can take the advice of most every top gun in the world who uses back-sighting. What's it going to be? Ever see the camera-mounted trapshooting and sporting clays videotapes on shooting? Do they show you sight pictures? They most certainly do. If you don't see a perfect sight picture, how will you know when to pull the trigger? Hmmm, is that why you are missing targets, pulling the trigger at the wrong time? We all do. If you're missing a ton of targets, it's high time to learn how to use the sight beads when shooting trap targets. Practice this back-sighting technique in front of the mirror often to firmly implant the technique into your mind. Yes, you can keep your eye on the target and still see the sight bead.

Now don't be dismayed when you try this out on the practice trap and find your scores sinking. It's a new technique that needs to be learned and all new things are hard to learn. Make it work because it's the proper avenue to precision shooting. In no time at all you'll feel right at home with the form.

When actually shooting targets, you should slow down just enough so you can learn to control this sight picture then later return to your normal timing. For one-eye shooters who wish to convert to two-eye or anyone experiencing intermittent cross-over there is a unique single-point, glowing sight bead that will help that doesn't appear aesthetically strange on the gun. See the *EasyHit* order form at the back of this book to order.

PRACTICE TIPS - Phase 4
We are going to do some "rifle shooting" with your shotgun. So, here goes.
1. Mount gun, call for target, looking down the sight beads as you would a rifle. Don't shoot the target! Track it all the way down to the ground. Do it five times. Note in your mind how the sight bead tracks the target.

2. Call for the target, still as rifle shooting, and this time you will fire, but only when the target peaks. Don't shoot quickly at your normal timing right now, just "deliberately" put the sight bead on the target and smoke the purgatory out of it. Close your eyes for a microsecond and envision what that sight picture looked like. Did you also see the target bending? You should have or you are not truly paying attention of the target's flight path. Try it again.

3. Now, shoot the rest of the targets within your normal timing, or at least as close as you normally can do. There will be some timing alterations (usually you will slow down) and this is good! Why? Because when you miss targets it is likely you have rushed them, and, absolutely, you have mispointed the gun. This is exactly the bad habit we want to resolve. Details! Details! Think of seeing details! Precision does not arrive by accident. I want you to see all the details of what is happening: flight angle, target clarity, target behavior, proper sight picture, and how the target broke. The only way to reliably implant these visualizations is to slow down your shooting into a slow-motion mode. We are training the eyes and mind, not the physical moves required to swing to the target. Slow down and open your eyes! Practice this until it hurts over a period of a few weekends, along with your normal mode of shooting.

4. Now that you have learned how to rifle shoot and to place that sight bead exactly where it should be, it's time to become more deliberate in your shooting. You will find it an advantage to incorporate a slight measure of rifle shooting into your pointing routine. We want absolute precision, nothing less will do. You can't get that without using the sight beads. Yes, you can get away with it at short-yardage, and to a degree on mid-yardage, then suddenly the sky falls in when you get punched back ever further from the traphouse. You can't just randomly point and expect solid hits. Some shooters can, but most can't, and those that claim they can still have sight beads on their gun! The next step, #5, is going to be dangerous. Yes, it can be very hazardous, but you are an advanced high caliber shooter, aren't you? You'll need to be, otherwise you'll develop a horrific bad habit of stopping the gun muzzles and temporarily disrupting your normal focus if you're a two-eye shooter. Be forewarned, if you are not an experienced shooter you could get beat up here pretty bad.

5. We're going to break the rules here so you can see the sight pictures. Call for the target as you normally would and shoot at your normal timing, but stop the gun's muzzles the moment you fire. This will implant in your mind the proper sight picture. It's going to take much practice. To avoid a habitual reoccurrence, don't over-practice this technique. Now, practice mixing in a bit of rifle aiming into your pointing, with one eye closed, just a smidgen right before you pull the trigger and stop the barrel's swing on a dime when you do pull the trigger. You should have your eye focused away from the gun when you call in the proper zone. You are only rifle shooting when the sight bead comes very near the target. You are learning how to build precision into your shooting. Your timing will go haywire at first and you'll feel uncomfortable, but once you get it down, precise aim will smoke more targets. Now practice shooting the targets at different distances from the traphouse, alternate between one and two-eye shooting. On the next round of practice, don't stop the muzzles, but do rifle shoot the target, looking with one eye intensely down the sight rib. On the next round of practice don't consciously rifle shoot, slow down your shooting a smidgen, keep your eyes solidly focused on the target, but recognize the ghost sight bead and where it truly is on or near the target. Take your time to break the target. You need to learn the art of double vision. Eye on target, but still seeing the ghostly sight bead, and pulling that trigger with absolute discipline -- pull only when the sight bead is right where it should be. If the ghostly sight bead just doesn't exist, or you can't line it up to the target, let the clay sail away. Precision must replace habitual random pulling of the trigger. Too many targets are lost due to this. No doubt, your shooting will slow down a smidgen, or much more, but that's okay. Speed is nice, broken targets are better. These techniques will help develop bead / bird relationship photographs in your subconscious. I did promise these practice tips would be unusual, didn't I? Another benefit you will receive is enhanced awareness which is so important for accuracy. Here's another tip: Have you ever shot a trap where the targets don't rise fully, tending to drop quickly right when you pulled the trigger, shooting over the top? Sure you have, especially on breezy days and you expediently popped a low score to boot! If you just point at a target like that, you will miss quite a few of them and deservedly so. I'll tell you what pointing can do. It has a built-in tendency to shoot where the target should be, not where it actually is as long as your eye is on the leading edge of the target. Call it a loaded lead if you will, or an automatic forward allowance. To hit diving targets requires more than just pointing, it requires the use of sight beads! It also requires an alteration in timing. You must deliberately swing to the target much more fluidity and slowly so you can truly see where the target is and how it is behaving. You can't be in a rush! You'll understand this the next time you do shoot targets like these, and the same is true with perpetually rising targets due to a head-wind. Slow down the swing and check target / bead alignment before slamming the hammer -- you'll hit more targets with extraordinary precision. Point at them and you may as well shoot for fun because you're not likely to punch a high score.

WHEN TO USE THE SIGHT BEADS
"Take dead aim!"

Every shooter has their own method of using sight beads. If you ask professionals, you will receive many conflicting answers. Some will tell you, "*Never.*" Others will say, "*Anyone who's been shooting handicap targets long enough will use them. If they don't, they have not been shooting for long.*" The best way to avoid debate on this touchy subject is to ignore the technicalities of theory and step into reality. The bottom line: it doesn't matter if you consciously use the sight beads or not, you are using them. Even if your gun has no sight bead, the mind will instruct the eye to use the barrel for a reference point to align itself to the target. The theory of solely pointing a gun is inaccurate, as you can't just randomly point a 8-pound 4-plus foot-long chunk of steel and wood and expect to hit all the targets all of the time. It must be aimed! The problem begins on the 16-yard line where the target is so close, and the shooter can simply point at the target. This is learned and imbedded deeply into the shooter's mind as the only way to shoot. It works on the 20 yard line too, and the 21, 22 and 23. Then suddenly, when the shooter is punched to the 24 or 25-yard line the cat is let out of the bag, pointing just doesn't seem to work as well anymore. This shooter may eventually win a few smaller shoots and get punched to the back fence, but watch out when attending the big shoots -- winning doesn't arrive very often! Poor shooting performance is often the rule. Precision shooting has never really been learned. Enough said.

Shooters who are in a slump, or just plain missing a tad too many targets, had better learn to return to using the sight beads to reestablish accuracy. Missing targets is a sign of a shooter who has lost visual awareness of sight pictures or is seeing the wrong sight picture. Write out a grid chart revealing an assortment of sight pictures. Pick those that relate to your gun's point of impact and timing. You have to see a sight picture if you want to break targets and you have to see the right sight picture. This is all so elementary to shotgun shooting, but amazingly, good shooters often forget the basics or have really never understood what it is that they have done right in the past, only now to have somehow forgotten how to shoot with dedicated precision. If you are a long yardage shooter, you need to start practicing "rifle aiming" the targets. Whether this be right or wrong is for you to decide only after you have tried it. The name of the game is "*Break the Targets.*" If you break more targets rifle shooting then do it! Stop suffocating yourself with all the rules and theories. You are beyond the novice stage. If you wish to progress, you must do it to advance and win. In trapshooting, whatever works, works! Everyone has their own techniques. Even if you do not like rifle-shooting a shotgun, you still need to do it to reestablish a precise sight picture. Or do you want to keep on randomly pulling the trigger when the target is not going to break? The choice is yours. Sight pictures are very important to precision shooters.

PRACTICE TIPS Phase 5
"What's it going to be -- reasons or results?"

1. You can aim a shotgun with one or two eyes. For this practice session I want you to do it with one eye. First, install an extra-full choke and shoot from your handicap yardage. Shoulder the gun; close one eye.

Looking down the rib, do you see the figure eight? You have to see a figure eight or the gun does not fit you. Get it fixed! You can never be precise with a gun that doesn't fit. Place the gunpoint on the far edge of the traphouse so you can see the target emerge clearly without obstruction. Keep your eye looking down the rib, don't lift the eye into the trapfield. Now call for the target.

2. Track the target with the sight beads and pull the trigger only when the sight bead is in proper relationship to the target. If you miss, keep shooting this way until you are hitting the targets. It may feel horribly uncomfortable and extremely awkward to swing the gun and see the target, don't worry about it. Just put the sight bead where it should be.

3. Now revert to your usual shooting form. See if any improvement in seeing the sight picture has developed. If not? Then try this: perform step # 1 then lift your one-eye up high into the trapfield, very high. Call for the target. You will see less streaking and a cleaner target. Now track the target with the sight beads and annihilate it. Do this for a least 25 targets. Then revert back to your old form of shooting. Any improvement? There should be! If not? Try this:

4. Perform steps 1 and 2 but track the target extremely slowly. Perform steps 1 and 3 the same way. Let the target get far away, but still rising, and track it down. Speed of shooting is not the goal at this point. All we want to do is reestablish how your eye and the gun sights relate to each other. Once you establish proper sight picture control, trigger control is next.

5. Let the target escape the normal zone you customarily shoot in. You can shoot with both eyes open now, or keep one eye closed if you prefer. You may need to maintain a slower speed of shooting for awhile to imbed in your mind and retrain you eye and body muscles to accurately perform to your will. The random style of shooting causing you lost targets must be abolished to the graveyard. A new form of shooting must take its place. Precise discipline is the goal! Aim that shotgun... until you get it right! Later, you can slowly revert back to your normal timing, but this time, you will be more "tuned" and break the targets with precision. Be aware to be smooth with your swing. Don't stab at the target with the muzzle! An unhurried shooter is a decisive shooter. Use the trigger word, *"Smooth."*

6. Don't forget; breaking the target is not the ideal. You must smokeball the critter into a ball of dust or technically you have missed the target. Never be satisfied with a chippy target. Precision shooting requires pulverizing the target. These practice tips are critical and you have to perform them as often as it takes to rebuild extreme precision shooting. You can't continue to randomly point the muzzle and pull the trigger out of sheer habit; then wonder why you missed the target. Use the trigger word, *"Aim."*

WHEN NOT TO USE SIGHT BEADS
"If you knew you couldn't fail, what would you attempt?"

Never use the sight beads, unless you want to win! If you are one of more than a few stubborn shooters who will not use the sight beads, then remove them from the gun's rib and toss them into the trash. You may believe you do not need sights because you point the gun, but you will soon discover how much you do use them once they are gone, especially in mounting the gun and in handicap shooting. When <u>not</u> to use sight beads is the point in time between gun is shouldered and calling for the target. Your eyes must always be looking out into the trapfield ready to acquire the target. The second time you never use the sights is when the ghost image of the sight beads (sight picture) is very near or locked onto the target. If you look back to the rib to double-check bead / target alignment you will certainly shoot behind the target because the muzzle will decelerate or stop cold! Even if you rifle aim a shotgun, this will occur if you shift eye focus away from the target to look back at the sight bead. Proper back-sighting will prevent this from happening.

RECHARGING THE BATTERIES
"Be careful what you think for it surely shall be yours."

Shooting takes a conscientious seriousness of purpose demanding intense mental effort. The depletion of energy must be restored to counterbalance the serious threat of exhaustion. This is best accomplished with good relaxation between events and a good night sleep. Fig. 13 reveals a sine wave chart of how you should raise and lower your concentration energy levels on the trap line between shots. If you stay high-strung with adrenaline you'll burn out and drop targets. It's why the last trap is often a disaster for many shooters. The same applies to use relaxation techniques between events. You will see most great shooters playing cards or just relaxing before and between events. Turn off the mind and give it a rest if you want to shoot your best. You'll notice the better shooters don't do too much of anything intensely between shoots. Some may play cards, others nap or simply prepare their gear for the next event. They seem to just take it easy. Others take a moment to visualize-out errors and mistakes that tended to creep into their shooting on the last event. Very simple, yet effective advice here. Don't push your energy levels to the max all day long. Learn to turn it on and off.

UNDERSTANDING THE SWING
"Good shooting requires a Fighter Pilot mentality."

Without a doubt, under-and over-swinging are the most habitual faults shooters encounter, resulting in inconsistency and lost targets. A precise shot requires expanded concentration; however it does not demand a long swing or excessive deliberate hand / arm action. Often the problem is **1)** The gun does not fit, causing the shooter to snap at the target, since an improperly fitted and unbalanced gun can't possibly swing smoothly. **2)** The gun is gripped too tightly or too loosely permitting the gun to be pushed around without body English controlling the muzzle. **3)** Poor foot and body stance forces the muzzle to rise over the top of targets on the swing and / or shoot behind the target. **4)** Eyes not smoothly following the target from the moment of call, usually caused by not being ready to see the target. The muzzle will leap randomly to the target in desperation without precision as eye-hand coordination timing is destroyed. **5)** Improper eye focus prior to the call will always disrupt the swing, as the target will appear to be a speeding bullet and the shooter plays catch-up, snapping the muzzle without precise aim to break the target. **6)** The shooter's mind-set is one of *"Hurry up!"* instead of *"Smooth and precise."* You must think precision to induce precision. **7)** Excessive follow-through on the target. This increases the desire to "Speed up to catch the target" which frequently causes the shooter to not properly acquire the target's true flight path. The swing commitment is made way too soon, before the target is visually acquired; **8)** The face is pulled away from the comb during the swing because the hips and body are not pivoting, but rather the arm pushing the gun. **9)** If the swing is not smooth the muzzle will wander or stop, or block visibility to the target causing the shooter to lift the head to see the target. **10)** The shooter has not developed a "feel" for the game; **11)** The shooter sways his body instead of turning in the swing. **12)** Shots are missed, lagging behind the target, indicating a timing / zone problem.

Here's a tip: imagine your arms were attached by some means to your hips. This forms one unit as your torso turns as there is little independent movement of the arms, thus making the swing true and controlled. Consistency comes from the large muscles of the shoulders and back as the arm muscles simply follow along. So again, don't push the muzzle to the target with your arm. Ensure your gun fits you, too. You can spend a few minutes getting custom fit, or you can spend a whole season wishing you had. You'll need to solve the problems above with your coach or through self-analysis on the practice range. Just bring this book with you and work on each phase until the problem is fixed. Not in one day! Spread the task over many weeks. Patience will take you further than haste.

If you keep slicing targets, your swing needs work. What is likely happening is the arm swings the gun before swinging from the body. To achieve the proper muzzle path to the target, you must initiate the swing, letting the body naturally turn in response to eye motion. All three must be smooth. As a rule, if you fail this tri-level motion, targets will be weakly struck and sliced resulting in over-the-top or behind missing. Head-lifting does the same. Here's a tip: When you stand on post, "Feel Tall." Try wearing a work boot instead of a loafer or sneaker. This will give you elevation to see the target better and will absolutely firm-up the stance, so you can swing on a reduced, elevated angle (vertical muzzle rise). Think about that. The shoes you wear can alter and affect the zone! When you "feel tall" confidence rises, so try that trigger word to give you a mental boost. It will help in shootoff situations.

Keep in mind targets may appear to be rising when, in fact, they are falling. Optical illusions. Primarily the extreme-angle targets as they bend ever so gently downward along the curved flight path. The moment you see the target where the trigger is pulled -- the target is no longer there, but has dropped in elevation. Targets are bending away not traveling in straight lines. The trick is to keep the muzzle below these extreme angle targets as you swing. Know your point of impact in the zone you normally shoot so you can determine the correct sight picture. Learn everything you can about all target flight paths. Once you finally realize targets are in fact bending away from your sight picture you will be able to compensate through visual awareness of these anomalies. Once you see these 'bending' targets you will reduce the optical illusions and finally be on the target where it really is, not where you thought it was. Awareness is the key. Here are more tips:

PRACTICE TIPS Phase 6
"I am that I am."

1. To feel a correct upper body move to the target, you must first close your eyes and swing the gun to become accustomed to the feel of the swing. Then open your eyes and swing at imaginary or fixed targets of your choosing. It could be the traditional wall- ceiling line or pasted objects on a wall. Get to know your gun and how it feels because it is vital to be at one with each other. Certainly, ensure the gun fits you by visiting a stock fitter less all you do is nothing gained. Proper gun fit is an essential link to good shot making, because swing styles, form and speed vary, so one gun can't fit everyone. A gun too heavy, too stiff and too high center of gravity makes a shooter work too hard on the swing.

2. Find the proper grip that allows you to swing the gun quickly, yet smoothly. This takes experimentation. Generally the trigger grip is snug and the forearm is very lax yet supportive. Recall that you only hold the gun against gravity -- you don't push the gun with your arm to the target. When you push you will shoot terribly. Often a slump is just that! Move your body to the target. Adjust forearm grip an inch or two forward for less muzzle swing response. Hold closer for quicker response. Less response is often better in handicap shooting for most shooters. Too many shooters with poor scores are pushing and not swinging the gun!

3. Insure your foot position and body geometry is proper on each post for the targets you will receive. When practicing, pay attention to the factor of swing ease. Was the muzzle dead-on the target or was it rising over the target? Trailing behind? These are indications geometry is in error. Now do you fully understand the critical nature of the setup? Shooters who establish a preshot routine consistently score higher.

4. Be *ready* when you call. Too many shooters simply have no routine except, "Hurry-up and shoot." Once the gun is mounted, lift your eyes to the proper zone and wait until all "feels" right. See Fig. 36 and 37. Don't wait too long though, for the longer you wait the more concentration falls. Generally, ½ to no more than 1 second is fine.

5. Pay attention to your eye placement and focus before calling for the target. You will notice if your eyes are focused the swing becomes very natural, unhurried and easy.

6. Think of precision. Use the trigger words in this book until they become fixed in your mind. They are a form of internal confirmations to trigger positive external physical results. Whatever you believe will be. Gentle reminders we all must use to prevent backsliding into bad habits. Once the trigger words are incorporated into your game, you will see definite improvement in scores. Confidence rises, which triggers a higher frame of mind to excel beyond your current abilities.

7. Too much follow through is not a good thing in trapshooting. It causes more problems than it's worth. Inconsistent, inaccurate moves to the target, are the usual result when excessive follow-through is employed. Some shooters way over do it, snapping the muzzle past the target long after the gun is fired. If you're doing this, good luck! Scores will improve if you smooth out your swing so any lead required is precisely tuned within your sight picture. If you are applying excessive lead, you are shooting too slow, letting the target get away and chasing after it instead of attacking the target. If you are shooting too slow you are not visually acquiring the target properly. The goal is "No lead!" Shoot fast in the zone and you'll need very little lead, if any. If you can't shoot fast at this time, then slow down your swing so it is precisely smooth. Over time, being smooth actually increases shooting speed, especially if you train your eyes to focus and acquire the target properly. It's not how fast you swing, it's how quick your eyes acquire the target. The secret is in the gun and eye holds.

8. Pay attention to cheek pressure. You must feel it at all times! Try shooting a round of trap just focusing attention on cheek pressure. You'll soon identify the forces being applied that cause your cheek to leave the comb or cause your head to rise. Knowing the source of the problem allows you to identify and correct the error. Be very certain you are not pushing the gun to the target. Use body English. Pivot by the waist and / or hips. So simple, yet many shooters have never learned this basic rule or have completely forgotten its importance. Ask yourself, "*Is my head moving with the gun?*" You can correct loss of cheek pressure by using your cheek as a pivot point to move the muzzle alignment to the target. Your cheek now becomes a critical force to move the gun and it will never rise again from the comb. Practice this and see how efficiently it works. Even if your eyes momentarily move away from the target, this method will allow you to use your cheek pressure to reacquire the target without lifting your head. You and the gun have become one. Think of your head having a miniature swing of its own. Simply force your cheek to drive the gun towards the target. Believe me, it works!

9. If your swing is not smooth, try a different foot position and stance. Usually the stance is excessively flexible instead of too stiff. The traditional five-past-three foot position may actually be causing you problems. It is a correct method, but instability has developed in the swing. To correct problems it pays to tighten up the body position so you can't swing the gun so easily. Now you'll see the problem of what you are doing wrong! Later, you can resort back to the stance you had, but you may not want to if the mistakes keep surfacing. Remember this: never take for granted that what you are now doing is correct. Over time, minute errors creep into form and style. It is vital the shooter constantly evaluate the setup and moves to the target. Bad habits slip in from nowhere, and before you know it you're in a deep slump with no way out! Question all, suspect everything. Simply start over as though it is the first time shooting. There is more than one way to break a target. Perhaps the style you now employ is not the form best for you. It is likely you have outgrown it and it's time for change. Consider this: everything you do is absolutely perfect, scores are dropping but you're not in a technical slump. Then you discover your weight has somehow shifted toward your toes giving rise to extreme flexibility and causing balance upset on the swing. Something this insignificant can throw the entire body for a loop. Worn shoes will do the same. Everything must be evaluated when problems arise. Weight distributed on the heels restricts range of motion and flow while weight centered will equalize a sound stance. Regardless of where you distribute weight on feet, don't sway from toes, arch to heel, from day to day. Be consistent.

10. Feel everything: the gun in your shoulder, in your hands, the swing. Practice getting in touch with the feel of shooting. Practice visualizing the feel of the gun moving to targets. Yes, daydream about how the gun should feel. Feeling the game will open doors to higher scores!

11. Tension is the killer of the swing. It will ruin your practice too. Most shooters don't know how to practice properly, flailing away at targets without real thought of what they are doing. It isn't long before the shooter can't make a shot or maintain consistency. Frustration builds and the practice session ends with nothing learned, or what is learned is completely lost from memory within minutes. This is all created by two things: **A)** Not having a practice plan and; **B)** Allowing emotions to rule the game. Develop a plan, then you won't need to suffer from emotions and the tensions they create. You may not be satisfied with the practice session, having a bad day, but you'll at least have learned what you set out to accomplish.

12. Loss of flexibility = loss of swing control. It also ruins speed and timing. When your game goes south, chances are it's faulty mechanics (setup), but may also be speed control! You must embed in your mind the day you shot so well, memorizing the feel of the speed in which you acquired and tracked the targets. Feel the rhythm! Timing and rhythm are usually ignored by most shooters, but they are critical elements for precision shooting. Timing is speed, it can be fast, but without tempo or rhythm the swing is less controlled and usually results in a fast slash misguided effort to hit the target. If tempo is too fast or too slow, accuracy is abandoned to chance. Think swing; not spring. The feel for rhythm can be developed at practice by establishing a consistent yet smooth flowing muzzle stroke. Breaking targets quickly in a zone is desirable, but not entirely necessary for all shooters, but the rhythm must exist. You know the feeling, you just need to get in touch with it again. It's perplexing to do, but with practice you can acquire the ability to recall it at will. After shooting a good round or event, always try to visualize the mood and feel. Then later in the day, bring back the sensation. The more you try this, the easier it is to do. Usually through eye fixation exercises the mood returns. But the timing of the shot is ever more complex because timing and rhythm can not be separated. If the mood isn't there you'll end up chasing targets all over the trapfield.

13. Timing is knowing where you break targets most reliably and returning to that point. Rhythm is the smoothness in which you do. Once you identify the zone, remind yourself to return to it. Often when you miss a target you'll become overly cautious and divert from the zone by slowing down or speeding up. Be careful doing this as it will certainly ruin the rhythm and timing you know works so well. It can take seasons to pass before you really understand and know the zone, timing and rhythm best for you. The first step is to find it. Do you know your zone? Are you aware of timing? Are you in touch with the rhythm? Can you feel it? Can you recall it? Practice and you will! Be aware a machinegun squad will destroy your rhythm and cause lost targets.

14. Do you feel there is no flow to your swing? Do you feel you are stabbing at targets? Do targets leap away from you with an element of surprise? Do you concentrate too much thinking about technique? If so, the likely cause is you are trying too hard to make the perfect move. And when you do this, did you know your swing rhythm slowed down, but timing has increased? It sure has. Timing and rhythm must be in synchronization. You may experience the inverse; rhythm increased but timing is slowed, allowing targets to leap away. Learn to feel, not think. Keep in mind that day-to-day our moods change. You may not be able to recall the zone and rhythm of the swing. This doesn't mean you need to experiment with new zones or alter swing timing. It only means you're having a bad day. When a bad day arrives the novice shooter commences to experiment too much instead of staying with what works. The experienced shooter tends to lock-up and refuses to experiment with new form and technique and ends up in a perpetuated slump. Don't fall into these traps. Feel your swing rhythm, timing and zone and learn to recall it whenever you shoot. Then make it a good habit.

15. Swing timing is a tempo in itself. You can increase swing timing without changing the break zone on the target. You can likewise decrease swing timing without changing where the target breaks. Confused? If you are it's easily correctable. The subject is complex, but I can best explain it by asking you to shoot on a windy day. The first thing you will notice is targets get away from you, often diving downward from the muzzle, and you shot over the top of the target. If you slow down your swing just a smidgen, you'll get to the target just as fast. How is that? Because when you stall the swing, your eyes acquire the target sooner and when that happens you'll still be on the target just as fast as you normally shoot. You'll have to try it to see it in action. The fact remains, the sooner you visually acquire a target; the sooner you will break it. This does not mean seeing the

target leave by focusing your eyes on the edge of the house. Wrong! Do that and you'll shoot even slower because the target will gain faster than the eye can track, or you'll shoot panicky fast missing a ton of clay birds. The trick is to keep your eyes up away from the house. Here you'll see that swing tempo is a matter of <u>where</u> you place your eyes, not how fast you swing the muzzle. That is the secret to a fast, accurate swing. Remember eye-hand coordination? Now you know what it really means in trapshooting! With experience, you will be able to manipulate this swing tempo to speed up or slow down simply by shifting eye hold points. In the wind you shift eye hold and focus downward to the grass about 30-feet beyond the traphouse. Now you'll track and swing to the target smoothly, and when it dips, you'll be there before it dips. On clear days your eyes are held and focused above the traphouse. Try practicing eye and gun holds and see the relationship between these holds and swing tempo. Use them to your advantage. Each post may require a different gun and eye hold, more so if the trap is not square or stations out of alignment.

16. Bear in mind conditions change from day to day: moods, attitudes, disposition, nerves, shoot-off pressure, energy levels. These variables will affect the speed, tempo and rhythm of your swing. This means you may never feel the swing exactly the same from one day to the next, giving rise to inconsistency. I mention slowing down the swing for good reason. You can't swing fast if you're not in a hurry! Speed kills if not controlled. Before you shoot, slow down everything you do, from walking, talking to eating. A calm deliberate mind reserves energy... and best of all, establishes control, dissolving a multitude of errors. For those who "think" on the line, this slow-motion mode of mind will flush thoughts and anxiety where they belong. Try it, it works. There is an <u>internal</u> anxiety not associated with the visible form of nervousness, an inner tension in the mind that is not felt, but will always reveal its presence in your swing speed. Once you understand this link-up between nervousness and swing you'll be well on your way to picking up the targets you likely would have missed. Once you feel the groove you can recall it, but it takes conscious effort to slow down and learn how to recall. If your mind is too focused on adjusting swing speed, zoning the target breaks, it's guaranteed you will produce jerky moves to the target. But if you flush your mind of thoughts with a deliberate slow-motion mind-set routine, you'll be smooth and break a high score. Rhythm is everything. Feel the game!

17. After you pull the trigger, stay in the gun. Don't take the gun away from your cheek until long after the target has broken. This is to prevent head-lifting and promote precision aim and control. If you don't do this, your head will lift ever so slightly in anticipation of recoil. Soon, it becomes a habit. What happens is the head lifts right when you pull the trigger or just before. Most shooters have this problem and don't even realize it. Feel that cheek pressure at all times and stay buried into the gun until the target breaks or say good-bye to a good score. Staying in the gun complements precision shooting. This also helps reduce recoil-related flinches.

18. Swing tempo, rhythm, eye hold points and focus all serve the trapshooter a solid hit target. For some shooters, shooting too fast is their problem, especially the long-yardage group. They need to shoot quicker, but not as quick as most believe. As a result they wrongly assimilate speed with body swing movement and end up *pushing* the muzzle to the target. This is a huge mistake seen repeatedly everywhere people go to shoot. Others shoot too slow, allowing the target to escape, creating a myriad of complications: pattern spread, excessive lead, shot drop, etc. The above practice tips, if applied, will resolve many difficulties and turn in some very impressive scores. Remember you can be quick and smooth, but never be quick and unsmooth. Learn your tempo, shot timing, swing speed, zone, eye and gun hold points with eye pre-focus routines. You cannot ignore these and expect to win tournaments with a measure of consistency. They are the inner secrets to precision shooting. Fact is, most long-yardage shooters need to slow down and drop their gun holds.

19. Maintain positive cheek pressure so you will not push the comb away from your face during the swing. Right-hand shooters suffer this on all right-trending targets, left-hand shooters on left targets. This is elementary but it's something a good shooter must constantly struggle with to maintain exact eye to muzzle alignments at all times, on all targets. Trigger word: *"Positive Pressure."* But this won't work if the shooter insists on pushing the muzzle, to the target with the forearm. Swing to it with body English especially the handicap shooters as they forget all about the swing, believing they don't have to. They do.

20. Never push the muzzle with your forearm to the target. You will fail to gain repeatability with this faulty technique. Body English must be incorporated into your approach to the target. Practice this now! If you push the muzzle, you will push the comb away from your cheek, shifting your gun off eye-level to the target. What is insidious is that it doesn't take much of a push to make this diversion and the shooter doesn't realize the gun is out of phase with the eye. Your cheek can even be tight to the comb and the muzzle will torque away when any push is enacted. Stand in front of a mirror, aim unloaded gun at your eye, push the muzzle and see it go off aim! It doesn't take much of a push to do it, just a slight one. That ¼" deviation can mean 2' off the target.

WHEN PERFORMANCE DISINTEGRATES
"The will to do what the others won't."

It is common to witness someone practicing and performing wonderfully smooth, well-placed shots, then once the tournament event begins the shooter forgets his form, chopping the muzzle at the sky like a fly swatter. What causes this? Many things, but predominately the shooter has failed to visually acquire the target. Good players look at the target. Poor players never look at the target. These are obvious flaws. What of the not so apparent? Numerous physical details can decrease performance and produce slumps: eye prescription changes, worn shoes, despair, etc. One of the most insidious causations may be unrecognizable to both the shooter and the coach -- "The Silent Headache." You don't even know you have one, but you may. So take a mild aspirin and see if your mood suddenly changes. Suspect this whenever you have a mood shift.

SCUTTLING THE FIRST TRAP
"Remain focused on the positive."

When the first, second, then third target is missed on the first trap, the prospect of a good score already appears grim and many shooters, at this point, mentally give up and cannot find the fire. There are many handicap wins with a 97 score and lower so this is no time to throw in the towel. Trap #2 comes on and two targets are missed. Now the score is 95, maybe a win but unlikely. Here are some tips to salvage the damage.

PRACTICE TIPS Phase 7
"Emotions in the cockpit will kill you."

1. When a target is missed, the mind instantly searches for a reason why. This is okay, but the eyes defocus and search lazily for the target and when it emerges the shooter often looks at the sight picture the wrong way by unconsciously looking back at the gun sights. The muzzle stops when the trigger is pulled and target is lost. This isn't the only reason targets are lost, but it certainly is a major one, along with head-lifting. Being overly cautious is the second reason, allowing the target to leave the zone to get a better look at it, or being too aggressive. Naturally, the answers are hard to come by. Best advice: learn to reset the mindset and realize you are likely shooting over or behind the targets and correct the problem.
2. The score is already blown, you know that, but you must learn to push past the pain and make all efforts to run the remaining traps. The incentive could be the option money you can still earn. It's time to get serious and aggressive, especially with the eyes on the target and timing. Don't forget eye and gun holds and swing dynamics, which often stray from the norm when targets are missed. Odds are you are stabbing at the targets from sheer desperation or excessive aggression.
3. Don't be astonished, surprised or angry. Salvage the damage. Quickly identify the error and turn on more visual and mental concentration. The core of the problem with bad scores is a loss of hope and motivation. This must be conquered less anytime a target is dropped early on a dismal score is guaranteed from sheer habit and learned expectation. When you have a bad trap or two, use this ill experience to recover.

4. Sometimes you can't recover no matter how hard you try. It's a bad day. But this is only an excuse, and if relied upon without finding the true reason for the poor shooting, it is certain to occur again, and again, often leading to a prolonged slump. It's time to hit the practice trap.

5. Write down what happened and how you corrected the problem, or couldn't. Save these index cards and review them. The act of writing them down reinforces learned experience. Write what you did when you shot well, then you can always pull out this Ace just before you go to shoot as a reminder, setting up the mind-frame desired to repeat the performance. It works more than it doesn't.

6. Often the best way to win is to forget to keep score. Just break each target, one at a time.

7. Are you aware of hugging the gun and feeling cheek pressure on the comb? This is stressed heavily in the "*Trap Shooting Secrets*" book and for good reason. You must feel the game, feel the shot, feel that gun: feel the moves. Good shooting is a "feel" not purely a technical formula. You and the gun must become one functioning unit.

8. Are you using Body English when swinging the gun to the target? Or are you still pushing the muzzle with your forearm? Back-fence shooters feel they only have to "push" the muzzle a tad because the swing is not excessive, but low and behold, they "push" the muzzle instead of flowing to the target using upper torso body movement. If you watch the pros shoot, you won't see them "push" the muzzle. There *is* body movement involved. It is slight and hard to see on some shooters, but it's there all right. If you are standing stiff as a rock and only pushing the muzzle to the target you'll know why it's wrong when you look at your score board. To break the habit, start moving your upper body to move the gun. You can rock and roll, but try to keep the shoulders from dipping one higher than the other. You can rock both shoulders as in the Bow technique as both shoulders tilt left to right on a level plane. Hey, now you're learning how to cant the gun for dead-on hits with hardly any muzzle swing at all!

9. Are you pre-focusing your eyes before you call for the target? Where are you focusing the eyes? If you don't want to keep "chasing" targets and "stabbing" at them, apply eye pre-focus.

10. Okay, you're on station #1. Where is your gun hold and eye hold point? If you don't know, find out. If you keep the same gun and eye hold on each station, you're likely losing targets because of it. Find the formula that works for you and don't be afraid to experiment. See the drawings for ideas. Eye and gun holds serve a purpose: to obtain maximum efficiency with minimum effort to break the target.

11. Where is your zone? You must know where it is. If you're shooting targets randomly you can expect random scores. Poor shooting is simply a loss of technique. Unfortunately, the vast majority of shooters have no technique. They just put up the gun, call and go for it. It works too, for a while, then when punched back to long-yardage they fall apart and wonder why they can't win those big shoots.

12. Do you believe you can win? Do you believe in yourself? Simple faith is the most powerful force in the universe. Learn your technique, then apply faith in your abilities. Don't miss out on this. Do you have that burning desire to win? Every professional trapshooter I've met has this inner flame. It's not a positive thinking thing, it's a real energy within to win the shoot. It comes with experience, but it also comes from practicing this mind-set. Do you *really* want to win?

13. Defeating the negative thoughts in your own mind is the winner's edge. If the mind is calm and stable, the body can respond appropriately. That's how you control nervousness. Use confidence. Think of your past victories. Don't think of the money or the crowd. Just climb within yourself and light the winning fire within you. Try this the next time you practice and see how it will help you shoot better.

14. Do you feel the trigger? Sorry, but if you do you're headed into trouble. If the pull-trigger is crisp, leave it alone. The more you dicker with it the more the trigger will divert your mind away from the target. Make your adjustment and then *conform* to it. Don't get into any trigger pull hang-ups. If you shoot a release trigger just let it go. Don't squeeze *any* shotgun trigger. Just pull it when the sight picture looks right. Don't yank it so hard the muzzle dances. Just pull the trigger with authority.

15. Having a hard time with a specific target angle, like the hard left, and keep missing? Stop thinking about it as being *hard*. Stop thinking and worrying that you are going to miss the target. Just call and you'll be surprised to see the target break the moment you stop fretting about it. Sometimes, trying too hard is self-defeating. Loosen up!

16. Want a stable platform to shoot on? Try wearing new work boots. They will allow you to stand a little taller to see the target better and will provide a firm footing and stance. Just try it and you'll see what I'm talking about.

17. Not shooting too well today? Take an aspirin. The *silent headache* is sinister and hideous as it ruins your mood without you even knowing exactly what is wrong. You just can't seem to find the fire. Try this the next time you find yourself shooting poorly. And don't forget to take vitamins and water. One more thing. Are you taking a deep breath before you call for the target? It will give you an extra burst of energy to the eyes so you can see the target clearer. It works.

18. How are you calling for the target? Does the muzzle dance? Does it upset your visual focus? Concentration? If you call too loudly, you're asking for trouble. It blows the entire setup and the shot. Develop a strong call, but not so strong as to disrupt your game. Many shooters would shoot much better by just changing their call volume, tone and timing routine. The sloppy shooter doesn't understand the importance of these seemingly insignificant things, but the precision shooter uses them.

19. Are you prepared for the extreme angle target when you call? Don't anticipate, just be prepared.

20. Do you feel lucky? It's not reliable. It's positive, but misleading. Precision shooting is not luck. It is learned. Once learned, then you'll be feeling lucky indeed. Lucky you learned how to shoot with accuracy.

CHAPTER 5
"Often we make no choice and that's our choice."

EYE FOCUS TRAINING
"Seek and you will find."

The following tips on developing eye focus are quite painless. We often ignore the fact we must also practice eye control along with trigger control, swing, etc. You may have developed your own forms of eye training or learned alternative methods and that's okay -- there is more than one way to see a target! Give these a try and see if they can improve your visual abilities.

DEPTH PERCEPTION
"You can't see a target unless you look at it."

First, depth perception is not required to shoot trap targets as you would with sporting clays, but it helps to practice seeing depth dimensions for eye training. Look at a string of telephone poles (poles close, middle, and far away). Let your eyes relax and feel the depth sensation. Notice the distance between the poles and the shrinking size of the poles with distance. Now focus your eyes on each pole completely blocking out the view of the other poles. This will help your eyes lock-on to objects of your choosing. It develops concentrated focus. Now close your eyes and visualize the poles and the chasm between each pole. Now try locking your eyes on any object. Select increasingly smaller distant objects. When you are at the trap, pull targets and lock your eyes onto them. You should be able to ignore all the background scenery, clouds in the sky, etc., even the shooters themselves. That's all there is to it for this exercise. You are now learning to use centralized vision.

Tip: The purpose of eye focus and hold point is to set up the eyes, so the target reaches the focal point in the zone. This way the target meets the eye and you don't have to search or chase the target. The target comes to you! This is how the pros shoot so fast. They are not chasing and tracking targets at random.

EYE EXERCISE
"A wise man will see more from the bottom of a well than a fool from a mountain top."

Hold your finger at various lengths as you move your finger slowly and smoothly. Focus your eye on finger then later focus on the tip of fingernail. At first your eye and hand movements will be jerky and you will see a blurry image, but as eye muscles become accustomed to flowing with the target you can speed up and the image will remain clean. The eye muscles must be trained and controlled to track moving objects while focused in central vision mode. This is something that is not performed on a daily basis, but it is a skill to be learned and of great value to the trapshooter. See Fig. 19.

EYE FOCUS INK BLOT TEST
"If I have seen farther than others, it is because I was standing on the shoulders of giants." Isaac Newton

Use these inkblots to learn how to focus your eyes and select spots without vision drift. Use distractions, radio, people in room, etc. See Fig. 19, Fig. 20 and 21.

Splash a dash of ink or motor oil on white cardstock paper. Look for interesting shapes to materialize from disorder. The more you focus the more imaginative you should become and suddenly the unseen becomes visible. Imagination is an important skill to develop, as it is a direct communicative link to the subconscious mind. Imagination is the sister to visualization. Both, if used, will open your mind to seeing the impossible materialize into reality. If you can imagine winning, you can. If you visualize winning, you likely will or at least come out with top scores. Now close your eyes and imagine the ink spot moving, changing shape to a traphouse. Watch the trap toss bright orange targets. Imagine yourself breaking them. Now dissolve the traphouse back into an ink blot, open your eyes. You have just transformed an inanimate object into a living breathing machine in your mind's eye. This imaginary transformation of objects will help trigger the concentrated visualization needed to dispatch targets with authority. You have just learned mind-control, the ability to see a target and force it to break in your mind. The message sent to your subconscious is powerful. Now you know it is possible to look at a target and know it will break even before you pull the trigger. Learn to respond to the target, not react to it. A response is conscious and managing the situation. You are ready for the target and when it emerges you confidently make your moves to break it. A reaction is being taken by an element of surprise. The target exits and you "react" with confusion or fear making unsmooth moves and often miss the target. Key word: *"Be responsive."*

ADJUSTING SWING SPEED
"Experience is that marvelous thing that enables you to recognize a mistake when you make it again." F. P. Jones

Swing speed should be the same for each target, but there are exceptions. Certain straightaway and hard-angle targets justify slowing down so you can get a good look at the target. However, this slow down is not performed solely by body moves, but through eye-mind control. Incorporating an unhurried, microsecond delay before making the move to the target is all that is required, along with the mental command to not rush the target. This delay is important, as it gives the eye time to acquire the target angle and lock-on. Many a missed target is due to advancing the gun swing prior to solid eye-target acquisition. If the muzzle advances prematurely, the body will often fail to make the necessary course corrections to align properly with the target. Eye-hand coordination and smoothness is lost.

Tip: Always lock the eyes onto the target before you swing. If you swing first, you'll likely keep missing.

EYE HOLD
"I believe in looking reality straight in the eye and denying it." Garrison Keillor

Keep in mind 80% or more of sensory input is visual. If your eye placement hold point is faulty, swing mechanics will fail. If the eyes fail to acquire the target properly (only you know what is proper or not) the body responds based on this faulty information. Say hello to another missed target. If you're struggling with your game and working hard with a particular technique, weak visual skills may be your problem, not your swing, stance, etc. You can work on the mechanics till eternity without meaningful improvements if your eyes are not seeing the target properly. Remember, it's your eyes that direct the actions of your hands. See a specialist in sports vision if at all possible. Contact: International Academy of Sports Vision, 200 So., Progress Ave.. Harrisburg, PA 17109 (717)-652-8080. American Optometric Assoc., Sports Vision Dept., 243 N. Lindbergh Blvd., St. Louis, MO 63141.

RESTORING A SMOOTH SWING
"Never confuse motion with action." Ben Franklin

Bad habits constantly creep in and the shooter is often totally unaware of the slippage until a feast of missed targets arise or a slump occurs. A smooth swing is usually the first to slip away, and once barrel darting begins it's hard to even recognize snapping and stabbing the muzzle to the targets. Shooters often fail to realize that they can shoot fast, even faster than they do now, if a smooth swing rhythm is maintained. This is why it is so important not to move the muzzle until the eye has locked on to the target so the eye can flow smoothly with the target. A jerky eye move will produce impulsive muzzle stabs. Keep in mind this all important fact; no matter how long you have been shooting, and despite past successes, you likely still have defects in your shooting form and there is always room for experimentation to improve. Remember, smooth swings and timing are linked to the eye. The better your eye can lock on to a target quickly and flow with the target smoothly, the higher your scores will climb. Here are a few more tips:

PRACTICE TIPS - Phase 8
"Education's purpose is to replace an empty mind with an open one." Malcolm S. Forbes

1. Check hand placement on forearm. Too far extended or too close-in will cause imbalance and erratic swings and loss of control. Do some experimenting here. You may find you are holding the gun wrong.
2. Have your gun balanced to correct uneven weight distribution. Weight should be evenly distributed between the hands or a tad heavier to the forearm.
3. Adjust foot position and stance posture until swing is the smoothest.
4. Check body English moves to the target. Pivot the gun using your upper body. The body must move the gun, not move after the gun has migrated. Pushing the muzzle will do exactly this and it is a deadly error.
5. Check swing rhythm for consistency. You'll need to feel the swing for it to be repeated time and time again. It's a mood and a state of mind when you feel smoothness.
6. Think slow motion! Smooth precision! The faster you try to hit targets the more hurried and uncontrolled you'll be. By thinking slow motion, being smooth and unhurried, you'll move to the target faster.
7. Ensure flexibility in the swing so muzzle can easily make coarse corrections, but not too much flexibility, otherwise precision will be lost. There is no need for excessive flexibility for trap targets since angles are not severe as in sporting clays and skeet. A solid rigid stance will wipe out many bad habits in the swing and will increase accuracy. Step to a full side-on stance to iron out the flaws. When shouldering the gun, lift the gun to your face, don't crouch down to the gun. Stand erect with a firm footing. If you feel stiff, that is good! If you

feel too comfortable and totally relaxed, you likely have too much flexibility in the swing. Once you determine the problem is resolved, you can then slip into a more comfortable stance and foot position.

8. Mount the gun slowly! If you mount the gun quickly, you're heading for big trouble. Shooters who mount quickly often fail to "feel the game," and they don't feel cheek pressure, and they often snap the muzzle to the target wildly. There is zero smoothness in their technique. Nothing is deliberate and eye focus is nonexistent. They are randomly shooting on luck. A slow deliberate mount prepares the mind for the shot and allows time for the eyes to focus, which enhances swing smoothness and repeatable accuracy.

9. Solidly lock the gun into your shoulder and feel the pressure. Differences in shoulder pressure upset length of pull, gun balance, eye placement to rib, eye alignment to sight beads, trigger pull, recoil, flinching, head-lifting and swing mechanics. Many shooters do not realize the importance of proper shoulder pressure. Wear a shooting vest! There are very, very few great trapshooters who wear no vest. Most professionals wear them as it is vital to the setup. Mount the gun slowly and feel the shoulder pressure. Push that gun forcibly into your shoulder and lock it in tight. This way the gun won't slip when you swing to the target. It can slip so slightly you'd never know it was happening. The sight picture may look good, but it's way off mark the moment you pull the trigger and the target escapes. Recoil a problem? Browning makes a great vest, the Reactar®, that has a gel-pad insert. You can purchase the Reactar® gel pad separately to sew into your own vest.

10. Hug the gun. The gun can never swing smoothly if it is just held in hand without a purpose. By hugging the gun, the cheek lies firm on the comb and the body moves the gun, not the forearm. A snug hug increases absolute control of the gun and increases smooth fluid precise motion. If the gun is not hugged, the muzzle becomes too "lively" and "loose fitting" which leads to wavering uncontrolled swing, head-lifting, eye cross-over, false sight pictures and too many lost targets.

11. Ensure the gun does not move until the eye has solidly acquired the target. The trick to good trapshooting is well established: eye-hand coordination, in that order. The moment you reverse the role to hand-eye coordination your shooting will never become consistent or proficient. The gun should just sit still until the eye has locked on to the target. This may upset your timing at first to rid yourself of a bad habit, but as you do so, your eye will acquire the target sooner and your timing will actually increase along with precise accuracy. Only the moving gun technique can violate this rule.

12. Practice eye exercises on moving objects. Eye muscles are not accustomed to tracking objects in centralized vision mode in daily life activities. They tend to lazily stare or jerk rapidly to see events around us. These muscles must be trained to lock on and flow smoothly. See Fig. 19, 20 and 22 to learn eye control.

13. Marginally slow pulls will upset swing tempo and destroy the readiness link between the eye and brain so moves to the target will be hasty and panicky. You must attack a target, not react to it. Slow pulls totally destroy the setup. Increase your call volume, and / or turn the target down.

14. Never memorize the do's and don'ts. If you practice all of the tips in this book and other books, video tapes, personal instruction by coaches, etc., you'll forget all you've learned, become confused, or both. But if you "feel the game" you'll feel all of the instructions and moves, and that is something you'll rarely, if ever, forget.

CHAPTER 6

"Good judgment comes from experience, and
experience comes from bad judgment."

EYE HOLD VARIATIONS
"If the only tool you have is a hammer, you tend to see every problem as a nail." Abraham Maslow

Eye hold points over the traphouse often do not change once you have mastered where to place your eye over the house, but they should change! Fig. 36 and 37 reveals the different eye hold points for various yardages. Notice the further back you go towards the 27-yard line, the lower the eye hold is on the house. Why? Because at distance it is easier to see the target leave the house. Targets streaking comet tails at long yardage are not as severe as they are at the 16 to 22-yard line. When shooting short yardage you are too close to the target and prolonged comet tails blur your vision to prevent clearly seeing the target. Lifting your eyes upward before calling for the target will reduce or eliminate the streak anomaly and focus your eyes better to the trap. It is easier to hit a clean target than a fuzzy one. Many experienced shooters shoot singles a bit too fast and wonder why they miss. Lift your eyes upward, take extra time to positively see the target clearly and you'll be better able to judge the target's angulation. There is no need to rush a singles target, or any target for that matter, for when you rush you are shooting more on nervous luck than skill. Precision shooting requires mental and visual relaxation and confidence in hitting the target. You can't do that if you're not 'looking' at the target. You can't look at a target properly if you're looking for it incorrectly. Practice these recommended eye hold points and see if it does not help you to see the target much more clearly. For once the target is accurately visually acquired, hitting the target usually is no miracle. Everyone is different, so you may find your eye hold point at the 16-yard line may be just as functional as if you shot the 27. But you'll never know for certain unless you examine alternatives. Here's a trigger word, "*Eyes Up*." See Fig. 38 through 41, 71 and 74.

SLOW MOTION SHOOTING
"When people say you cannot do it, you try and discover you can."

Have you ever noticed when you are shooting outrageously well, the target and muzzle appear to be in slow motion? Everything seems so silent, in perfect control. Flipping the coin, when you are shooting badly everything appears to be happening too fast... out of control! Wouldn't it be grand to recall at will the feeling and mode where everything slows down and you shoot at your best? The good news is, you can! It's not as hard as you think it is. At first it does take some practice, but it's still easy to do. Much easier than you believe. Easier than shooting the way you do now! There are two prime factors that cause slow motion effects: 1) Deep concentration and 2.) Fixation -- resulting in deep concentration. Fixation is the "trigger" firing off perfect concentration. When fixating, use the trigger word "*Slow Motion,*" a very simple phrase with potent results. You already know how to fixate to trigger deep concentration, but let's do a practice run. Each time you mount your gun, look up and fixate. Repeat the words, "*Slow and Precise*". The meaning of these words will be this: As the target rises, I will move the gun slowly and smoothly to the target, forever watching and expecting the target to deviate from its flight path. I will watch the target perfectly, expecting it to drop instantly under the muzzle as if a breeze may push it downward. I will not pull the trigger until I am certain the target will not descend. That's all there is to it! This extra focus time builds precision and the ability to truly see the target.

What you are doing is complex, but to explain with simplicity, you are concentrating so hard, so abnormally hard on the target, it appears you are rifle shooting, watching the target to see if it is going to change direction. Now that's close and intense visual awareness! The amazing thing is you trigger the slow motion effect, which may seem as if you are shooting too slowly, but in reality you are shooting very near where you normally always shoot the target. It's a good illusion to get used to. By rifle shooting the target, you can also trigger this slow motion effect, but it will not work without fixation and concentration prior to calling for the target. Practice slow motion shooting by purposely making yourself swing to the target in slow motion. Of course, by now, I assume you know the difference between back-sighting and rifle shooting. If not, see the illustrations in this book and the book *Trap Shooting Secrets*.

Key to slow motion. Prefocus your eyes intensely on an object prior to calling for the target. Experiment with raising or lowering your eye hold, raising usually works for most shooters. Gun hold can have an influence so make adjustments, usually by dropping the gun hold a smidgen. The trick is simple, by raising your eye hold with an intense prefocus, the zone compresses and the target locks into the central visual receptors in the eye. The eye now does not have to search for the target and it slowly and smoothly tracks the target with utmost ease.

Also, the target, when acquired in this means, is actually traveling slower as it is acquired beyond the streak zone. Once you learn the technique, intense focus will not be required. Why? Because you have trained your eye to prefocus. It's like curling a 50-pound weight. At first it's hard strain. Later, it's easy to do. So it is with the eyes. Prefocus is a strain at first -- then, it feels like a soft-focus once it is learned.

Here's another tip. Check your swing speed. I bet you swing the gun too quickly. It may feel normal for you, but it may be all wrong. To trigger slow motion shooting and to be comfortable within its confines, you must learn, believe, and conquer... not rushing the target. How do you do this? Just practice not shooting the target in your zone, but practice relaxing as you swing to the target as if you had plenty of time to hit it. In fact, you do have plenty of time, even the hard left and right angles. The key in this practice routine is to trigger the slow motion mode so you can control all the physical motions needed to hit the target. Control? Yes, perfect control. You develop this by intentionally 'slowing down' your shooting, aiming like a rifle, feeling all of your body moves. This creates awareness of the muscular moves required to hit the target. I bet you never practiced that before! Let's do one.

Mount the gun (you can practice this at home if you wish) and aim the gun like a rifle. Now find a spot on the wall and swing to it. Don't point the gun rapidly, move very, very, slowly. Feel your body moves. If you only feel you arm muscle swinging the gun, you are pushing the gun by the forearm. You'll miss a truckload of targets if you don't stop this bad habit. Now try swinging your body by the hips to the target, in slow motion. Notice how smooth this is. Now as you know, targets do not travel in straight lines. So let's imagine a target curving along the wall. You can draw a line on the wall if you wish, but it is better to imagine to develop visualization skills. Track this curve in slow motion, still looking down the sights as shooting a rifle. Notice the slight cant on your gun muzzle. If there is no cant, then you are likely tracking the curve wrong. Draw a line or tape a string on the wall and try again. To place the sight bead exactly where it should be on a curving target there will be a smidgen of cant on the muzzle. If you don't apply a touch of cant, precision will be lost. You *can* shoot without canting, no doubt about it, many do. But I'd like you to try canting the gun so you can feel "Body English" in action. You have to feel your body moving to the target! You and the gun must feel at one with each other. You don't hold the gun... you hug it! It has to feel like it's an extension of your body, a part of you that cannot function alone. Use your body to move the gun, not the arm alone!

Many shooters have no inner sense of the gun being a part of themselves. It's just a gun put on the shoulder, pointed and fired. Go ahead, shoulder the gun. Now pull the gun snugly into your shoulder, place your cheek down and hug that gun. Now move slowly to the target. If you "feel the hug"' you will never ever lift your head up from the stock! You'll have a sense of using your cheek to steer the gun to the target. That's how you stop head-lifting! This one tip alone will now pick up your scores to impressive levels. Here are two of the reasons to use the bow technique. **1)** The head stays down and body English can be felt, so the gun and shooter are both compatible to each other. **2)** You and the gun are partners and neither one alone nor the other can break the targets. It takes two to score.

CONVENTIONAL WISDOM
"You can't put the mule behind the cart and expect a good pull."

It's time to discuss what is right and what is wrong. Conventional wisdom is often wrong. If you watch the pros shoot, they all have there own distinct style. There is no standard mode. Yes, principles apply, but rules can be broken. In fact, in all disciplines in sports, when rules are broken... new world records are established! Every great invention ever made broke the rules of conventional wisdom of the day. The word wrong and impossible should be taken out of your vocabulary. There are many Hall of Fame trapshooters who use unorthodox shooting methods. Where you get into trouble is following the crowd, shooting just like they do. Continue to do this and you will be shooting just like them. When you consider most in the crowd lose, that's not an ideal goal to set your eyes on. *"Trap Shooting Secrets"* encourages developing your own style of shooting. Take it one step further. No matter how you wish to shoot, all you need to do is put that little bead on the target and you'll have a dead target. It doesn't matter if you cant the gun, use the bow technique, or any other form of getting the gun to the target. Just as long as you can put that bead on the target consistently, you're going to come out a winner. That's not saying ignore wisdom, but to expand your thinking and be bold to try new things, anything that will break targets. A trapshooter should shoot quickly, but before you can master quick shooting, you must know how to shoot in slow motion. So, slow down and track the target properly so you can reliably repeat each and every move to the target.

THE MIND'S EYE
"You've heard the phrase, *'I've seen it in my mind's eye.'* Say what?"

Remember a happy moment in your past. Close your eyes and replay the film of events. Try to pick out details of the scene. Now try it with your eyes open. Detail will be lost, but if you fixate on an object and concentrate you can catch glimpses of the event. For some people, this can be difficult for not everyone has the ability to visualize, though it can be learned. Let's try it.

Place a penny on a tabletop. Stare at it examining every detail: the date and mint stamp, Lincoln's facial expression, the words, "In God We Trust" and "Liberty". Notice if the penny is bright or dull. Now close your eyes and force you mind to reproduce the object. Don't expect instant results, it may take some time for the penny to materialize. Breathe deeply and smoothly so you can hear your breathing. Do not let the eyes search behind the eyelids, keep eyes focused dead center. Don't think of anything. Let the object come into view. You may notice a white fuzzy object trying to materialize into something, this is the penny. With practice it will arrive. If all you see is blackness, try staring at the penny again, but this time shine a bright light on it. A flashlight will do fine. If this still fails, take a pencil and paper, close your eyes and draw the penny. Don't worry if the artwork is terribly sloppy, just draw as best you can. Keep trying to visualize as much as you can and one day, out of the blue, the penny will emerge in your mind's eye.

You may find you can visualize the penny (or better yet, a clay target) with your eyes open. Even if you are totally unsuccessful at producing the object visually in this practice exercise, you will be inducing concentration. You may not see the object, but your mind still knows what it is. Close your eyes. Can you see targets flying out of a traphouse? Practice this with eyes closed, then with eyes open; practice imagining breaking the targets hard. Sometimes, no matter how hard you try you can't seem to visualize anything. No problem! By performing the exercise the ideal end result will still be accomplished... breaking more targets!

Again, the mind's eye is a very powerful tool, but it can be a dreaded enemy. Be certain when you see another shooter lose a target you "reset" your mind-set, transforming the target into a broken target. When a target is lost, watch the target fall all the way to the ground before you shoulder the gun. When it breaks up on the field, repeat the trigger word, *"Dead!"* After you see that this method works you can just say the trigger word without waiting for the target to strike the ground.

SWING TIMING
"A bad habit is always a bad habit even when it feels right."

When you are shooting awfully bad it is not simply a mood change to blame, but rather a timing problem. Trigger timing is best explained and described as a habit of calling for the target and instantly shooting simply because your internal time clock convinced you to shoot. Trigger timing comes into play when you believe the sight picture is correct, then the trigger is pulled. It is often too fast and too wrong resulting in lost targets! Shooting within the internal time clock (See *Trap Shooting Secrets* book for explanation) is important to maintain consistency but not at the expense of accuracy. In other words, timing has to be performed properly. Observe a decent shooter having a bad day, missing targets, and you'll notice the trigger is pulled out of habit, because it has worked more often than not for the shooter, so instead of taking corrective action, the trigger is pulled out of synchronization. The eye sees the target, trigger is pulled, but the muzzle is nowhere near the target! It is lagging behind or "pushed" somewhere else. The problem is mood, and reflexes are not as reliable as we wish them to be to our internal time clock. For some shooters a severe slump occurs, lasting months or years, all due to timing problems. Just because your internal time clock invokes you to pull the trigger doesn't make it the right thing to do if you're going to miss the target. There is another factor to consider and it is "Swing Timing."

Swing Timing is the time required to point the muzzle to the target. For the shooter having a bad day, notice the gun's swing is no longer smooth but "stabbing" at the target as if in a panic. Shooting has become very habitual, relying on luck of the draw, hit and miss, panic shooting. The muzzles are "pushed" to the target instead of smoothly "flowing" to the target. If you watch pros shoot, it appears they shoot awfully fast, but in fact it is slow motion to them. They are just so proficient in their trigger and swing timing they can speed up the process, but in their mind the target is actually traveling in slow motion and they have plenty of time to swing to the target. To prove this, observe the fluidity of their gun's muzzle to the target. It's fast, but very smooth and moreover, extremely accurate. What they are truly concentrating on is precision, placing that sight bead exactly where it should be. And when you slow down your swing timing so you can better see and track the target's flight angle, you have a clearer view of the correct sight picture, resulting in broken targets. Likewise, when swing timing is decelerated, trigger timing is also decelerated and visual focus on the target increases, equiviling enhanced sight picture. Slow down, don't speed up! This may appear to be a contradiction from my book, *Trap Shooting Secrets*, explaining to speed shoot, but it is not. A novice needs to speed up, a proficient shooter needs to slow down! Why? Because you already have the body moves down pat, you know where to break the target, it's just that you have lost precision. To regain precision you have to slow down all you moves to the target to get into the "slow motion" mode. When you do, you will later find there is little deviation from when you used to shoot the targets, maybe breaking the targets a few feet distant but now breaking more of them.

The key to understanding trigger and swing timing is that both are separate and distinct to themselves. One cannot be used without the other. When both are in synchronization, targets will be annihilated. If trigger timing alone is used, you will find yourself snap shooting, attempting to shoot too quickly, aimlessly yanking the trigger. If swing timing alone is used, the gun will feel like trying to swing a lead mallet horizontally, resulting in shooting behind the targets. If the swing and timing are too rapid you'll shoot over the top of the target. If you swing and shoot purely out of habit, "*But this is where I always shoot the targets,*" then you are zone shooting, and since targets are slipping by, you are likely stabbing the muzzle at the target, which means an absolute loss of precision aim! And there is one more factor, Visual Target Acquisition. You can't accurately visually acquire the target's true flight angle if you have lost control of trigger and swing timing. Why? You're shooting so fast or out of pure habit, concentration is diminished and there is no clear sight picture.

To enhance swing control and consistent trigger pulls, insure the gun's stock-grip fits your hand properly. Your trigger finger should be aligned on the grip so it pulls back in a straight line. Custom fitting the grip is a simple process (for the experienced stock fitter) of reshaping contours to match your hand dimensions. For shooters with sensitive trigger finger pulls, increased precision of trigger dexterity arises. In most cases, the upper forward section of the comb is the culprit and the grip itself too thick. Again, many shooters do not truly shoot a gun which properly fits them and then wonder why targets are lost here and there.

Buttplate or heelplate. When shouldering the gun, occasionally under certain weather conditions or otherwise, the butt-end of the gun will slip a smidgen. This too may occur on the swing, causing a lost target. The best recoil pad in the world can't help you if it's slipping or sliding as it seeks equilibrium. The novice shooter will hardly recognize such minute irregularities, but the experienced shooter should! A curved recoil pad will make huge improvements, but even then a slip can occur. A recoil pad with serration's will resist slipping on the shoulder or vest pad. Shooting with a shirt alone? When you perspire the shirt will slide on the skin and the gun will slip out of position. Another method is to apply a thin layer of closed-cell foam rubber or spray a fine coating of anti-slip glue (used to tack throw-rugs to floors yet easily removed). Often the cure is even simpler by just applying increased shoulder pressure, hugging the gun snugly to insure a solid mount. Somewhere down the line you may have become a bit too relaxed, taking gun mount for granted, and it's causing you to have some bad shooting days. Precision shooting demands a decisive gun mount. A good practice tip: shoulder gun and swing muzzles in all directions, then draw your name with the muzzles on a imaginary blackboard, keeping your attention focused on any tail slippage, then level the gun to see if the sight bead stacking has changed. Best tip? Hug the gun firmly!

PRACTICE TIPS Phase 9
"Believe in yourself. Believe you can."

These practice tips will smooth out kinks you are having in relation to trigger and swing timing. You will discover initially all slows down and it is uncomfortable. Later, everything will seem to speed up again as you become acclimated to the new slower, yet highly accurate swing speed. Now you'll be shooting with greater precision than you thought possible. To invoke this mind-set at will use the trigger word *"Smooth and Slow."*

1. Don't plan to break the target in your usual timing. Call for the target and track it slowly until the sight picture is right on the money. You'll smoke the target. Do it on all stations.
2. Don't rush the target. Relax. You have plenty of time to shoot. Keep this thought in your mind.
3. Think slow motion.
4. Think: Precision! Precision! Precision! Accuracy governs trigger and swing speed.
5. Be smooth to the target. Muzzles must flow smoothly as if in slow motion.
6. Targets will appear to fly unhurriedly. If not, you are stabbing the muzzles to the target again.
7. Control your eyes to lock-on to the target and just watch it for a second before swinging the muzzle. This will help you to see the target cleanly and test the slow motion effect as you slowly move the muzzle to catch the receding target.
8. There is no hurry or rush to break the target. An accurate sight picture takes priority over habit!
9. Force yourself to pull the trigger only when the sight picture looks absolutely fabulous. You miss because you are not truly looking at the target, and if you are not looking at the target, the muzzle cannot align. Although the alignment is in error, habit forces you to pull the trigger due to uncontrolled timing. Discipline yourself to pull the trigger only when the sight picture is correct, even if you have to track the target beyond the zone you have established to break the target. There is no excuse for random, habitually sloppy shooting. Think precision! Be precise! Don't rush the target! Slow down if need be! Once precision is reestablished, speed will naturally increase over time.
10. Try various sight pictures, pulling trigger when you see top of target, bottom, left, right, etc. This develops precision trigger control and visual focus. Strict discipline increases scores.

PERFECTION
"Think the unthinkable; you'll do the impossible."

Your shooting disposition must change from mediocre, *"I'll shoot and hope for the best,"* to perfectionist, *"I'll break them all."* And mean it! You will see many shooters too relaxed in registered competition, as though they were having fun at another practice session. The shooters who are deliberate in their shooting usually win or at least score high, taking their due share of the option money. Too many shooters are just shooting and not shooting with dedicated precision. They have not fine-tuned their technique or don't know how to advance to the next level of proficiency. They wrongly believe, the more they shoot the better they will get. Often, improvement is made but it is always a hit 'n miss affair with choppy scores revealing gross inconsistencies. The advancement process to perfection is a very complex affair and severely unaccommodating. It begins with a total reevaluation of every aspect of your shooting style, stance and technique and ends with a new style of shooting. Growth and change is imperative. You can't continue to keep shooting wrong no matter how right it feels. For some, a total overhaul is required, while others may only need develop a more serious attitude or simply slow down their shooting so they can deliberately burn that sight bead on the target. Sounds easy, but as you know it is painfully troublesome to do. Shooting is 90% mental and visual concentration until you become proficient, thereafter shooting requires 110% of your undivided attention. Here are some pointers:

PRACTICE TIPS Phase 10
"Is it conceivable you are using the creative power of mind to limit your abilities?"

1. Practice mounting the gun with eyes closed and opening the eyes after gun is shouldered. You need to see the sight beads stacked and aligned perfectly, not once in a while, but all of the time. You should feel the gun mount process. Even before you open your eyes you know it is right! Failure to perfectly mount the gun is perhaps the most routine error the vast majority of trapshooters make. They just don't practice it!
2. Foot position and stance posture should be aligned to the traphouse. Regardless how you position your feet, it must be comfortable. Maintain perfect balance when swinging the muzzle with no muzzle rise or drop when swung to the target. More targets are lost due to improper foot position, stance and swing technique than most shooters realize. Those who feel this is unimportant are usually the ones that need correction the most and are often hit n'miss shooters or experience prolonged or repeated slumps.
3. Evaluate every aspect of your setup. Leave no stone unturned. Ask yourself, *"I do it this way, because ..."* If the answer is not related to aiming the gun properly and reliably to the target, then learn why you are doing things the way you do them. Every motion must have a purpose, a goal, a reason! You just don't do things because other shooters do it, or because you have always done it this or that way. **Examples**: why do you place your cheek on the comb where you do? Could you improve if the length of pull on the gun were changed? Why do you mount the gun as you do? Could a more efficient process be better? Why do you feel cheek pressure on the comb before calling for the target? Do you know how much pressure is required to prevent head-lifting? Why do you swing the muzzles to the target so rapidly? Would a slower more controlled approach increase precision? Evaluate everything, and do this while you are at a practice trap. It's the only way to become finely tuned and at one with yourself and the gun.
4. Slow down the entire process. When you enter slow motion mode, errors in technique are easier to identify and correct. **Examples**: If you mount gun fast, slow down so you can "feel" every muscle in motion. If you swing muzzle quickly, slow down so you can see if the sight bead is tracking the target accurately. Feel every muscle from cheek pressure to the tips of your toes. Know what it feels like to be shooting right or wrong. Everything must be felt, otherwise, you are simply going through motions with no purpose of design. Targets slip away due to errors in the setup! Targets slide into the horizon when technique is flawed! Lost targets don't happen by sheer accident, they are created by human error or poor technique.

5. Perfection and precision shooting walk hand in hand. Why do you pull the trigger when the sight bead is not on the target? Think about that! Do you know how to stop doing such foolish things? It's really easy, just go practice a round with only one thought in mind, *"I will pull the trigger only when the sight bead is perfectly aligned to the target."* Use the trigger word *"Trigger Control"* or *"Eye Control"* and it works magic. Why would anything so simple produce such remarkable results? Because trapshooting is a mind game, a game where we need constant reminders to repair a derailed mind. If you really focus all your energy into putting the sight bead right on the target (or lead in the proper place for hard angles) the target will break. If you do this and the targets still do not break, then you must reevaluate all aspects of your setup and swing dynamics. Make changes through experimentation until the targets dust hard. Remember, slow down your shooting when you do this. Accuracy is more crucial than speed! Work on this one practice tip and you'll see a tremendous improvement. It's easy, so mark your hint card to work on this next time you practice.

6. There is more, too much more to list here but you have the idea and the plan. Every motion must have a purpose. Every motion develops a "feel" so you will always know when something is wrong in the setup or technique! Hug the gun so you and the gun are one and the same. Go ahead; try it. If you're snug with the gun, you will see great improvement in your scores. Head-lifting vanishes and you'll be placing the sight bead deeply onto the target with precision. A snug gun will respond to your body moves more than a loosely held gun. It will eliminate shooting behind targets! If the gun is not firmly socketed to your shoulder and your cheek is not down snugly as you swing, the target will always appear to be getting away from you and the gun lagging behind. This produces a quick reflex reaction to hurry up and catch the target causing you to stab or jerk the muzzles, often missing the target. If the gun is snug, you can be very smooth and unhurried. Allow your body to move to the target, not just pushing the muzzle with your arm, especially the back fence shooters. Adjust eye and gun hold so you don't have to stab at the targets. Be quick, but do not rush targets! Get that sight bead onto the target before you pull the trigger. Do not shoot out of phase with a false time clock in the mind telling you to pull the trigger because it feels like the right time. Make sure the eyes tell you when to pull the trigger.

MOVING GUN TECHNIQUE
"It is not worth an intelligent man's time to be in the majority. By definition, there are already enough people to do that." G. H. Hardy

Is it right for you? You'll never know lest you try. What is the purpose of a moving gun and why do some shooters use it? 1) The muzzle is in slight movement when the shooter calls for the target. 2) Primarily it developed as a habit with no true understanding or discipline as to why they do it. It's just something they do. But is this a bad habit? Depends on the shooter, but reexamine the status quo of conventional wisdom that frowns on moving gun techniques. There is much to be said positive for the form!

Consider the aspect of target speed exiting the house. It's fast! Your gun is stopped and to get it moving requires an instant shock or burst of electrical energy to the muscles to overcome the gun's dead-weight inertia. This can cause a shooter problems. 1) First comes the impulse to stab at the target, to force the gun to move quickly lest the target get away. The muscles must be totally energized in one impulse, thus when inertia is overcome and the muzzle swings, the muscles must apply braking effects to decelerate the swing. 2) This tends to cause the shooter to push the gun violently instead of smoothly to the target. The swing becomes uncontrolled and energy is expended to constantly adjust and correct muzzle swing speed resulting in erratic muzzle movement. 3) This knee-jerk reaction can setup the shooter's nervous system to flinch. The muscles are bursting with energy and are tense. Tense muscles are not easily controlled and may suddenly discharge energy with a flinch due to nerve impulses. 4) The trigger finger muscles tend to tighten and lose smoothness. Anticipation sets in and often the trigger is pulled at the wrong time, resulting in a clean miss.

Now take a peek at the positive side of a moving gun... all of the above are greatly diminished! The more you think of moving the gun as you call for the target, the more logical sense it makes. The muscles are not subjected to a sudden explosion of energy, they are turned on smoothly, and when the target appears, less energy is required to move the heavy muzzle to the target. Inertia is managed and under control. Think of the timing factor, it's smooth and quick and the muzzle will reach the target sooner, an advantage not to be disregarded. You could imagine a ton of benefits a moving gun can convey. It's logical and therefore practical to develop the technique within your setup. The problem arises as to what is a good moving gun technique versus a bad form? And how does one develop comfort with the technique?

Wrong Moves. Generally speaking, a moving gun is wrong if: 1) The movement serves no purpose to derive the above mentioned benefits. The move must have a purpose with a plan and a design. 2) Gun is moving in a horizontal direction that will clearly move in the opposite direction of a target. 3) The movement is performed on a impulse reaction instead of a deliberately controlled move. 4) Movement is unsmooth. 5) Stance is rendered to a state of imbalance which fails to produce consistency when moving the gun during the call routine. 6) Excessive mental energy is required to control the movement (this happens when learning the technique, but should dissipate as moves become second nature). 7) Muzzle control is lost due to faulty moving gun technique. 8) Too much or too little movement upsets timing and concentration. 9) The technique can't be made comfortable no matter how much you try with practice. 10) Targets do not break hard and scores are punishingly low. 11) Muzzle rise or fall upsets the ability to track muzzle to target on the correct flight path.

Good Moves. Obviously, you have a good moving gun technique if the above do not come into play. Despite the obvious, a good moving gun technique should have smoothness built into the form, a relaxed nature where the muzzles effortlessly flow to the target. With body muscles already slightly energized this smoothness will occur. A good moving gun technique should; 1) Be controlled and managed with ease. 2) Result in hard target hits. 3) Advance the body muscles to easily flow to the target. 4) Be repeated with accurate consistency and 5) Feel comfortable and creates higher scores. 6) Muzzle cants slightly or pushes forward when calling for target (advanced moving gun method, most shooters should maintain a still gun when calling for target).

TWO MOVING GUN TECHNIQUES
"Part of being sane, is being a little bit crazy." Janet Long

A gun that does not move, yet must reach instant acceleration from a dead stop, is at a disadvantage to a gun that is already in motion. Like pushing a stalled car, it takes great energy to overcome the vehicle's inertia, yet little energy to keep it moving once the wheels are rolling. You may find developing a moving gun technique awkward. Join the club. It is annoying and frustrating to learn, as everything new is. Try it. Work on it. You may incorporate into your style. If not, the fact you have practiced it will give you a deeper understanding of the game, and that is encouraging news! Through experimentation you learn and progress.

FORWARD STAB. Many skeet and hunting type shooters use an exaggerated form of forward leaning with the knee bending the body forward that can be used in trapshooting, to a degree. Problems arise when the forward lean is excessive and unrepeatable. To move the gun forward to accomplish a moving gun, simply lean forward 1". There is no need to lean 6" or an entire foot! A small 1" slow motion advance will setup all the muscles to turn on. The muzzle should not dip, waver or rise. Just move it <u>slowly</u> forward. Be aware, this will upset your timing, as the target may appear at the forward motion of the gun at differing points. At first, it will appear horrifically impractical and discomforting, but it will work if you make it work. The rule is 1" but you may eventually find more or less desirable, but any movement over 2" is not recommended; otherwise repeatability will suffer. The extent of muzzle forward movement can be determined by the duration of your call.

If the target does not appear before you reach the end point of muzzle travel, say 3 to 5 degrees you have a slow pull... don't shoot it! Likewise if target appears before muzzle begins moving, you have a fast pull not to shoot. Adjust your call timing. One-half inch of gun movement is a good place to call. **Tip**: Use your cheek to push the gun forward to eliminate head-lifting. This will help you get deeper into the target by making certain your eye is pinned solidly behind the sight rib. Use your cheek to assist in swinging the gun. Apply unrelenting cheek pressure at all times and more targets will break. A good method to practice is to feel your forearm hand push upwards while your cheek applies pressure to push the muzzle back down. When both are equalized the gun will remain steady and will be properly fitted to your body, if the gun fits you.

ROLLING GUN. Here, as also described in *Trap Shooting Secrets*, the gun is rolled slightly onto its side to apply a minor cant to the muzzle. One-quarter inch of pre-roll when calling for the target will accomplish the mission of incorporating the rolling gun technique into the moving gun format. Extra cant doesn't adversely affect the rolling muzzle since pre-cant is built into the moving gun when you call and less cant angle is required to maintain accuracy during the swing. Naturally, the pre-roll remains left for left-hand shooter's and right on right-handed shooters on all targets. Do not pre-roll more than ½" for ¼ " is sufficient and recommended. Adjust call timing and pre-roll speed accordingly. The roll must be slow and smooth. Yes, you can roll and push the gun forward using both techniques. It's very accurate and you'll see the fast and slow pulls, though it is difficult to learn. Canting is is not wrong if it is performed properly.

CANTING THE GUN
"A lie told repeatedly becomes truth."

Times are changing. Years ago instructors would never ever suggest canting the muzzle of a gun to hit a target. Today, it is taught in sporting clays by notable instructors and used by professionals. Trapshooting has been left in the dust as it is predisposed that no new techniques could be possibly discovered. Canting is not new, it's been around for a long time, usually used by shooters who unknowingly cant the muzzle. When an instructor or coach sees it, the shooter is told it is a flaw in technique. And it is! For the shooter was canting the muzzle without a purpose, it was an error in swing technique being revealed by the degree of cant. This put a bad label on canting the gun. *Trap Shooting Secrets* explores the cant technique, so time won't be spent here on the subject. For precision shooting purposes, try canting the gun, especially on the targets that are giving you trouble on specific posts. A smidgen of cant may allow you to catch up with the target instead of forcing extra lead in the swing. Of course, for canting to work, to control the direction and angle of the shot string, you must have a high point-of-impact gun. If your gun shoots flat, the shot cannot be controlled. As with all new forms, canting is not easy to learn, but it can be fun to experiment with it and even more fun to reach the point where your shot will fly more powerfully and accurately and bite the targets hard.

Remember, if you do cant the gun never use your wrist to twist the muzzle; always use body English by gently bowing from the hips and upper body and steer the gun with your cheek. Be smooth. It requires very little body motion to advance the muzzle which is why when observing shooters who use this technique, the muzzle appears to hardly moves at all. Canting is the ultimate form of accuracy a shooter can learn, yet the most difficult to master. The best way to learn it is to not incorporate the technique so quickly. Practice it, toy with it. Go back to your original style of shooting, then little by little, over many months, apply a touch of cant. The transition will be less painful. When scores drop? Immediately return to your original form of shooting, then evaluate the degree of cant and your body moves in relation to original form and proceed slowly to cant again. That is how you discover errors in this technique. If you don't revert back to the traditional trapshooting stance and form for a reference point, the confusion can be hellish. Canting allows so much muzzle control the ever slightest deviation will send the muzzle scuttling all over the trapfield, which is why canting is destructive for a novice.

But for the precision shooter, canting can be the answer to prayers. Try it. If you don't like it you will learn more about seeing the true target angle and muzzle control that will certainly help you regardless of the technique you have.

The purpose of canting is to shape the shot by directing the shotstring on a "curving" trajectory directly in line or arc ahead of a "curving" target. All trap targets bend on a curved flight path. The result is a massive head-on collision! See Fig. 64 and *Trap Shooting Secrets* book for details. Canting also reduces body movements and accelerates the muzzle to the target. If you want to shoot fast, cant the gun! Mechanically, there is no faster way. It's so quick, you must convince yourself to relax and slow down or you'll be unmindfully snapping at the targets. When learning, your mind is on canting but once learned your body will automatically perform canting for you without thought. However, the moment you think about canting, watch out! Scores tumble as missed targets sail into the kingdom of the lost. Never think of it, do it. Just let it happen. Rule? Less is more. Excessive cant can't break targets.

CHAPTER 7
"If you don't succeed you haven't failed!"

MISSING TARGETS
"Trust in God, work hard, believe in yourself."

You have often heard, "*Shooting is easy, we make it complicated.*" True and False! Shooting is easy; precision shooting is not. To smash handicap targets for high scores takes more than pure habitual shooting, it requires a blending of many techniques. Targets will always be missed due to human error, one day or another. The goal is to minimize the misses to bare bones. The reasons for missing targets are so complex no book or coach could possibly weed them out. See Fig. 63, 64, 65, and 51 through 56. It's more of a personal thing between the shooter and the target. *Trap Shooting Secrets* does a good job on this subject, so the basics won't be repeated here. We'll take it a step deeper.

More targets are lost due to not paying attention, not keeping your eye on the target at all times, improper setup, fatigue, discomfort, target illumination, angle, speed and visibility, not being ready when you call for the target, slow and fast pulls, disruptions in concentration, lost eye focus, heat-induced barrel walking, shifting POI, choke size and shot pattern, eye focus in wrong place, improper foot position and body stance, incorrect swing technique, rushing the target, inexperience, worn clothing, inadequate shot size and velocity deviations, vision deficiency, stabbing the target by pushing or pulling the muzzle, diverse backgrounds, no visualization., thinking, weather conditions, seeing a lost target, faulty point of impact, inconsistent timing, flinching, unsmooth swing, fear of missing, being too aggressive or too cautious, faulty trap settings, improper sight picture and leads, emotions, fast squad rhythm, mood and state of mind, etc. The list may indeed be endless.

So how do you hit more targets? With serious concentration. When you are in deep concentration the subconscious mind is energized, allowing your thoughts to converge and execute all you have learned without thought, focusing on all the right things. Maintaining unyielding concentration on each target is the magic. This is where the shooter must leap from the nest and face reality head-on. The best advice is to practice concentration and learn two things: 1) Feel concentration as a mood. Practice concentrating on objects every day so you can recall the mood at will. Some days you just won't be able to find the fire to recall the mood. To recall properly, you'll need to begin this process after you have shot well. Capture the moment! When the trance-like feeling dissipates after shooting, stop what you are doing and pretend you are being called to a shootoff and turn on the mood. **2)** Visualize as often as you can, swinging your gun and aligning the muzzle to targets. Visualize perfect shots. Now feel the mood.

Once you develop the ability to "feel the game" accuracy will increase. You must feel serious, professional, confident, and certain you can and will break the target. You also have to know what you are doing. There must be elements of situational awareness, knowing what's going on. You can't put a gun to shoulder and pull the trigger on hope and luck. So many shooters do this and miss out on high scores. The target is broken long before you pull the trigger! The plan must be in place so you will know exactly what to do when the target emerges. It's not difficult to do, it's just effortful to remind yourself to setup a plan when shooting a specific station.

Missed targets create more missed targets. If you miss, don't even think about it unless you know exactly what went wrong. That is the trick to learn. To develop the ability to quickly recognize your mistake so you can correct it immediately. Often, we don't know what we did wrong and drop a few more targets. Then later, we realize the error, but it's too late to salvage the score. This ability requires inner knowledge of the game and a total understanding of your technique. It takes time and many hours of practice, sometimes years, to reach this stage of instant error recognition. But it will never arrive if you don't begin now to consciously develop the skill of instant recall. Know why you missed! Know why you hit targets!

It is important not to apply too much pressure upon yourself. You will miss targets because you are not a machine. Most great trapshooters have blown as many tournaments as they have won, if not more.

KNOW YOUR TIMING
"Timing is everything."

Timing is a complex subject. It's something you have to develop on your own. This doesn't mean it is difficult. In fact, it is easy once you understand how timing is broken down then combined into a solid well-functioning form. Timing is difficult to learn, but it's critical to good shooting.

SETUP TIMING
"For every human problem, there is a neat, simple solution; and it is always wrong" Mencken's Metalaw

Be aware of the time it takes to perform the setup. You don't want any deviations. If it takes you six seconds then work on maintaining this interval all of the time. Once you deviate, you'll open the gates to lost target city. The setup speed should be slow and deliberate, especially so the eye can pre-focus. Those who setup too quickly or are inconsistent with setup timing often keep missing targets they shouldn't be missing. You can get away with it shooting singles, but in handicap you'll pay the price. See *"Squad Timing"* and you'll see why.

CALL TIMING
"Time is the wisest of all counselors." Plutarch

Call timing is the interval of time after the gun is shouldered, cheek is down solid, and begins when the eye is pre-focused ready for the target. Once the eye is focused the call is made. But it goes further than this. The way you call has great importance. The tone, volume, intonation, length of time -- are all critical. Each shooter must experiment to find the ideal call. Some call all the way to the target while others issue a brief staccato sound. The prolonged call is great, but it has dangers. If you call and discover when you pull the trigger the call volume changes or tone shifts, you'll end up pulling the trigger on timing only... when you hear the octave shift. That tonal shift triggers the brain to yank the trigger even when the target is nowhere close to being hit. It's a vocal flinch! To call all the way to the target, the voice must be monotone all the way to the target. A short call is fine, but beware that brief calls tend to burst from the throat, often causing the muzzle to dance. Keep these points in mind when developing your call routine.

SWING TIMING
"This time, like all times, is a very good one, if we but know what to do with it." Ralph Waldo Emerson

Swing timing is difficult to explain. It's not fast or slow, it's "smooth." The gun and eye hold points are critical to establish proper swing timing. If you swing fast, you'll end up pushing the muzzle with your hand, but it can accelerate smoothly by using body English, using the upper torso and / or shoulders to swing the gun. If you are shooting fast flying targets such as on the East, South or West Coast areas, you'll have a tendency to swing faster. This is wrong. Swing smoother, being less hurried will produce more hits. When shooting soft slow targets you can accelerate the swing by raising your eye and gun hold. Use eye and gun hold to adjust swing timing and always think of the trigger word "*Smooth*." If targets are not rising, lower your gun and eye hold. This will adjust swing timing to avoid overshooting the targets. Swing timing is not a matter of adjusting speed of the swing. Watch shooters who have inconsistent swing timing, they speed up the swing when a target gets the jump on them -- often stabbing and missing. They react to the target instead of smoothly attacking it. To perfect swing timing you must truly pre-focus your eyes and be ready for the target when you call. Do this and all will be smooth. If your swing is inconsistent it is not smooth nor is it repeatable. The problem is eye and gun hold and eye pre-focus, not the swing speed. The error is in the setup.

SQUAD TIMING
"Lose time and you'll never find it again."

Have you ever noticed you start well on the first trap then slip and fall on the second, third, or forth? Squad rhythm, in the common sense of keeping a good flow, is not the only timing problem you must be watchful of. When you shoot to a squad rhythm, you are likely focused on a "hurry up and shoot" mindset. What it does is destroy your setup routine and your eye pre-focus. You know the dangers of a machinegun squad, so maintain your own setup timing. Six seconds is plenty of time to mount and call. Be consistent and play your own game. But now going to the other traps, the squad will have other influences upon you such as: where they break the targets may be distant to where you break yours. If you're not careful this will influence you to slow down, especially when you miss a target or two. Don't get over cautious. Maintain your own shoot timing. If you look back on a bad event, you'll likely see your timing has altered from trap to trap. You may even be influenced to the point your call progressively deviates from the norm. This too will cause lost targets. Now you know how to prevent that from happening again.

Another thing you'll notice is when the squad first starts shooting they don't break the targets so close as they do after a couple traps have been shot. This quick shooting of the targets is gradual and you must watch out for it or you'll get caught up into it. This is when the targets begin to slip away intact. Play your own game. Pace yourself. Stay focused, and pay attention to that squad rhythm so it will not lead you into a dead-end situation.

SHOOT TIMING
"Such power there is in clear-eyed self-restraint." James Russell Lowell

There is an internal time clock within each shooter that wants to break the target very quickly. Listen for that inner voice telling you to shoot, for once you discover it you'll be well on your way to shooting in a tight zone. This internal time clock is the subconscious mind, often screaming, though the shooter fails to hear, to "*Shoot! Shoot!*" When you practice, call for the target and you'll notice your mind wants to shoot the target faster than you are doing it. But if you try it you'll end up pushing and stabbing the muzzles, snapshooting and missing. Why? Because you can't shoot to the internal time clock until you make accommodations to your foot position, stance, eye and gun hold, swing dynamics and call routine. Only then can you shoot the zone your mind wants to shoot. That's how the pros shoot so quickly and accurately. They know the zone, and they've made the changes necessary to adapt to the new timing. There comes a point in time you will need to discover your zone, where you will break all the targets. See Fig. 23, 31, 32, 33, 34, 35, 51, and 78. If you are breaking targets, some close in and others far away, your shoot timing is undulating from target to target, station to station, and trap to trap. Now you know why some days are good and others are bad. It's your timing! Find the zone and make all the necessary changes required to break the targets in the zone. It's going to take hard work, but it's time for you to advance onward to better scores and true consistency.

TURN-DOWN TIMING
"Prudent, cautious self-control is wisdom's root." _{Robert Burns}

Timing is everything. Slow pulls will kill scores and destroys everything if you shoot them. Zone is ruined, reaction time, eye focus, nervous system is supercharged to push-stab muzzle, mind is confused, sight picture is blurred, head-lifting occurs, and the list goes on. You must learn to recognize a slow pull when you are calling. If the target does not appear when it should, turn it down or you'll miss more than you deserve. Bad pulls will get you! Pull control is timing too and more important than you may believe. Turning a target down is not a sin if it is a slow or fast pull. If the pull isn't right, *learn* to turn them down or desensitize so you can shoot them by being totally ready for the target when you call. If the rules allow turning down, it is legal. If you have an exhausted or lazy puller, replace the puller. If you can't? Then extend the duration of your call tone and expect the target to exit "somewhere" within the tone. This will greatly help when getting horrible pulls. It reduces the element of surprise and that keeps your head down on the comb where it belongs. Fast pulls will have the same effect but worse, because the target exits before that time clock in your head tells you you're ready to see a target. So, you have to turn down bad pulls if you want to hit all your targets.

Professionals will not shoot a target they know they can't hit. Now, that certainly is not *chasing* targets, it's *attacking* them with a prescribed plan. When you learn how to control turn-down timing, you are now executing that plan, knowing way before you pull the trigger if the target is broken or not. That is fine-tuning the setup and those targets don't stand much of a chance when you use the technique.

Now, you can end up a neurotic if you become too sensitized to the insidious slow pull and there's a cure for that. You call for the target, but don't start the internal clock until you *see* the target exit. This means you may have to use an extended call duration so you won't sense gaps in the interval of time delayed. Now if you run out of breath when calling and there is no target, that was one heck of a slow pull! There is no corrective action to take on a fast pull except to not shoot it. Until voice-activation launches targets, you will have to learn to turn down targets. It's not easy to do, but it must be done if your setup is being destroyed. Proper training and frequent rest breaks for pullers, is required. Competition is business, not solely fun and games. Voice call systems is a must for the sport to flourish professionally and fairly for all players.

Practice tip 1. At the practice trap, concentrate on setting up your preshot routine by paying attention to the time intervals of target release in relation to your call timing. Setup a timing factor in your mind when you want to see the target emerge from the house in direct relationship to the time interval of your call duration. If you use a short staccato call "*PULL*," you may want the target on the "U," but on the 4th "L" if you use an extended call, "*PUUUULLLL*." This is only half the story.

Practice tip 2 Now that you have a general idea of the pull timing you want, you must now "see" the target in a specific zone to stitch the technique down. If your eye hold is too low, the zone is expanded and your eye is seeing too much field of view and the pulls will appear too fast or slow, so start raising your eye hold to *compress* the zone's field of view. This will help reduce sensitivity to miniscule pull variations. Shooters using voice activation systems, adjust the gain control and direction of microphone to insure proper pick up of your voice call.

Now you have the basic formula. Pull timing within the mind's internal clock will tell you the pull is slow or fast, and the eye will verify the pull condition when the target enters the zone. If the pull was good, it will *feel* right and the target will be in the zone. If the pull is slow, the target will not be in the zone and it will *feel* wrong. If the pull was fast, the target will give you a 'serious jolt of surprise' upsetting this timing formula. It all sounds elementary until you begin to practice this formula, then you will see just how impressionable it is and how difficult it truly is to not only learn but to "refuse" to shoot.

You can't hit all of the targets or be machine-like in your shooting if you are chasing targets all over the place out there. You have to establish a zone to shoot the targets so you have very few sight pictures to memorize and less swing motions. No zone equals targets being shot in too many zones so timing and swing errors will creep in to create missed targets. Watch a new shooter and you'll see this "no fun zone" taking place. Watch a pro and you'll see a tight zone. If you have never practiced this before, you will find it difficult to manage at first, but it will "click in" quite easily once you try. The mere fact of testing the technique gives you this valuable inside knowledge.

Practice tip 3 Try a moving gun technique. You can tell a fast or slow pull by the degree of gun movement. If you pre-cant, the gun's barrel will roll too far over and you have a slow pull. If you use a forward stab, the muzzle will move too far forward and you'll *see* and *feel* the slow pull way before the target enters the zone. Moving guns have inherent benefits of timing the pulls and breaking static momentum so you gain incredible control of the gun and the target.

Practice tip 4 Remember to learn how to shoot a target that escapes into the far reaches of the zone. Just in case you do shoot the target and it was a slow pull... you'll' know how to hit the target anyway. This may be difficult to understand, but learn how to perform a "two-stage" swing. The typical swing is one smooth move to the target. The two-stage is: you swing, but realize the pull was slow and you shouldn't be in this position. But now that you are committed... you accelerate the muzzle, at this point of recognition, to dispatch the target. This not an easy trick to learn. I've seen a lot of pros us the technique and you have, too, but have likely not recognized it when they do it. It's used on all targets and most certainly on hard angles that have taken the shooter by surprise. It is often used to apply that "extra push" of the muzzle to lead the target. Yes, it is a *push* and the *only* push you should ever use when shooting trap... and even then the body moves with the push. Remember, if you push a gun, even softly, it will surely shove the rib out of alignment with the eye, spelling disaster. It's one of the craziest things trapshooters persist in doing. Sadly, most shooters don't even realize they are doing it! That's how powerful the habit has become.

Practice tip 5 If bad pulls are driving you crazy, there are some tips you can use. **1)** Raise your call volume, but not so loudly to cause muzzle-flip or the eyes to defocus. **2)** Try the rolling-gun technique. As you apply cheek pressure to the comb, the gun rolls on its side slightly during the call. If the target does not appear when the muzzle has rolled 5-degrees, the pull is slow, so turn it down. **3)** Ask the puller to stand closer to the squad. 4) Replace the puller if s/he is suffering fatigue. **4)** Use a whistle instead of your voice. **5)** Locate a puller you know who can pull on time. **6)** Adjust sensitivity and delay on voice call systems.

CHAPTER 8

THE TEN BIG MISTAKES
"I did not miss the target… it eluded me!"

If you have low scores, it is likely you are making the TEN B-I-G MISTAKES many good shooters make. **1)** Stance and foot position is improper for the post. **2)** Mounting the gun is too fast and it is shouldered improperly or the gun does not fit the shooter. **3)** Improper or nonexistent gun & eye hold points. **4)** Gun hold is too high so target's track cannot be acquired with gun & eye hold points improper or nonexistent and failure to establish an effective zone. **5)** Failure to pre-focus eyes prior to call causing eye-flitter movements to target, not seeing the target in slow-motion and establishing an improper zone with eye disengaging from the target. **6)** Call volume too loud causing a visual concentration crash and muzzle ballet, call volume too soft or call timing error shooting at slow pulls. **7)** Muzzle is pushed with no body English moves. **8)** Not steering gun with cheek ruins swing, accuracy and creates head-lifting. **9)** No back-sighting to establish precision shooting annihilates trigger timing. **10)** Not staying in the gun causes head to lift from comb when trigger is pulled and begins the flinch process.

If you were to just take these 10 items and scribe them on a 3x5-index card, bring them with you to practice sessions and seriously work on them, you would see amazingly rapid results.

SUBCONSCIOUS TIMING
"Few minds wear out; more rust out." <small>Christian Nestell Bovee</small>

"*I shoot subconsciously.*" You've heard that a million times. It is a mistake! If you find yourself just mounting the gun, calling and shooting with no plan or thought-line, you may shoot well enough, then one day you can't hit anything. It's okay to shoot subconsciously, but you have to be in total control of the subconscious commands. Here's why. When you miss a target, the subconscious will have learned how to miss and it will do it again and again. It's the same effect as seeing a lost target and most, if not all, shooters then miss their targets too! The subconscious mind is a powerful machine and it has no conscience. It will do right and wrong without a care. Total subconscious shooting is 'dumb shooting' and it will only get you into trouble more often than not. There are exemptions to the rule, but they are the minority. Most shooters will not be precision shooters shooting blind; they get lucky and win, get punched a yard, then find themselves impaled at the back fence hardly ever wining anything! Precision shooting was never learned. It was never understood. Through concentration and precision shooting techniques you will develop the ability to prevent the subconscious mind from playing it's own game, the game of losing. You must control the subconscious or it will control you. You must be in the process of repeatedly teaching it to do the right thing; otherwise it will tend persistently to do the wrong thing. It's what slumps are all about. Slowly, errors creep in and you find yourself in a deep slump. Blame the subconscious mind, for it is deviously full of mischief. The point made is to learn how to shoot with precision and the subconscious will learn and obey. Know your setup timing, gun and eye holds, etc. Be aware of what you are doing and know how to break targets. Simply calling and letting the body do it's own thing just won't cut the cake, for eventually you'll lose control and fall into the abyss of the slump. And it's not an easy thing to teach an old dog new tricks. If this sounds like you, then you are well on your way to dissolving bad habits and beginning a new learning experience... you break the targets, not the subconscious mind or anyone else. You do it with technique, developing your own timing and brutal willpower.

Tip: The more you concentrate on your set up, the more targets you will be hitting.

FLINCHING AND NERVES
"I fear, fear is to be feared, I fear."

Everyone experiences flinching at one time or another. It can be reduced, but never eliminated on a perpetual basis. Some days you'll experience no flinching, while other days, it rises like a rattlesnake destined to ruin your day. *Trap Shooting Secrets* delves into flinching and nervous reactions. Here are a few more tips to unload the burden.

Install or adjust your trigger to a heavier setting. Try a 5-pound pull. Keep in mind, the use of a release trigger is no guarantee flinching will dissolve or scores will rise. If the trigger pull is too light or too tight or lock-time drearily slow or too fast, it will not only encourage a flinch, but also transfix your mind's attention to the trigger. Once this happens, you'll end up fiddling with trigger settings till the end of time. To dissolve trigger attentive disorder, simply tell yourself your trigger is just fine as is, and adapt to its settings and feel. Stop squeezing the trigger, "pull it" with a solid jab. Don't yank it, just move into it with authority when the sight picture is right on. The moment you see the proper sight picture, the trigger is pulled. This is not a "thinking" process. It's a subconscious reaction. If you think, you'll miss! If you concentrate on only seeing the target you won't be thinking of your trigger or other distractions. Diverting your mind away from the trigger is critical, and the best way to do it is to focus your attention where it belongs... on the target. Regardless of trigger pull tension or lock-time you can adapt to anything if you put your mind to it. Don't become "sensitized" to details of lesser importance. This is not to say trigger tension setting is unimportant, just don't get too hung up on the trigger.

Simply installing a higher rib on your gun could dissolve a flinch. How? Sometimes flinching is a reaction caused by not seeing the target in the sights properly and your nerves will cause you to randomly pull the trigger misleading you to believe the target is escaping. The next time you flinch, see if this is what you are doing. The trigger may not be the culprit, but rather your diverted mental focus, over-sensitivity, and failure to not truly see the target. When you don't pay attention to the target, your mind will divert full devotion to the trigger... and everything else you can think of, too!

Nerves: It's a problem everyone experiences, some more than others. The best means to dispel nerves is through concentration. Yes, concentration on the target! The mind can't think of two things at the same time. So if you think of seeing and breaking the target, nerves dissipate. Experience tranquilizes the mind. Enough said.

EXPECTING TO MISS
"He who makes no mistakes usually makes nothing."

How many times have you stepped on line knowing, just knowing you will miss a target? Likely plenty of times. This bad habit must be arrested. I know it is direly difficult, especially when you've given all your best to a round of trap and still miss, but it is important to keep telling yourself you will not miss any targets. Even if you do miss one or two, you must tell yourself, *"That's enough! No more!"* It's a real mental war-zone but you can't surrender to the enemy if you wish to arrive to the point of not missing the targets. When even this positive thinking fails you, it's time to begin believing in yourself. Of course, if your shooting form is defective, or gun doesn't fit, nothing will reverse losing targets. But once you have arrived to the point in your shooting career that you are only missing one or two targets per trap, you can pick up the lost targets with pure self-confidence and faith. Put a tad more aggression into the targets to boost your visual attentiveness and progress will be made. Never expect to miss a target. In fact, if you visualized hitting all of the targets before you stepped on line to shoot, odds are you will. If you miss a target and it comes as a huge shock to you, you know you are on the right track to success. Targets will slip by occasionally even for the pros. But if you are not overwhelmed with astonishment when a target is lost you need to focus more on precision shooting. When you are precise, targets smoke, and when you miss it's a tremendous shock. Don't condemn yourself if you have an off day or two. Think about what you did wrong and correct the problem as best you can. Then step on the line with renewed confidence, with the attitude you will not miss the target. Believe you can hit them all. Have faith.

First you must learn, through forcing your conscious mind, to stop expecting to miss targets. Rationalize with yourself that there really is no reason to miss since you've hit every angle thousands of times. It's reality. It is also reality you will miss a target occasionally. People generally tend to bestow upon themselves more confidence than they actually have. As you know, confidence alone won't get the job done, in fact, it can even be a hindrance. The true goal is developing real confidence, not a pumped up adrenaline rush that can never be sustained. How many times have you stepped on line shooting well beyond your expectations? Then a negative thought arises, "*Something isn't right, I'll miss one or two soon, maybe on post five I'll get clobbered.*" Confidence is more than confidence, it is an expectation you will break the targets! If you expect to break them, like you have thousands of times before, you will. Raise your expectations! Step on the line knowing you're going to annihilate the clays and smash a great score. Convince yourself of the reality. Believe in yourself.

Here's an example of how the mind works. You're watching a movie, say *Indiana Jones*, where he's suddenly surrounded by snakes. Suddenly, you too 'feel' snakes are eminent in your presence, you feel the actor's tension. If something brushed against your leg at this moment you would leap. The mind visualized snakes and your nerves are predisposed to react accordingly. Expectations function in the same way to tune you in and focus on the job at hand. The more you expect, the more you will receive. So expect to perform well and you will. With visualization included, closing your eyes and visualizing smashing the targets with ease will setup your mind before you even pick up the gun! It has just raised your expectations and hence your performance. Trapshooting is a mentally demanding sport, it's all in the mind after you've learned the basics of shooting.

BACKGROUND SCENERY
"It is foolish to tear one's hair in grief, as though sorrow would be made less by baldness." Cicero

Many shooters complain of busy backgrounds for losing targets. It is a good excuse and often a legitimate reason at that, but in reality these shooters place too much emphasis on the backgrounds instead of the target. Certainly, a cluttered and multi-colored backset will obscure the target, making it more difficult to see. This is all the more reason to learn to use your eyes correctly with centralized vision focus. Perhaps, you have not learned how to central-focus your eyes, and when you face a busy background you don't see a three dimensional image of the target ahead of the backdrop scene. If you don't use centralized vision to focus hard on the target, the eye will wander away from the target to the background objects. Another fault is the shooter is very likely to rifle shoot these hard to see targets by looking back to the gun sights, which loses the three dimensional view, allowing the target to blur into the scenery. Perhaps you have not learned how to ignore backgrounds and other shooter's comments about the horrid conditions?

Backgrounds can make a target appear to be traveling faster than what it is as it blurs past the scenery. This, too, can upset your nervous system and causes an acceleration in timing, often with erratic moves to the target. The shooter is shooting faster than his ability and targets slip away. If you keep your eye solidly pinned on the target with central vision and high concentration, the target will slow down! Targets speed up when the eye shifts focus away from the target. This means if your eye momentarily shifts to the background or the gun sights, expect to see a perceived acceleration in target speed. You can't truly see two things at one time. This is why the eye constantly shifts and flickers from object to object in daily life. Learning how to focus and move your eye smoothly requires dedicated practice. Have you practiced it lately?

I've included Fig. 27, 28, 29, 59, and 60 on shooting busy backgrounds. No matter how much shooters complain, the background will remain, so what can you do? **First,** analyze the background from the post you will shoot from and visualize the basic three target angles and where you plan to break them. Where you break them can make a big difference. By altering your timing slightly you can break the target in a zone that favors and enhances target visibility. **Second,** keep your eye solid on the target and nothing else. Just don't look at the background at all. **Third,** you may want to change shooting lenses to a lighter shade as the background can blend with certain lens colors. Dark brown and gray are worst. Light purple, bronze, vermilion and orange is better. **Fourth,** don't confuse background problems with lighting variations. If a cloud passes by your eye will tend to shift to the background as the target becomes less bright and appears as a razor blade. In this case, breaking the target quicker, before it enters the background scene, is a good strategy. In fact, it is the best way to shoot trap targets under all conditions. Shoot a tight zone and consistency increases.

INCREASING YOUR SCORE
"Failure has a habit of repeating itself."

All shooters eventually reach a plateau of consistently hitting, say, 93 - 95% and can't seem to notch up the scores. Ability indicates the shooter is doing a lot of things right to be so consistent. There are many reasons for this shortcoming and here are a few to consider.

1. Slight errors in misjudging the angle of the target, failing to acquire the target at the proper time, eye and gun hold off a smidgen, not being ready when calling for the target and shooting a slow or fast pull. Work on this until you have complete control of the setup and the game. Not knowing how or when to turn down a defective pull is frequently the problem leading to errors of miscalculations and upsets timing.

2. Timing has been altered. Maintain the timing routine from the setup to firing the shot. Discover the zone and stay within it. Timing is everything. If timing is off, the sight picture will change to center-hit the target.

3. Learn to center-hit targets, not just break them. Precision demands gnat's eye accuracy. If you're just shattering targets erratically and near-miss chipping and slicing, the error in aim will be exposed and targets will slip by. Practice with a full or extra full choke to build precision aim. The goal is to dustball the target decisively or mentally self-declare it a lost target in an effort to improve marksmanship.

4. Most of the time a degeneration of concentration is the true reason for losing targets along with nervousness. **First,** learn not to keep score and have only one thought on your mind, *"Break this one target."* There is only one target, not 100. Do this and your scores will increase. **Second,** don't concentrate on concentrating, concentrate on seeing the target. **Third,** convince yourself you can break every target. **Fourth,** use a mental checklist before you call for the target to focus your mind to the job at hand. This will improve concentration, remove mental blocks, diminish choking and distractive squad influences. **Fifth,** beware of shooting from sheer habit in place of a plan to break the target. **Sixth,** be highly aggressive, but be smooth to the target.

5. You may be having a problem with a specific post or target angle. Identify the targets that are slipping away and find the solution. Often, when this is done, another angle or post arises from the ashes to give you problems. It seems to never end. This always happens when you shoot targets out of the zone, as you'll keep forgetting the numerous sight pictures. Shoot the zone and you'll be able to identify what is wrong and reduce sight picture memorization. If you don't shoot a zone, you can't learn all the sight pictures. There will be too many.

6. Ask someone to help you find a new way to break troublesome targets. Yes, there is more than one way to break targets. Experiment with gun cant, hold points, foot position and stance geometry, moving gun techniques. Call to mind, each post usually requires a different method and plan of attack. If you're shooting each post the same, errors will persist. Know the formula to break the targets on each post.

7. Understand what your gun is doing, where it shoots. Adjust point of impact to match your timing. The goal is to put the bead on the target with as little lead as possible. Let the gun advance the lead so you don't have to

make these complex calculations which will only increase miscalculations. Does the gun truly shoot where you look when shooting the zone? Are you shooting a zone? Is your timing and swing correct?

8. Each target should feel like hard work to break it. If the feeling of ease sets in, targets slip by. Are you too relaxed? Too confident you won't miss? Not putting in the extra effort? Not aggressive? Every pro will tell you effortless subconscious shooting is wrong. You must work hard on seeing and breaking the targets insuring you see the proper bird / bead relationships. When you miss the same angle twice or more, you know you're shooting subconsciously or with the eyes only. The subconscious can learn how to miss targets and will be hard to correct at the moment when needed. It can be corrected with solid concentration and using the sight bead to insure a correct bird / bead relationship. You have to use sight beads at long yardage. Sorry, but it's true. Some back-sighting is required so you're not just shooting with your eyes only.

9. Are you using the right shells for your gun? Maybe #8 shot will work better than #7 ½ shot. Perhaps your choke is too wide open or too tight for the yardage you shoot. Is velocity consistent? Usually the choke constriction is too large and will not "smoke" a target; therefore, holes will develop in pattern, especially shooting beyond the 24-yard line. Experiment to find the optimal ammo and chock combination. You'll know it's right when the targets smoke time and time again.

10. Are you stabbing at the targets? If so, you are thinking of shooting fast instead of thinking of shooting the zone smoothly. If you visually acquire the target properly, you'll be in the zone and you'll shoot smooth and fast without thinking of shooting fast. It just happens. Don't let the targets surprise you. If they do, turn them down because it was a slow or fast pull, or you were not ready when you called. Don't shoot slow or fast pulls. You may believe you can handle them, but it upsets timing and allows targets to slip away. Adjust your call duration so you'll know when a pull is early or late. See Fig. 14 thru 17 and 64. The target must appear when you call.

11. Your attitude and mindset may need adjusting. You've likely been stuck in a plateau for quite some time and have not yet convinced yourself that you can do better. It seems the harder you try, the lower the score. Not trying so hard may be the cure for you, then again, trying harder may, too. Trying harder means to try harder to see the target, not physically pushing or swinging the gun with undue force or being tense. It's a mental aggression. If the aggression shows in your call or in your swing, you're not doing it right. Watch the pros and you'll see how it's done. A solid sense of authority generates controlled aggression.

12. Understand that this may be the limit of your shooting ability at this point in time. As time progresses, with extra effort and willpower on your part, progress will be made. Give experience time to grow. Excessive expectations can be the cause of your stagnation. Think out the problems and resolve them one-by-one, over time. With experimentation you will find the cause and solutions to errors. A good coach will save you time and money. It's an investment to consider.

13. Consider equipment modifications or a new gun with modern features as a last resort. A simple step rib, high rib gun will allow you to pick up the targets quicker. Try a high rib gun first before you buy, and consider an adjustable rib gun to zero-in the point of impact. The step rib is an abrupt rise of the rib which naturally leads your eye down the sight plane. Be certain the gun is well balanced and swings smoothly. Regardless of the type of rib, be certain you are not looking for the target with your eye drastically away from the sight plane. See Fig. 50. Above all, have confidence in your equipment and it will take you to higher levels.

14. Evaluate the obvious basics: head-lifting, prescription eyewear, recoil flinch, clothing, gun fit, setup, etc. You may even want to consider holding a low gun on the house or visa versa on all or specific posts.

15. A bad timing habit can form where the shooter pulls the trigger just because it is time to do so. When an odd unexpected angle appears or a slow / fast pull, the trigger is still pulled without looking at the target's true condition. Moving the muzzle vertically or horizontally when no target exists is often the cause of a timing upset. Make certain you see the target before initiating the swing. Freeze until you see the target.

16. Stay away from the score board before you shoot because the only scores that will change will be yours... likely downward. And don't count the hits or losses keeping a mental tally of your score as you shoot. Take one target at a time, for winning always comes by surprise even when you *know* you may win.

17. Extend the call tone time when dealing with slow pulls and don't start your inner time clock to move to the target until you see the target exit. Anticipation destroys timing ferociously.

The above listings are only suggestions. If you try them all in one week, no doubt your shooting will tumble. Try one at a time over a long period of time. Ultimately, the best advice to pick up your scores is to recall everything when you were shooting well and write it down. You will notice the targets appear big, bright and slow when concentration and vision is right on. This indicates the main problem with inconsistent shooters is improper use of the eyes. You must focus sharply on the targets. If you are using a wide-angle and soft focus the targets will appear small, dim and fast. So go back to finding the proper eye and gun hold points. Use a chart to log in these points. See Fig. 30.

YOU AND THE TARGET
"It's a one target game."

Ever wonder why you run a trap and on the next score a low 20, or worse yet ,18? The bottom just fell out and you forgot how to shoot? Could be a spell of exhaustion, but it is more likely the trap settings are the culprit, especially when you recover and score a 25 on the next trap. Go back and take a look at that trap that stole your win and you'll see why this happened. **1)** The lighting and therefore target visibility may have been poor. **2)** The targets are not thrown square and true, flying on steep or shallow angles with little to no face and target speed is fast or slow. **3)** Target speed variations from trap to trap, slow or fast, will radically upset your timing and sight picture to the degree you will feel you have forgotten how to shoot. What happens is your zone shifts, rising in elevation. See Fig. 23, 31, 32 and 33. **4)** Target height is not correct to standards, flying too high or too low. **5)** Look who's pulling and see if the pulls are timely. The puller may be lazy, literally sitting down on the job. When you see this the next time you shoot, ask the puller to stand up! **6)** When the squad leader calls, *"Let's see one,"* pay attention to the target. If the target is not where it should be, don't shoot the trap as is. The pros don't for good reason, they know better. Ask for the traps to be reset if it's throwing weird flight paths or speeds. If this can't be done, then compensate with stance, gun and eye hold variations.

LEARNING TO BREAK TARGETS
"Learning and doing is a bridge safely crossed."

You can break a lot of targets, but the day of destiny inevitably arises where you must no longer do, but learn how to break targets. There is more than one way to break a target! Once you begin to focus on the details of what you did right to dustball the target, more will follow and scores will increase. Too many shooters are just doing it, shooting, hoping to have a lucky day. You can tell by watching slivers or the target breaks into huge chunks. These are lucky hits. A precise shot will annihilate the target, and this should be your goal. Work out a plan to do so on every target angle on each post. Keep trying. Precision breeds precision. It's a must at handicap shooting. It's the only way to bring your handicap scores up to your singles levels of achievement. As you increase yardage from the trap, the targets appear smaller and slight variations of target behavior are harder to visually pick up. Small mistakes in aim are compounded vastly at distance, so precision is an absolute necessity. You can't just keep pointing and shooting at handicap targets. You have to use the sights more than you believe, or have been told, to get the sight picture dead on so you'll know when to pull the trigger. You can get away with it in singles and doubles, but handicap is an entirely different beast to ride. Don't play the singles game when standing on the handicap.

All the books, videotapes and personal instruction in the world cannot help a shooter who is not willing to learn new things. Adopt a learning or quality improvement mindset to expand awareness, and this will link the subconscious mind to the conscious. Focus on precision and it will take you where you want to go. Think precisely.

SUNSET AND SUNRISE SHOOTING
"Some persons do first, think afterward, and then repent forever." Thomas Secker

Depending where the sun is, you will have to lower gun and eye hold to see the target exit the house. Often a black speeding target will be seen. If your eye hold remains high above the trap in low light glare, the target will snap out of the house and you won't even see it. Razorblade targets are hard to see. The sun may be in your eyes or only lighting up half the target. Changing eyeglass lenses can certainly help, but the eye hold is the key to acquire the target as it leaves the house. It's not a good idea to shoot the first or last squad. Why shoot and fight the obvious detriment? Clubs recognize the problem of pros knowing these advantages and use a lottery system of squad order so you can't pick the time to shoot. So, you'll need to learn to shoot in any light or weather condition. Extra eye pre-focus will often do the trick. If the light is really bad, you'll miss targets and that's just the way the cookie crumbles.

CHAPTER 9

"Attempt to pursue excellence."

DEPARTMENT OF CORRECTIONS
"To develop correct form you must reinvent yourself."

Duplicating a professional shooter's form and style of shooting is encouraged to a degree. Still, it is essential to allow your own form to mature. Unfortunately, many shooters have developed an individualistic style of shooting that is totally incorrect, loaded with deadly inaccuracy and bearing wildly fluctuating performance with devastating scores. To identify your own mistakes, learn to be a silent critic by evaluating other shooters' blunders. Evaluation originates from insight. Mistakes are easy to correct once you have developed the ability to identify faults. Be big enough to admit you are wrong and you'll become a member of the small group of elite shooters.

Take a good look at the back-fence shooters and you'll see more defective forms than you would believe possible. How could this be? After all, they are the elite handicap shooters and they had to win many times to arrive where they are today. Pure luck... not true skill! Many have won earned yardage from attending small shoots, then fail miserably in the State and Grand shoots. You'll see these defective shooters at the big tournaments wildly stabbing at the targets losing not only the event, but their option money too. Head lifting? Sometimes, but more often than not you'll see horrendous setup problems. Here are a few examples to evaluate. Remember to keep in mind you may be doing the same thing. If so, correct the problem. Watch the pros and you'll see the right way to do it.

PRACTICE TIPS Phase 11
"Cheer up, the worst is yet to come." Philander Johnson

1. Foot position and body stance are upsetting geometry to the target. The stance is often out of alignment to the traphouse and the swing too flexible, allowing muzzle sway. The cure is a return to a basic foot position, a solid and stable stance, and a firm hugging of the gun close to the body. Balance is often way out of whack with some shooters' feet moving when shooting! If it's too comfortable it could still be wrong as you are comfortable with the wrong foot positioning and stance posture.

2. Gun mount is excessively complicated and totally inconsistent. The gun is mounted too rapidly to insure a proper cheek pressure and 'feel' of the shouldered gun is nonexistent. The cure is to reduce the gun mount procedure to a simple 3 step form. **A)** Smoothly mount the gun in a circular motion to the shoulder and firmly lock it into place. **B)** Slowly lower cheek to comb to ensure proper cheek pressure and sight bead alignment. **C)** Keep eyes up and away from the muzzle and focused before calling for the target. Often you will see shooters rapidly mounting the gun out of habit instead of deliberation. There's little to no chance for the eyes to focus. The gun if mismounted, will devastate your scores and demolish every attempt to be a precision shooter, dominant defects producing lost targets. If you observe shooters closely, you will see many errors in the setup and gun fit. It is here you will discover the gun fits or not. <u>Thousands</u> of experienced shooters shoot guns that don't fit them. Are you one of them?

3. The moment the gun is shouldered, the target is called, often even before the gun is truly socketed and the cheek dropped to the comb! This is a devastating flaw in technique. Be a machine, not a machine-gun! These shooters are in a hurry and rely on blessed chance to hit targets. Some days they are very lucky, but most can be easily whipped on the score sheet by a deliberate shooter. The cure is to stop rushing yourself and to take setup procedures seriously. A rushed setup produces a rushed shot which leads us to:

4. Don't move the gun. Hold the muzzle still when you call for the target and never begin your swing until your eyes have 'locked-on' to the target. If the muzzle moves the moment the target emerges, and the eyes have not acquired and locked-on, the muzzle will 'snap' to the target instead of smoothly flowing. The swing must be smooth. Smooth does not mean slow. You can swing fast yet still be smooth once you learn not to move the gun until your eye has locked-on, a major cause of lost targets. If your gun is in movement -- horizontally or vertically -- your eyes will not acquire the true trajectory of the target and you'll track a mirage. A linear gun move or rolling (canting) the barrel are okay as moving gun techniques usually, if properly performed. Do not disrupt visual target acquisition or swing geometry since the muzzle is not tracking the emerging target -- it is setting up the gun for the target.

5. Often, the moment the target emerges the shooter internally panics pushing the muzzle with a mad stab to the target. Or the swing is smooth, target is visually acquired, then suddenly the muzzle leaps to catch the target. Repeatable accuracy is difficult to maintain pushing the gun with brute force. The move to the target must be smooth. In fact, the entire setup should be performed in slow motion, the swing smooth right up until the target breaks. Slow down! Learn to incorporate smoothness by using the shoulders and upper body to swing the gun to the target... not pushing the gun with your forearm grip. Then suddenly, with practice, the smooth motions accelerate into one harmonious fluid motion. You'll shoot even faster than before but now with superior correctness without the arm pushing the muzzle. Watch how many shooters push the gun around with their forearm instead of using body English. Watch the pros and you'll see they don't 'push' the muzzle. Their upper body flows the gun to the target, by pivoting the hips and / or shoulders. If you push the muzzles, **A)** You will push the muzzle off the target's line of flight; **B)** You will push the comb away from your face which will trigger a lost cheek pressure signal to the brain, causing your head to rise from the comb to visually reacquire the target; **C)** The muzzle will be pushed, or pulled, away from the rib sight plane, misaligning the sight beads and rib from your true line of sight. You simply miss the target because your eye and the sight bead are out of synchronization. The next time you pull the trigger when the bead is on the target, suspect any or all of the above errors occurred.

6. Panic shooting. When a target is missed, shooters often begin to speed up or slow down. They become too aggressive or overly cautious, and two prolific mistakes. They don't understand 'timing.' When timing is altered, expect to turn in a poor score sheet. Know your zone! Know your timing! Know what you are doing! When timing is consistent, you'll see impressive scores consistently, even on windy days. Timing is complicated, difficult to learn, and even more troublesome to maintain. Remain calm as panic shooting creates trigger flinch, pulling the trigger when the target is not visually acquired. Excessively cautious shooting slows down the brain and nervous system giving rise to more errors than can be listed here. Target distance then alters sight pictures to increase complications, so many sight pictures you can't remember them all.

7. Shooting without a plan: You can see shooters react with astonishment when the target emerges. They have not set up a plan to break the target before it emerges from the trap. They react to the target instead of attacking it. They don't know where to break the target. The breaks are at random distances. They are simply not mentally and visually prepared for the three basic angles to emerge. The target always gets the jump on them by surprise. Their muzzle will 'leap' to the target, leaving smoothness behind along with a good score.

8. No delay to focus eyes. Shooters shoulder the gun too quickly, then call for the target before eyes focus. Shooting this way is shooting on luck, not exactness. Sometimes these shooters will have very lucky days, but a precision shooter wouldn't even consider them as valid competition. You've heard the saying, "*He has good eyes.*" It's not what you think it is. Good vision does not make a precision shooter... properly focused eyes do! Too many shooters 'see' a target but don't 'look' at it. If you don't focus your eyes for the target before you call, you will never truly 'look' at a target. You'll 'see' it slip away unbroken. When you focus your eyes the target will appear; **Brighter, Larger** and in **Slow Motion**. This will trigger 'smooth' moves to the target. The targets will be easy to hit and you'll feel relaxed and confident for the next shot. Try it... it works.

9. Out of rhythm. Shooters who shoot to the squad tempo are shooters who miss targets. Watch the professional shooters. Notice how they maintain their own setup pace and shoot beat, yet they do not disrupt the basic flow of the squad. Watch most shooters and you'll see they have little sense of their setup routine. They believe it is more important to pull the trigger than setup properly and consistently. Play your own game! Shooting out of rhythm also means breaking or missing the targets at inconsistent distances. This sloppiness will generally produce missed targets. If you're ready for the target when you call, and you already know where to break the target, this disorder will dissolve.

There are numerous errors to observe. It is easy to behold others' mistakes, though difficult to see our own. By observing and studying shooters bungling you will be erecting a mirror, a reflection of your own performance. Ask yourself when you examine a slip-up, "*Do I do this?*" It is vitally important to be critical when evaluating shooters. It's how you learn what is right and what is wrong. Watch the pros! If you have any of the above deficiencies, you can resolve them one at a time. Don't say, "*Well, it's my style.*" Wrong is always inaccurate, right is always precise. If you want high scores... work hard to perfect your setup and your swing and your visual focus. This means you must practice with a plan, a goal, something to perfect. Believe me... when you practice your setup and visual skills... targets will smoke!

Don't practice hitting targets! That's what everyone is doing and it is wrong! To just step to the practice trap and call for targets to see if you can hit them is just a waste of time and money. You'll learn nothing much of true lasting value. If you do well, you'll likely have forgotten what you learned by next week. Most shooters shoot at targets hoping they break them. They rely on only one thing... eye / hand coordination. This too is dead wrong! Excellent trapshooting is more, much more, than this. You will never develop superior eye / hand coordination through undisciplined practice. Maybe at 16 yards, but not in long-yardage handicap where precision shooting demands precise aim, focus and feel.

While developing form and style, it is vitally important to realize basic fundamentals, and technique still must apply to the form you develop. If you have been shooting for years and have reached a plateau where scores are not increasing and are erratic from shoot to shoot, you must come to the truth. Your form is defective. It's time for change. In some cases, an entire overhaul. It's not as difficult as you may perceive. Scores will tumble at first, but if you make the changes in the winter months, you'll be ready for the spring, summer and fall shooting season. Changing styles is actually fun. It's exciting to see how small deviations in form can create solid hits on targets or outright misses. You really have nothing to lose by experimenting with new swing techniques, new setup procedures, eye focus, etc. If you don't change, you have already lost next year's events. That's not a fun way to shoot trap, not at all. Read *Trap Shooting Secrets* to help you experiment with varying forms and techniques. Best advice? Watch the pros and incorporate their style into yours. Make it work for you. Don't be shy or embarrassed to experiment with new forms. You will receive criticism from other shooters. For your sake, change, change, change styles until you find something that feels good, and more than feel, breaks the targets! Then when you do finally get it down, change again to improve your performance. Learning never ends. The moment you cease to learn, inconsistency surfaces. That's why new shooters seem to do so well in their first couple years and old shooters get stuck in ruts.

READING A BREAK
"You earn what you learn."

Pay attention to how you break targets. It's important to fine-tune accuracy. You know if you chip a target you really missed it, but most shooters breath a sigh of relief and go right on without second thoughts about it. You know if the target isn't dustballed, you missed it, but again, shooters do nothing to correct the inaccuracy, being grateful they hit it. Never be satisfied or be complacent with choppy breaks, because they are revealing errors in aim that will soon result in a lost target. You need to move forward now to fine-tune your accuracy. No deep explanation is needed here. Strive to dustball the target, every target, every time, so when an error does arrive you'll still break the target. Precision shooting requires you break the target in the hot central core of the pattern. And to do this you first have to have a hot central core. Get rid of the modified and improved modified choke beyond the 20-yard line. They are doing you a great disservice. Sure, you can break targets, most of them, but can you break *all* of them with open chokes with reliability? Nope. When you shoot with open chokes you shoot on sloppy luck. Now you know why you miss targets... accuracy truly isn't imbedded into your shots. Read your breaks! Use a light full or full choke. You may even have to progress to an extra-full choke to get that 25" hot core.

You can break a target with any choke size, with any shell, at any handicap distance. Try it and you'll see it's true -- but it's not reliable. However, the proper choke will procure consistency. Reading breaks can be deceptive because if you dead-center the target it will break clean even with an improper choke. And if you miss aim, the break will be choppy, so you can't rely on visual results only. Looks can be deceiving. The pattern board is helpful to measure effective pattern spread, so you should strive for a tightly packed 25" pattern. When you see a target smokeball, don't believe for a minute your pattern is too tight; it's likely just the way it should be, as the 25" spread is probably right on the money. All chokes have hot cores depending on distance even cylinder chokes at 10 yards. You want to see smoke, not chips, at handicap yardage and singles, then you know reliability is built in. If you never see smoke, then the choke is too open. This may be a simplistic explanation, but there is no need for technical prattle here. The results will impress you more with less confusion. And contrary to general opinion, the full choke will allow for miss-aim in handicap by as much as a foot or more and still break the target. Why? The pattern is denser and the shot column is more elongated. The more open the choke, the more accurate you must be. It's like shooting targets with #9 shot. You can't break them unless you are dead-on. So the choke with a tight core will always be dead-on even if you are slightly off aim. Pattern for 25" spread, not 30." Olympic shooters use tight 25" cores to increase accuracy and obtain repeatable reliable breaks. Put it to use, it works.

SHOOTING OVER THE TOP OF TARGETS
"Cheers! You have yet to shoot your worst score!"

Of course, you know how to read a target break by observing the chips. Chips fly up, you hit under the target. Chips down or you see dust, you shot over. Chips moving left, you hit right. Chips pushed right, you're on the left. Now, how many times do you ever see chips flying upward? Hardly ever. Just about everybody shoots over or behind a target... never under the target, and that goes for seeing dustings too. The rim of targets break clean into defined chips, so you're dusting the fast *rising* top "dome" of the target... shooting over the top and shooting too soon. You also don't miss a straightaway target by pointing straight at the target, you miss it because you *thought* it was straight. You're supposed to shoot to the left or right of the target and under it. And you better not shoot it too quickly. Let it get out a way. If you rush them, they escape. There is no such thing as a straightaway target. They all drift and bend away on curved flight paths at handicap yardage. Newton's law of gravity causes the bending. Fluid aerodynamics creates drifting. The sooner you *learn* this, the better shot you'll be because you'll be watching for this drift and arcing of the target. That's why we shoot over the top of targets. There are more reasons.

Watch out for target and shot drop. Extreme angle targets are falling by the time you get your bead on them (for most shooters) and the shot is also dropping, to a degree, depending on POI settings and timing. Gravity is at work here to help you miss. Also, if you are pushing the muzzle instead of using your cheek and body to steer the gun, swing dynamics will cause you to swing over the target or right on it. Usually, we shoot right at the target but we should be swinging the gun *under* the target to compensate for swing winding-up a muzzle rise and to compensate for the falling target. Extreme angle targets lose angular momentum rapidly and do so aggressively especially if the target is thrown with a tailwind.

Adjust your point of impact. How many shooters do you know who have actually adjusted their POI? Too few indeed. POI may be set too high. Adjust your timing and zone so you won't overshoot targets. Double and triple-check your foot stance and swing dynamics. Your swing geometry is out of kilter if you swing and the muzzle rises. Perform these tests on post #1 and #5. Bear in mind, the muzzle only need rise ¼ inch or so to shoot way over the top of the target. Keep your head down. If you don't feel cheek pressure you'll shoot over. Is the butt riding too high on the shoulder? Get a concave recoil pad. Is the comb set too high? Trigger set too light? If trigger is set too light (less than 3-lb. pull) it will cause you to shoot too fast and off time. A tight, crisp, releasing trigger allows you to get deeper into the target. Try a 5 to 8-lb. pull.

Loosen up your forearm grip, it's too tight. It should just support the gun. The trigger handgrip should be a firm snug-tight, not an iron grip. You're shooting too fast, slow down... slow way down. Relax, the target is not going to escape if you track it! Ride the target a little bit more and you'll see precision increase. Pros shoot fast, but they don't pull the trigger until the sight picture looks right. If you watch very closely, you'll see their zone is not as tight as you first thought. There is a bit of room for making aim / error mid-course muzzle corrections. Your gun hold is too high, lower it. Raise your eye hold so you don't see streaking comet tails which induces premature muzzle advancement. The muzzle must never move vertically until the target has escaped the house and you see its angle clearly, so stop rushing the targets. The bloody gun doesn't fit! If it doesn't fit you can *never* consistently shoot straight, never.

And here's one more that is very important, too: stay in the gun after you pull the trigger. Too many shooters lift their heads and dismount the gun right after firing, as if the gun was burning their face. Stay in the gun until you see the target break. If you don't, you'll actually be lifting your head at the moment you pull the trigger starting the gun dismount process sooner than you may realize. You may swear you are not doing it, but if you videotape yourself shooting or see a coach, you may be in for a rude awakening. Recall, you often cannot see your own mistakes. Many mistakes are performed without conscious thought; so therefore, you don't recognize them happening. A coach sees from the outside in, looking at the big picture. And these are only a *few* of the reasons why you may be shooting over the top of targets or behind them. It would take an entire book to just handle these two topics alone. That's how involved it is. And that brings us to:

HIRE A COACH!

"A goose flies by a chart which the Royal Geographical Society could not mend." Oliver Wendell Holmes

Don't be foolish and think you can learn to shoot all by yourself. You'll spend *thousands* of dollars over the years and with lucky wins at small events get yourself punched to the back fence, then you'll fall apart and stagnate for many, many, years. How many times can you say you've won handicap events at the big State shoots, competing against hundreds of shooters? That should tell you something. It's time to hire a coach or attend a shooting school specializing in trapshooting. Were you trained in your job? I was a bass guitarist / singer and lessons took me to Las Vegas. I was an engineer and school did that. I write screenplays and training was (and still is) required. The learning process never ceases. Once you stop learning, you lose touch with the creative process and fall into slumps. You can practice shooting every weekend for 20-years and still imbed bad old habits making the same daft mistakes over and over again. Our veteran shooters should shoot way better than they do, but they don't because they don't *believe* in education. Another problem is, in America, shooters don't place emphasis on attending trapshooting schools or clinics given by professionals. But in Europe it's the status quo! No wonder they shoot better than we do. USA Shooting trains the Olympic shooters and that is great!

So, when are you going to make your appointment to see a shooting coach? They are listed in *Clay Shooting Magazine, Pull,* the *ATA* and *Shotgun Sports* magazines. (If you do not subscribe to these magazines you are losing out on valuable knowledge!) Make your appointment for next year if you can't afford it right now, but do make an appointment so you'll begin to budget and prepare for it. If formal classes are still way out of line financially, then seek out the best shooter you know and start there. Any coach is better than no coach if the shooter knows how to shoot and can explain why s/he shoots so well. Read books, keep reading books and magazine articles. Buy videotapes, keep learning and apply what you have learned. Talk to professional trapshooters. Don't be shy, talk to them! No question is stupid. Don't ask a dozen questions, ask just one or two, then write the answer down or you'll forget it. Take the lesson to the practice trap and apply it. Make it work no matter how long it takes. If you do this, you just hired a coach for free! This still won't compare to actually taking lessons, but it's better than nothing.

MUZZLE TRANSITION

"You can't shoot fast and be smooth, but you can be smooth and shoot fast."

When the gun is shouldered and you call for the target, it is of prime importance that you do not move the muzzle. Don't take this rule lightly. Allow time for the target to fly, so your eye can identify the flight path angle. If you don't, you'll wildly chase the target. Sure, you'll hit a lot of targets, but the targets you miss will be the price you'll pay. It sets you up to follow no track-line to the target so you can't perform a proper follow-though execution.

If a target exits fast, not from a fast pull, but just getting the jump on you because you called and were not truly ready for the target, don't rush the target. Learn to relax, swing to it smoothly. Don't worry, you'll catch it. In fact, you should practice letting targets escape the zone so you can see for yourself it's not going to get away. It's a big mistake to rush any target.

All handicap shooters need to slow down their swing to the target. The muzzle is moving too fast and way too many are being *pushed, shoved, jerked,* wildly. So if you're dropping targets, slow down the swing. Slowing down the swing does not mean slow shooting. Read the questions and answers section for an explanation on slow-motion shooting. When smooth is perfected, precision speed is realized.

Swing, swing, swing. I bet you forgot how to pivot from the hips to execute the swing. Oh, back-fence shooters don't have to swing. Sorry about that, but they do, many don't and many won't win the big shoots. Just walk the line and observe how many shooters are *stabbing* at the targets, *pushing* the muzzle with the forearm, snap shooting the targets and missing. These are the "pointing shooters." They believe pointing the shotgun is the only thing that matters and shoving the gun around with the forearm works just fine. After all, it got them to the back fence, so it must work. The truth is, the vast majority of back-fence shooters won yardage at the small local town shoots, not the big State or Satellite Grand tournaments where high scores are required to get punched. What happens? If you get to the back-fence too soon you get into trouble, unless you're very talented, have taken shooting lessons, etc. Most haven't. So the pointing and the pushing of the muzzle gets more imbedded, snapshooting takes over with *false* timing within the zone; and there go the targets and the money to the better shooters. Walk the line and see it for yourself. Many of these shooters posting low scores have never learned precision shooting methods. Ask them what back-sighting, zone compression or target arcing is and most won't know. The point is, now is the time to slow down and swing smoothly to the target. No more pushing, no more snap-shooting, no more rushing targets; and learn how to back-sight shooting off the end of the barrel. Get "*Body English*" back into the game.

How do you know when you're shooting smooth? When you see targets in slow-motion. How do you do that? With eye pre-focus and proper gun holds. When the eye locks on to the target in *centralized* vision everything slows down. Remember the days when you shot so good it was hard to miss? Remember how everything looked like it was in slow motion? Of course you do. Your eyes were really working for you that day. You can bring it back again, at will.

SWING SINS
"I despise I became what I hated."

The major problem with muzzle transitions to the target is not seeing the target properly in centralized vision. **1.)** Failure to impart eye pre-focus. **2.)** Faulty eye and gun hold points, **3)** No swing in the muzzle to track the flight path of target. **4)** Eyewear lens color too light or dark, not enough contrast. **5)** Squinting eyes when calling for target. Call volume and duration is improper. **6)** Muzzle-dance when calling. Call is too loud or shouted with stomach or chest muscles expanding. **7)** Taking eye off target. **8)** Squeezing the trigger instead of pulling it with authority. **9)** Timing the shot is out of kilter. Shooting faster than ability. **10)** Shooting an improper zone or no zone at all. **11)** Improper foot position and stance. I could go on. Let's end it here.

Muzzle transition to target for most high gun shooters, well, is just plain wrong. Every shooting coach worth his/her salt will tell you, you have to *swing* to the target on the target's flight path. Many, many high gun shooters are not doing it. They are holding the high gun straight out, letting target rise above the muzzle then moving the gun horizontally left to right, or right to left. Draw the target angle on paper and you'll see making a move like that requires that you hit the target dead-on; otherwise, you risk shooting over, under, to the left side or right side. The game is now working against you, big time. Here's how to do it:

Drop the gun hold a few inches so you can see the target *sooner* and see its *angle*. Now move the muzzle below the target and track it down the line of flight of the target. Presto! You're swinging again and you won't shoot over or under the target so often. All you have to worry about is placing proper follow-though or lead to avoid shooting behind. The odds of hitting the target have just increased in your favor, and your aim does not have to be dead-on. Your entire 25" hot-core pattern is now going to work for you. Analyze this and you'll see the light.

Watch the pros shoot and you'll see the same method. Yes, *tracking* the target with the muzzle, like on railroad tracks. It's subtle, but they do it. And it allows you to make mid-course directional changes to get that sight bead where it belongs. Neat, isn't it? So, all you have to do now is start shooting a lower gun hold. That's the key that sets up all the other moves. The next step is to swing the muzzle using the hips to generate the smoothness. Never push the muzzle with the forearm alone. Get your body moving. Pre-focus the eyes, call and swing *slower* to the target. Sounds simple because it is. Backfence shooters will argue, "*Slower? No way.*" But it's true. You actually swing slower, not faster. Watch the pros, you'll see how it's done. They shoot so smooth it appears fast, but it's really slow motion shooting. It's an illusion requiring study and personal experience to see the reality of it. Read the question and answer section. You'll learn a bit there.

I'M TOO OLD TO LEARN
"What you believe, will be."

Keep saying that and you'll eventually believe it. Regardless of your age, you can still learn. You can absolutely learn to shoot better than you do now, and that is going to make shooting a much more enjoyable experience for you. It's no fun sulking around the scoreboard gazing at your name at the bottom rankings and telling your friends, "*Oh, I had a bad day, as usual.*" Or fabricating excuses, "*Ah, my eyes are not as good as they used to be.*" That may be true, but you did hit some targets didn't you? And you smoked a few into huge black balls of dust? Of course you did. You hit more than 50 of 100 targets? Yep. So, the ability is there. Don't cheat yourself thinking otherwise. Just a few lessons to get rid of some silly kinks in your setup and your scores will go back into the 90's sooner than you may believe. No kidding! And this applies to *everyone*, regardless of age.

CHAPTER 10
"Could trapshooting be the Garden of Eden?"

ERGOGENIC AIDS
"Health is better than wealth."

A complete and balanced multimineral multivitamin pill such as Centrum® along with Energize® will help replenish your body to prolong the dreaded fatigue that may occur. An energy food like Power Bar® [800-444-5154] may be beneficial to provide a burst of alertness and endurance. Anything, within reason, that can offer you a mild energy and confidence boost is certainly to your advantage. All competitive sportsmen use legal ergogenic aids since they <u>do</u> give a competitive edge. Most ergogenic aids are more hype then reality, but there are some that are essential and may give you the edge needed to win. Certainly anything listed here when used in moderation may furthermore benefit your general health. The prevailing rule is: all things in moderation. Never overdo anything. Not less than 100%, never more than 300% of the USRDAS daily recommendations. Some megadose formulas can be harmful, containing more than 10 times the USRDAS rule and they do not provide extra benefits. In fact, large doses of Vitamin A and D will cause liver damage, nausea and bone / muscle pain. Even excessive dosages of vitamin B_6 can cause nerve damage, tingling of hands and feet and numbness. The most effective is a combined multivitamin, multimineral single dose. Taking a handful of various pills can cause a secondary deficiency. For example, taking calcium alone can result in a iron and zinc deficiency. The examples are endless.

Always take supplements after a snack or meal, with the exception of iron which is assimilated better on an empty stomach. Time-released supplements may do you little good, as they often dissolve so slowly they are expelled from the body before they've had time to be absorbed. Keep in mind this is not a nutritional guide, but a brief viewpoint of important factors trapshooters should not overlook. Though simple in origin and often neglected, a tired vitamin & mineral depleted body isn't bound to help you hit targets. Although not as copious as a tennis player, still, considerable energy is depleted while shooting and replenishment is essential before you 'hit the wall'. It's no secret Arnold Palmer endorsed *Green Magma*® [800-777-4430] a nutritional supplement. Vitamin Research Products, 3579 Hwy., 50 East, Carson City, NV 89701 (800) 877-2447 has unique formulations to heighten vision, alertness, concentration and endurance. You may want to try their 'Energize' product. It's a potent vitamin based formulation to boost natural mood elevator dopamine excitatory neurotransmitters. Be sure to read the product caution notice before using. Ask for a catalog. *'Energize'* is all natural and it packs a mild long-lasting punch that is quite remarkable for sharpening awareness, concentration, and endurance. Their *'Blast Off II'* product is ever more powerful and contains caffeine and fructose, which is overkill for trapshooting purposes. *'Energize'* is a perfect moderator for the trapshooter who could use a mild continuous boost of energy with a solid dose of A and B group vitamins. There are other products on the market so try the ones that work for you. Use caution, of course, when taking any supplement.

There are several supplements which may enhance your performance. Choline is a nutrient consumed in foods and produced endogenously. It is essential for the production of phosphatidylcholine, a phospolipid and an important constituent of cell membranes. Soy lecithin is a good source of choline and has been used in studies of memory formation and concentration. When lecithin is digested it splits off into its constituent parts into phophatides, inositol, and choline, which are all important in nervous system function. For shooters who sip the brew, it has been discovered lecithin can prevent and even reverse cirrhosis of the liver. This disease has no other effective treatment. Vitamin Research Products has choline+B-5 available.

Magnesium is beneficial as it is a necessary cofactor for enzymes needed for energy production. Magnesium aspartates have been found to increase endurance in athletes. Most people are deficient in magnesium. Vitamin Research Products has an herbal formula which research has shown to improve visual acuity. Bilberry extract and Ginkgo biloba extract have both been studied and found effective in this regard. A general supplement providing ample dosages of the B vitamins, especially B-5, necessary for proper function of the adrenal, and found to enhance endurance could be of value to you.

Controversial, yes, but caffeine in coffee, cola's and tea releases fat from tissues which gives a long-lasting energy boost. By consuming two or three cups of coffee two hours before shooting, carbohydrates are slowly metabolized which prolongs the time the shooter punches a hole in the sky due to exhaustion. Caffeine can enhance performance in the proper dosage. Too much caffeine can cause nervous flinching along with a general case of jitters. Many people are sensitive to caffeine and should not use it if adverse affects are noted. For others, caffeine produces a sharp boost of heightened awareness. Caffeine is a diuretic, increasing urinary output greatly magnifying your vitamin and fluid needs and if not replaced you can expect lost targets due to preliminary effects of dehydration fatigue, even on a cool day.

Though not a direct performance booster, antioxidants can help reverse the effects of reactive compounds found in air pollution, including the inhalation of burning gunpowder fumes which are prevalent on trapfields. Hard rock miners are familiar with the 'nitroglycerin headache' that constricts blood vessels. Modern double-base gunpowder fumes have unfriendly consequences as nitroglycerin cellulose fumes are known to increase tension. An aspirin along with an antioxidant vitamin helps counter the physical effects. You may not feel the effects, still the adverse influences are present. The "silent headache" is one reason for having an off-day mood and a bad score. Moods are trickier yet and there is no pill or magic stew yet brewed to legally, safely and reliably enhance performance. Oxidants can alter moods toward the negative frame of mind if one is exposed to them in sufficient quantity over a period of time. Fumes of any sort are suspect. That means gunsmoke and the nitro-headache. Any tunnel digger or hard rock miner will confirm that!

Insure your multivitamin pills contain at least 100% of USDA recommendations. These vitamins are key to maintaining stamina and good vision. Inadequate vitamin A intake can produce dry eye symptoms which every shooter experiences at one time or another. A good source of vitamin A is to carry a few apricots with you for snack food. Apricots will contribute an energy boost without the 'high' followed by a 'crash' sugar will often give. Vitamin E prevents vitamin A from being attacked. Nuts are a good source of vitamin E. The B group of vitamins will enhance resistance to stressors, maintain fluid balance, aid nerve transmission and muscle contraction -- very important for a trapshooter. A deficiency of potassium will cause muscle weakness and uneasiness including mild depression, the enemies of all competitors. Sodium of course is salt. Natural and processed foods have plenty of salt. A pinch may be required on humid days when perspiration is severe or shooting in hot dry conditions.

Most all of the above vitamins can be had in two products, *Centrum*® and *Energize*® and you will feel enhanced energy, awareness and stamina. Don't neglect to snag a meal between shoots. Eat well, perform well. However, overeating induces lethargic moods, ruining performance.

FLUID REPLENISHMENT
"The only way to keep your health is to eat what you don't want, drink what you don't like, and do what you'd rather not." Mark Twain

Water is the most vital nutrient, though frequently overlooked. Most shooters don't drink enough of it during competitions. Dehydration will create muscle and body fatigue. Keep in mind, thirst is not an indicator of fluid needs, so you should drink twice as much water as it takes to quench your thirst. Drink at least eight glasses a day spread throughout the day, especially before and during the competition and more so when shooting in hot weather. Remember, dehydration occurs rapidly and you'll drop targets before you recognize the symptoms. A pinch of salt or a snack bag of potato chips will help retain water. You can die of thirst drinking from a spring in the middle of the desert without salt to retain water in body cells.

Water is the body's largest component. It's physiological function serves to maintain body temp. Water and salt intake was -- at one time -- thought to be the only recommended form or fluid replenishment to maintain proper blood volume. As fluid is lost through perspiration or exercise. A decrease in blood volume reduces oxygen to working muscles and may induce listlessness, causing performance to suffer. For a trapshooter the muscles affected can be the eyes and arm. Incomplete fluid replenishment can have adverse affects on muscle contraction and utilization of energy sources. Most athletes, including trapshooters, fail to consume adequate fluids before, during or after events to regulate body temperature and replenish loss fluids. Thirst is an unreliable indicator of fluid needs. To determine proper fluid replenishment requirements simply weigh yourself before and after each event. A 1 pound loss of body weight equals 1 pint of fluid lost. Taking 16 oz of *Poweraide*® replaces that loss. Here's where sports drinks such as *Powerade*® (800) 343-0341 (the official sports drink of the Olympic Games & World Cup Soccer) can be beneficial to the trapshooter, particularly on a blistering summer day shooting nonstop for an hour or more. A loss of 2% of body weight equals a 3 pound loss for a 150 lb. individual which is equivalent to six 8 oz. cups of water. This fluid loss can cause a marked decrease in concentration, coordination, strength, and stamina. Replenishing lost fluids is vital. Drink water with one sports drink. They are not substitutes for water. Drink lots of water when shooting in competition, especially in warm weather.

Carbohydrates, recognized as sugars, are the primary source of energy. Muscles rely on glycogen as the first and primary source of energy. Depletion of muscle glycogen is one reason for fatigue. Glucose polymers (maltodextrin, high fructose corn syrup source of fructose and glucose) are converted by the body to energy sources for working muscles during endurance events. Sodium enhances fluid absorption in the small intestine. One of the roles of carbohydrates in sports drinks is to help improve performance during prolonged continuous exercise -- 60 to 90 minutes or longer. Electrolytes maintain water balance and enhanced fluid absorption. Minerals are especially needed to retain are sodium, potassium and chloride, better known as salts. Sweat contains and expels electrolytes. Though the amount lost during ordinary exercise can generally be replaced with a balanced diet, a sports drink can subdue the thirst sensation while replenishing sodium, potassium and carbohydrates. As we all know, trapshooting events don't always have balanced diets readily available, nor do we have the time to eat well when the squads are on the move. Drinking water alone is not adequate and ingestion of plain water may actually diminish the desire to continue drinking, resulting in dehydration and exhaustion with secondary effects of loss of concentration -- the trapshooters worst foe. *Poweraid*® delivers rapid fluid delivery which is critical for optimum performance, leaving the stomach quickly to the small intestine for absorption into the bloodstream. Fluid volume in the blood is maintained, as well as water. Of course, a sports drink is no substitute for a well balanced diet, though it certainly can help you persevere a grueling event or shootoff at high noon. More gun clubs should have these drinks readily available to shooters as water, soft drinks and alcoholic beverages, straightforwardly, can't muster the advantages a sports drink can deliver... shooters retain more energy to break more targets!

HOT WEATHER SHOOTING
"Your health comes first; you can always hang yourself later." Only Kidding

Keeping cool when temperatures soar is vital to ward off heatstroke, but the shooter need not become overheated before the body will begin shutting down mental and visual alertness and muscle movement, and exhaustion sets in. Common methods to compensate for heat are to drink plenty of water, with an occasional pinch of salt to retain water in the body's cells. Dress light, slow down when walking, seek out shade between events, wear a hat, sunglasses, blinders and take a multivitamin pill. These all help and are important, but once on the line firing in a blazing heat wave there is a product that works extremely well. It's a gel collar. It is a simple cloth collar filled with water absorbing crystals. Soak it in water, it swells up, place around your neck and overheating is remarkably abated. The water collar chills blood to the brain, retaining your alertness as though you were shooting on a cool day. Your body may feel like you're in an oven, but your neck and head are cool. The product works. You can buy them at most Western region registered shoots or sporting supply stores. You can make one yourself. Arts & Craft stores sell the magic crystals which are commonly used to water plants and retain moisture in soil. You may have to crush the pellets to a smaller size, as the grains will swell a bit too large for a water collar. Place some crystals in a 1 ½" wide cloth tube, sew the ends with straps extending to tie the collar, soak in water and you have a fine refrigeration system to keep cool on the trap line.

Sunburn is common, especially out West in the deserts. A sunblock cream will help ensure you can last through a multi-day shoot in the sun. There is little worse than pain to take your mind off the targets. However, sparingly use sunblock on your forehead, as it will surely migrate to your eyes at the moment you need to smoke the target. Wear a hat with a visor and blinders to shade the eyes and face. Use a sweatband if perspiration migrates to eyes or vapor smudges accumulate to distort view through shooting glasses. Preparedness is meaningful if you desire to rank superior scores. Maximum comfort and relaxation with minimal psychological diversions are required to shoot commendably. If you do get sunburned, don't use aspirin for pain relief as it dilates blood vessels and can make your skin hurt even more. For pain relief, use non-aspirin, acetaminophen pills, anesthetic cream or an aloe-based product. Avoid oil-based moisturizers. Keep in mind the sun's UV rays can penetrate most loose-fitting thin summer shooting vests so sunscreen protection may still be required. The sun is strongest between 10:00 a.m. and 2:00 p.m., and UV rays can penetrate cloud cover. When shooting in bright sunlight conditions, use eye drops 30-minutes prior to shooting to keep the eyes cool and focused.

COLD & ADVERSE WEATHER SHOOTING
"Empathy… the disease nobody cares about."

I'll keep this short and sweet as *Trap Shooting Secrets* handles this subject. In cold and rainy situations scores normally fall. Would you like to raise your scores? Okay, remove the insulating material from your heavy jacket where the gun is shouldered to maintain the gun's length of pull. It will restore your point visuals, swing and trigger timing. Enough said.

BREAKING THE LEARNING BARRIER
"The best defense against the hydrogen bomb is not to be there when it goes off."

Learning new things is not as simple as you perceive it to be. We have been repeatedly told to practice, practice, practice, through repetition trapshooting is learned. Practice makes perfect. Not so. Rigid practice sessions will only lock you into a rut, relearning only what you believe is correct, which may be dead wrong. A new way of thinking must be implemented about the purpose of practice. Without it you are only reinforcing old habits that makes progression and improvement difficult at best. Are you ready? Here goes. **1)** You must take in new information… or else practice only becomes a repetitive rehearsal of old habits. **2)** You must be responsive to change and enjoy the experience of learning new things. **3)** Conventional practicing and learning must be altered to push abilities forward. Again, learning new ways to break targets gives real knowledge. Knowledge that can be used to expand your abilities. **4)** Repetitive practice is devoted to repetitive automatic behavior that stifles creativity, creates a mind-block and frigidness to deviate from the norm. This invokes failure as boredom sets in and mediocre performance is the end result. **5)** Robotic practice of previously learned technique over-and-over again-and-again is self-defeating depriving you of your full potential to expand into precision shooting techniques. **6)** You must expand your thinking, widen your knowledge base, discover the hidden wisdom within yourself, and that means even disregarding what your teacher has taught you, to a degree, so you can advance past the teacher's abilities. If you don't, you can never excel beyond the teacher's own ability. A fact of life. **7)** When you experiment with differing shooting methods and techniques you will surpass your greatest dreams by unleashing new knowledge. If you don't experiment with new things the mind becomes bored, inflexible and limiting. **8)** Perform the basic skills learned differently. Fight the urge to break targets the same way, over and over again during practice sessions so you can create new ways of solving problems. **9)** The learning experience should be fun, an adventure into the unknown.

Now how do you do it? Easy. Don't get into a groove when practicing. Walk on the wild side by trying different gun and eye holds, swing timing, call tones, foot positioning, zone variations. Be creative and don't get bored. Never shoot for score when practicing, as this is only a rehearsal where nothing new is learned. Get the drift? Knowledge is power and high scores; consistency and precision can't be obtained without experimentation. With the expanded knowledge, you will be able to discern problems quickly at competition shoots and stop the lost targets before they get too far out of hand. Be patient, but persistent to learn new things. Going stale, being bored and using mindless practice sessions will only produce identical poor results. Be creative and push yourself past the barriers that have been holding scores down.

A MESSAGE TO CLUB MANAGERS
"Good targets generate revenue."

From the shooter's point of view, if a club has a lethargic attitude toward properly setting traps, with eyeball-only adjustments, poor spin on targets, improper trap machine settings and installation, the better shooters will steer clear and attend shoots where club management performs to higher customer service standards. What is worse, the pros know how to shoot these wild situations and everyone else posts ruinous scores. Eventually the club acquires a reputation of being a difficult place to achieve good scores, causing more shooters to slip away to greener pastures. Improper trap settings, poorly trained or "burned out" pullers are damaging to the shooter's score average and the "fun factor" dissolves rapidly as the trip to your shoot become a total waste of time, money and effort. Once the reputation sets in and persists over a period of years, it is nearly impossible to bring back the crowds without fancy and expensive marketing. I've seen good clubs lose shooters one-by-one just for these reasons alone. Make sure your pullers are properly trained or your shooters will suffer low scores!

Liquidation is a huge problem in some areas of the country where too many shoots are taking place in close geographic areas and all the clubs experience low turnouts. Club managers should communicate among each other to schedule shoot dates, and agree not to compete with registered shoots, by scheduling non-registered "fun shoots." The clubs and the shooters lose, nobody wins if liquidation exists.

Treatment of people is a huge problem at some gun clubs and it needs to be addressed. Courtesy is of the utmost importance, reverting to the tried and proven concept that the customer is always right (even when wrong). Accommodate the shooter's needs at all costs. Each shooter has a measure of "juice" at his own gun club and if this shooter is offended, often an entire group of out of town shooters will not return. Just ask yourself why you won't shoot at certain clubs and you'll find the solutions. Nothing kills a club's reputation faster than internal conflicts that offend members. Instruct your volunteers and workers to be courteous. Properly train your trap help and rotate them so monotonous exhaustion does not upset the quality of the event.

PROMOTING THE SPORT

"Committee--a group of men who individually can do nothing but as a group decide that nothing can be done." Fred Allen

Each of us has a responsibility to promote the sport. Introduce a friend or neighbor to the sport. Make a suggestion to club management to purchase a loaner gun so visitors can try out the game. Gun clubs are fearful of environmentalists and shy away from broad media exposure. In this case, distribute a flyer specifically aimed at a certain employee group to post on the employer's bulletin board. From a machine shop to heavy industrial sites, selective marketing works. Advertise to industry for company picnics and offer trapshooting as recreation, competition between the various company departments. Industry is always looking for recreation, so don't overlook this as they pay good money to rent the facilities!

Another idea is to have "open-house" day where every club member invites a neighbor or co-worker to try trapshooting. Give visitors a taste of trapshooting and you'll attract members. Every club member who succeeds in having the visitor join the club, paying membership dues, wins a prize -- case of shells, five free rounds of trap or free meals. This could be done twice per year, spring and fall perhaps. Another method is to set up a competition between high school or college students as a school event. That's how to get the sport into the new generation and attract parents to the sport, too. People are looking for "something different" to do, let them know you have this unique sport for the entire family to play.

Contact an RV association, a motorhome club/group, or magazine publisher such as; *Trailer Life* and *Motorhome Magazine* and let them know you will host "free camping" at your gun club for all RV'ers who want to try the *new* sport of trapshooting. Advertise it as a "new sport" as it *is* new to most all who know nothing about the sport, which equals *millions* of people. Public announcement ads like this are free. You can post your schedule with dates, hours and restrictions (if any, such as: must own RV or motorhome) with a directions "map" on highway rest areas. You'd be surprised just how many RV'ers will pull in out of curiosity and for free camping! Let them stay a couple days or a week. Believe me, the word of mouth goes out like lightening with these folks and you'll have plenty of new shooters. You'll need a few loaner guns. There is money to be made here. If you don't want RV'ers to camp, post ads at RV parks promoting your seasonal events. RV'ers have money, are usually bored and looking for something very different to do -- and always looking for new friends to meet. Trapshoots and RV'ers are a perfect match.

All of this can be performed without local newspaper advertising for clubs who do not relish the idea of regional exposure. Gun clubs need to begin advertising if the sport is to grow. Make a flyer with a coupon for a free round of trap, skeet or sporting clays and place them in waiting areas at local businesses. You'll be surprised how many people will be showing up to shoot! Many will become long-term members.

BUYING THE NEW GUN
"To err is human, but to really foul things up requires a new gun."

As stated in *Trap Shooting Secrets*, buying a new gun is an instant formula for disaster for most shooters. Make certain when you do purchase a new gun the gun is *custom* built to fit you and the point of impact is ordered to your specifications. Before you buy, make sure you get a written guarantee the manufacturer will correct any improper specifications. If you ordered a POI of 80/20 and it's shooting 70/30 and to the left of aim... you'll want that gun to be brought back into specs. However, you must custom order the gun spelling out the specs. If you do this, most gun manufacturers will correct the problem. If not, you may be on your own. You can give specs to a gun dealer, but the dealer is not authorized to commit the manufacturer to binding contracts, so make your custom specs available to the manufacturer prior to placing your order and before you deposit any down-payment funds for the gun. Get the agreement first.

Don't buy a new gun unless you know what you are doing. Too many shooters are looking for the magic bullet gun and can't shoot the gun when they finally buy it. The gun works fine at the practice trap to test it, then when they get home they discover scores are dumping and the gun does not fit, etc. Buying a new gun is no easy matter. It's expensive and you must custom order the gun to fit you or have it fitted later. Now, a new gun can do wonders if it it's the gun causing the problem in your shooting. That's a hard call to make. Most shooters go through a few guns until they find the right one. Just do it intelligently and do it for the right reasons. A new gun will destroy your scores until you learn how to shoot it. Expect a long learning curve and at least 5,000 shells to get the feel of the gun, even 10,000 shells or more may be required. Often it's not the new gun, but a new gun that still does not fit like the old gun! Get your gun fitted when new out of the box!

Look at what the pros are shooting and go from there. Shoot many guns so you'll know what you need, not just what you want. Want is too generalized. We all want this or that brand of gun, but do you *need* high rib? Adjustable comb? Adjustable point of impact and what range of impact settings? Some guns will not adjust POI down below, say 6" high... and that may be too high for you and sometimes the rib can't be drilled to compensate so you're stuck with a multi-thousand dollar gun you can't shoot and nobody wants to buy. Single barrel or Over & Under? Do you need 30" or 32" or 34" barrels? Pull or release trigger and what lock time is required? There is no easy answer except this: Do not rush into it. Keep thinking about all the specifications you need and in two or three years of shooting you should have a general idea of your needs. Talk with pros, gunsmiths and stock fitters before buying the gun to see what sort of problems they have. Each gun has unique quirks and one of them could just end up being some sort of adjustment that can't be made which you desperately need altered. Not everything is fixable or practical to fix. And for heaven's sake, make sure the gun fits and shoots where you look. Way too many shooters buy guns that don't even come near to fitting and certainly do not shoot where they are looking. It's so criminal it should be outlawed. To sum it up, a new gun is a product of the untalented, sold to the utterly bewildered. But such is not always the case.

CHAPTER 11
"Learning is everything unforgotten."

A QUICK REVIEW OF THE ILLUSTRATIONS
"A new technique will never feel right 'till it becomes old."

Let us take a quick ride exploring the illustrations in this book. This is a book in itself!

Fig. 1 through 3. Explores the basic stance. If you look at a lot of shooters they just have a horrible stance, some even employ the typical skeet shooting and hunting stances. Trapshooting is a "different" game and it requires a unique form. How to get it right? Stand like the professionals do. It's that plain and simple. You have to break old habits if you want to shoot well.

Fig. 4. A reminder: do not move that gun until you see the target clearly. If your gun is jumping or moving in any way as you call for the target, you're just asking for a missed target! It's one of the best means known to wildly stab at targets. There are only two acceptable moving gun techniques, rolling the gun as in the Bow Technique or a slow forward stab of the muzzle as you call for the target. Both techniques prepare the gun to move by annihilating dead-momentum so the swing to the target can be smoothly executed. It stops stabbing of the targets and gets that gun moving. Try these techniques because they will fit your form if your gun is dancing or dipping when you call. Change your call routine if necessary as the call may be causing muzzle ballet.

Fig. 5. What is your plan? Eye pre-focus and gun holds are important. If you don't use them how can you expect to get that extra edge of precision required to win shoots? Winning may come by surprise, but hardly ever by accident. Get serious with your plan. Where is your zone? Is your timing correct? Or do you have no plan and just call for the target and go after it? Develop a plan and you'll see your scores rise. When you stand on station you should have a basic plan of execution to attack the three basic angles from that post. Each station may require a deviation on the theme from other station posts. Likely, you are not using a specific plan for each post. Most shooters don't. Most shooters shoot terribly on a consistent basis. They come to a shoot already knowing they will lose. They have no technical plan to apply.

Fig. 6 and 7. Trap setting is important to recognize. When you are assigned your traps, take a walk and look for trap variations at these traps. A trap set low will streak a target at longer distance before your eye acquires the target. The zone becomes flatter and deeper in depth and if your gun hold is not lowered a smidgen, the target will appear to not rise above your barrel. You may have to raise your hold if you hold a low gun. Distance is the enemy of trapshooters and this trap will push a target out of the zone, upsetting your timing and no doubt slipping past your shotstring for a lost target. There's more to this, but this is all you really have to be aware of for now. You'll figure out the rest as experience will teach you. Eye hold lowered will compensate.

Fig. 8. If the trap is offset and you don't compensate, all the geometry of your swing is flushed away. Look to see if the trap is to the left or right of the stations. And look to see if the trap itself is throwing the straight post #3 target from the center area of the traphouse. If the target exits to the left of center, move your gun and eye hold to the left to compensate. It's that easy. But if you don't recognize the problem, and many shooters never even consider it, targets will be missed and you'll be scratching your head why. It's important to walk the line and see the traps you are going to shoot. At least, arrive early to your traps and check them out. You can also readjust geometry of the swing by moving your foot positions a tad to the left if targets are shifting left. Move right if targets are shifting right. Trap misalignment is often subtle, but to the trained eye it is easily recognized.

Competitive rules require you cannot step off center line when shooting, so to compensate you change your foot position, body stance, eye and gun hold points to compensate. The next time you shoot a specific trap and perform terribly, take a look at the trap. Odds are high the trap was improperly set creating *strange* target angles which did not complement your setup. A misaligned trap upsets the geometry of the swing and pushes the zone into unfamiliar territory. Walk the traps before you shoot and observe, or at least take notice prior to stepping on station to shoot. Not all traps are alike.

Fig. 9 and 10. Draw the figure-8 with your gun without lifting your head from the comb. Certainly this extreme motion is not used in trapshooting, but if you can steer the gun like this, you'll be well on your way to learning how to keep your head snug-tight to the comb. Learn to steer the gun with your cheek. Let your body move, tilting side-to-side to draw the figure-8. Then later try drawing a circle, then a semi-arc like tracking a curving target. Again, let your body move so you can learn how to make the gun and yourself one movable unit. Now you're learning Body English. Shooting becomes more fluid when you use your body to steer/swing the gun. Accuracy increases because your cheek stays down tight to the comb, naturally.

Fig. 11 and 12. These exercises will do wonders. Fig. 11 will help you with trigger control and swing separation along with eye focus.

Fig. 13. Concentration must be managed. Many shooters don't even know how to control their concentration. They apply too much concentration throughout the entire event, never shutting it off. Many walk around like zombies when changing traps. The pros know how to turn it off and turn it on at will, which gives them that powerful edge to beat us. If you manage concentration, you won't tire out on the last trap. Burn-out is a major problem for most shooters because the mind cannot continue to function at 100% energy levels. Makes sense doesn't it?

Fig. 14. Through 17. Call timing is essential to the setup. It helps you maintain your zone and timing. Calling for the target with no other purpose but to see a target exit is going to cause you to lose focus and chase targets. You don't chase targets, you attack them, with a plan, within your zone. That's how the pros shoot with such consistency. *"The target is lost or scored long before you pull the trigger."* If your setup is ignored expect low scores. Precision shooting requires precision, preparation and execution. The call is important to attack the target within the zone and maintaining consistent timing of the shot.

Fig. 18. Visualization is no secret to professional trap shooters. They take a moment to take a *picture* in their mind of where that target will be broken before they call for the target, usually right before they shoulder the gun. It's fast, but it's done nevertheless. Are you doing it? That's the question. Are you breaking the target in your mind's eye before you call for that target? Learn to do this and scores will rise. It adds a necessary boost of confidence and conviction with energy to accomplish the act.

Fig. 19 through 22. Simple eye exercises to smooth out the jitters in the eye, to control eye movements, and to focus. Here you will see why you are stabbing at targets because your eye is jinxing around trying to acquire the target. Discover the power of centralized vision focus and smooth eye motion. If the eye motion is smooth, the swing will be too. This is why eye hold points are important, to slow the target down visually so you won't be chasing the target in a mad dash. At practice, try raising your gun and eye-hold higher than normal, then lower than normal and see the changes taking place. The zone changes and timing are altered. If you want to be a smooth shooter, get that eye hold right and let the eye smoothly glide to the target. Rapid eye movement is a lost target in the wings. Are you shooting on pure 100% eye/hand coordination without specific intent? Yes, trapshooting employs eye/hand coordination, but it's not all that is required, precision is needed. The eye will move slower and smoother if you shoot a tight zone and your gun and eye holds are positioned in or close to the zone (for high gun shooter). Low gun shooter -- put the eye in the zone and gun low down on the house or slightly above it.

Fig. 23 and 24. Eye hold determines the zone. It is like a bubble floating around the end of the muzzle. You can now see why it would be very difficult to obtain precise shooting if the zone kept shifting on you each time you called for a target. One hundred zone shifts are a killer and requires great luck and skill to hit 'em all. But if you select a eye (and gun) hold for each target to focus the zone, you can readily see the advantage. Consistency rises. Neat trick, huh? So, zone shooting is a requirement you must not only learn, but apply to your game. It's not easy to learn, it really isn't, but it can be learned as long as you want to learn it. Now you know why pros shoot so perfectly. By using a zone, they eliminate many of the disadvantages.

Fig. 25 and 26. These are the basic three angles you should visualize prior to shooting any target on any post. Certainly there are intermediate angles between the three, but at least you are prepared for them. This setup routine is a mental reminder of the targets you will receive and helps reduce the *surprise* factor when the target leaves the house. Complications decrease when you are certain of the approximate angle target to be delivered. Of the three angles, the most difficult is the hard left or right angle. This is the target you should set up to kill, but without anticipating that angle, only being *prepared* for it to emerge. Excessive anticipation sets up a shock to the nervous system when the wished-for target fails to materialize, causing you to make fast snappy moves to the unexpected target -- lost targets often result.

Fig. 27 through 30. Busy backgrounds often cause a shooter problems. You are supposed to keep your eye on the target at all times, but backgrounds can cause optical illusions, distorting target speed. A target with no background appears to float *slowly* while a busy background creates a *blur,* fooling you into believing the target is traveling *faster* than it really is. Depending on the background, the target can become dissolved and hidden. If this is the case, you can compensate by shifting your zone away from the blinding area. When you shift the zone your timing is not upset, only the place where the target will be broken is changed. Raise or lower eye or gun hold points and the zone will shift where you want it to. Often, eye pre-focus points can be of help.

Fig. 31 through 35. The text is self-explanatory. Zones are important to learn in trapshooting. You are shooting a zone now and may not even be aware of it, but it may not be the proper zone. If you are unaware of shooting a specific zone, you are likely shooting too many zones from target to target, trap to trap. A big problem. Determine the ideal zone and make all setups on each post conform to the zone. You only want to shoot one zone, not two, four, fifty or one-hundred. Watch the pros shoot. They shoot a tight zone. They don't break targets at varying distances from the traphouse. Zone shooting takes time to learn, but it will serve you well to employ the method.

Fig. 36 and 37. It is true if you raise your eye hold you actually reduce the zone. The imaginary bubble floating around the muzzle actually compresses, tightening the zone. You would think it would be the opposite, but it's not. Raise the eye hold and the targets will be near their crest points and where they are actually slowing down, making them easier to hit. But at the long-yardage posts this is not acceptable as distance and shot pattern spread now work as a disadvantage, so the eye hold is lowered. To explain all the variables here would require a hundred pages of text. Just remember to drop your eye and gun holds a smidgen for each yardage punch you receive. Some shooters, those who hold low gun to the house, may want to raise the hold points as distance increases from the traphouse. As long as you understand the principle here, experimentation will discover the ideal zone for you to shoot in.

Fig. 38 and 44. These gun and eye holds are all variations on a theme. You can use differing holds than shown for each station post, whatever works best for you. The idea is to experiment with these hold points to better prepare you to see the target and to react to the three basic target angles and to adjust the zone and timing of the shot. There is more than one way to break a target. The best way is the right way for you. Just being conscious of your gun and eye hold will help you acquire the target much better than you are likely doing now. Every professional will tell you the importance of gun and eye holds if you ask them. Trying them will convince you just how important they can be.

Fig. 45. This drawing reveals a simple sight picture frozen in time, sort of like spot shooting the target. There are many ways to attack targets; spot shooting, pull-away, swing-through, sustained lead. **Spot:** (a.k.a. snap shooting) is like shooting the first target in double-trap whereas the gun hold is positioned in the zone where the target is to be broken and waits for the target to "flash" by the muzzle. Trigger is pulled, target broken. **Pull-Away:** the sight bead is put on the target and pulled away to allow lead. Good trapshooters use this method on hard angle targets that were giving them problems, because there is more time allotted to setup the sight picture which diminishes the tendency to stop the muzzles in mid-swing. **Swing-Through:** allows the muzzle to flow from behind the target, tracking it, then breaking the target. It's the preferred method in trapshooting because it complements surprise target-angle shooting, even though the gun must move faster than the target to catch up to it and sight picture must be precise and quick to align. This method develops momentum to help reduce muzzle freeze (stopping the gun). **Sustained Lead:** the muzzle always stays ahead of the target, never tracking it from behind. This will give the most time to setup the sight picture but causes a huge problem of freezing the muzzle. Of the four techniques, Swing-through and Pull-Away are used in American trapshooting, but use Spot Shooting on double-trap's first target. You can use Sustained Lead on the double-trap's second target or Swing-Through or Pull-Away. Choice is yours.

Fig. 46 and 47. More gun and eye holds revealed on attacking the hard (extreme) angles. Canting of the gun is not shown, but you can readily see the advantage of doing so. Setting up for the hard angle on each post is something the great shooters know all so well to do. Are you doing it too? Go to practice and work on this formula and you'll see the angles become less intimidating and have less reliance on luck shooting.

Fig. 48. Seeing the sight picture is critical, critical, critical. It tells you *when* to pull the trigger. There would be no form of shooting such as Spot, Pull-Away, Swing-Through or Sustained Lead if sight pictures were never needed. Don't argue; just do. Seeing the sight picture is a must for the precision shooter. No sight bead? No broken targets. Certainly, you can take the sight bead off and shoot, but then the muzzle becomes the sight bead. Okay? You can't just shoot with your eyes and rely on eye/hand coordination in handicap shooting. Remember to stand in front of a mirror starring at your eyes (the target) as you wave your index finger back and forth. That is the sight picture you should see. Eye on the target but the finger (sight bead or muzzle) is readily seen moving into the target's kill zone. Now you're zooming in and shooting with intense precision. You won't be wildly stabbing at the targets. The next step is setting up your gun's point of impact to take advantage of the sight picture. Shooting the zone keeps all the sight pictures down to a reasonable level to easily memorize. Eye and gun holds then make the job easier to acquire the target in the zone and maintain consistent timing. See how it all comes together?

Fig. 49. Don't argue with eye pre-focus, just do it. Once you acclimate yourself to seeing targets cleanly and in slow-motion you won't have to pre-focus so intensely as when first learning the technique. It all becomes natural as the eye knows now how to lock-on to the targets. Okay? It is a fact the pros see targets much differently than the average shooter does. Now you can learn this two ways. 1) You can shoot 20,000 shells a year for many years to learn how to see targets or 2) You can learn to pre-focus your eyes and get on with building higher scores right now. Take your pick.

Fig. 50. It is better to change your gun hold point than to shift your eye too far away from the rib. But some shooters can do it with no problem. Use this guide as a starting point. You will find more precision in your shooting if you eye stays within the rib zone without straying too far from it. It makes perfect sense.

Fig. 51 through 56. Getting that bead on the target is a tough one to do. An adjustable rib gun can alter the point of impact to get the job done, but your timing and zone must be tight to do it. The pros make it look so easy. If you have no adjustable rib, have fun. Canting the gun to apply automatic lead (if point of impact is high) does the trick, but that too is a tough technique to learn, but it can be learned if you apply yourself to make it work. The goal is to get the sight bead so close to the target that very little lead is required to smash the target. If you can accomplish this, with many trials and tears, trapshooting becomes much easier. It's never easy.

Fig. 57 & 58. Many shooters have never adjusted their point of impact and that's good news for the precision shooter (daunting bad news for those who don't know or set their POI). You already have a great edge on your competitors (the targets, of course) if your POI is set properly. If you have never set your point of impact, now is the time to do so. Too many shooters buy a gun off the shelf and start shooting it, learning how to shoot the gun, making themselves conform to the gun. You make the gun conform to you! Make that gun shoot where you want to break the target (zone). It's a frustrating experience adjusting POI, but if you want to shoot well you need a POI setting that is complementary to your shooting style, timing, zone, etc. This POI business is serious business and the pros know how important it is as they custom order their guns to conform to the desired POI. Make the gun shoot where you look.

Fig. 59 & 60. Here's an elementary rule of thumb you can use to determine your eye hold at a new gun club. It will get you close to where you should be. It's simple and effective. Try it. Remember, eye holds are important and will determine how you will see the target and where the zone will be to break it. No eye hold equals poor scores.

Fig. 61 and 62. Trapshooting requires knowledge, not just getting "out there" and seeing what happens. That's okay if you want to lose the event. Of course, luck plays a role, but not much of it, so don't rely on luck, place your bets on skill. To be a precision shooter you first have to declare to yourself that you want to be. Then you will have the inclination to work at building precision into your game. It's simple faith in action. First desire, then willpower and then accomplishment follows. You bought this book to learn precision shooting and to raise your scores. The information is here to do so. The rest is totally up to you. It's your decision. So, what's it going to be?

Fig. 63. As long as humans push the release button, slow and fast pulls will occur. There is a method you can use to help block out slow and fast pulls to a good degree but not the gross violations. If you're getting too sensitive to the pull timing and it's just a bit too much of a smidgen off? Extend your call duration and if the target doesn't emerge at the half-way point, then you know the pull is way too slow and turn it down. If the pull is fast, it's obvious as the target emerged prior to your call. Most important? Be absolutely *ready* for the target when you call. Slow and fast pulls simply destroy the setup and shock the nervous system. That's why you must learn to turn them down. Until the rules change, that is.

Fig. 64. Here, gun canting is demonstrated. It's a controversial subject among American trapshooters, but some stateside pros do use the technique. It's a sound form, but it's no picnic to master. To learn this technique you should observe a professional in action. Videotape the form and get cracking on it. You can learn it yourself. Just remember to *bow* gently at the hips to produce the cant and don't crank one shoulder up and the other down. It's okay to rock the shoulders left to right as if they were both welded together. You don't have to cant if you don't want to. Okay? It's just that canting has very powerful abilities to dead-center targets and to get on them faster and smoother. It's a moving gun technique if the cant begins while you are calling. Get the picture? If the degree of cant is a few degrees past normal, you'll know you have a slow pull and can turn it down.

Fig. 65. This is a good example of a zone. A bubble floating around the gun. If you raise the gun the bubble should rise, but it won't rise if your eye hold remains the same. It's your eye hold that controls what you will see. If you raise your eye, the zone decreases, becomes small even though the target angles appear wider. What happens is the zone closed up, not allowing the extreme angle into view. Understand that now? So, to tighten your zone, raise your eye hold, and your gun hold too. You want the eye close to where you plan to break the target in the zone. Peripheral vision will see the target leave the house and the target will enter your centralized focus. It works for those who hold a low gun on the house too. Just swing to the target smoothly.

Fig. 66 through 69. Those buggery traphouses can mess you up long before you even shoulder the gun. Look at these guys! Some short, some tall, skinny or wide. It has adverse effects on gun and eye-hold points and timing. If the traphouse is tall, you can lower your gun and eye holds. If the trap is small, raise your gun and eye hold. If the trap is wide, determine where the targets are exiting in reference to the traphouse. If trap is thin do the same. You may have to hold your gun off the house on a thin one. And hope the traps are set properly too, if not, there are more compensations to be made by shifting your gun and eye holds left or right.

Fig. 70. Here we go again on the pointing issue. You can't keep pointing your gun, shooting with the eyes only. Now you can if you want low scores and want to shoot on luck alone. After all, you got back to the 27-yard line on the "lucky days" at small shoots. Sound familiar? Now lets get down to reality. Just how good are you performing at those big shoots when all the top guns arrive? Are you getting into the shootoff's? If not, you need to learn precision shooting. You have to use the gun sights. Back-sighting is critical and key to precision. You can point or you can aim. Those who aim win the trophies and money. That's what precision is, precise alignment of the sight picture. You can't do that without seeing the sight beads (or muzzle) as a reference point. You can do it subconsciously or consciously, but you're doing it nevertheless whenever you find yourself shooting well. Now if you can learn to see it and control it, you're a precision shooter. It's really simple.

Fig. 71. Help for one-eye shooters. The one-eye shooter should hold a low gun on the house so as to see the target exit. You can hold a high gun too. You can learn to do anything you want to do. In trapshooting, there are rules, but none are chiseled in stone. When dealing with talent, rules are often violated with great success. Sure there is more gun movement holding low on the house which could cause some errors to surface, but many one-eye shooters have won numerous championship shoots. It's not a disadvantage. In fact, there are many terrible shooters you get whipped time after time at registered competition and they could probably start winning if they shot with only one eye! It's an ego thing. Oh, well. One-eye shooters can zero in to very tight sight pictures, clear as clear can be. Try it sometime. Controversy will go on forever on this subject. Who cares? S/he who breaks the most targets wins. That's the bottom line. Try every technique. Who knows? You may decide to convert to one-eye shooting. And why not? If your scores are trash and one-eye shooting can raise your scores… well, what are you waiting for?

Fig. 72 through 74. Eye holds and focal points. A good subject, but too intense to brief here. You can see how easily a target can be acquired in centralized vision if eye hold and pre-focus is used. There are way more photoreceptors in the central area of the eye and that's where you want the target to be. It all makes perfect common sense and it works just fine, too. Seeing is believing. No magic here.

Fig. 75 and 76. More gun hold tips for one-eye shooters. Holding the gun below the far edge of the traphouse causes two problems. 1) Eye is held too low into the target streak zone. 2) If trap is short in height, it upsets geometry of swing. Holding the gun a tad higher over the edge of traphouse may tend to obscure target leaving the house, but it really doesn't as the zone is much higher.

Fig. 77. Shooting short and tall traphouses can upset the geometry of the swing, especially for one-eye shooters. The two-eye shooter still must make adjustments in eye hold, especially on a high traphouse. General rule: Lower gun and eye hold on tall traphouse; raise holds on low house. This is so you can shift and compress the zone upward on the tall house and shift the zone down and expand the zone on the short house. Remember, it's the eye focal point that shifts the zone, not just the gun hold. Move focal-point down, the zone rises. Confused? The higher the eye focus, the smaller zone becomes in size; the imaginary bubble becomes compressed. If eye focus is lowered, the zone expands; you see more, a wider field of view. This may sound strange, but if you try it you'll see how it works. A low eye focal point will always require more gun movement to track the target because the zone has expanded. One more thing. Each shooter has a differing technique, so the opposite rule may apply in your specific case.

Fig. 78. Here, we are not primarily talking about expanding or contracting the zone, but shifting the zone up or down. The gun hold is used to shift the zone in conjunction with the eye hold to expand or contract the zone. It takes some practice to understand the principles, but you'll get the idea quickly. Timing is everything in trapshooting. It's why you must *feel* the game. Feel the setup, cheek pressure, call timing, swing, etc.

Fig. 79. Be aware of the psychological impact of trapshooting. Understand how internal thoughts towards the external environment can affect your shooting performance. Trying to ignore external distractions through conscious effort is a mistake, as it expends energy to maintain the isolation. Rather, perfect concentration actually makes you *more aware* of distractions, but they are harmless and do not bother you.

Fig. 80. Good vision is a must, so get your eyes checked. Use shooting glasses with a lens tint that will complement your ability to contrast the target to the background. Frustration is a phase you will never grow out of, so you may as well learn to deal with it. You won't win every event no matter how good you are. Timing is everything in trapshooting. Watch pros and you'll get a good dose of how timing the shot is accomplished, then start developing a *feel* for timing. If you're pulling the trigger and missing targets, yet it feels like the right spot to be in, you can shift the zone and the point of impact of your gun to break the targets right where you want to. Adjust POI, eye and gun hold points.

Fig. 81. Trapshooting expense form comes in handy to tally expenses. Remember, if you shoot for money you can use trapshooting as a business expense and write off such on taxes.

Fig. 82. Catching the three basic target angles requires a proper eye and gun hold set up to take maximum advantage to reduce the surprise factor, comet tail effect, eye flitter or eye shock -- and to get the gun onto the target's line of flight. If you can imbed into your mind these target angles and visualize them prior to calling for the target you will find you will be absolutely ready for the target! Talk to excellent shooters and they will tell you their prime concern is; *"Making sure I am ready for the target when I call."* Now you know how to do it. Prepare your set up for the widest angled target, but do not anticipate that angle will appear otherwise, you will become momentarily surprised and stunned and react hastily. Another technique is to prepare for the widest angle, then incorporate an instant backup plan in case the opposite angle appears. Just knowing these inner secrets of setting up the shot will give you plenty of inside knowledge to work on in your practice sessions.

Fig. 83. High-gun crossover is a major mistake so many shooters are making. Simply watch the general population shooters and you will see this deadly crossover in their swing. Watch the pros shoot and you will see they have eliminated crossing-over. It takes a fine eye and an informed shooter to recognize it when seen. Study the pro shooters in very fine detail and you will learn much. Smoothness and precision shooting are partners, whereas sharp angled moves of the gun or eyes -- is the target shooter's prime enemy. Find these abrupt moves in your shooting style and work to smooth them out. It's really easy to do; just slow down your shooting and you'll see that you may be shooting too fast causing these straight line vectored moves to materialize. Shooting a hard-right-angled target, using a clock dial as an example, the pro does not move the gun on a straight horizontal line to the target from 9 a.m. to 3 p.m. They move the gun from 9 a.m. to 2 p.m. "tracking" the target's flight path. The crossover angle is not as abrupt and way more precise.

Fig. 84. The higher the high-gun shooter holds the gun the worst things can get. The target's angle increases and this requires even more crossover which gives rise to more missed targets! Way too many shooters are crossing over, especially the long-range handicap and Olympic trap shooters. Crossing over eliminates swing! If there is no swing, too many errors occur and targets will be missed by the dozen! Hit and miss -- or hit, hit, hit, miss is the result. A choppy performance. Best advice; if you are a long-yardage shooter? Get rid of the crossover immediately and develop a proper smooth swing. Make sure you are seeing that target's line of flight so you can smoothly catch its track and ride it for a proper follow-through shot. You must incorporate a swing move to do it. You can't just crossover because you hold a high-gun, you must find and ride the target's track and be smooth about it. No pushing of the muzzle whatsoever is allowed! Use body English moves in the swing. Pushing the muzzle is a bad habit that will destroy scores and must be eradicated from your game if you wish to shoot accurately, as professionals do. Can you see in the illustration the low-gun shooter's advantage? No crossover. The gun is set up and ready to follow the target's true flight path from the start. See Fig. 85.

Fig. 85. The illustration shows a high-gun shooter (right side) holding a lower gun over the house. You don't have to hold it this low, just dropping your normal gun hold an inch or two will allow you to reduce crossover and catch the target's line of flight. This simple adjustment in gun hold solves so many problems to list here! It will reduce crossover to a major degree and increase accuracy and repeatable precision. It allows you to naturally establish a "swing" into your move, eliminating "muzzle-pushing." Incorporating a raised eye hold with this muzzle drop will trigger the slow-motion effect that every handicap or Olympic shooter must acquire, as the target is smaller and more distant and moving fast. This is a great shooting tip to employ.

DOUBLE TRAP TIPS - EXPLANATIONS TO ILLUSTRATIONS
"We cannot experience more than we can accept, but we can expect more than we have been experiencing"
Earnest Holmes

Here we continue with a brief overview of the illustrations in this book. Refer to the illustrations for details. Although some tips can be incorporated in other clay target shooting disciplines, remember we are talking ATA double-rise and Olympic double-trap here, so do not employ these techniques when shooting single targets such as ATA, DTL, or Olympic trap, unless stated otherwise. Double-rise is a game with it's own peculiarities, so do not use the techniques here with any other game. Some tips here can be incorporated in Automatic Ball Trap (ABT, known in USA as Wobble or Continental trap), but not all advice here applies to ABT, for it too, is another peculiar game with its own set of rules and procedures. Think double-trap and you'll be okay. Unless otherwise stated, the following tips focus on the shooter shooting the straight target first, on each post.

Fig. 86. Be careful if you hold the gun off the house. It is generally is not recommended, although some top-gun shooters have found success with the method. Also, in doubles, you <u>can</u> shoot the angled target first. Richard Faulds of Great Britain, a prestigious Olympic-medallist double-trap shooter, always shot the angled target first on each peg. This means it works. It is a viable and proven technique. It may or may not work for you. Try it and see if it does. Generally, you can make anything work if you practice and apply it.

Fig. 87. Where you hold your eyes and gun determines the pick-up point of first seeing the target, and the zone you will likely dispatch the target. The general rule of hold points is to find the hold point that allow you to see the target sooner and clearer than you do now. Double-trap is an eye-movement game. The faster you can move your eyes to the second target, the sooner you will see a rise in your scores. This smooth, but fast-switching of the eyes from the first target to the second, allows you to not have to rush the first, to break the second. Never wait to "see" if the first target breaks. Get the eyes moving to the second target the moment you pull the trigger on the first target. Time is of the essence. Delay makes it harder to shoot the second target.

Fig. 88. Here is shown the "V-dip" swing method. The gun, after firing the first straight target, dips slightly before the swing to the second angled-target, ("V-dip method") or during the swing ("U-dip" method). It is better to "V-dip" before the swing to the angled-target, when first learning the technique. The illustration shows a sharp dip of the gun's muzzle, but you may use a softer "U" shape flow to the second target. The point here is to dip the muzzle a bit, so you can catch the track of the second target for a normal follow-through shot, and to reduce the risk of crossing-over off the target's line of flight. See Fig. 82, 83, 84, 85, 98. Many top-gun shooters simply swing the gun on a horizontal line without dipping. Both techniques work. Finding the right one for you is the name of the game. The long-range handicap shooter who fails to eliminate crossover in the swing will suffer terribly on double-trap angled-targets, despite standing on the 16-yard line!

Fig. 89. Train your eyes to "flow" smoothly from one object to another. No jittering allowed! You can switch the eyes fast and still retain flow/focus control. Make sure the eyes switch first, before the gun moves away from the first target. Eye control is a must when shooting all targets, including double-rise targets. Smooth eye movement and clear eye focus is two prime areas to perfect. This tip applies to all disciplines of clay target shooting.

Fig. 90. Double-trap timing must be smooth; a rhythm established with fine control of the eyes and gun. The tendency of most shooters is to "rush" the shots, but in reality, speed comes from smoothness first! Practice moving the gun smoothly from target-to-target. As you do this, speed will increase. It will appear you are shooting very slow, but it's only that you have trained yourself to be smooth and quick. The professional must always remind himself to slow-down. Is it right for you to begin the slowing-down process? If you have been shooting for over 2-years, it's time. You are probably rushing your shots and destroying precision and consistency. All good shooters have learned to slow down and stay in the proper groove pertaining to timing.

Fig. 91. Flash-shooting, is a technique of spot-shooting. You set up the gun and eye hold, so when you see the bright flash of the target exiting the trap, you pull the trigger immediately -- then switch your eyes to the second target and shoot it as you would a singles trap target. This method allows you to rapidly dispatch the straightaway target first, to give you plenty of time to get on to the second target. You need to know where that first target will exit the house so you can set up the eye and gun hold for that specific peg (post or station). The gun does not move at all, or very little vertically. Most shooters should lower the gun hold, so the muzzle can rise a smidgen to insure a precise hit. This makes it easier on the nervous system.

Fig. 92. Double-trap usually requires a double-gun for ultimate reliability and accuracy. The bottom barrel is used for the straightaway target, as it usually has a higher point of impact to catch a fast rising target. The upper barrel shoots flatter, as the more distant angled target is not rising as quickly. An autoloader shotgun can only shoot one POI setting. If you plan to shoot all the angle targets first, then use the upper barrel first, lower barrel last, but you can barrel-select anyway that works best for you. Most will find the rules in Fig 92 here to be best. Of course, you must check your double-gun to see if the upper and low barrels conform to differing POI's. If both are shooting the same POI use any barrel first, but it's best to set up the gun, as mentioned here, so you can have the gun working for you, not against you. Custom chokes can change your POI for each barrel.

Fig. 93. You may want to lessen the angle of your stance, so you are facing the trap more than you would to the side as shooting single target trapshooting. This will allow your body to be facing the trap more squarely so you can swing in both directions, left and right, equally. Of course, the first straight target requires no horizontal swing, so you set your stance a bit more in the direction of the angled target. Stance is not chiseled in stone, so make the adjustments that works best for you, but do experiment to see if stance can get you on the targets quicker and with more precision in the shots. Everyone is built different, so alter your stance to fit your body's moves. The point here is to make a stance adjustment, for each peg if necessary, to maximize your effectiveness. Doubles is a different game than single-target shooting, so make adjustments for it. If you don't? Your scores will reveal why you should!

Fig. 94. Here's a surprise for you. Shooters who believe they are gaining advantage by holding the gun higher, to be closer to the target to reduce swing distance, are making a big mistake. Hold the gun closer to the house when shooting wide-angled targets, such as on post #1 and #5. The top-gun pros do this. Shouldn't you? The danger is; if you hold further away, you now have to crossover to hit shallow-angle targets! This gun hold rule applies to all disciplines of clay target trap shooting -- and to some degree, sporting clays.

Fig. 95. Make sure your gun is aligned properly to the flight path of the target. If the gun is held too high, you will not be able to perform a precise follow-through shot, and this will permit too many chances for you to miss. The shotstring and swing geometry will be working against you. Stay on the line of the target. Never crossover against a rising target or the geometry of the shotstring and target will be off line from each other. Follow-through demands you track the target's line of flight, as it allows you room for error, yet allows you to still be able to hit the target squarely. Now you know why the set up, your stance and eye and gun hold points, is so important! Shooters who ignore the set up will certainly pay the price of continuous low-score frustration.

Fig. 96. Gun-fitting is complex to explain. It is always best to see a professional to have your gun fitted. Interviewing scores of professional shooters, all have strongly advised having the gun fitted. It's a must! If you have not had your gun fitted you are truly wasting time, energy, money and increasing your frustration trying to score high in the clay target sports. You will miss way less targets with a fitted gun. It pays to be fit! Surprisingly, few shooters who compete have a professionally fitted gun. The smart shooter who wants to rise above the competition does two things, **1)** Takes shooting lessons and studies the intricate details of the sport. **2)** Has the gun fitted to insure the gun shoots where s/he looks. This simple two-step process is the key to ultimate performance and success. Fact; most all pros have taken lessons. Shouldn't you? A list of schools and instructors is included in *Trap Shooting Secrets*.

Fig. 97. Two methods to practice swinging to a target and instill trigger control. Use <u>both</u> methods. Remember, targets never travel in straight lines. Gravity bends the flight path into an arc flight path. Even the straightaway targets will drift left or right from wind, eddy currents, target irregularities, etc. The "straight-line" method helps to establish the new shooter to learn how to swing the gun, without deviating the swing off the target's line of flight from an improper stance or body English move. The "curving-line" method is an enhancement to fine-tune the shooter to track the target precisely on its true flight path, for a direct-center-hit shot. Learn the "straight-line" method first then advance to the "curving-line" to increase precision.

Fig. 98. A classic example of a crossover error. This is why the "V-dip" method in Fig. 88 works, as it allows the gun to drop a tad, so you can then raise the gun along the line of the angled target's true flight path for a perfect follow-through shot. Actually, the "U-dip" method (not shown) has more control and less abrupt moves to make the transition from target to target. Just dip the muzzle in a gentle "U" movement instead of the sharp "V" angle. Practice with the "V" method first, as it is easier to grasp the concept. Later you can smooth it out. This won't work with ABT as a low-target and skyrocket-target must be expected. Use this tip only on double-trap.

Fig. 99. Here's some tips for the finely-tuned shooter. When you get to this point where you are reading your breaks in minute detail, you have built true precision into your game. Keep tuning up, tweaking your technique until perfect target breaks become routine. This tip applies to all disciplines of clay target shooting.

Fig. 100. Shooters with high POI guns will find themselves shooting over the top of targets when they miss. Shooters who miss under the target usually have a timing problem, POI set too low or not swinging the gun. Do not push the muzzle to the target with the forearm alone. Use body English. Keep your eye locked onto the target. The moment you look back at the gun sight, the muzzle will freeze and you will shoot under or behind the target. Be aware, it is good to know why you missed a target, but it is better to concentrate into your routine why you do hit targets. When you miss, concentrate into your mind for the next shot, the sight picture you need to hit the target. If you spend too much evaluation time on why you missed, you will likely keep on missing and become confused. Focus always on what you do right, <u>not</u> what you are doing wrong. Switching your thought-focus when missing targets allows you to recover -- and the sooner the better!

Fig. 101. Eye control is paramount to clay target shooting. It's all in the eyes. There are six eye methods to be employed in clay target shooting: **1)** Eye hold point; where you hold the eye in relation to the trap when calling for the target. **2)** Eye-prefocus; the degree of clarity or narrowed tunnel vision prior to calling for the target. **3)** Eye-switching for double trap, ABT and sporting clays; the ability to switch eye from one target to another quickly. **4)** Eye-flow for smooth tracking of target and the eye's ability to remain clearly focused on the moving target. **5)** Trigger control; the sight picture controls when to pull the trigger. **6)** Backsighting; seeing the sight bead or muzzle and the target simultaneously with the eye focused strongly on the target. Train your eyes when you practice. You will experience a huge improvement in scores. All of the above must be incorporated for precision shooting. Start with one technique then progress to the others. It takes time to learn all this.

Fig. 102. Mind control. Controlling thoughts is critical; flushing the negative to replace with positive will build faith in your ability and generate confidence with relaxation. All that you have in your life began with a thought. Thoughts are creative and will manifest in material form exactly what you believe. What do you believe about yourself pertaining to target shooting? Shooting skills? Forthcoming score? Control your thoughts! Think professional, be professional. Control emotions or they will lead you astray to the land of lost targets.

Fig. 103. Reading target breaks finely tunes your shooting skills. You will find that slicing or missing targets is often due to some error with the eyes not staying locked onto the target. Have you noticed when you are shooting well, your eyes are locking on and flowing smoothly with the target? When the eye locks to the target, everything else seems to be on autopilot and a good score develops. Capture this when it happens, so you can recall it at will, when needed. It's a feeling, a frame of mind sort of thing to develop precision shooting on demand.

Fig. 104. ATA traps do not have markers, but other countries and disciplines allow them. If no markers exist, use imaginary ones. It is good to place markers on a practice trap, as it will give you a jumpstart in learning how to pick up the target and supply reference points to gun and eye hold placement.

Fig. 105. Chokes: no rules. Whatever works for you is fine. Shot size: same thing, except don't use #9's. Selecting the double trap target you wish to shoot first is a personal preference. You can shoot the angled target first on all pegs if you wish, no rule against it. It can be better for the shooter to do this if scores are low and never improving. Why stay in a rut? You may find the technique works better for you! Too many shooters are copycats, mimicking other shooters. **Example**: ATA pros generally shoot the straight target first. Many shooters copy the technique, yet some Olympic-class shooters do not. Both techniques are acceptable as each has advantages and disadvantages. What others do may not be right for you!

Fig. 106. Swing speed is adjustable. Many shooters need to understand how to do it. This illustration explains how. Remember, speed is developed when you learn how to see targets move in slow motion. When you panic things slow down in the mind; falling down seems to take forever and you see every detail all so clearly during the fall. Fast moving accidents happen the same way. You can trigger this slow motion mindset simply by adjusting your eye and gun hold points. Once initiated, you think you are shooting slow, but from those on the outside appears you are shooting fast. Slow down your shooting, as you may be shooting fast already, but it feels slow to you! Now you know why top-gun shooters have to keep reminding themselves to, "slow-down."

Fig. 107. Eye separation for the low-gun shooter. Here we can see the advantage of raising the eye hold point. In fact, you can hold the eye much higher than shown in the illustration. Experiment to find the eye hold location that suits you best for each station peg. Each station may require a different eye (and gun) hold location.

Fig. 108. Eye separation for the high-gun (and low-gun) shooter eliminates "eye shock" and "surprise factor". Eye separation or hold point is not raising your head or cheek from the comb, but as shown in the illustration is simply looking up. They eyeball moves, but the eye remains centered down the rib where it belongs.

Fig. 109 & 110. Backsighting is the technique to learn for consistent precise shooting. Once backsighting is learned you will be shooting the target quicker and with authority, dustballing targets like a habit. Use a mirror to establish the procedure. See *Trap Shooting Secrets* book. See Fig. 116 for the calendar method.

Fig. 111 & 112. A list of double trap tips you can use before you shoot the program.

Fig. 113, 114 & 115. Double trap gun swing practice tips with relation to targets.

Fig. 116. This calendar shooting tip will greatly increase control of the eyes, swing and trigger control. It seems simple and easy at first glance, but once you try it, you will discover serious errors in your ability to control the gun you never knew existed until now. Keep practicing with the calendar and you will be amazed at how much precision and control will be developed in just a few short practice sessions!

THE POWER WITHIN
"It's hard to look at reality and call it a liar."
Within you lies the power to achieve great things if you will only forget yesterday's failures.

Every shooter faces a series of "firewalls" to extinguish and the first is, failure. When learning anything you will make mistakes and in trapshooting these mistakes do result in low scores and losing shoots. But there comes a time when you must separate the amateur from the professional and for you... that day has arrived today! This is not positive thinking, but actually letting the past slide away and begin a new journey into the professional arena. It all begins with the *thought* and this thought then materializes into reality.

Look at everything you own. Each item was obtained by a thought. Call it desire. And once this desire was imbedded and acted upon the material object appeared. The money just came one way or another, but you do have the item, right? Well, a simple thought of wanting to be professional in your shooting will produce the same identical results. The thought will act, often in mysterious ways, but it will perform and allow you to gain the knowledge necessary to reach the goal. There is high power in thought!

So you have to change your thinking today... today... today! Your past failures were only the learning phase, but today it all comes together. This is the day of reckoning where you pass from the amateur phase to the professional phase. Got it? With this thought fully embedded in your mind, think of it often and think like a professional trapshooter would. Don't act like an egotistical pro, but *think* like an egomaniac pro. You have just begun the process of changeover from amateur to pro status. Your scores may still be down in the pits, but your mind, your thoughts will pull them up over time. This is the process. You have to make the decision today. If you don't, how can you ever expect to become professional? When your scores rise? Nope. It works in *reverse*... when you decide to shoot like a pro scores rise. It all begins in the mind with that one solitary thought and a decision to make the transition, then the miracles begin as you begin to believe you can. Only then can we dance in the flames of life!

THOUGHT
"What you think you will be."

Have you noticed something different in the top gun shooters when you talk to them? Something you can't seem to put your finger on, but... something is different about them. It may be the confidence they radiate, their conviction to win, professionalism, etc. They have tapped into a source of power within themselves, which gives them the ability to shoot to kill and win.

The better tip in this book is right here. Read this book: "*The Millionaire Joshua*" published by; DeVorrs & Company, P.O. Box 550, Marina del Rey, CA 90294. It's going to change your life for the better! This book only costs about $12 and is worth more than it's weight in gold. Do order it right now, it's going to do wonders for your trapshooting and much, much more. Trust me, it will. The book is available on our web site.

Most trapshooters attend a registered shoot knowing they will lose. You can hear the tone in their voice when you tell them to hit them all, "*I'll try.*" "*Well, the way I've been shooting lately...*". It's hard to look at reality and call it a liar.

The fact is, as we think we are. There are mental barriers we must push through to excel. If you believe you will shoot poorly based upon past experience (scores) then what chance do you have of ever punching a good score? Little to none. You see, you are what you think! Now if you were to dare to believe in yourself for once, just believe that you will break more targets today than yesterday... you will! No strain, no effort, no sweat-dripping concentration required... just believe. That is faith, simple faith in action and simple it is, okay? Faith is the most powerful force in the universe, it moves things, people, events, mountains in your life.

Ready? This is what is called an affirmation, a personal statement to yourself. If you let these words sink into your thoughts throughout the day, every day for a couple weeks you will begin to see "things move." You don't have to understand how or why it happens, but when you see improvements you'll know you're onto something, something you can't put your finger on, but something good and finally welcome. Here's the words to say;

THE TRAPSHOOTER'S PRAYER

"I have lived my life in a circle of circumstances which keep repeating themselves, a negative upon a negative, a problem upon a problem creating frustration in my life. This repetition is created by the way I think, negative and wrong thinking creating a total disregard of my true inherent abilities. For as I think I will be. I believe there are invisible powers thriving throughout the universe. I feel the power of gravity, I see the miracle of trees to the diversity of life and the abundance of it all. I see these miracles for what they are and I now believe the life-force who has given life to all is giving power to now act in my daily life. In a small way right now, but getting stronger day-by-day. My old life is leaving me as I enter my new world of opportunity. I have nothing to lose and everything to gain to simply believe good things are now happening to me regardless how bad my current life situation appears. It's my simple faith in action. My trapshooting scores were not very impressive, but not anymore. My scores are rising, I Am getting better, and I Am hitting the targets harder and more accurately than I ever had before. Despite the evidence of what I have seen in my past and in my present situation, I will dare to believe that all negativity I see is a lie. What I am seeing is a product of my own thoughts which have become reality. And my thoughts of disbelief in my abilities and good have created a belief in a misconception of the truth. I will dare to believe by my expecting good to come upon me, I will produce powerful results in my life and good will come. I can, with my thought alone, produce the direct opposite result. From this day forward, my life is new and I await the good to arrive today. I will put forth effort to my best ability. I shall seek and I shall find it. I already notice a change, I can't put my finger on it or explain it, but I know something good is beginning to happen today, tomorrow, next week, next month... it's all getting better. Yesterday ended today. I believe I can believe. Those targets are now mine... thank God!"

AFFIRMATIONS WORK
"I Am... the creator of my own world."

The above affirmation is a really good start. It begins to break that vicious circle of doubt letting in the light of possibility that change can occur, that the experiences we have in our life right now and in our past -- were and are -- all caused by our thought. How? It's like a magnet that like charges attract each other. Negative thinking or lack in faith in yourself is a negative charge. As long as that charge exists it will attract negative things in your life, like a magnet! You don't have to know how or why, it just does!

Now this is way more than positive thinking. Those self-help positive thinking books don't really work very long. The moment you forget to think positive the bottom falls out and you're right back where you started. This method is extraordinarily different and way more powerful. It is a deep inner belief and a desire to see good changes come into your life. You don't have to keep telling yourself to think positive, you just do it by believing in simple affirmations. Simple faith! You will get what you expect! Expect a poor shooting performance and you get that. Those horrific scores will come to you like a magnet.

Now you can choose to believe in yourself, to believe there are powers at your disposal, powers that will provide positive results in your life or you can choose not to believe and be satisfied with your shooting scores and the score of life you live now. Simple faith requires no effort, no forcing of the issue desired. It's believing in the truth and the truth is, you can change your expectations and when you do you will see change. It's that simple. Without going into details, you are invoking powerful immutable laws. God gave you powers you may not be aware of, the power of free will and the power of thought. Every prophet spoke of these powers, yet they are not so well commuted in this society we live in, but the power is real, hidden from the eyes of many, but real it is and accessible to you. You'll learn a lot about these powers and how *fast* they do work when you read *The Millionaire Joshua*. I know the title sounds like some positive-thinking, get-rich-quick book, but it isn't. It will teach you the ways to prosperity using biblical demonstrations and personal life histories, including your own, but it teaches you how to tap into influential unseen results-generating powers. Seeing is believing and you will see.

You know trapshooting is 90% or more mental in origin to shoot good scores. You have probably tried many concentration techniques, and even the advice in the book you now hold in your hands. Knowledge is important, no doubt about it in trapshooting, but without the inner conviction, the belief in yourself and the expectation of good in your life about to happen... well, you know the results. So, give it a try. Just believe you will break the targets, one by one, and you will. When you miss tell yourself, *"I saw it, but I don't believe it's going to continue."* That will get you back into that right frame of mind. The point is, you will see immediate improvement in your shooting when you believe in yourself and believe you will hit the targets. Certainly you will have some bad days, everyone does as we are not machines, but just watch your average rise higher than it would have otherwise! All you have to do is believe, then count your blessings.

Remember we talked about trigger words? Those simple phrases to help you set up your shots properly? They are mini-affirmations. Now, they do work don't they?

CHAPTER 12
"I had the answer but I forgot the question."

FREQUENTLY ASKED QUESTIONS & ANSWERS
"You are only one thought away from winning or losing."

Shooters frequently ask questions. Some answers will be noted here. There are so many myths in this sport and that it would be helpful to separate fact from fiction. You may want to jot these and some of your own questions down to ask a pro when you meet one. The answers each can give you will expand your knowledge. Keep in mind, this book and the following questions and answers pertain to handicap trapshooting only because there are substantial technical differences between singles, doubles and handicap.

One of the better ways to learn is by using simple questions and answers to "real world" problems shooters face. Here's a collection, in no specific order, to help you understand the principles of trapshooting. It is also one of the most enjoyable methods to learn something new. You will learn much here and really open your eyes to the realities of the game. Let's get started.

1. What is most important in trapshooting?
Setup, point of impact, timing, visual and mental focus, gun fit. Perfect these six criteria and you'll be way ahead of the crowd. Here are a few more tips: overhaul and evaluate everything you do. Efficiency of setup, swing, tempo, rhythm, etc. There should be no wasted movement like using elaborate gun mounting procedures requiring four or more steps to get the butt on the shoulder. Look for shortcuts, as less maneuvering equals dependable repeatability. Through self-evaluation, awareness is enhanced and a streamlined form is developed that is technically sound and efficient. Simple motions, though complex to learn, are easy to repeat under pressure. A sound technique will develop a smooth, unwavering swing that will hit the target squarely. They say 100 chips are better than 99 smokeballs, but the chipper will hardly ever get the 100 except on a blue moon as true accuracy is nonexistent. Think and shoot with precision.

2. Tell me the fastest way to learn?
Be a specialist. Lawyers, engineers and doctors do, so can you. If you want to be an excellent handicap shooter, then shoot the handicap events only. Forget the singles and doubles until you are proficient in handicap. Each event requires a differing technique. I personally found it intensely trying to learn how to shoot all the events all at one time. I couldn't do it. Maybe you can. Fatigue was a big factor. I'd do well in the singles then poorly in handicap and fall to pieces in doubles. I just couldn't sustain the intense concentration and maintain the technical disciplines, plus I'd get confused and lose the sight picture, forgetting how to shoot. To learn quickly is your goal, then specialize. Shooting one event forces you to become serious and focused. All energy is expended on the handicap. Others may not agree, but it works for me and others.

3. How can I interpret this book when the rules have changed?
Assuming rules such as introducing a 30-yard line handicap, or the use of 1 oz. loads of lead shot, or worse yet; steel shot. Once you learn the basics taught here, it will be common sense with a tad of experimentation to make the adjustments. You'll have the inner knowledge to know what to do and know what to look for to make your patterns, zone, chokes, timing, eye and gun holds, etc., work for you. All of the principles, standards and goals will still apply with some small deviations, so what you learn here will never be outdated. Rule changes affect everyone, but you'll have a enormous edge on everyone right from the start.

4. People tell me that to be a good handicap shooter you must shoot all the events, singles and doubles. True?
Shooters do not understand that singles and handicap are two separate games with unique skills required for each, more so with doubles and ever more true with handicap shooting. Be a surgeon on the trap line, not a general practitioner. It is difficult to learn three things at once. Focus on the one game you love the most! When you perfect it, then go on to the next. This guidance may conflict with some shooters' advice, but it's the advice I follow myself. It makes too much sense, for in all areas of life if you wish to be good at something you need to specialize in it. If I'm wrong, at least I do know you'll be one terror of a shooter on the handicap events. It all depends on your goal. If you wish to be a great all-around shooter, then by all means shoot all the events, that is, if you can financially afford to. If you shoot only for fun, shoot the entire program and have fun. If you shoot for money, shoot the handicap. Trapshooting has always been a money game.

5. The more I shoot the better shooter I will be?
Trapshooting is an invitation to a dilemma of sorts. Shooters like to shoot, but few wish to apply the intense effort to be a precision shooter. Most shooters simply shoot not knowing what they are doing. Many practice only what they do well and this is a huge error. It's pure tunnel vision without hope of expanding the horizon. They believe the more they shoot the better they will become, but this is not true. Most will reach a plateau and stay there, relying on lucky days to win events. The less you shoot this way the better off you'll be. It's not quantity, it's <u>quality</u> of shooting sessions. Practice with a goal and a plan and for heavens sake, experiment, explore, evaluate; otherwise, you will not improve and imbed old bad habits ever deeper into your form. Natural ability only takes you so far, then you plateau and require technical ability to push on. In the 1996 Atlanta Centennial Olympiad 6,500 coaches and trainers were on site. Get the idea? Competitive trapshooting is not a victory waiting to happen. You have to make it happen. This means you need that extra edge of precision other players don't have. You can learn it yourself with experimentation, but a coach can accelerate the process. Read as much as you can about the sport and <u>apply</u> the knowledge learned. Success arrives from your ability to recognize and solve problems. How can you do that if you only know how to shoot one way? And what if that way is the wrong way?

6. Should I hire a coach?
If you can, you should. If you can't, keep experimenting with different ways to break targets until you discover the best most efficient way of breaking each target angle on each post. Talk with professionals and ask questions, don't be shy. Watch the pros shoot and try to incorporate their stance, timing and form into a style you feel comfortable with. A coach will identify bad habits and form immediately. If you come to the point of total frustration in your shooting career, a coach will pull you out of the slump and back to winning again. So if you plan to quit the sport, don't do it until you give yourself a chance with a good coach or trapshooting school. Just do it and you'll be glad you did.

7. How do I find a good coach?
Recommendations are fine; however, many shooting schools exist and are published in the shooting magazines. Some professionals also give lessons. At first glance the price may seem high, but it really isn't when you consider the money you will win for years to come and the self-satisfaction you receive from shooting high scores which simply can't be rewarded with material possessions. There is always a price to pay for excellence. You can find shooting schools on the Internet and in the *Clay Shooting, Pull, ATA* and *Shotgun Sports* magazines. If you don't have a computer your library likely does, so go visit the web there.

8. What ammo should I use?

The shells that reliably break the most targets. Velocity must be consistent. Here, a pattern check can help, but is not decisive in itself. What you see on the scoreboard will ultimately determine which shell is best for you and your gun. Seeing results is believing reality. Don't forget to match the ammo with the ideal choke. Choke to smoke. Don't choke to erratically break targets. You'll keep missing targets you do not deserve to miss. Build precision aim into your game!

9. What choke should I use?

The one that hammers the target hard. Choppy breaks give rise to complacency and lost targets. Extra-full when practicing, but verify POI hasn't shifted from choke-to-choke or you'll learn nothing. You need a tight pattern to zero-in your sight picture for precise hits. Later you can switch to a light-full or a full choke in competition to help compensate for shallow errors in aim. Don't use modified chokes, because if you do you will keep dropping targets here and there because you never really learned how to shoot with precision. Keep the choke clean of carbonized wad material as POI will drift. Be careful that chokes are lubed and tight, if they loosen a barrel explosion can result. Use a wrench not your fingers! Extended ported chokes will give you better patterns from wad-stripping and wad slamming effects. For 16-20 yd use improved modified; 21-23 light-full; 24-27 full choke. Or, use full choke on all yardages. Depending on your barrel peculiarities you may even have to use an extra-full choke. The goal is the 25" hot core pattern. Only then when you put that bead to the target you know it's going to burn. Scores keep *slipping* downward as the pattern expands above 25 inches. Get away from that 30" pattern if you want to see reliability of target annihilation.

10. The best shot size to use?

At 16 yards some shooters use #9 shot but they would get more reliable breaks and harder hitting velocity with 8 ½'s. To make life simple use #8 shot for all yardages powered at maximum legal dram limits to maintain velocity and timing. Many shooters switch to #7 ½ at 24-27 yards as speed of shot is faster than 8's, hit harder and patterns remain tighter at distance. I don't know of any better formula than the above that is practical and effective. You can develop compound mixed-shot loads and other crazy reloading formulas but you run into serious timing and POI problems when you run out of ammo and have to buy factory loads.

11. What about gunpowder?

They are all good. Patterns are primarily affected by the type of powder used but chokes can compensate for many discrepancies. Perfect pattern board pictures don't mean anything because they are one-dimensional, whereas the shotstring has height, width, depth and time traveled. Holes appear even in the best patterns due to shot atrophy (disorder). I believe pattern and powder relationships are way overblown in relation to precision shooting. What matters most is the shift in POI from powder-to-powder. Selecting new shells will also have similar POI shifts, which is why some guns don't like certain shells. To rephrase, it's why shooters don't like certain shells because they are too lazy or fearful to reconfigure the POI / sight picture relationship. Once the mental adjustment is made, including POI rib adjustment and choke selection, most new shells will perform. Shooters without adjustable POI guns must then use alternatives such as selecting powders, wads, primers or certain brands of shells to perform. My best advice is not to fall head-first into reload mania. This is the simple reload formula I use and it works: Federal Gold Medal hull, 3 drams Clays powder, Federal 12S3 wad, #8 shot (or 7 ½ shot size). When I switch to new Federal shells there is no POI shift or timing deviation. I just shoot as I normally do. No complications. Your gun may break targets with other brands. You won't know until you try. Many shooters are stuck on a shell brand that may not be right for their gun.

12. Is a fast powder better than a slow-burning powder?

To maintain tight patterns and simultaneously reduce recoil, a slow-burning powder has the edge, to a degree. There will be less pellet deformation due to setback shock waves, but recoil may remain as it takes more double-base powder to reach the identical velocity a single-base powder requires. However, *perceived felt* recoil may be reduced with the double-base slow-burning powder. In all practical reality? Use the powder you like that breaks the most targets. Keep the shot speed to match standard factory loads. You don't want to run out of reloads and buy a box of factory ammo then lose the shootoff or event due to timing and POI shifts. The powder that breaks the most targets is the best. I know that's subjective but it's a real world test and that is what is recorded on the score sheet. Don't let powders set you off-balance. It's not the powder... it's the shooter who breaks targets.

13. I'll shoot well when I buy a good gun.

A new gun will not help you learn precision shooting, not at all. It may set you back months or devastate your scores for the next two years or more. I've seen many shooters buy expensive guns and never learn to shoot them! If the gun you now own fits you properly, shoots where you look, and has at least a full choke, you have the right gun for you. Expensive guns are custom-built machines. You never buy one off the shelf. You have to know the POI you want, balance, feel, fitted properly, and have the gun built to the desired specifications. Many shooters buy expensive guns believing it will improve their scores, but never had the gun built to specs. They learn to shoot the gun instead of learning how to shoot. First, learn how to shoot with precision, then, have the gun built to complement your shooting form, style and technique. This is important. The perfect gun isn't out there, it's inside you waiting for you to discover it. You may already have the gun in your hands. I shot bad a few days at the PITA Salem Grand. I became so frustrated I told Dan Orlich I wanted to sell my gun. He gave me a well-deserved scolding that I was looking for the easy way out of a personal problem, not a gun problem. He was absolutely right then and today. I never sold the gun and I still shoot it at the time of this writing. You have to *learn* to like your gun because if you don't you'll never shoot well with it. I had a hard time doing that. I kept thinking I needed a gun the professionals shoot which is a wrong approach. First you have to learn how to shoot! Of course, an inferior gun not designed for trapshooting is not a bargain if it doesn't help your game. If an $18,000 gun doesn't fit or shoot where you look, what good is it?

14. I'm a good shooter and now ready to buy a prestige gun. Which do you recommend?
Personal preference and affordability rules. See what the pros shoot and go from there. Just remember this, what you see in America as being the elite guns may be faddish or market share dominance. Everyone follows the leader syndrome. I can tell you this, Browning and Beretta O & U are hot in Europe and the pros shoot them religiously. The clay target trap games Europeans play make our trapshoots appear as child's play. Substantially more forbidding! It's not the gun that wins, it's the shooter. Then again, having a gun that doesn't fit or is terribly out of balance isn't going to do you any justice. Yet be aware, the most expensive guns can be a useless stick if ill-fitted and not setting up properly; point of impact, eye plane alignment, balance, choke, pattern performance, depth of field relative to pointability included. Price does not include the above unless exactly specified. Most shooters just buy without knowing what they need and that's what makes buying expensive guns a formidable process, usually with poor results for the shooter. At first the shooter may even shoot well when testing out the gun, but this is a false sense of security. Usually, the high performance is a momentary boost in concentration and it's not the gun at all. Then when comfort sets in, scores drop and sometimes never return to respectable levels. Be very careful about changing guns, any gun. The switch-over is difficult and horrendous if you change to another ill-fitted or improperly set up gun, you gain nothing. Seek professional advice when you wish to switch guns!

15. Multi-barrel guns are heavier than single barrel guns so why shoot them?
There are many single barrel guns heavier than O&U guns right out of the box. Look at the single barrel guns and you'll see barrel weights attached, stock weights inserted or heavy metal mercury recoil-reduction devices. The weight is now equal or more. A heavy gun is desirable to smooth and slow the swing by adding a touch of momentum (resistance) upon take-off, and, to decrease muzzle stop after pulling the trigger for follow-through. But if too heavy, the gun will swing like a fence post, tire you out and fatigue will take its toll on scores. A lighter gun has magnified pointability, but if the shooter is not well disciplined he'll find himself stabbing at the targets and missing more than he bargained for, and recoil increases too. Balance is part of gun fit and no set weigh-number works for all. If the gun's center of gravity is centered between the shooter's hands, the gun will be too lively for trapshooting. A muzzle-heavy gun adds momentum and smoothes the swing. In any case, the gun that is comfortable and shoots where you look is superior regardless of design factors or price.

16. What is the most effective modification I can make on my gun at the lowest cost?
Change the recoil pad. It's that simple. A curved recoil pad will help you mount the gun properly every time without it slipping away from your shoulder. A soft recoil pad is a mistake to use to get rid of recoil and many shooters do make this *huge* error. Why? When the pad rebounds from the initial recoil jolt it causes the comb to rise striking the face. Now you will, or soon will have, a subconscious head-lifting problem. Isn't shotgunning full of surprises? Here's the formula: soft recoil pad = more comb rise = face slap = head-lifting = missed targets. And you didn't think recoil pads were important? So this brings us to what is the best recoil pad on the market? Bar none, at this time of writing the Kick-Eez™ brand made of Sorbothane® rubber. It's soft but has delay-controlled rebound. Do buy one. Now the shape of the recoil pad is important, but so is its position. A slight cant helps some shooters get the gun lined up. You can easily adjust the length of pull by using spacer or washers, adjust pitch, etc. etc. A stock fitter is best to be consulted. If recoil is a problem, install a compression-type recoil reducer to your stock and get the misery of being beat to death behind you. Oh, one more thing. Make sure the gun fits you. That's the most *important* modification of all. And, one more… are you gripping the stock with your trigger hand firmly? A lazy grip always creates face-slap. Is the gun socketed firmly into the shoulder? Is your cheek down on the comb. Not down to the bone, but close to it? Is your gun backbored to .745 with lengthened and smoothly tapered forcing cones? Barrels and chokes ported?

17. Is timing the shot unforgiving?
Never. There is always room for time to readjust sight picture to line up the shot. You must insure you do this even if shooting a tight zone. If you can't? Your zone is too tight. Open it up a bit so you won't be snapping at the targets. The zone is supposed to be flexible, not a rigid frame which you must break all targets in the parameter. You must allow yourself this extra bit of time to get the sight bead (or muzzle if you shoot off the muzzle) to the target. More than you may believe, the pros have to "ride the target" a tad before pulling the trigger. It may look like their zone is unforgiving, but look very, very, closely and you'll see the variations and mid-course corrections they make. When you're behind the gun it may seem like an eternity when you let a target escape the inner

ideal break point in the zone, but that's an illusion. The perception of time slows down when you shoot. To observers, it still looks like you shot the target mighty quick. Use the zone and timing to your advantage. Don't let the zone or timing force you to pull the trigger when the sight picture is not right.

18. I can't get my timing consistent. I keep missing targets. Why?
You are shooting too fast. Slow down. Back off. Every handicap shooter believes they must shoot faster because the target is further away. That's not true. Fact is, you can take more time than you may believe is possible. See the above paragraph for an example. You can see the target better at long yardage even though it is smaller, and you don't have to swing as much as short yardage shooters. This means you have an elevated opportunity to make adjustments to the sight picture. Now it is true you have to shoot faster than the 16-yard shooter theoretically, but not in actual practice. Too many handicap shooters shoot way too fast, over and beyond their abilities to snap shoot targets, which is bad to do. They watch pros and believe they must whack the target the moment it exits the house. No way. They must learn that shooting is a slow-motion mode and what looks slow is not slow, but acutely fast. When you think fast you'll shoot too fast! Start thinking "*smooth and slow*" and watch what happens... you begin hitting targets with ease and all within the zone too!

19. Are you saying that what we see and do are two separate realities?
Yep. When you see other shooters on your squad whacking targets fast you are in "real time" mode. This sets you up to shoot as fast, but it's a big mistake, as your scores will verify that it is. When you shoot a zone you have established a reference point to break the target. This zone looks huge in area when shooting, but it's very small to the other shooters. So what you see is an illusion and everything slows down yet, it's all really happening very quickly from the other shooter's perspective. When you understand and apply this trapshooting secret you'll be able to slow down your shooting and ride the target a little bit more than you thought possible and still break the clay in the zone. Simply raise the zone a tad and you'll be breaking the target at the close-in area of the new zone. It is adjustable. Most back-fence shooters are shooting way too fast, wildly missing targets. It's not the distance, it's misunderstanding zone, timing and slow-motion shooting. So they snap-shoot at the targets, push or erratically jerk the muzzle instead of swinging to the target.

20. There is very little swing at the back fence. It's not required.
So you're the one telling kids there's no Santa Claus? I'm going to tell you something many back-fence shooters will be appalled to hear. If your scores are low the biggest culprit is you forgot how to shoot by swinging to the target. True, there is less swing, but there is swing nevertheless. Pushing the gun is the #1 problem for long-yardage shooters. The body must move to the target pivoted from the hips. The upper body with the gun is like a solid mass of steel welded together. The gun must not move unless the upper body pivots to create the smooth swing. And that's a fact. Even the pros pivot and do so with deliberation. It may *appear* they don't, but with a trained eye you'll see it. I'll bet you forgot how to swing to the target. It's a very common and insidious ailment long-yardage shooters suffer from, and rarely diagnosed by the shooter. A coach would correct this problem right away. Ask a pro to watch you shoot. Bet you they tell you your swing is defective or nonexistent, shooting too fast, improper stance, poor gun mount, fatal setup, pushing muzzle, poor call, no target acquisition time, a total wreck of a shooter who doesn't stand a chance. Just too many serious errors working against you. But all this can be *easily* corrected. Really!

21. What is call timing and delay?
See Fig. 14 through 17. I'll say this. Make sure when you call that the target exits within a certain expected time duration or turn the target down. Slow (and fast) pulls destroy the entire setup. The call delay? Extend your call tone a bit longer than normal, or call all the way to the target. One more important point. As you call and see the target exit the house, don't move the gun immediately. That's rushing and creates stabbing at the target. Delay. Remember, you are in a slow-motion state of mind, so a ¼ second delay may feel like a whole second to you. Your eyes must acquire the target and know its angle before that muzzle budges an inch. This is a conscious act you must learn if you want to break high scores. Practice this, okay? Be rock steady or use a moving gun.

22. I keep thinking too much. How can I stop it?
Concentration is a tough cookie to eat. If you concentrate all of the time, your mind will shut down, disengage and will "think" to protect itself from going insane. That's the best explanation I can give, though it may not be psychologically correct, of course. I use a very simple method that many good shooters use while standing on station waiting turn to shoot. I watch the targets. I watch them explode and follow a chip. This is relaxing to me and I find I don't think much, except thinking of the break and the chips. To me, it's sort of like a fireworks show even with a few inner "*Ohhh's*" and "*Ahhh's*." Now if the target does not break I watch it fall to the ground and hope it crumbles. I look for, "Boney." S/he's out there and I just pray Boney will eat the other shooters' targets. If you don't know Boney go to question # 213. Now if you're thinking just before it's your turn to shoot, usually bad thoughts, think of the

sight picture and visualize the target exploding. Use trigger words, as they always work. If you are shooting over targets keep reminding yourself to "*Stay under the target*" each time you mount the gun. Trigger words are good to use.

23. Once I miss a target my mood dumps, especially on the first trap. What can I do?
Have another beer and get drunk. We all love an intoxicated mourner crying out for sympathy. Only kidding. It's hard to learn not to get wrapped up when a target escapes. The trick is to forget about it and become more mentally aggressive and tuned-in for the next target. If you know what you did wrong, correct the problem right away. Reminisce, you are likely shooting too fast, over the top or behind the target, and not looking at the target. Remind yourself of these primary errors and any others you have refined. You have to *force* yourself to be positive when feeling negative. How else will you succeed? You have to learn to do this.

24. How should I deal with a bad puller?
On the first instance you turn around and give the kid a dirty look. If s/he does it again yell and scream until the kid gets it right. Well, that's what some shooters do and it works. Best method? Be polite and ask the puller to stand a little closer so s/he can hear the calls. That usually does the trick. If the puller is tired, ask for a replacement. It's a hard job pulling and a slow pull will happen even from the best. Try it sometime. Extend your call duration, that's what I do. Sometimes a short, loud call works better. Make certain the puller can hear you call for the target! You'll have to learn to turn down targets if the pulls are horrid.

25. Wind gives me a problem. Any tips?
Trap Shooting Secrets book delves into adverse weather shooting. Gun hold is the trick. Suppressed targets require a lower gun hold. You can still keep your eye hold high, believe it or not. Rockets require a higher gun hold. But in the wind, it's direction is usually shifting so the low gun hold will work best. Swing slower, not faster in any wind. Ride the target a tiny bit more than usual, I mean a tiny bit so you can see where the target is, not where you think it is. Don't shoot faster. That's a common error. Relax and enjoy the ride. The targets will slow down or speed up, jink, turn on their side and dive and bend away. When the target slows down it will really act wild, so keep the zone reasonably tight with a bit of room for making adjustments to the sight picture. Sounds simple, but shooting in the wind is just like playing sporting clays or automatic ball trap. That's a good frame of mind to have when shooting in the wind. It's no longer trapshooting as you know it.

26. I'm stuck in a rut. What can I do?
Get a shovel and dig yourself out. You're the only one who can, along with a good coach. Stop trying to spot-shoot the targets or intersect them. High gun shooters tend to forget about riding the track of the target. They swing the gun side to side using interception methods to head-off the target at the pass. Don't work that way. Every good shooter tracks the target with a controlled swing movement. Get back onto the flight path. Hold a lower gun than normal. It's likely you have, over time, raised your gun hold so high it feels normal when it is not. This question can be best answered by reading books and magazines and taking lessons. It's just too broad and complex to answer here.

27. I keep chipping targets. Why?
Many things cause this. Here's a few suggestions. Gun must fit. Adjust point of impact. Adjust swing, trigger and zone timing, gun and eye holds. Pushing muzzle, forearm grip too tight, looking back at the sight beads. Last, but likely the culprit, you're using the wrong size choke or shell combination. Get that 25" hot-core working for you and start learning how to back-sight when shooting. Adjust your zone so you can get on the target. Chipping is a sign something is very wrong in the preshot setup.

28. My scores are going down. Help!
You're coming on to the target too fast, shooting over it. There's more, but I'd look at this first. Smooth out your swing and make sure the swing is following *something*... the flight path of the target. Gun fit, POI, etc., all play a role. Attitude needs alteration. You're frame of mind is likely in poor condition due to the slump, which is a self-fulfilling prophesy. Go back to the basics. Foot stance-to-sight picture. Leave no stone unturned. The problem will be found in the setup and how you execute your shot. Get a coach. If you have no coach, then hit the practice trap and iron out the problems as best you can.

29. I attack targets and keep missing. Why?
Mentally attack the targets, not physically. You're too aggressive, which is an emotion and that leads you astray. Anger does the same, causes a burst of adrenaline that stiffens the muscles, upsetting everything. Then you'll rush the target, afraid it's going to escape, and nervously snap at it. Be smooth. It's a fine line to walk. Are you pushing the muzzle? Are you seeing the targets in slow-motion mode? Focus aggression into the will of the mind to burn the target.

Tip: Are you seeing a sight picture before pulling the trigger or are you pulling the trigger on timing alone? Make sure you see a clear sight picture. The eyes must pull the trigger, not the mind nor a feeling of timing. Practice until the eyes take control!

30. You say I shouldn't shoot with family and friends. I don't agree.
Not in tournament shoots, it spells disaster. Recreational weekend shooting at the club is one thing, competition is another. I'm talking about close friends and relatives, not distant acquaintances. When you shoot with people close to the heart, you feel their lost targets, gun jams, low scores, frustrations, etc. Emotions and moods surface. It's a major psychological straightjacket. Squad building with out of town friends with known ability whom you meet at the shoot is a professional relationship and that's a different matter entirely. That's okay. I've seen gun club friends shoot together and when they somehow get separated or bumped out of a squad, their scores usually rise. Shooting with the same ol' friends can create a safety-blanket mind-set and produce low scores if the squad has a newcomer on it. It may be 'fun' to shoot with the buddies, but the scores are usually not much fun to look at. Learn to shoot with any squad and you'll build higher skills and confidence and meet many more friends too! On your next shoot sign up with a strange squad and go to work. If scores drop, don't blame the squad… you are responsible for your own timing!

31. I'm shooting too fast. How do I slow down?
Just don't get into a panic mode. Most rushing results from believing the target will get away. Believe that it will not, even when the target gets the jump on you. If you pivot by hips and swing that way, you'll catch that target. If you shove the forearm you'll play the hit 'n' miss game. Shooting a gun that is unbalanced, too light at the forearm end, makes for a lively gun. Extend your forearm grip so the gun won't accelerate so quickly. Add a muzzle weight if need be. The trigger could be set too light. A heavier set trigger allows you to get deeper into the target. Mentally, you're thinking or convinced you must shoot faster, when you should be shooting slower. There's a lot more to this, but the above should be investigated first.

32. What is a trigger flinch and how do I get rid of it?
It's a jerking of the muzzle, a loss of control the moment the trigger is pulled. Everyone has one and here's how to see just how bad you have it. Mount gun and _slowly_ swing gun to a wall calendar. Pull the trigger on a specific date. Did the gun jerk off course or stop moving when the trigger was pulled? Likely did. Just keep practicing this and control will be established.

33. Someone misses a target and then I miss. What gives?
You must learn to be a determined shooter. Recognize that the subconscious mind will repeat what it sees. That's why you'll see everyone on the squad miss in quick succession. You must tell yourself you are going to break this cycle and that the target is dead. This little affirmation will do wonders. Remember, when you get lazy that's when the subconscious mind takes over and all Hades breaks loose. Shooting is not a subconscious act, it's an act of precision. Some elements, like when to pull the trigger, are subconscious, but sight picture alignment is not. You have to be constantly aware of that first, then the trigger will be pulled subconsciously. If you find yourself pulling the trigger and the target was nowhere near where it should be, you're shooting on timing alone. You're out of phase with your inner time clock and the zone / sight picture relationship. When everyone misses each target and it is your turn to shoot, it helps to watch the last intact target fall to the ground, and say, "_It's dead_" or "_it's broken_" before you call to break this mysterious, yet real, syndrome.

34. I tried back-sighting and it doesn't work. Now what?
You're doing it wrong. You're looking back at the sight bead or end of muzzle. You never look back. Your eye always stays on the target, but you are seeing the sight picture (sight bead or end of muzzle) clearly approaching the target. Once you learn how to do it, don't think too much about it. You may be putting all your energy into back-sighting instead of shooting the target. Relax, swing smoothly, see the picture, and shoot. It's hard to learn. It's an advanced shooting method and it takes determination and proficient maturity to make it happen.

35. Timing is big problem for me. It's messing me up bad.
Timing the shot, working in the zone are tough nuts to learn. If timing is confusing you should then forget about timing for awhile. It will come to you in time. At least you are now aware of timing, which puts you ahead of the majority. Later, it will come and when it does you'll see how it all makes sense. Then the scores go way up. Don't try to learn too much in one season or one year. You can't learn and apply all of the information in this book in one year. Don't even try. Once step at a time. There is just way too much knowledge here to absorb. The best means to learn timing is through using various eye and gun hold points. You don't think timing when shooting, only when learning at the practice trap. Timing is only a reference, not an absolute. The only timing that is perfectly correct is the time you pull the trigger and that is _controlled_ by the sight picture. Timing is nothing without the sight picture and the sight picture can't be _consistently_ obtained without timing. So, you adjust the zone via eye and gun holds first then call and you'll be up and on the target quite quickly. Eye and gun-holds are the secret and now you know it.

36. I get worried about certain targets and then I miss them. It's terrible.
And it'll stay that way, too. If a target is giving you trouble, hit the practice trap, figure out what's causing the problem and resolve it as best you can. In competition you must train yourself to not give any specific target or angle or station post preference. They are just targets. No more, no less. Even if in the face of reality you are having problems with post five, you simply put faith into action and believe it will not be a problem, even if you miss one or two. Just keep believing in the impossible for now. You will surprise yourself and likely run the station and then start dropping targets that were no problem at all before. You know what I'm talking about because you've experienced this. The moment you worry, it's all over before you even yell, "*Pull*." So work on this, okay? You are likely having this problem because somewhere along the line you came to believe a specific target is harder than the others. They are all hard to break. Once you think otherwise a problem will result with certain targets. One month it's a hard right, next month it'll be a straighter target. It never ends until you defocus attention on these targets and treat them all as equals. It's a mind thing you have to learn and it's all based on reality… it's just a target like any other.

37. Should I shoot every target with the same timing?
No. Many shooters simply do not understand timing and zones. They think they are rigid parameters and in reality they are not. Every target requires its own timing. The right timing is the time you put the bead on the target and smoke it. So be flexible on each target. The zone is only a reference out there in the field of view where you plan to burn the target, and it usually gets burnt there, too. Trapshooting is not spot shooting like taking the first target in doubles. You should practice letting targets get out the zone so you can experience this flexibility. You're not a machine so don't even try to break each target based on timing alone. It doesn't work. Just set your zone with the eye and gun hold and get that bead onto the target smoothly. Forget about timing. Timing is a learning phase, not a shooting phase. Once you learn timing it just happens naturally as part of your form and style. If you think too much about timing in competition you will lose.

38. Which gun would you personally like to own?
I shoot a Browning Citori Plus O & U in all events. One gun does it all. If you talk with professionals, they will tell you to stay with one gun. Many pros have owned less than a handful of trap shotguns in their entire career! I personally like the Ljutic Olympic rib model. They have the features and the appearance I like in a gun. Maybe I'll own one some day, but I have to break more targets than my Browning! At this writing I'm sold on what I own. The future could change. Never say never. The perfect gun must be custom built. I like the Berretta high-rib gun and the Perrazi too. If I had to pick between the three in a pinch, I'd go with the Berretta.

39. You shoot a gun Browning doesn't make anymore. Why is that?
I have discovered people who bought the Citori Plus, which is a highly technologically-advanced state-of-the-art gun, didn't know how to set up the gun, specifically the point of impact. The rib has two phases of adjustment on the muzzle-rib and a progressive adjustment on the receiver-end and the minimum setting is 3" high POI. It's confusing to the novice shooter. Adjustable rib guns can be a terrorizing experience to shooters who are unfamiliar with vertical lead tuning. Point of impact adjustments can drastically affect a shooter's timing and can alter sight pictures. The gun should have sold like hotcakes, but shooters were not ready for it as they didn't understand the marvelous features of adjusting POI and they found they couldn't score high with the gun. The big problem was the shooter, not the gun. Most owners never even bothered to set the POI properly because they really didn't know how to do it. My book "*Trapshooting Secrets*" explains how to take advantage of rib adjustments. It makes shooting so much easier once you discover your timing and have the gun to match it. The Citori-Plus punches targets very hard with gentle recoil. That I like. Problem is, Browning stopped production on the gun, but a lot of good used ones are out there with low mileage.

40. Do you adjust the rib on occasions?
Yes, but not as often as friends tease me about. I make minor adjustments, usually 1" POI adjustments, higher or lower depending on target behavior and trap setting conditions. If it's windy and the targets are suppressed, I'll drop the POI so I won't shoot over the top of the targets. If the targets are fast or lofty I'll raise the POI to insure the shot rises to hit the target. Doing this, my timing remains the same, always, and I'll score more targets. I don't shoot an absolute zone. I prefer to keep a fairly tight zone with a bit of wiggle room for sight picture flexibility so scores tend to be consistent despite weather conditions or moods. I'll make a very minor ½" adjustment depending on my physical disposition. If I find I'm not swinging to the target at my usual speed for some reason, I can compensate with a POI adjustment. Most of the time I don't need to fiddle with the rib. In fact, the less you tinker with it the better off you are. Once it's set, you can leave it alone, which most of the time I do. Pros don't fiddle with the rib.

Adjustable rib guns are advantageous once you know what you are doing. They are very innovative. To the unskilled, it's a nightmare come true. People who don't shoot adjustable POI guns fail to understand the concept behind the innovation. This should not prevent you from buying one. Good coaching can get you set up quickly. Rib adjustments don't exclusively adjust POI, they can be used for precise eye alignment, to lift your head square to the rib, produce accurate swings, curtail head-lifting, increase target visibility, reduce felt recoil, enhance gun fit, hold and balance, decrease flinching, design shotstring accuracy parameters (muzzle canting), reduce distorting heat waves, adjust shooter's timing, etc. There are a lot of features here totally unrecognized by many shooters. It's amazing what an adjustable sight rib can do. It's almost like cheating.

41. What sort of rib should I use?
That's personal. To each their own. Here are some options: An adjustable rib can set point of impact in quick easy steps. A high rib performs wonders as it allow you to see the target arriving from under the barrel sooner, reduces head-lifting, reduces felt recoil and much, much, more. Read "*Trap Shooting Secrets*" for all the details. It is true you don't need a rib at all to shoot trap but you had better be extraordinarily talented. Every gun has a rib and sight beads so it's to your advantage to use them, especially for the setup to insure the gun is pre-mounted properly and when seeing the sight picture before you pull the trigger. A high rib gun has great advantages, and if adjustable, even more. I'd say get both.

42. I see a chip fly off the target, but they call it lost. That's not fair.
What you are seeing is the wad or dust from the target's dome, or it could be the beer has gone bad. I know, I see it, too.

43. I tried using the sights and I keep missing targets. Why?
You're not using the sights properly. Your back-sighting routine is likely causing you to look back at the sight, causing the muzzle to stop. That's the biggest hurdle every shooter must learn to overcome when learning how to back-sight. Unfortunately, you have to learn it, so keep trying. Stand in front of the mirror and practice developing sight pictures as instructed. See subchapter *"Seeing the Sight Picture"* for instructions. It's easy once you know how to do it. Also see the illustrations on finding the target.

44. Why is trapshooting so complicated?
We make it so. The physical act of shooting is really easy, but like bowling it's hard to run strikes each time. There are always one or two targets that escape and finding the flaw in technique allows complications to set in. Shooting may be easy, but it is very hard work to punch consistently high scores. There are many ways to break targets and most shooters break them using a multitude of techniques whether they realize it or not. If you watch the pros you'll see they only use one technique where their timing remains consistent. You have to find the 'groove' that works for you. Finding it is a complicated procedure riddled with hours upon months on years of trial and error. There are other factors which evade technique like wind, razor blade targets, target speed and angles, etc. Then the most baffling of all is mastering the gray matter between the ears. It is a complicated mind-searing sport. It's a beast to learn, but once learned it all makes sense.

45. I read magazine articles, but I don't seem to learn from them. Why?
Most shooters do not realize the importance of the article. They are simply not ready, or have not opened their mind to the writer's instructions. When I began shooting, I read articles and couldn't relate to the subject as being so important. Who cares about foot position, stance or gun hold when you're trying to put the bead on the target? But you must have the above nailed down before you can put the bead on the target! I've witnessed a multitude of shooters who don't practice properly and few, very few, ever doubt their stance is improper. They simply don't relate to anything but calling for the target, point the gun and pull the trigger. It's all wrong. The key to success is in the setup, not the final act of shooting the target. Read articles with due seriousness and tear yourself apart by experimenting with the techniques the writer is disclosing. You don't learn by reading, but by doing. Get rid of the security blankets and evaluate everything. If your scores fall apart, then you are on the right path to learning. Most shooters refuse to try anything new for fear of seeing scores drop. This fear immobilizes any future progression. It's a self-inflicted injury. Bring the article with you when practicing and do what it says. Practicing the wrong way can produce more harm than good. I see a lot of shooters shooting, but few practicing. Practice with intelligence.

46. Tell me how to practice.
At no time shoot for score, shoot to learn. You must walk away from the trap knowing you have learned something, anything, but learned something of importance. Then sit for a moment, think, let it sink in. Write it down for future reference. Keep a diary or log sheet. Then go back and put what you have learned into use. Never shoot for score when practicing unless you are 'polishing' for a tournament. Practice is where you can make mistakes and should, too! Through mistakes knowledge is gained. If you strive to not make mistakes and constantly shoot for score to impress club members, you'll never learn the inner secrets required in trapshooting. Those secrets are deep inside yourself waiting to be discovered. Through experimenting with differing techniques to break targets the process of elimination takes hold until the best form is discovered to dispatch the targets. Try different foot positions, gun and eye hold points, swing tempo changes, timing, canting, calls, gun mount, etc. Feel what you are doing. Practice the fundamental elements. Don't be afraid to try new things and stop shooting for score, start shooting to learn! Practice with deep thought of what you are learning.

47. What is the fastest way to determine proper gun and eye hold points?
Simply keep raising your eye hold until targets are easily seen and broken. You may want to start by placing your gun hold over the far-edge of the traphouse roof and start from there. You never know, your current gun and/or eye hold may be way too high as is, or too low. You'll have to find the hold points. Nobody can really show you how. We can get you into the general area to determine a zone, but only you can fine-tune the hold points. Everyone is different. When on post, hold your fist out over the top of the traphouse and pick a finger that would make a good hold point. Use this as a reference point for gun hold. See the drawing in this book.

48. I tried pre-focusing my eye on a twig in the background and I didn't even see the target. Why?
Many things could have happened. It takes some practice. You likely focused okay, but in the wrong spot. Likely too high. Try lowering your focus somewhere between the center field stake and the traphouse and you'll see the target. Then raise your eye focus point in small increments. Each gun club may require a different eye and gun hold due to background and target settings. It's tricky stuff, no doubt about it, but once you get it down the targets smoke. If the sun is setting at an angle to the trap, the lower the eye and gun hold the better; otherwise, the target will slip under your point of view, especially the extreme angles on post #1, 2, 4 and 5.

49. I've tried other techniques and it really messed me up bad. Why is that?
Creatures of habit that we are. Experimentation will annihilate your game. A temporary element of confusion will set in. Once you are in touch with the feeling of the game, you can change techniques on a dime without second thought. The more you do, the more you can do! Scores will fall apart and when that happens shooters panic and immediately revert to their old 'comfortable' shooting, which isn't very impressive to begin with and will only lead them to the road of perpetual frustration, repeating the same mistakes time and time again. This subtle error is magnified exponentially. As many such errors accumulate, a sizable error is introduced. Then the excuses arrive, "*I can't shoot like that.*" Train hard; play hard. Success often rises out of the ashes of failure. You have to look beyond failure. Practicing can be a barrel of fun trying out new techniques, and it is very rewarding with the knowledge gained, as it can be applied when needed. There is more than one way to break a target and you should learn these ways. The more experimentation you do, the easier shooting and learning becomes. In a short spell of time you'll get so good at it, experimentation won't mess up your game. In fact, it's the dues required to increase scores.

If you want to keep losing events... just keep on doing what you are doing now and your wishes shall be fulfilled. Present choices determine future rewards. Too many shooters are stagnant, stale, and sloppy because they don't realize there are defects in their form and style that need the rough edges honed out. If you never experiment, you'll never discover the defects. Experimentation is like looking in a mirror seeing your defects, then suddenly you can step through the mirror to make adjustments to what you see is wrong. Knowledge gained is useless unless applied. Having no knowledge is even worse. Keep trying new techniques until you find the solution, then keep learning. If the mind becomes bored it's slump time.

50. You say patterns should be 25" not 30." This goes against the grain of traditional wisdom. Why?
Mathematically the formulas are a bit complex and the laws of physics do not change. Every pattern has a hot center core. There is no such thing as an evenly spread pattern. No matter what choke you use the core will be hotter than the fringe area. Sorry, but that's the way it is. When shooting handicap, edge-on targets are broken at 40 to 45 yards out. Cone expansion of the shot will fill a 30" pattern, but not *effectively*. Only the inner 25" of the pattern is *reliable* to break targets. It requires 3 to 5 pellets to break edge-on targets. Place a target on the pattern board and you'll see where the hot-core area becomes *highly* effective, whereas the fringe is too scattered. So, you must use a full choke on the back fence. If you use a 1-oz. load you're dead. The core dies at that distance despite an increase in speed and so will your scores die as chipped targets soon become missed targets. So, at 16-yard you should use an improved modified not a modified choke, 20-23 yards a light full choke, and beyond a full choke. If you pattern this with 3-dram loads you should see an effective 25" hot-core and that's what you want and need. Automatically, it fills the fringe area with a respectable amount of shot and that, too, is what you truly need. Even the European and Olympic shooters know this. Why it's such a secret in American trap is a mystery. The most effective shot pattern will always have a hot-core due to ballistics. If you pattern to open up this hot-core to fill a 30" pattern, you're shooting yourself into low scores. Here's another eye-opener for you, even with an effective pattern of 85% in the 30" pattern board you still only have a 14 to 16 inch *effective* pattern at 45+ yards. So you can see why precision is absolute when shooting long-yardage. It's a tad too complex to explain all the details in this book. It's not necessary. Just accept the fact and use a full choke and shell combination to get that 25" hot-core and the fringe area will take care of itself. Reverse your thinking. Don't think fringe; think effective core.

51. Everybody gives me advice. I'm confused.
Every man and his dog will give you advice. Add to the basic reluctance of humans to accept advice and hard-headedness sets in rapidly. *Shotgun Sports Magazine* is the best source of trapshooting advice I've seen, along with *Clay Shooting Magazine*, *Pull* and the *Trap & Field's ATA* magazine interviews of professionals. Serving the PITA a magazine called *On*-Target covers some

shooting advice, too. The best advice is to talk with pros and to study them closely when they shoot. Too much advice is a bad omen, but a little here and there is beneficial. Also consider the shooter who is giving the advice. The trapmen that shoot the worse always seem to have the answers to your problem. This is not to say to ignore advice, not at all, but to listen and see if what they say does make sense. Always remember the coach is never better than the athlete, and the pros do not take lessons from other pros. But a coach has knowledge the athlete does not have. When you become very proficient after many years of shooting, advice is something that is taken lightly and solutions must come from within, unless you have an outstanding coach. I've learned things from novice shooters. Haven't you? Listen and you'll learn. Everyone can give you insights that you've never thought of before.

52. When I see pros shoot it makes me sick. I'll never be that good!
That's their job. They shoot for a living. If you talk with them they will tell you just how terribly they shot when they first began trapshooting. They may appear superhuman today, but nobody is born with a shotgun in the cradle. Many pros shot worse than you did when they first started. There is one major difference between you and them. They wanted to be professional and they put in the dues of hardship to get where they are today. You can do the same if you put your mind to it. When learning and advancing, frustration often builds and we seek shortcuts. Patience and intelligent practice is required. If you're still unhappy about your performance, perhaps you are expecting too much, too soon. You never find happiness until you stop looking for it. It's a mistake to compare yourself with a pro who's been shooting for 30+ years. Be optimistic, greater things are yet to come.

53. I've talked to professional trapshooters but can't apply what they say.
It takes years to learn all the little tips and secrets. Many pros can't even tell you why they shoot so well because they don't know themselves. How can you take thirty years of experience and put it into words? However, if you read between the lines, listen to what they are saying, you will pick up treasures of knowledge. The trick is to apply this knowledge by actually doing it, not just listen and walk away. I've never heard of a pro giving bad advice. Even pros contradict sometimes if asked the same question because each has developed their own theory and technique, but the advice is sound regardless.

54. How can I reduce recoil without changing anything on my gun?
Shoot a 2 ¾ dram load shell. But you sacrifice speed, so you'll need to be aware of placing more lead, more swing momentum, and adjust your timing and zone to compensate. Usually you raise the zone (expanded view) when shooting a slower speed shell. If you try to shoot quicker to make up for the loss of velocity, it won't work. Take out the targets when they are losing velocity in a deeper zone area. Let the target get out there a tiny bit more than usual. It's a price to pay for not having a recoil device installed on your gun. Wear a shooting vest with a good shoulder pad. Browning® makes a good gel-pad shock absorber. Make sure your gun fits you or you'll forever be socked with recoil problems.

55. What is the best method of reducing recoil on my gun without buying a recoil device?
Simply add weight to your gun. Each pound of weight can reduce recoil as much as 10% or so. But this weight gain may have adverse affects on the swing and balance of your gun, and your scores. The best method of reducing recoil is to have the gun fit you properly. It will spread the recoil to the shoulder, where recoil belongs, not pounding away in your face. If your face hurts, the gun doesn't fit. Another thing, are you mounting the gun properly? Maybe the way you hold your gun to the shoulder is causing the comb to rise on firing. Check this out and a new recoil pad may just be the answer. Wear a shooting vest with a gel-type recoil absorber like Browning vests have. Now add these up: add weight to gun + shooting a lower dram shell + gun fit + vest = a smoother ride. About a 50% improvement in the ride! That's nothing to sneeze at. If recoil is a problem, it *is* a problem. It will cause flinching and head-lifting = no fun shooting and no fun scores. Seek a stock fitter and spend the money to get it right.

56. Why should I use hard 7 ½ shot in long-yardage handicap shooting?
Besides the obvious of pellet energy, speed and tight patterns, consider these: Targets can be cold, wet, old, or new and they may not be placed properly on the trap arm, generating *less* spin which makes them *harder* to break. You are also shooting edge-on targets so little to no face is showing. It's harder to break an edge-on target and it requires more than one pellet to get the job done. Mid-yardage shooters should shoot 7 ½ shot if the above conditions exist.

57. What is your opinion of barrel porting?
It reduces muzzle flip and perceived recoil to the face which is a sizable reason shooters lift their heads from the comb, but head-lifting is usually more another problem than recoil, primarily an improperly fitted gun and unsuitable rib/eye alignment with stance/swing mechanics defects. Porting is great in doubles or any game requiring a second shot to prevent muzzle leap, but in trap it is also useful to smooth out the harsh expanding gases prior to the wad leaving the barrel. Patterns will be more consistent. An extended ported choke with barrel porting transforms your gun to hit the targets harder with increased pattern reliability.

58. How do you deal with match pressure?
Sometimes I can't deal with it. I have a sensitive nervous system and I get the shakes really bad. Often for no reason! It's just me. How I push through it is I've noticed when I do get nervous I rarely drop a target. I remind myself of this and tell myself I can break the targets. After a few stations are run, I tend to calm down because I'm focusing so hard on the target it displaces the jitters. That's the secret, focus on what you are doing 100%. When I'm truly focused I don't get nervous at all. I also regulate smooth and easy breathing to control nervousness. Here's another tip. Yawn! You can't be tense and yawn at the same time! As for crowds, opponents and shootoffs, they don't exist, only the target. The best competition is with yourself... just you and the target. The danger is placing too much pressure upon yourself, which erodes confidence and can create a scar that may never disappear. Reverse your thinking! Apply the butterflies. Channel nervous pressure to breaking the target. It'll help you stay within yourself. When you are nervous, concentration and awareness can increase if you let it happen. Trapshooting is a game of confidence. It's all on the mental side once fundamentals are learned and polished.

59. I get stuck on a short-squad and my scores dump. Why is that?
Rushing the targets! Timing is incredibly important in trapshooting. If you have three-squad shooters, it's hard to tell the other two to slow down between firing. They will machinegun in rapid succession. The best thing you can do is not get caught up in such a squeeze, but if you do? 1) Try to be squad leader so you can take that extra time delay before it's your turn to shoot: 2) Maintain your own timing regardless how fast the others are shooting: 3) Concentrate extra hard to just break the targets. 4) Pretend it's a shootoff. 5.) Play your own game.

60. I can't put the bead on the target yet. What can I do?
If you can't shoot fast enough to put the bead on the target, you can shoot using lead. How much lead? Swing through the target putting the sight bead about one target diameter ahead of the target. This usually gets the job done. You can see the target size better than seeing inches. Buy an adjustable rib gun or have one installed or work extra hard to establish your timing.

61. I'm never happy with my trigger setting. What can I do?
Desensitize yourself. You can use a bandage on your pull trigger finger or even wear a thin leather glove. If that doesn't work try slapping the trigger briskly instead of gently pulling the trigger or squeezing it. If none of this works, then get a release trigger and end the misery once and for all. You shouldn't be dickering with your trigger unless it is obvious it is malfunctioning. Some shooters become fanatical over the trigger and most of it is in the mind, not the trigger. Trapshooting will do one thing; it will reveal how the mind will constantly play tricks with you, from blaming triggers to fiddling with magic reloads and shell selections. Anything to get your mind away from taking responsibility for yourself. Now is that true or what?

62. I'm having a terrible time lately hitting the extreme angles. Help!
This book and "*Trap Shooting Secrets*"have the answers for you. But I'll tell you one more not previously discussed. You are likely stopping your gun in your swing. You may deny it all you want, but I bet you that's where your problem is. Go back and follow-thorough with a nice intentional sweep of the target and see what happens. Get that muzzle way ahead of the bird. If this isn't it, the problem is likely in your setup, not what you do after you call for the bird. Seems like you forgot how to shoot. Join the club. We all do at times. You may also not be holding your gun below the target as these targets are falling, not rising, even though they appear to be rising... they are not. They lose angular momentum the moment they leave the traphouse. The only time they don't is when they are flying into a wind. Then they rise like kites. You still have to keep the muzzle under the target though.

63. I try to be a perfectionist, yet I am far from my goal. Why?
You are placing way too much pressure on yourself. You're expectations are not human, but machine. First, forget perfection. When you get too perfectionistic you'll end up convincing yourself you can't play until you get it perfect and you'll deceive yourself thinking when you shot well you hit the targets with perfection. It's a psychological trap. Loosen up. Be kind to yourself. Don't' force your body to do unnatural stints. You'll shoot a lot better if you defocus on perfection and focus on precision. They are not the same. Perfection is perfect flawless action or thought, precision is simply breaking the target. I watch pros shoot and they are not perfect even when they run 100 straight. I see unintended variations in the setup, foot position, stance, timing, call routine, etc. Far from being a machine, yet they run the targets. They focus on precision. That's what's important. The more you think of perfection, the less precision you'll achieve. It's like trying to hit the targets with all your might. The harder you try, the lower the score. Have you ever noticed whenever you try to perform a task with perfection you begin to fumble? Try mounting the gun with perfection and you'll see all sorts of errors creeping in on you. That's why I say, *"Feel the game."* You can get very close to perfection with feeling yet very far away with thought. Shoot your targets with feeling, not emotion, not thought. It's all a feel, and it's something you have to get in touch with if you wish to post high scores.

64. What do you mean when you say to be aggressive?
Be aggressive towards the target, not the squad or events taking place around you. Don't just look at a target; kill it! Many shooters are less aggressive than they realize. Too many shooters seem to be playing cat and mouse with the target instead of the war it really is. There must be a slight degree of ill thoughts, for that miserable target because it is the enemy to be destroyed. Otherwise, the opponent will destroy you. There is only one winner; will it be you or the target? The aggression is mental not physical. You have to separate the two otherwise the aggressive nature will spill over into the swing and you'll stab at the beast, often missing. You can incorporate this aggression into your concentration. In fact, it will trigger concentration. Competition is aggressive. It's serious business so you have to be serious about it. What I see the most is the misuse of constructive aggression. Cussing, scolding targets is still a sin in more ways than one. It upsets concentration. Worse yet, scolding and blaming others for missed targets will absolutely guarantee you will lose the event... it rarely fails! Anger is not aggression. It is of the same family, a distant relative, but it's anti-competitive. Never get angry. There is no need to be a raging beast and it is harmful to the setup. You can get disgusted, but anger is a powerful emotion that only brings destruction to the bearer. Aggression is pure focus with intent to accomplish a task... annihilating the target. Some shooters will do better not to use aggression, but to learn how to relax and focus more on confidence and awareness. Ever notice that fear makes for higher performance? Fear releases adrenaline, producing the element of aggression. You have to learn how to turn aggression on and off and to focus it where it belongs... on the target and only the target. Shoot with an attitude! Remember, authority is better than aggression for it promotes precision shooting!

65. How does a high rib gun help stop head-lifting?
The prime reason for head-lifting is being somewhat surprised by the target exiting, or a wicked slow pull, and you can't see the target. You're looking for it and it's suddenly elsewhere or nowhere. The head rises and you miss. The high rib gun helps you see the target rise under the muzzle for high gun hold shooters and for low gun shooters it keeps the head down, too. If the head is already in an upright-like position, well, it's pretty hard to raise your head up any more (but it still can be done).

66. I don't see many shooters canting the muzzles and they have fine scores. Why?
You don't need to cant to hit targets. It's all a matter of personal technique. I do because I'm controlling the shotstring plane for dead-on hits. I want the target in the hot central core of the pattern. This increases the odds that if my aim is off, the target will still be in the dense annular ring and the target will break with reliability. Reliability is the desired goal. Less room for errors and lost targets. If you look closely, everyone is canting the muzzle a tiny smidgen whether they know it or not, that is, if they are truly following the curved flight path of the target. Most do and don't realize they are doing it. If they added a bit more cant, dustballs form in the air. The trick is to not over-cant. It's a tricky method to learn. It's not for everyone.

67. What is the real secret of catching the straightaway target?
No target is straight. You have to shoot to the left or right of the target. Shoot under the target. Don't rush the target, let it enter the far end of the zone. Taking the shot too quickly is tempting, and that's what causes the miss. But there are two more. Improper anticipation or surprise will cause head-lifting. Panic sets in and the mad dash commences. These are the big culprits. If the gun doesn't shoot where you look, then get the gun fitted, adjust point of impact and use a full choke to get the 25" hot-core pattern. Straight-trending targets are perfectly suited for slipping through holes in a shotstring.

68. What do you think of just before you call for the target?
Nothing. I clear my mind of all thought once the gun is shouldered. I focus my eyes and call. However, prior to calling for the target I struggle to insure my setup is perfect. If I make a mistake here I'll lose the target. I rely on feel. Everything has to feel right. If not, I'll dismount the gun and reset the process. It is critical to be self-conscious of the setup. Accurate shots begin with accurate alignment. You must align the gun and your body squarely to the target at the point the target will be broken. With proper alignment, the muzzle will travel on the target line into and through impact. My thoughts are totally on the setup. This can include specific "trigger words," but I usually use these after I see a sloppily broken target and remind myself of certain things during reloading or changing stations. But when the heat is really on and there is only one post left to run, I know it's hard to not count down the targets left. I have to talk to myself using trigger words to force my mind to "pay attention."

69. What sort of practice routine do you do at home? Do you own a trap?
I practice mounting the gun at least twice a day. Keeping the unloaded gun in an accessible location, I visualize targets and shoot them. When I'm outside doing errands I often stop and focus on small objects, items smaller than clay targets and often further away just to maintain vision focusing skills. I don't own a trap. It's not necessary to own one and practice day after day after day, but I admit it would be neat to have to iron out inefficiencies. If you are thinking of going to pro status, owning a trap may very well be the way to save on practice costs. Not everyone can afford this or has the land space to do this. Going on the circuit to tour is an effective alternative and in my opinion preferred for real world competitive challenge reasons.

70. What sort of plan do you have when you practice?
During the week I always discover some discomfort I have with a certain target I can't break with absolute reliability. I'll formulate a plan in my mind or on index cards of how to attack the target. Then I practice everything I know to make it happen. I'll change foot position, body stance, gun hold point, eye hold point, deviate timing if need be. I prefer to maintain timing and change only the physical positions and movements. I want to blow up the target no more than ½ second after I call. I have to keep reminding myself all targets are equally difficult to break and not focus on just one specific target angle. I always plan on learning something new at each practice session.

71. I shoot left-handed and I can't catch those fast hard rights on post one. Now what?
You can do many things. Turn your foot stance to the left a bit. You could hold gun off the house a smidgen, but you have to be careful here for the other two angles. Not recommended unless the traphouse is short. Generally, practice is better. If the gun just won't move you can bring your forearm grip in closer to you. This unlocks the elbow and makes the gun come alive, but it also makes it easier to stop the gun when pulling the trigger! Best bet? Don't use strange methods. Just go back and practice. In time you'll get it right. Watch the pros do it. You may have to take the target out of the zone for awhile until you gain smoothness.

72. How can I learn to shoot that fast?
First, you must know your gun's POI. If the POI is not correct, too flat shooting, you can't shoot quick. In this case, you can only shoot when you know the target will break. I keep raising the point of impact until the sight bead touches the target and it smokes in the ½ second time frame. But quick shooting is more than POI adjustments. You have to train your eyes to acquire the target quickly. It's easier to see a target at mid and long yardage than at short yardage. Yes, the target appears smaller, but you can see it emerge from the traphouse without a blurry comet tail. High gun holds are not the key. I've held low on the house and can break the target as quick as anyone holding over the house, even though the gun must move a further distance I've visually acquired the target sooner. The next secret is to lift your eyes up away from the edge of the traphouse and look into the field. You would think that placing eye focus on the traphouse would help you acquire the target faster, but it doesn't work that way. You'll tend to stab at the target and you'll only see a blurry comet tail. Get your eyes up! And that includes all the targets, hard angles, etc. To shoot fast, practice shooting fast, but you must first learn how to shoot slowly with true precision. This means you'll need to learn to focus hard on targets, then begin speeding up gradually. You will need to adjust POI to compensate for the new timing factor. At this point, most shooters cave in due to complications of timing and gun alterations, hence the benefits of an adjustable rib gun! Those with the capability to adjust POI need only learn the new timing factors. Speed must feel natural. You can't force it; otherwise, you will shoot beyond your abilities. With practice speed will unfold. If you shoot in slowmotion mode you will shoot fast, but it will feel slow.

73. Do you shoot with one or two eyes? Which is better?
I shoot one-eyed. I've tried two but I have a severe crossover problem and a weaker focus when I use both eyes. I see there are benefits in one-eyed shooting; a stronger focus on the target is one. A low gun hold on the house gives me a clear unobstructed view of the target leaving the house. The move to the target is precise as I see the target angulation clearly and sooner. Two-eyed shooting also has its merits, but if one-eyed shooting breaks the targets, I'm sold on it. I don't believe one technique is superior over the other in trapshooting. We only use peripheral and central focal vision. There is no need for depth perception as you would need in shooting sporting clays. It doesn't matter if you use one or two eyes for trapshooting. There are pros that use one-eye shooting. I suggest if you can, shoot two-eyed. If you can't, then shoot one-eyed. Both methods break targets. If eye crossover is a problem, then definitely shoot one-eyed or find the solution to the problem.

74. I'm a cross-dominant shooter. Is that okay?
Cross-dominant means a right-handed shooter uses his left eye to sight the target. A left-handed shooter would use the left eye. Good luck! The gun must be mounted on the shoulder of the dominant eye (unless you use side-mounted sights). I had to switch from right-handed to left when my left eye became dominant. It's not as difficult as you believe it is, awkward at first but not totally destructive. For me, I found it easy to point the gun with my right hand since I am naturally right-handed. You can do anything if you apply yourself. If you don't know which eye is dominant you need to find out. Most experienced tournament shooters can give you a few eye tests. If you have to switch over, do it. You pay now or pay later, the choice is yours. A temporary reduction in score is a price I was willing to pay to ultimately increase my scores. It's worth the effort.

75. I suffer from eye-crossover. How can I stop it?
If your eye is switching from the line of sight down the rib, you should shoot a tighter zone (raise eye & gun hold). Less muzzle swing will often do the trick. If this ultimately fails, you can shoot one-eyed. Or apply a patch over the opposite eye's shooting glasses. Do some eye training exercises to see if you can build up more strength in the dominate eye. Are you certain you are shooting with the dominate eye? You may want to switch your gun mount to the opposite shoulder to really find out for certain or

visit a stockfitter or coach for some advice. Try swinging the gun much slower and smoother. You may be swinging and shooting too fast. The *EasyHit* gun sight will do wonders for you. See the order form in this book.

Tip: Nothing repairs eye crossover better than shooting on the proper shoulder to the master eye.

76. Any devices on your gun or lucky charms that help?
I repent. I do have lucky charms. I may buy a new glove to give me that little inner spark. Or a new hat that feels new. I like new things. Sometimes friends give me a lucky pebble, penny or whatever to take to the shoot. I do it because it's fun, and I believe it helps - at least to build a happy mood-set. Don't we all shoot better when we feel good? I do wear my first silver belt buckle from the first handicap event I won. It was at the Eel River Trap Club in Fortuna, California. It has always been my lucky charm to this writing. As for gizmos on the gun? None really. I like extended ported chokes, if you want to call that an extraordinary device. It helps maintain tight patterns diminishing wad-slam that can bounce the shot out of the cup. I use *Briley*® chokes as of this writing.

77. Why a ported choke? Doesn't that reduce power?
Wad slam. When the wad exits the barrel, the gasses wallop the wad, bouncing the shot out of the cup. This changes the point of impact a small but significant degree and disrupts the shotstring flow to the target. I use ported barrels to assist in pre-release of muzzle pressures for the same reasons. Any power loss is negligible, as shotstring momentum is fully established midway in the barrel before reaching ported barrels and chokes. The targets are still annihilated with ease as long as I don't miss. Not all disciplines will allow ported barrels or chokes. Check the rulebook.

78. What is the best advice you can give me?
I asked Daro Handy, a Top-Gun handicap ATA Hall of Fame shooter the same question years ago. He smiled, "*Put the bead on the target.*" Sounds so simple, but when I tried it, I kept missing targets. I found my gun was not shooting where I looked because I didn't really have a zone to shoot in. After adjusting the gun to fit and setting the point of impact to match my desired timing and zone, Daro's advice worked. Now I just put the bead on the target and pull the trigger. It's so simple once you tune in. But it's still hard to break them all!

79. What is your view of coaches?
If you can find one with a solid reputation of coaching skills, make your reservations! Professionals in all sports have coaches. Keep in mind that coaches need not be professional shooters. You don't see pros being coached by other pros, do you? That's not reality. Coaching is a 'talent' in itself. Coaches are competent, but not professional in the game they teach. It's a different world many people fail to understand. The shooter looks from the inside-out, yet the coach sees the world outside-in. The best coaches are not as proficient as the athlete they train. Fact of life. Every Olympic champion will confirm this.

80. What are the primary reasons why you miss a target?
If I knew I wouldn't miss any! Usually not paying attention, losing my focus, letting the target get the jump on me, slow and fast pulls, advancing the muzzle before eyes lock on to the target, taking my eye off the target. Usually it's just me, my mood or something, or just a plain dumb mistake. If I don't feel well, I can't shoot well. My moods affect my shooting ability. Sometimes I just can't seem to concentrate. Other days I can concentrate very well yet my body won't move to the target. Go figure! Just part of being human. We are all going to miss targets as we are not machines. We all make mistakes.

81. Targets get the jump on me. How can I stop it?
If you find targets are taking you by surprise when they exit the house, causing you to jerk, snap or overreact try this: **1)** You have to know where to break the target before you call to energize timing of the shot, so preplan your tactics before and after you shoulder the gun. Learn your zone so you can acquire and break targets in the same place time and time again, or at least close to the zone. **2)** Be absolutely ready to see the target when you call and do expect the worst angle to occur. Many shooters are really not ready to see the target and simply call because it's their turn to shoot. **3)** Get your eye's central vision up away from the traphouse so you won't see streaks causing you to move the gun before your eye has locked on to the target. **4)** Pre-focus your master eye before you call for the target. This way your eye's focus doesn't shift producing a mirage effect of shooting where the target is not present. Some, if not most, shooters with low scores need to slow down their timing a smidgen and pull the trigger when they know the target will be burned. Too many are 'mentally flinching' letting the target jump them and they react hastily, pushing, stabbing the muzzle losing precision. **5)** Raise your gun and eye hold points so you see the target and not the comet tail. An eye hold too low will enhance the 'Jack in the Box' syndrome, surprising you when you call. It happens because the eye is forced to 'jerk' and change direction too rapidly and body coordination follows the eye. The swing becomes too stab-like, the eye loses focus and the sight picture fades. It also causes flinching.

82. I get too many slow pulls and other shooters don't. Why?
I have to keep the answer short here because I could write a few chapters on this, easily. If you shoot a high gun, like most trapshooters in the USA do, you must lower your gun hold. The higher you hold the gun, the more the target appears to be a slow pull. The trick is to lower the gun so you can keep your eye pre-focus out in the field. Another method to use, and it may do you wonders, I just don't know, is to look down with peripheral vision through your barrel so you can see the target rise up under the muzzle. If you're a low gun shooter, call louder. That includes high gun too.

83. How do you deal with targets and thoughts on winning or losing?
A positive attitude helps, but it is definitely not a cure-all. I never think about winning or losing option money when shooting. There is only one thing I focus on and that is breaking the targets, one at a time. I don't like to think of anything else when shooting. When thoughts do enter my mind I flush them out immediately. When I see someone on the squad drop a target, especially when a chain-reaction string of them develops, I purposely wait until the target hits the ground and reinforce in my mind the target is broken. I find if I don't tell myself the target is dead, I'll miss it, too. That is the only thought I let into my head when shooting. Sometimes when I'm on my 25th target on a trap I may tell myself to break it, but I don't like to think like this, but sometimes pointless thoughts arise out of nowhere and I have to remind myself to not be psyched by it. It's just another target to break. There is nothing special about it no matter how much money resides on it. Easy to say, hard to do. Try to be a machine as much as you possibly can. No emotions! You should have a burning desire to win. That's the state of mind, not a thought process. A high level of knowing you can, and will, break the target.

84. What is the most important thing I can do on a tournament shoot?
Be yourself. If you are normally a quiet person, be quiet. If you're an extrovert, be lively. But always take the time to sit alone somewhere and visualize yourself breaking each and every target dead-on. Visualize the sight picture! This way you'll know what you are doing out there and how to handle the targets. It kicks the subconscious mind into overdrive. Get very serious about breaking the targets. Don't go out there to horse around, hoping to break targets. Be aggressive and take no prisoners. Don't let the squad influence you: timing, rhythm, lost targets, disruptions, etc. Stay focused. You may want to shoot a squad behind a professional as they often insist on shooting traps they know are solid and well set. This can be an immense advantage. Don't shoot traps that are not set properly. You can't be consistent if the traps are inconsistent, and this advice includes practice sessions at the local gun club. Suppressed targets are dangerous to shoot as you'll shoot over the top of the target.

85. Is it advisable to hit the practice trap before shooting an event?
I think it is for multiple reasons. It gives you a chance to see the total environment and get a feel for the targets. You'll not be distracted by backgrounds, traphouse, target and field cosmetics, etc., in the actual event. You don't want any surprises. Practice acclimates the body to flex the muscles and tunes your eye focus to the target. It also removes the 'misses' you would have made in the event. However, this is a 'to each their own' situation. Some shooters don't need practice. Some find it unnerves them when they do miss a target in practice and it throws their game, setting up fear for the real event. Sometimes I don't bother practicing to warm up, other days I do. Overall, I think it is a good thing to do, especially if you get punched back a yard or two; you'll need the practice for sure.

86. How often do you clean your gun?
I'm not big on cleaning. Pure laziness I suppose. It's really not necessary with an O & U with chrome plated barrels. I don't bother cleaning the gun after each day's shoot. I'll spray clean the receiver to remove light fouling, lube the working parts and clean the ports on the choke and if fouled I'll brush the choke clean. I don't bother punching out the barrel religiously because it basically stays clean. That's the extent of it. The choke must be clean, otherwise, you'll see a POI shift. I have tremendous faith in my gun to perform and it does just fine even when dirty. I'm not a gun collector and I'm also very hard on my gun... it's a working gun and I treat it as such. I have no contemplation of resale value. When it breaks, I'll fix it or buy a new gun. It's just a gun. I'll shoot in the rain with a coat of oil. I just don't care about a tad of rust or a ding in the wood. I want it to break targets; that's all I want it to do. I'd treat an expensive gun the same way. It's like a mechanic with a hammer and pipe wrench, tools that are designed for a purpose. Both are not for good looks. That may be unorthodox, but that's me. I try to focus my energy in proper perspective in relation to functionality. These are not rifles. I keep choke tube threads and all moving parts well oiled with Break Free® brand oil.

87. I thought holding a high gun had advantages and you say it doesn't over low gun?
Everything is a tradeoff. Low gun always sees the target better and faster. High gun has less moves to the target, less swing angle, but surprisingly -- very few high gun shooters actually swing the gun properly and miss way too many targets. They are shooting intersections, or what is called horizontal-line shooting with little vertical lift. It's all wrong and it doesn't work reliably for consistency. If you shoot high gun you have to drop your gun-hold from the straight out horizontal down a bit. Then when the target passes by the muzzle you can see its angle. Buy yourself a bit of time to acquire that angle and then swing horizontally and

vertically following the same flight path of the target. Don't just swing left to right, etc. That's intersection shooting and if you draft these angles on paper, you'll see why it's working against you. It's like trying to hit a missile with a missile at right angles. Too tough for our organic gelatin computers to do. You have to get back into the *swing* of things and slow down. Frankly, there are very few shooters who really have mastered the high gun technique. They could if they just dropped the muzzle and swung to the target smoothly on the target's flight path. It's as simple as that. And don't forget to slow down.

88. You mentioned in *Trap Shooting Secrets* to practice snap-shooting. I disagree.

It's explained in the book why. It's to tone up the nervous system to acquire and shoot fast and to discover the internal time clock where you should be shooting the target, discovering the zone and dissolving flinching. After you do this and return to a realistic speed, everything goes into slowmotion and targets become easy to hit once again. Certainly, you could pick up some bad habits, but that can happen by not even trying to improve your shooting. Any bad habits learned are usually easily discarded after snap shooting exercise is over. Another argument is there are a lot of handicap shooters snap shooting who never even practiced it. They do it because they are mislead that they must shoot handicap targets faster than the sixteen's. That's a bad habit. Go figure.

89. How do you deal with the heat on extremely hot days?

I use a water-collar and a gel sweatband. The gel-filled necktie and band swell when soaked in water to keep you cool. They really work. Some shooters don't like anything around their neck or forehead. I got used to it. I believe anyone can adapt to anything if they put their mind to it. Heat rapidly delivers fatigue. My scores go up when I'm cool and comfortable, which is true for everyone. Try it for yourself and see the results. Contact: Sweat Tamer / Medical Direct Inc., 11230 Gold Express Drive, Suite 310-147, Gold River, CA 95670. On hot humid days when even the gel devices fail, I've learned the hard way to drink more water than you believe you need. As a trapshooting friend told me, "*Let your body leak.*" Drink 2-gallons of water or more per day with a pinch of salt twice a day, and don't forget taking a multi-vitamin supplement. Nothing can take the place of plain water, even if you do use sports drinks to replace electrolytes. Caffeinated beverages and sugary soft drinks and full-strength fruit juices obstruct internal body cooling by concentrating fluid in the digestive track. Eat light and consume foods high in water content: fruits, salads and soups. Mother has spoken.

90. Do you use reloads when you shoot?

Yes, I do for practice shooting. Nothing fancy, no special formula. I load Federal Gold Metal plastic hulls with Federal 12S3 wad, Federal 209-A primers and 5% antimony magnum grade shot. I currently use Clays powder to maintain 1200 f.p.s. 3-dram loads on everything I shoot. I like #8 shot on calm days on dry targets. Otherwise, I'll shoot 7 ½'s. I like the speed of 7 ½'s and the authoritative impact they have on the target. When the big event arises, I'll buy new shells if there is any psychological doubt of losing the event. If you can afford to shoot new shells, by all means do so. If you can't, then reload to factory specifications with OEM components in quality hulls. You'll reduce the chance of shell-to-shell ballistic deviations, and if you get into a shootoff and have to buy new shells, they will still break the targets. If you play around trying to cut costs on components, you risk losing targets and shootoffs. Reload to meet factory specifications of new shells.

91. Can recoil cause permanent damage to the body?

I know of no one who has been damaged from trapshooting. The loads used are low power. If the gun does not fit properly the comb will rise up and punch you a few times to bruise or even break the skin covering the cheekbone. The recoil does not induce neck or back spinal problems that I know of. More people get pulled tendons and muscles playing golf. Trapshooting in this respect is safe. If you don't wear ear protection you'll lose your hearing. Eye protection is a must in case of any chamber leakage. Other than that, it's really safe, unless someone shoots you, accidentally, of course.

92. Should I study other shooters' styles at tournament shoots?

Oh, yes. For two reasons. First you should walk the traps you are assigned to shoot to check the backgrounds, quality of the puller's, target settings, target flight behavior, station to house alignment, etc. Secondly, watching other shooters' mistakes will help reinforce into your mind not to make the same mistakes. It takes a fine eye to see others' mistakes, and when you can see them you'll be more able to discover your own. I like to analyze the many different styles of shooting. Some little techniques I've stolen from the pros, but they borrow systems, too. We all do and we all should! It's good to share knowledge.

93. What do you mean when you say it's just you and the target?

Just what it means. Ignore everything around you. When I shootoff, I see and hear nothing but the target being released. Sometimes when I've locked horns with a shooter and he drops a bird, I may remind myself to "*Be precise.*" Other than that it's just one target at a time, not 1 or 10 left to go. I have to blow up the target and to do that I must focus and pay attention 110%. Anything less and I'll lose. I've lost my share, too. Don't we all?

94. What exactly does back-sighting do?
It helps you to shoot off the end of the barrel. If you see the sight bead coming up on the target, that bead is at the end of the barrel. You're not looking all the way down the rib as if seeing a large plank with a bead sticking up from it. The muzzle bead is uplifted in relation to the rib. It also helps you to fine-tune your sight picture to a micron. The trick is to learn how to do this without looking back at the sight beads so the swing will not be stopped. Practice in front of a mirror moving your finger as you stare into your eyes. Now getting away from the mirror, try holding the gun, raise your eye hold away from the gun's rib and just raise and lower the gun pretending you have a pin standing upright on the end of your muzzle and you want to puncture balloons floating above the gun. That is sort of how you shoot at the end of the barrel. That's the best way I can explain it

95. What does it mean to swing to the line to break targets?
It's a European phrase. It simply means, to obtain the required lead and prevent shooting over or under targets, you simply use the follow-through method of tracking the target's flight path. In this way you also reduce the chances of shooting behind the target. Follow-through is not just pushing the muzzle through and past the target, you have to ride the flight path first, then pass the gun through the target and pull the trigger once muzzle is ahead of the target. It's a technique a good measure of American trapshooters are not using, except the better shooters, that is.

96. What's a quick way to test my swing?
You already know about tracing the wall / ceiling line with the gun. Now try balancing a Styrofoam cup of water on the rib and swing slowly. Awkward, and sometimes messy, but it does work. When you pull the trigger, you will see just how bad of a trigger flinch you have if water spills from the cup. Everyone has a trigger flinch! Best you can do is learn to manage it.

97. Which is better, a taper or parallel rib?
The choice is one you have to make. Some say the rib makes no difference and it's true you shouldn't be looking at the rib, but a tapered rib is going to give you a tunnel-effect, fashioning the rib to look longer than it is. For some shooters it will have a tendency of making you look at your rib and back to the sight bead. If this happens, then taper is not the way to go. A wide parallel rib is just fine, but some shooters prefer a thinner rib to improve accuracy to the pointing routine. A higher rib is always better than a lower rib in American trap. But I wouldn't argue with any pro shooting a low rib gun who eats hundred straights for breakfast. For most shooters, the high rib will help them a lot more in many areas of shooting.

98. What's your opinion of those bright florescent sight beads?
I like them. They do work. It really helps you to see that bead coming onto the target without looking back at the sights. Some shooters will balk and never be able to use them because they don't understand back-sighting and how it's used to define precise shots. They are shooters who only "point" at targets. It's a great training tool and comes in handy when lighting conditions fade. Like anything, you can adapt to anything if you put your mind to it.

99. Can getting advice from shooters confuse and ruin a shooter?
Yes, it can. Assimilating too much knowledge very quickly is the culprit. Shooters need to learn patience, for patience will allow you to reach high levels of expertise in due time. Learning trapshooting is grueling and very punishing for those who wish to excel. A good coach can help walk you through the minefields. Advice is important, even bad advice! Experimentation will ultimately leave your trapshooting friends behind as you pull forward. Ultimately means, in due time. Have patience and try everything and anything. Whenever you accumulate enlightenment it is good for many reasons. Inside knowledge aids you to break out of slumps and readjust to variant shooting conditions because you've learned many techniques and when and how to apply them. Experience is a fine teacher.

100. How to practice properly?
First, disregard the old fables *"Practice makes perfect."* And here's another, *"Keep shooting, and shooting, and shooting."* Many shooters permanently embed flaws and mistakes the more they shoot. The goal of practicing is not to shoot and see how many targets you can break, but to learn, to improve, to resolve a difficulty. Practice for most is nothing more than a physical exercise, but true productive practice involves the brain. You need to take your shot and analyze visual and sensory feedback, get the feel of the moves you made and embed these criteria into your mind. If you memorize, you'll surely forget. That's why it is so important to feel the game. Shooters are too conscious of the results of a shot when they should be seriously analyzing every move to the shot. Think and feel. Shoot as though a $3,000 purse lies on each bird. Be that serious! Pay attention to every detail. The more you feel the game, the better shot you will be. Feel the setup, the swing, the timing and eye focus that dustballs the targets. All of this takes place in less than 7 seconds: 6 seconds to setup, ½ second of call, ½ second until the target breaks. Be aware you may think you made a good shot but in reality you didn't. Always question yourself. Consistency will tell you whether you got it right. If it's hit and miss it's all wrong and you need to do something to alter the end result. Don't just try again, do something different,

experiment, use your creativity and imagination to dream up new methods to break the targets. Failure to experiment and feel the game usually produces poor results in competition. It would be better to spend your time watching and learning how the pros shoot than practicing in a mindless way, because improper practice is simply bad habits reinvented. Poor practice is worse than no practice.

101. Help me out on this. I feel changing styles and experimenting are self-defeating.
People find it difficult to change in all areas of life. Most of us have become so discouraged by trying and slipping back so often we dismiss the possibility of change. The resistance factor is so high. We all want instant results, forever searching for the big turning point where we can say, "*Hey, this is easy.*" That day will come only through experimentation. It's intensely disheartening to see your scores in the garbage dump when experimenting and trying new things, but the inside knowledge learned is incredible. I've received extraordinary jeers by highly experienced shooters during my research phases with many telling me, "*You're all wrong, nobody shoots that way, you're taking this game too seriously, trapshooting is not that technical,*" etc. Now they buy my trapshooting books. It's no miracle that increased knowledge increases scores. Stagnation develops if you do not change! That's what a rut is all about and too many shooters are neck deep in ruts and slumps. Life is change. Stop rationalizing everything and start doing and you'll see improvements. But you'll need to endure the low scores for a few months. It's the price to pay to defeat mediocrity. If you look at it as being fun it helps ease the pain.

102. Explain a few new methods I could use at practice.
First, get in touch with how the gun feels in your arms, feel the setup, feel everything. Do it with your eyes closed so you can feel the whole complex. Call for the target and shoot. If you miss, think! You must know what you did wrong, otherwise, you can't correct the problem. If you shot behind the target, alter your stance so your body's geometry can easily acquire the target to accelerate the swing. Forget the conventional rules! This is the time to break the rules. If you have to stand differently on each post then do so. Experiment! Change gun and eye holds, swing technique, readjust your timing. These few tips alone will keep you busy for a few months of weekend practice. It would be best to stop here. If I reveal more, mass confusion may arise.

103. I am very confused. How do I solve disorientation?
Time heals all wounds. Confusion for the novice shooter -- and even accomplished shooters when learning new things -- is normal and to be expected. Patience is the key. Be kind to yourself and break the difficulties down into tiny segments. Believe me, it's going to take hard work to become a precision shooter and it will take time. If you keep striving, little by little, huge improvements will materialize. The more you think about problems and how to resolve them, confusion vaporizes to enlightenment.

104. I've had days when I've actually forgotten how to shoot. What gives?
Me too! It happens when we think too hard about shooting and seeing sight pictures. It happened to me on the practice trap at the Oregon State Shoot. I forgot how to shoot the hard lefts. I dropped three out of five and it darn right scared me. I practiced again and could not find the sight picture and dropped four more! It just would not materialize and I randomly shot it. It devastated me psychologically. Making the best of a tough situation, I resigned myself to logically forget about it (with great trepidation I may add) and shoot the event on a pure subconscious level. I won the handicap event. Lesson to be learned... don't think, do! I also discovered a timing problem. The hard lefts were not breaking in the ½ second zone I want to shoot in. All the targets obeyed except the hard left. I'm a left-handed shooter, left-eye dominant so naturally my stance was incorrect, upsetting the angle of attack. I've changed my foot position and stance to face further to the left on post 1, offset the gun hold a smidgen along with eye focus toward the left to resolve the problem. When you forget how to shoot, suspect a timing problem along with the setup. That's where most of the problems reside and can be fixed. Problems are not shooting at the target! Once the target leaves the house, the setup determines if you'll break the target, not the physical act of shooting, as a general rule. Good health also is a criteria along with a proper diet. If you're not feeling well, how can you shoot well?

105. I find competition shooting is stressful. What can I do to about this?
Welcome to trapshooting! If you don't feel any stress you'll probably lose the event. If you're overstressed you'll also likely lose. Competition is tension shooting. A lot resides on the outcome. Over time, this stress can be managed, but it is always present and it should be to a degree. A surge of adrenaline and a touch of fear invoke the body and mind to outperform its limitations. Look at stress and fear as a positive trait because it is. Through perfect concentration and focus on the targets, you can dissolve much of the negative stress. If you tell yourself repeatedly you enjoy the stress, you will. Or at least you'll be able tolerate it and push through its damaging factors. My problem is jittery nerves, I hate it, but there is nothing I can do about it. At least I've not found the cure yet, but I'm still searching for a resolution.

106. My scores are so bad, I feel like quitting tournament shooting.
Don't quit before the miracle happens. Everything in life is hard, nothing comes easy unless you hit the lottery. You are focusing on score and performance when you should be hard-pressed to keep your eye on the target and perfect your shooting form. Learn to feel the game and you'll see scores will rise. Get serious when you practice. Develop a plan of action as to how you will annihilate the three basic angle targets on each station. And keep your cheek locked down tight to the comb. Trapshooting is not random, it's a planned process. Practice visualizing often. This will open big doors for you. At times I felt I would never improve and wanted to quit. We all have feelings of inadequacy. These are just temporary barriers to punch through. It wouldn't be fun without the challenge. Even the pros have bad runs and slumps. Those who love the game and accept the personal challenge to excel, will. Winning isn't everything, have fun, too. Life is too short not to enjoy the moment.

107. I'm in a slump. How can I get rid of it?
It's very complicated as it's an individual thing. Go back to the basics, examine every avenue from foot position, stance, gun and eye hold points, eye focus, swing timing, zone defection, and feel. Often the problem is a simple one originating in the setup. Something has changed, throwing the entire chain-reaction off kilter. It could be worn shoes or vest, even a mechanical shoulder slip on the gun; comb cast, pitch, butt cant causing a POI shift in the gun. Weight gain or loss can upset gun fit. The internal slump is more difficult to identify and resolve. If you believe you are in a slump you certainly are. If you raise your expectations, you may break through it. *Trap Shooting Secrets* gets into the full details of slumps and how to break free. It's a highly involved process. Don't be emotional when you do slump as it feeds the fire. Believe me, the solution may be difficult to find, but once you do find it you'll be kicking yourself in the pants, as its causation is usually so elementary. You may not even be in a slump, you may be just having a few off days where you can't find the fire. Don't think slump as soon as a few bad days of shooting materialize because that too can induce a mental spiral slump. Stay focused and remain confident. Here's a secret: the more you experiment with differing styles of shooting, the easier it is to identify problems when they arise as knowledge is increased. If you shoot out of pure habit, without true thought of what you are doing and what is really happening out there, it's like a blind man trying to lead another blind man. If you do slump do something about it... hire a coach! Don't suffer for years on end as many shooters do. Remember this, you start shooting badly and it progressively gets worse. The harder you try to demolish the slump by trying hard-hearted to hit the targets, the less accurate you become. Every man, woman and child will offer advice, but you have to find the solution within you.

108. What's your feeling about advice?
Good advice is always good advice. So is bad advice. Bad advice is better than no advice at all (only kidding). We all learn from our mistakes. It's part of the living experience. A new shooter should listen and learn. But the day will come you must hold your feet to the fire and listen to yourself perusing past experience. It's your number one source. The problem is most shooters believe that day has arrived but it hasn't. The more you learn, the better shot you will become. Knowledge is power. All good tournament shooters have learned to dig themselves out of their own holes over the years. When the game goes sour, they can adapt by tapping into a vast knowledge bank. Don't just read about trapshooting, study it! Become sensitized to target speed variations, color and flight angle, flare (degree of face visible), target height, backgrounds and field slope dimensions, trap to station positioning, atmospheric conditions. When you see these things, you can use your past experience to identify small shifts in form and timing to break the targets. It is here, within you that you'll receive your best advice. Don't allow yourself to be overwhelmed with advice, yet don't close your ears. Strike a balance here. The best advice? Talk with professionals. Ask questions and do what they say to do. Write it down lest you forget. This game is more complex than most shooters believe it is.

109. I've read trapshooting books, magazines and videotapes. None seem to help. Why?
Information overload. I've read articles in sporting magazines and the writer has jammed so much information into the subject that confusion forms. I've read great articles and so have you, but when was the last time you saw anyone take the article with them to a practice trap session? That's the problem. It's fine to read, but learning is by doing. It's great to have the knowledge, but it's more productive to apply the knowledge you have. I also believe the majority of shooters deep-down believe that they can't learn from reading or watching a video. They could if they broke down the information into small manageable segments. There is a huge vacuum out there, void of knowledge on how to shoot trap. As a writer I saw this black hole and personally wished I had a book to help me shoot. I wrote *Trap Shooting Secrets* to help shine light on the subject. Based on testimonials, it's doing its job in a big way. Many shooters write me, telling how they won with the book's advice. Another factor we should not overlook is that shooting is a highly personal experience. It's a subjective concept that is very difficult to communicate.

110. How aggressive should I be when calling for the target?
Internal aggression is preferred over a militant ear-splitting call. The louder you call, the more air moves from the diaphragm, and like a cough, the muzzle will dance. This gun movement can be severe enough to distract concentration or worse -- momentarily drag your eye back to the muzzle, allowing the target to spring out of the house. You'll end up reacting to the target instead of

aggressively attacking it. You're also expending too much energy in the call instead of eye focus and mental concentration. Go ahead, focus on an object and cough. You'll see your eyes lose focus. A deafening call does the same. Remember to maintain internal aggression, not external. You need to work the target, not snap randomly to it. By working I mean getting the sight bead on the target at all costs. You need to expend tremendous internal energy to do this.

111. Why is eye focus prior to target release so important?
Where you focus your eye determines if the target dies or survives. The physical moves to the target are governed through eye sensory input. If the input is faulted, the shot will be defective. If you can learn to acquire the target cleanly and keep your focused eye on the clay, your body will make all the moves required to align the bead to the bird. It will even pull the trigger for you. You need to look for the target when you call. Then you need to really look at it, not just see it. You do not need good eyes to shoot trap, you need good eye focus with central vision, and anybody can do that with practice. Eye placement is critical to activate precise eye-hand coordination. With proper eye focus and placement the target will appear as in slow motion. When that happens, shooting gets to be real fun and scores rise sensationally. Proper eye focus triggers deep concentration. It's all to do with the eyes.

112. Inner motivation. What is it?
In brief, you must strive to outperform yourself. To lose a target is comparable to a slap in the face; it's insulting. That's how I see it. When you apply all the energy you have to break the target, more will break. There must be a reason why you want to break the target. Not just a monetary purpose, a personal rationalism. I literally can't stand the sight of a intact target hitting the ground, whether it's my target or someone else's. I actually feel pity for the poor shooter. It's like a war out there, me against them clay birds. They have no mercy on me, why should I have any with them? Shooting is a feel, a personal experience. That is how I put feel into the game. It's part of a plan and purpose. Who's going to win today? Me or the targets? When I miss, they win. It's unnerving, but it's so important to not let emotions get into the game; otherwise, the targets wins again. Just imagine the target slipping away from you laughing. That will stir your juices to get even. And they do laugh, too -- not the targets, those who post the high scores; they laugh all the way to the bank! After crying myself to sleep too many times, I decided enough was enough so I got very serious in the game. I think you can relate to that.

113. You didn't talk much about flinching in this book. Why?
Trap Shooting Secrets handles that subject in great detail. It's the inner time clock out of synchronization. Flinching is not just caused by recoil or nervousness. It has multitude causation, Everything from improper eye and gun hold, improperly shooting the zone, snap shooting, to undisciplined trigger control, etc.

114. Do you like to shoot or is it just for the money?
It's the money and a bit of fun. It's absolutely not fun being out there on line when your money is on the table, knowing you're going to give it away to the pros. Tournament shooting is not fun in the common sense of the word, at least it isn't to me. It's hard work! It's like punching a time clock. There is a business side to trapshooting not to be ignored. A return on your investment is how I view it. What I do consider fun is traveling to the shoot, meeting friends, socializing. That is the main reason why I got into trapshooting. Then I saw dollars and became ruined by it. Let's face it, it's expensive to shoot trap. If I didn't win, I'd have to give it up long ago. The same rings true with other shooters, too. I didn't want to give up, so the only alternative was to get good enough to make a little cash to pay expenses by playing the options. If I break even, I'm satisfied, it was a fun shoot. If I lose badly, I can't say it was truly an enjoyable experience. And I do love shooting for the sake of shooting, but tournament shooting is serious business. It's not a matter of wanting to win, I have to win or score well to qualify for the options to pay expenses. Trapshooting is more than a game. The fact remains, money and prizes draw crowds to registered shoots like a magnet. If the money wasn't there, attendance would drop considerably. It's always been a money game. Competition is always serious business. Ask any top-fuel drag racer or athlete. It's a fun business. If you want to shoot for fun, don't play the money options. Competition is not entertainment.

115. So, shooting is not a fun sport?
We live in a competitive world. The trick is to blend business with pleasure. You can have fun with seriousness. However, it is important to not lose sight of the prime reasons why we shoot trap, the great feeling you get when targets explode. I have fun watching other shooters win, too! It's the competition, but winning isn't everything. I lose my share of events like everyone else, and sometimes I have a terrible year like everyone else. The nice thing is you always have another day to surprise yourself. Shooting for pure fun is something I can't do in competition, but to me it still retains an element of enjoyment; otherwise, I wouldn't be there. Competition is serious business and it's all about money. Trapshooting may be an enjoyable sport, but it is a serious one. Never shoot practice rounds for plain old festivity, because it'll often weaken your ability to recover from a disregard of concentration. If you can have fun, too, that's great. The pros are out there "working hard." The fun comes later when you win or score up some option money to pay expenses. It's a business. So it is the trap clubs trying to make a profit. Why not the shooter,

too? Everyone has their own reasons for shooting trap and that should be respected. It's fun for some and business for others. It's just life.

Tip: It is fun to shoot a respectable score even when you lose the event. However, losing is not fun as any winner will tell you. Instead of complaining about the pros being too good and winning all the time, become a professional yourself in your own way.

116. Playing options is confusing and I don't understand the formulas and terminology.
You're not alone. Many shooters don't comprehend these complex and baffling accounting systems. I suggest you purchase the book, *"Trap Options"* by Scattergun Press, 4919 Westview Drive, Austin TX 78731 (512)-419-9345. The author has broken down the formulas so shooters can finally decipher shoot programs and the book explains each option; Ford, Purse, Jackpot, Calcutta, Lewis, Perpetual, etc. A very good book!

117. I've read you must point a shotgun, never use the sights, yet you use them. Why?
Shooting singles at close range you can point and get away with it, even at short yardage handicap. But when you enter mid-and long-yardage frontiers, pointing will only cause you grief. Precision is required! Of course, I'm not saying to rifle-shoot, the eye stays on the target, but you must clearly see the sight bead moving in on the target like a ghost, and you have to learn to "control" that sight picture, not just move it randomly close to the target. You need to be precise. This means the swing must be smooth and accurate. It's really a subconscious phenomena, but when learning you'll need to rifle-shoot to see what the sight picture looks like. Once you get it down, it's easy to do. If you keep dropping targets, you had better learn how to use the sight beads or live with the low scores.

Shooters who have won many competitions use the sight beads. It's all in peripheral vision but they do use them. You know that is what makes handicap shooting so difficult for shooters. They keep believing wives' tales that you need to point the muzzle not aim it. Handicap shooting demands more skill than just pointing alone; it's a different game than singles, requiring entirely new techniques. Like Daro Handy told me long ago, *"Put the bead on the target."* Well, how are you going to do that if you don't even see a sight bead? Now you've heard the story of the fellow who shot well only to discover his sight bead was missing. This is used by "pointing converts" to prove you don't need the sight beads. That's ridiculous. The man was highly experienced and he likely used the muzzle-end or rib for a reference point, and he was probably shooting singles, not long-handicap events. For true eye-hand coordination to take place, the eye must lock onto the target and the hand must move to it, but the trigger must be pulled at the right time. When is the right time? When the sight bead is on the target! When you miss, the sight bead was not on the target. No mystery here. If the sights were not important, every professional shooter's gun wouldn't have them. They are subconscious reference points, at the very least, the subconscious mind is using the sights or muzzle-end without the shooter being aware of it.

118. Eye training seems complicated and I'm not certain I can perfect it. What can I do?
You can see a target, but unless your eye is focused you can't see clearly. Eye training really is not difficult, just different. You simply need to stop seeing as you normally would walking down the street. That is a soft focus. In contrast, if you stop along the way and closely examine a flower your eye is now kicking in to central vision. If you focus harder, you'll see the flower brighten and hidden details suddenly become visible. If you look at targets this way you'll see an increase in scores. Practicing fixation triggers central focus and mental concentration that produces a slowmotion effect. It's the dream-like state you felt when you were shooting well. With practice, you can reinvent the mood at will. When you do, you'll be amazed how high your scores will leap! Look, don't see. That's the key. If you're really looking at the target in central vision, you'll see the ghost sight-bead approaching the target very clearly. Don't look for instant results, just practice looking at objects and targets and the mind will take care of the rest for you. Every day we see things, but how often must you look at speeding targets? Only on the trapfield. This is why you should practice kicking-in central vision at least once per day so your eyes can learn how to adapt when you do shoot.

119. I can't help thinking I know I'm going to miss a target. How can I stop this?
Expecting to miss a target is a predisposition to failure, but I suffer from the same thing. It's a bad habit! You can tell yourself, *"I won't miss."* Then when you do it's a letdown. The best policy is to keep telling yourself you can kill the targets without using the trigger word *"Miss."* When a target is missed, don't think of score or say, *"I can get a 99 if I don't miss anymore."* All thoughts and all emotions will lead you astray. Just concentrate on one target at a time because there is only one target!

120. I'm shooting great, ran three traps, then fall apart on the last trap. Why?
Pressure. You're letting match pressure get the better of you. You are placing special emphasis on these last few targets when in fact they are just ordinary targets like the others you shot. Your mind has now drifted to the end result, thinking of score, money, winning, achievement. It takes experience to disconnect yourself from the importance of running the last trap or station. Recall, it's

one target at time and only one target is the game, not 100. Practice this mind-set on the practice trap so you can recall it when you really need it in competition. It's that simple. A machine does not think!

121. You recommend O&U guns, but few top shooters in the USA shoot them. Why?

Watch the Olympics! They shoot O&U shotguns. In Europe the top guns use them exclusively, and the games are considerably more vexing than American trap: Olympic trap, Universal Trench, Down the Line, Automatic Ball Trap. For practical purposes, the novice shooter should buy an O&U to control expenses and promote flexibility to shoot doubles. The single barrel gun has superior pointability and balance over the O&U and that's why pros in the USA use it. I explain this in *Trap Shooting Secrets*. It's not the gun that breaks targets, it's the shooter. A pro could break hundreds straight with your gun, any gun. As long as it fits and shoots where you look, that's the gun for you. I've seen many shooters win tournaments with O&U guns. Haven't you? The moment you believe the gun wins tournaments, you're on the wrong highway. If that were true, then all the pros would be shooting identical brands and models. We know this is not reality, they all shoot different guns. One day, I may exclusively shoot a single barrel gun, but that doesn't mean the O&U can't take you to successful wins. It's all personal preference.

122. I seem to shoot better at some clubs than others. Why is that?

Many reasons. To condense the answer, it is often the way the traps are set up. Some clubs throw fast targets and other soft. Visibility is a prime reason for fluctuating scores too. The background and flight angle of the targets, trap positioning in relation to the sun, elevation, field conditions all these play a key role, and more.

123. What is the best advice you can give an experienced shooter?

Read, study, experiment! Be your own worse critic. Learn precision. Be precise in all that you do and get very serious when you are shooting. Pay attention! It's one target at a time and don't quit the sport. If success were easy, everyone would be doing it and like Dary Handy say's "*Put the bead on the target.*" To do that you need to adjust your timing and point of impact and learn back sighting procedure.

124. Is trapshooting all in the eyes?

Yes and no. If you're looking, really looking at the target, sensory input from the eyes will command the body to move to the target and pull the trigger when the sight picture is dead on. That is the core of eye / hand coordination. But there are times, even when visual and mental concentration is perfect, a missed target is dealt. This is caused by a tiny error in the setup that the eye cannot compensate for. It is also caused by "attitude" of the shooter swinging the muzzle too fast, so swing tempo is disturbed. I use these trigger words, "*Setup, look, smooth precision.*" Precision shooting is much more than simply looking at the target. Learn to incorporate all three criteria, smoothly. Above all, think precision. If you don't think precision, it won't happen. The word precision is a powerful trigger word in itself. But keep in mind this strange yet beautiful fact, the target is seldom the target!

125. Explain more about shooting with the eyes only.

Way too many shooters look at the target but fail to notice its forward motion. If your eyes are fixed solely on the target, you'll miss it! Why? You have to know where it is going, where it will be after you pull the trigger. Your eyes must not just look at the target, they must "flow" with the target. That's one reason targets are lost even when the sight picture was dead-on the target. A 1 inch miss at a foot (muzzle end) can be well over a 30 inch miss at 40 yards. If your eyes don't flow with the target, usually on the leading edge or ahead of the target, the muzzle will likely stop when you pull the trigger. This is not follow-through, it's predetermined lead as the eye / muzzle rib bears down on an accurate sight picture. If the eyes don't flow, the sight picture will evolve to an incorrect sight picture by the time the shot arrives. This explains why shooters miss even when they employ drastic follow-through swings. Remember this, the target does not stop just because you pulled the trigger. You have to be looking ahead of the target too! Learn to pull the trigger only when the sight picture is perfect. Don't shoot out of habit.

126. You mention many shooters should change their call. Why is that?

How you call for the target has serious implications. It's so critical to find the right call tone to set up the mood, maintain timing, gun stability and efficient pulls. Too many shooters are using the wrong call and find their muzzles flipping around like a fish out of water or getting erratic pulls. Usually the word "*Pull*" is the culprit, especially when shouted loudly upsetting the setup. The use of vowels (A, E, I, O, U) will get the job done without heaving the chest and arms. Or a brief, "*Huh*" or "*Ha*" can be used. The shorter in duration the call, the better for most shooters. Now I like the long call "*Puuuull*" all the way to the target, but I get timing problems. If you do this, you must consistently break the targets in a specific, unchanging zone; otherwise the call duration will keep changing and that can be devastating. What happens is you'll end up getting into a bad habit of pulling the trigger, say on the fourth "u" of the word, blowing accuracy to pieces. The timing may be perfect, but the target is nowhere in sight! Trapshooting is a very sensitive sport and the feel must be perfect for perfect scores. Experiment with different call tones and durations. Remember, your eyes will lose focus if you call too loudly or use excessive muscular force to execute the call. Keep in mind the zone is not only adjustable but when the eye acquires the target is where the zone should be. Pros shoot quicker because they see the target bird/bead relationship sooner than the average shooter. Sometimes it looks like they shoot in a tight zone, but they are really only shooting the target as they see it! Shooting a zone is a practice technique to help you see the target relationship sooner than you do now.

Tip: The purpose of the call is to get the target out of the house, that is all. The problem is, some shooter's calls are disruptive to themselves by calling too loudly upsetting eye focus, concentration or creating muzzle-flip, etc.

127. Do women suffer more than men in trapshooting?

I don't believe so. They get teased, but not to any large degree as the men also bait each other with jokes, etc. I see women struggle with guns that are way too heavy for them and get beat up with guns that are not properly fitted. I also see too many husbands / boyfriends trying to coach the lady or their children and in most cases it just doesn't work out well. This also applies to father & son. We need more women in the sport and more are joining and I like that. The best advice is to not over-coach them. Let them learn through enjoyment with small tips here and there. Don't hover over them in public, nobody likes that. Give women and children a gun that is light and well fitted. That applies to men, too! Above all, trapshooting has to be enjoyable or they will lose interest. The worst teacher is a competitive tournament shooter with no coaching skills. They instill a sense of guilt and embarrassment when the shooter makes a mistake, and I've often seen parents become disgusted, angry and scolding. Let them be free to learn and enjoy and send them to a shooting school so they can learn the right way to shoot. Family should not shoot together on the same squad, as deep and complex emotions always arise to ruin everyone's game. Never underestimate a woman. There are lady shooters who can outshoot you! Annie Oakley was only the first to do it. Women are intimidated by men who hit higher scores, just as men are intimidated by women who beat them. I've not seen any open rivalry. All are treated equally. Fact is, the women I've met seem to have a better attitude toward the game than many men, and their presence is a fine moderator to attitudes. Trapshooting is a family sport, and the more women we have the better our sport will be. Long live the Queen!

128. I've asked good shooters questions and get vague answers. Are they holding back secrets?

A few probably are, but most good shooters I've met don't have the communication skills to communicate ideas and learned experience. If you ask why they shoot so well, you'll get a blank stare and some quip remarks such as: *"Practice." "Take lessons." "Concentrate."* Many shooters are intimidated to speak with professionals for the same reason, they believe the pro is simply not interested in sharing knowledge. And when you consider we see the pros at the shoots, they don't really want to talk about trapshooting especially when they are preparing for their turn in the barrel. Trapshooting is a complex game, and it is quite difficult to explain the myriad tactics even when they are known. To explain it in simple conversation requires skills of a different kind. There are very few trapshooting books, so that should give you some insight here as to how difficult a sport it is to communicate. In the last 60 years how many trapshooting books could fit in your hand? I've asked good shooters questions they could give no answers to. More than a few have told me they simply don't know why they shoot so well. Some call it talent. I lean to say it's retained knowledge executed without thought. They shoot well because the years have taught them well.

129. I have a lot of inside knowledge of trapshooting but I still can't shoot as well as I should. Why?

Knowledge is power only when applied. That's the secret. It's hard to apply all that you have learned and even more difficult to remember what you have learned when shooting. Once you step on line and the target flies, it seems all the theory flies out the window and primal instinct takes over. The key to applying knowledge is to feel what you have learned. If you're a weekend shooter don't expect to shoot as well as a someone on tour regardless of how much knowledge you may have of the game.

130. How come I see so many writers writing about trapshooting but the pros remain relatively silent?

Friends joke with me saying, *"You wrote the books, so how come you didn't win today?"* Keep in mind professionals shoot for a living, it's their job! A writers' job is to capture this knowledge and transform it into an easily communicative form (a very daunting task). There are shooters and there are writers. Many articles you have read on trapshooting has not been written by a professional. To simplify, how much effective practical knowledge did you obtain from professionals who did write articles or books? The skills are two different animals. Taking it a step further, a professional can give private lessons, but will this make the shooter equal to the teacher? Hardly. Trapshooting is a highly individualistic mind-game, and only writers and pro-teachers can hope to communicate the required skills as best as we humanly can. Just as top-gun shooter struggle into a sweat to write and communicate their secrets to success, the writer is not be capable of taking on the pros in the arena. There is another factor to consider. Writing articles -- and especially books, which takes years of writing and rewriting -- is grueling work, which few have the talent and patience to endure. I believe pros could write some great books, but they don't have the time and energy to dedicate to the task along with the awful responsibility of communicating their intangible inner knowledge to legible discernible form. How much do you owe to shooting well from reading shotgun sports magazine articles and trapshooting books? Pros shoot, writer's write... that's our job. The end result is beneficial to you.

131. What about cheating? It exists doesn't it?
Yeah, it does. There are sandbaggers, turndown artists, mind manipulators and reload cheats. The A.T.A and P.I.T.A. have good rules covering behavior and technical factors, so cheats can only go just so far. Eventually, they get caught and are disciplined. There is one way to beat a cheat and that is with precision shooting. I like what Richard Rawlingson, Editor of *Clay Shooting Magazine* had to say about cheating, "*A reputation takes a lifetime to earn and a minute to lose.*" If you are aware of cheating, you should expose it, because it robs you and others from obtaining the win you deserve. Believe me, trapshooters are not shy if they suspect cheating and the losers are always suspicious! Before thinking someone has cheated, be very certain you understand the rule book. Example: Someone turns down a perfectly good pull. The A.T.A. allows one failure to fire! Rules can change, so always check the most current rulebook for updates. Sandbaggers every sport seems to have and the cure is most trying and quite impossible to curb.

132. What features of trapshooting stand out from other sports?
Longevity! In golf, bowling, tennis, etc., the games require fast, unnatural and often distorted body moves. Where age stops others cold, trapshooters can go on shooting as long as the eyes hold up. You don't have to be a contortionist to shoot trap as you would with golf. The golfer must corkscrew his back, twist legs, tilt shoulders, swing briskly ending somewhat off balance with a foot half or clear off the ground, twist waist and neck, etc. It's a major problem for age and joint pain limits these motions. I think limited motion is one of the best longevity features trapshooters enjoy next to the tight camaraderie of social interactions shooters enjoy.

133. How to shoot in the wind?
Shoot where the target is, not where you think it should be. Maintain a lower gun and eye hold than normal so you can be smooth to the target and not overrun it. Above all, relax. Don't let the wind upset your nerves. There's a roar on the trapline and it's not the sound of shotguns. It's the battle between your ears!

134. I suffer from head-lifting and can't seem to stop it.
Then do something about it. Too many shooters know they lift their heads yet do nothing to terminate the affliction. You have to take deliberate action. The answer is too complex to go into full details, but if you do this one thing, much will be resolved. Use your cheek to steer the gun to the target. To give you an idea, mount the unloaded gun and face it to the ground just ahead of you. Now draw a figure-8. Notice how easily the gun wants to leave your face. Now, try steering the gun with your cheek along with your upper body. The gun won't leave your cheek! Do this when shooting and head-lifting will be greatly dissolved, if not permanently cured. Be innovative in your search to resolve difficulties. Through experimentation, answers await you. If the affliction persists, get a high rib gun that fits you.

135. I'm flinching. Help!
Flinching is a bad habit learned. It can be unlearned, but sometimes it's not worth the pain and suffering to cure the problem with mind control alone. Some shooters simply can't stop flinching. The release trigger does work, but it's no guarantee because there is more to flinching than meets the eye. There is recoil flinching where the brain anticipates recoil, causing a random pull of the trigger; lock-up flinching where the shooter can't pull the trigger; timing flinch where the trigger is pulled when the sight picture is not correct, indicating a zone and timing problem; escape flinch when the target gets the jump on the shooter and a panic stab to the target is made. Nervous flinch happens when the shooter's arm or hand suddenly jerks violently, which is caused by fear of missing the target. Eye-aversion flinch happens when the eye just leaves the target or eyes close, stopping the muzzle. Trigger flinch happens when the shooter's thoughts are on the trigger, not the target. Flinching is not as easy to cure as most shooters believe it to be. The release trigger, fortunately, resolves most problems over time because one flinch leads to the others. Get rid of one and likely the others will dissipate as concentration is restored. Slap-shooting by pulling the trigger with a solid slap also works at much less cost, so will wearing a thin shooting glove. The main problem with shooters who flinch is 1) They are too aware of trigger sensitivity and 2) They have a timing problem. A release trigger does not guarantee your scores will rise if you still retain a timing / zone problem or you are not looking at the target. If the release trigger helps you, then be grateful it did for you. For those that find it doesn't work there are alternative areas to research to identify the problem as I've cited above. Flinching can be cured. Once in awhile you will get one though. It just happens.

136. Visualization and performance. Explain this.
There are benefits to perseverance. Intensive training can make up for a lack of innate ability. This often does not mean the intensity of training must focus entirely on the physical, but more on mental-rehearsed techniques to boost focused concentration. It is a proven fact, mental practice alone can improve motor skills and performance to a high degree. For many trapshooters, this vital element is missing in their practice scheme. So are muscle relaxation exercises, and setting realistic obtainable goals to accomplish when practicing. Relaxation exercises will enhance concentration, helping the shooter to recognize the muscle tension that can and will upset technique and ultimately defeat the accuracy of shooting the target. This relaxation mode is coupled with the act of

visualizing yourself executing perfect target hits. It's all so simple, yet very much ignored, except by the better shooters. It's important to visualize before each target is shot. At the same time the shooter must be aware that he must compete with something, not necessarily someone. Athletes, runners for example, do perform better when competing against someone instead of racing a time clock. For trapshooters it's not a good idea to contend head-to-head with a human opponent, setting up emotional blocks because you can see the opponents' targets breaking and inducing bad elements to undermine concentration and confidence right when you need it the most. Compete against the target and see yourself breaking it, long before you even shoulder the gun. The moment the gun is reloaded, visualize the three basic target angles and explode them in your mind. With practice it becomes second nature. Be certain to reserve at least five minutes of your time to visualize shattering the targets on each post before you go shoot. This will enhance your scores.

137. Give me a few more tips in a nutshell.
1) You have to know what you are doing by having a plan of attack on each target. You must reach down deep inside of yourself to find that level of authority and element of aggression, conviction and courage that breaks targets and builds confidence. 2) Nearly every swing fault can be traced to a problem with foot position, posture, grip, gun fit alignment, balance and eye / gun hold. 3) Professionals do have secrets but they are not magical, hidden or mysterious. They have learned through extraordinary measure of practice over the years. 4) Five prime factors affect precision: gun fit, muzzle speed, muzzle angle to target, timing and eye focus. 5) You'll miss angle and straightaway targets more often by shooting over the top of them, so keep the bead on the bottom leading edge. You'll miss most targets by stabbing at them, not acquiring the flight angle, loss of eye contact and allowing target to escape your zone. 6) Be very conscious of your pre-shot setup routine, physical and mental. Both must be trained through repetitive practice to focus and relax. The entire process must take less than six seconds. Call too fast or slow and you'll have no reliable setup. 7) Before calling for a target, take a deep breath to energize the body's neural networks and visualize in your mind pictures of the target breaking. This also helps eliminate negative or intrusive thoughts which lead to nervousness and other maladies causing lost targets. 8) Practice gun mount and swing in front of a mirror. Often what you think you are doing doesn't correlate to what you actually see. The feel may be wrong and you're repeating mistakes. 9) A smooth accurate swing to the target will actually increase your timing and speed. A higher or lower eye hold will do the same. Thinking smooth increases accuracy. Thinking to shoot fast with deliberate action will produce stupendous errors. Speed is a technique, not an effort. It naturally arises when eye focus and timing is mastered. 10) Use a moving gun and you'll shoot quicker.

138. Some days I simply forget how to shoot. How is that?
Some days are just off days and you'll have to accept human limitations, but this is not to say you should excuse yourself for a bad performance. Something technically is wrong. If you're ill there is nothing much you can do, but if all feels fine and you're shooting badly you have lost visual and mental focus, sight picture and timing. You'll find the answer in the setup. To prevent a repeat performance on the next event, practice visualizing breaking targets perfectly, then take a test ride on the practice trap to work out the bugs. It's perfectly normal to discover that you have lost your edge. It happens to all of us. The moment you stop worrying about it your shooting skills often return. Sometimes it is good to forget. Just pay attention and shoot. It's so easy to get caught up in technical thoughts, especially after missing a target or two at the practice trap before a tournament. Forget about it.

139. Some shooters tell me never to practice at the practice trap before an event.
Maybe they don't want you to win? Or perhaps they don't understand the psychology of practice trap blues. Not infrequently when you shoot badly at the test trap before an event, panic sets in knowing you're going to fumble the tournament event. Then you begin to "think" too hard, grab another box of shells and try again often with similar results and magnified anxiety. The purpose of the practice trap is not score, but to loosen up the limbs and acquire the sight picture and timing for the next event. If you miss a target or two or three or four... don't even think of it! Don't "think" of the backgrounds, target angles and settings, flaws in technique, etc. Just relax and warm up and practice concentrating and be smooth. Lost targets should be viewed as, *"Flushing the misses out of the game before the event begins."* Many shooters stay away from the practice trap due to the adverse psychological affects it can have. To beat the blues, never shoot for score when practicing on this trap. If you can't take the heat, then don't practice before the event. Many top guns do not require rehearsals and clearly don't fancy anything to agitate their mindset, competence, confidence or courage. Overall, I believe a warm-up is a good thing for most shooters if they follow the rules I've just given.

140. I try so hard to shoot well, yet I make little progress. What can I do?
You will have tough times ahead, as we all. You are likely trying too hard and seeking perfection in all the wrong places. Trapshooting requires the character trait of patience, for without it you cannot become a consistent shooter. Patience is the key to success. In whatever you do in life you need patience, dedication, determination, discipline and perseverance to win. These in themselves are individual skills to be learned. As the years troll by, these skills emerge, self-activating with little effort on your part. Progression is not a matter of "trying harder" but "shooting smarter." Think of trapshooting as an intelligent game, for it is. Work out a technique and a plan to break the targets. Don't just call and hope for the best. Know what you are doing, be wise to the

game. There are only three basic angles on each post. You should know how to break them even before they emerge. Examine the setup and insure your gun fits you so it will shoot where you look. This is often the number one reason why shooters don't progress. Don't beat up on yourself. Relax and play the game with discernment. When should you really try hard? To see the target and keeping your eye solidly on the target. That is where all effort must concentrate.

Tip: Ambition is good, but it can be destructive if you force yourself to learn too quickly. Learn slowly over a period of years.

141. There are so many techniques. Which should I use?
Try them all. Incorporate the features you find works into your own form. Only through lasting experimentation will you stumble upon the perfect mix. On a deeper level, form should express feeling and attitude. You have to develop your own individualistic style of shooting that fits your personality. There are shooters with unorthodox techniques who are very successful. Great inventions are found through experiments gone bad, from synthetic rubber to light bulbs, the list is endless. Top notch athletes each have a unique style, but they all conform to the basic fundamentals with personal modifications. The best vacation is the one you never planned. Experimentation is like that. Enlightenment arrives by surprise.

142. What is the difference between good shooters and lesser ones?
The better shooters control the gun. They attack the target, not react to it. The assault is smooth and calculated. The lesser shooter relies more on instinct and becomes mesmerized by the targets instead of visually focusing with a definite purpose. Play the game, but don't let the game play you! The better shooter has a smooth setup that absolutely stands out, screaming precision. Better players look at the target and look at it hard. They pay attention and awareness is elevated. Lesser shooters are not serious, have low convictions and expectations and primarily shoot for fun, exclusively hoping they may get lucky and win something. Luck is never reliable nor should a shooter hope for it as it erodes confidence, even though luck is often an element in winning.

143. I'm shooting well, then everything falls apart. Why is this?
Primarily fatigue, loss of concentration and visual contact with the target. Stamina must be raised, but it should be elevated slowly, which is why I believe a shooter should only shoot a specific event (or two at most) at a registered shoot until stamina rises. The first to go is the eyes. Once the eyes become lazy, the body will respond to the false information the eyes will supply. Vision training will definitely improve your performance. If you want to run five miles, you start with one, then two, etc. If you keep trying to tackle the five-mile run, you just keep hitting a wall and nothing is gained and the goal eludes you. If your swing suddenly falls apart and becomes erratic and timing is ruined, look to the eyes for the solution. Weak vision skills are often the culprit upsetting eye-hand coordination. When you grow tired your body will try to reset itself by reverting back to its old lazy form of shooting. You'll revert to old mistakes that you thought were vanquished long ago, but suddenly rise from the ashes. It creeps in very slowly, then suddenly takes control so you have to be very conscious of your limitations of endurance and shoot within those parameters.

144. Some clubs may be upset hearing those words.
Perhaps, but it benefits both the shooter and the club in the long term. How many shooters have you seen quit the sport due to mental exhaustion and frustration? Too many shooters are trying to win all the events when they should specialize and focus all they have on the event they want to win. If this means only shooting the handicap events, then so be it. It is better to perform respectably than to exhaust yourself by shooting beyond your limitations and win nothing at all. That's a fine way to wreck confidence, and when confidence and hope is shattered, people eventually quit and take up another activity. I see too many disgruntled shooters after day's end embarrassed with their scores. If they only specialized, they would see tremendous improvement and win more money and attend more shoots! The shooter and the clubs both win and, best of all attendance increases.

145. I'm still confused. Everyone is telling me never to use the sight beads.
This debate will never end due to ignorance and differing techniques. It's most like the argument between shooting trap with one or two-eyes... both work fine! Use the sight beads, rifle shoot when learning precision shooting to imbed in your subconscious mind what a proper sight picture looks like. Once you see it, you can then keep your eye solidly on the target and the subconscious will take over observing the 'ghost' image. You can see it with your conscious mind but only if you take your eyes off the target which is what you don't want to do and where confusion sets in. It's like developing a double image, central vision of the eye on target while peripheral vision reveals the ghostly sight bead / target relationship. It all happens very quickly, which makes it difficult to explain and even for the shooter to recognize when it is done properly. If you stand in front of a mirror with your arm extended about 6" from your nose then move your index finger past your nose while you are staring at your eyes you'll see a perfect explanation of this ghost image. It's quite clear once you recognize it. So, at last, your finger in this test is the sight bead and that's how you align to the target. Practice this by a mirror with your finger, then use your gun in a mirror and you'll soon be pointing the gun with precision, putting the sight bead dead-on the target.

146. What about the days I can't seem to hit anything?
It's just one of those bad days. Actually the reason is as complex and mysterious as the mind itself, and it is the mind playing its own game at your expense. Every good shooter visits slump city, though eventually redeeming qualities purge form and technique sins. There are no easy answers, but a coach could locate transgressions. Often, it is one or two small errors creeping back into your setup. You have to go back to the basics to perform an evaluation of everything you are doing. If all is well, it's just a bad day. If the poor shooting continues on to the second day and you find your technique is okay, then there is a self-defeating mental attitude developing where you are thinking of what you do wrong instead of what you do right. And there is the mood factor. There will be days you just don't feel like shooting, the thrill isn't there, or you have other things pressing on your mind. Don't panic over mini-slumps. We all get them. And one more, don't try so hard. Relax and put all your energy into seeing the target. The harder you try, the tighter your muscles become and you lose your timing and swing rhythm. Check your gun. Did something slip out of adjustment?

147. I patterned for 25" but I can't hit the targets. Now what?
It doesn't? Are you sure? Okay, try this. 1) Try a quality choke, extended and ported. 2) Adjust your point of impact. 3) Adjust gun and eye holds. 4) Try a 3-dram or 2 ¾ dram charge. 5) Learn to shoot with precision. That last one is likely the real reason it's not working. Make sure you're not head-lifting and all those other stupid things. It happens when trying out new things. You want to get a good spread of pellets in the 25" circle. Yes, the core will naturally be hotter, but there is nothing you can do about it. Just get that spread in the 25" circle. It'll work, believe me.

148. Why use extended ported chokes?
Less deformation of pellets the longer the choke. Porting depressurizes accelerating gas, so shot is not *bounced* out of the shot cup to upset pattern from wad-slamming. And maybe, they look mysterious and sinister to the squad members (wishful thinking). You don't have to use them if you don't want to. A choke won't break a target if you're aim is off. These chokes only give you an edge, that edge you may need to win that extra target or two. To give you a tighter more reliable pattern. Many pros use custom barrels so they don't need removable chokes for straight trapshooting. Others do use chokes for double-trap.

149. Which is better the high gun hold or the low gun hold?
You may not want to hear the answer, but here it is. There are many, many, many shooters who use the high gun hold and keep losing, losing, losing. In all reality, there are quite a few - compared to the majority -- who really know how to shoot a high gun hold. You have to have snappy and very finely-tuned reflexes to acquire the target with such precision to crack those high scores consistently. The zone and angle of interception to the target is very small. It's an ego thing that many shooters shoot a high gun because they want to be seen shooting a high gun, but a vast majority of these shooters show little increase in their performance. They are stuck in a rut always performing on a plateau. *"Hey, the pros shoot high gun and I want to do that, too"* mentally sets in. Well, there are many pros who hold a low gun too! The high gun requires fewer moves to the target, but there is very little, repeat, very, *very little* room for error to make any tracking adjustments. If you're a tad off the mark, it's precipitous to compensate to get the bead back on the target where it belongs.

The low gun allows you more time to track and align the target *smoothly* without pushing or stabbing the gun. The swing accelerates *smoothly* to the target and course corrections can be made, and it's harder to stop the muzzle when pulling the trigger. Bottom line? Many high gun shooters who have reached a rut could very well benefit from holding a lower gun, even down to the traphouse. Many high gun shooters may squawk, but it's true. Less gun movement requires faster reflexes and a ton of practice to maintain skill proficiency. To obtain the advantage of a high gun hold requires a very steep price for many shooters who really don't know how to shoot the high gun method. I told you, you wouldn't like the answer. I'm not going to fib to appease the multitudes. It is a reality. Who is really seeing the target better coming out of the house? Low-gun or high-gun? Shoot low gun and you'll see the angle of the target *right now*. No waiting for target to rise up under the barrel, no blind spots, no surprises, enhances swing corrections, more follow-through, no having to look through the gun searching for the target. Now the pros can shoot high gun because they burn 20,000 shells a year to maintain their form and reflexes. Do you? If so, go right on and shoot high gun. If not? Start dropping your gun hold a little bit at a time so you'll gain more swing, see the target better and not have to *rush* the target. Yes. You have to rush the target with a high gun hold and that's why so many people are *pushing* the gun around with their forearm because there is no more swing in the swing. Sorry, but it's true.

150. So, you're saying a 27-yard shooter should drop his gun hold to improve scores?
Absolutely, positively. Try dropping the gun hold just 1-foot lower (or less) and you'll open up a time window. Swing from the hips (you likely forgot how to do this), not by pushing the muzzle, and you'll even break the target sooner. At the 27-yard line the gun should not be held straight out at eye level. The line of sight should be lowered and the gun hold, too, so you can compress the zone. Only the pros can hold straight out due to incredibly super-human polished technique and lots and lots of shooting time in the

trenches. Most shooters would benefit from a lower gun hold. Many times I've given advice to shooters who were missing targets and told them to lower the gun a few inches and presto! Good results. **1)** You have to see the target leave the house immediately. How many All-American shooters have told you that before? **2)** Whoever sees the target best often breaks the target. **3)** Don't shoot a form that requires intensive skill you can't maintain. Shooting once per week just won't maintain the form. **4)** If you have mastered the high gun technique, simply ignore the above. **5)** If you haven't mastered the form, lower the gun and eye hold. **6)** Why keep destroying your opportunities of winning events when the form is too harsh to maintain? I'd like to go into more details on this but space is a limitation. Maybe, book number three?

151. How do I shoot fast targets?
Coastal areas have high humidity and dense air so the traps must be set for power to reach the field post. Speed increases and confusion breaks loose. The key is to raise your eye and / or gun hold to maintain your timing and to reduce the extended target comet tail. If eye hold is too low, the target will blur and the eye can't lock on and you'll shoot a mirage. It's also harder to judge the target's true flight path angle. Most shooters change nothing and end up chasing the targets with poor scores in the process. To shoot fast targets, raise your holds and slow down your swing. Don't worry, you'll catch the target if your eyes are focused properly because the targets perceivably will slow down. You'll break the target in your normal zone or just beyond. Just keep your eye on the target, it's the golden rule. Remember, you adjust timing by raising or lowering your eye hold. If you raise the eye hold your timing will increase. Lower the hold and timing decreases. Why? Because you won't move the gun or shoot until your eye has a good solid view of the target. If your eye sees comet tails, the clock ticks until your eye can refocus to see the target clearly. If the gun / eye hold is too low, the target escapes the zone. The inverse may be true for some shooters. Discover how gun and eye holds affect your shooting.

152. Explain eye holds a bit more. Doesn't the zone shift, too?
Yes. The zone does shift because the zone is in relation to the gun and eye hold, not the traphouse. Fig. 23 and 33 shows a zone related to the distance from the traphouse to illustrate what a zone looks like. But in reality, the zone begins where the target first passes by the gun's muzzle and ends where the target breaks. If you raise the gun, you can raise the entire zone. Think of the zone as a bubble floating above the gun's muzzle. See Fig. 65. This is where the targets will be broken, inside the bubble. See Fig. 24. You can adjust the zone without disturbing your timing, because everything looks the same regardless if the hold is low or high. The only thing that changes, is what your eye will see, the condition of the target. Lower the hold and you'll see comet tails and the target will escape the zone before you can shoot it. The trick is to adjust the zone (gun and eye hold) so the target is seen clearly as it appears near the muzzle, which is exactly where your eye's centralized vision is focused, along and above the sight rib. If your eye is pre-focused, the target slows down, becomes brighter and is easier to hit.

153. What do you mean the target slows down?
The target in real-time doesn't decelerate, but it appears to because the eye, when pre-focused, catches the target in centralized vision. A perfect example is to watch cars passing by with a lazy gaze and you'll see blurs. But if you quickly "focus" on one car and follow it you'll notice how clear and bright the car becomes and it's easy to track. So, by pre-focusing your eye, the target will enter the centralized segment of focus. You will see the target clearly and smoothly and you'll feel no "rush to break the target." This technique helps eliminate the target getting the jump on you, which results in a mad rush stab at the targets. And the back-fence shooters better listen up here because they are the worst culprits of stabbing at targets. If you have ever watched Daro Handy shoot , you saw a smooth machine. All the pros have this smoothness, and it's because they see targets differently than the average shooter. They are using eye prefocus techniques whether they admit it or not. And they use back-sighting. Many top guns I've spoken with can't explain why they shoot so well. My books attempt to do that speaking, so you can learn the techniques the pros unconsciously have learned over the years. Once you master eye pre-focus, natural eye/hand coordination becomes much smoother and precise. Just another secret the pros use and don't talk too much about. Did you read "*Little's Trapshooting Book*?" It advises to watch as many targets as you possibly can. What Frank Little was getting at; was to learn from practicing observing targets how to look at targets in your centralized vision. That's eye pre-focus.

154. Must I see the target leave the traphouse immediately?
Yes and no. Yes, in relation to peripheral vision. You want to see the target leave so you can adjust to the angle. No, in relation to centralized vision. You want your eye hold up high, far away from the edge of the traphouse so the eye will not chase a blur and focus and refocus, constantly trying to zero-in on the target. You want the target to come out and meet the eye. The eye should be pre-focused so when the target comes into the zone you see it very clearly. If a one-eyed shooter holds a high gun resting on the top edge of the house as in Fig. 71, some peripheral vision is lost, but accuracy often increases due to seeing the target better with less vertical muzzle swing and shooting the target quicker. Find the eye / gun hold that helps you see the target the best. It's not a difficult thing to do. The holds may need to change from station to station and trap to trap.

155. I feel very uncomfortable and awkward trying new things and my scores drop. Why?
The hard part is discovering the little secrets. Once you do, then giving them a good workout with an open mind and allowing yourself to pass through the initial discomfort will perform wonders for your scores. Everything new you try will feel unpleasant. Push past the pain. If it makes sense, then make it work. Discomfort is subjective, for once learned it becomes comfortable. Shooters who never progress avoid pain and embarrassment. Those who are willing to always keep learning and trying new ways to break targets will push ahead of the crowd.

156. Any advice to gun clubs?
Every gun club should have a loaner gun available to introduce the newcomer to the sport. There are multitudes of people who have never tried trapshooting, have come to the club to check it out and end up leaving because they have no gun to shoot. Shooting is addictive but without the gun they can't get hooked. I believe trap help should be better trained, especially the pullers, and they should be rotated frequently with rest breaks so crisp pulls can be consistent. Fatigue wears the puller down and here come the bad pulls. Remember, the shooters subconsciously blame club management for bad pulls and improper trap settings and attendance will gravitate to the club that does a better job. Every club needs a suggestion box to get a feel for how the shoot transpired in the minds of the shooters. Feedback is important, for once a club gets a bad reputation it sticks for years. A simple market survey form induces attendees to respond. For shooters, they should try running a shoot before criticizing management too harshly... it's a tough job and compliments are direly needed, too! One grumpy employee can ruin the day for a hundred shooters. Keep friendly staff.

157. Why must trapshooters use tight chokes?
Reliability. Too many shooters are using modified chokes on singles events and improved modified on handicap and they are losing not only accurate sight pictures, but effective pattern density. There's no perfect pattern but here's a tip. Stop using the 30 inch pattern board and drop it down to 25" and choke from there. You'll see a hotter effective central core but that's okay, but you'll also notice a stronger annular ring full of pellets too! Now you have a consistently tight repeatable and reliable pattern. As accuracy increases to adapt to the snug pattern you'll see your scores leap with a mighty bound. If you're scores are in the 80's in handicap you had better reevaluate your choking scheme and I'll wager the choke is a major nuisance. Many shooters don't know how to pattern. They believe an even spread of pellets throughout a 30" circle is "best" when in fact it is "defective." You must have a hot-core shooting edge-on trap targets and the best patterns always will. In handicap, you'll keep on losing targets and events if you rely on evenly spread patterns. Full choke or light-full should be used and even extra-full if more targets break with increased reliability, but full choke seems to work best in trapshooting. Never ask the choke to do your job. Be accurate when you shoot. A loose choke invites incompetence. You never have a 30" pattern, you only have 25" on account of only the 25" pattern will "reliably" break the targets, especially at long yardage or breaking *any* edge-on target at 40 to 45 yards distance. Open the choke and you invite disaster as the reliable central core weakens.

Example: Shoot a pattern at 20 yards with modified, then 40 yards with a full choke. Both patterns have hot-cores and weak fringe areas. Where do you think reliability is? It's in the 25" heart of the pattern. Remember, if you dead-center a target with any choke it will smoke. You can't defragment the central core as ballistics physics won't allow it, but you can tighten the fringe. What you want is an effective 25" core. Don't concern yourself if too many pellets are in the central eye, count the pellets in the 25" circle and ignore everything between 25-30 inches. Get as many pellets into that 25" circle by using the tightest choke you can. You should be aiming your gun as though you are shooting a small bullet not a huge pattern because that enormous pattern simply doesn't exist. All you really have is 23" to 25" and you need way more than one pellet to break the target. It's a never-ending subject, but if you do this, your scores will tell the truth and you'll take home more wins. That's the bottom line.

158. I concentrate so hard I get a headache.
That's not concentration, it's hitting your head against a wall. The hard work is getting the sight bead on the target. That's where most of the energy is expended when concentration is performed correctly. Yes, shooting is 90% mental, 10% equipment, but that's just an analysis of the general status of the game. You can concentrate hard and mentally exert yourself into exhaustion. It's a balancing act between the mental process and physical. You must use both so they compliment each other. It's a matter of having good mind control to which the body responds to execute the shot. Very hard to explain these subjective matters. Try directing a bit more energy into the physical moves, and take an aspirin.

159. I've tried full chokes but I miss too many targets. Why?
Certainly flaws in aim are instantly exposed and most shooters shy away and go back to their open chokes which is a big mistake. But it may not be the main reason why targets are missed. Point of impact often shifts when changing choke size and becomes ever so obvious the tighter the choke is. Once you readjust your sight pictures to the POI shift or make a rib adjustment, you'll be on your way to higher scores, that is, you still must now learn to shoot more precisely. The back-fence shooters all use full chokes, and so should the 20-23 yard shooters, too! If you find it too difficult at short and mid yardage then use a light-full choke.

160. Why must I use hard shot with 5% Antimony?
Because hard shot maintains a tighter pattern due to less deformation of the pattern, and the shot string length is shorter than soft shot so there will be less chance of holes developing in the pattern. The nice thing is that it works. Soft shot (lead without a hardening agent) is not useless, but just not as reliable at handicap shooting distances. Using 6% antimony shot is good stuff too. Any higher percentage begins to take away the energy of the shot as Antimony is less dense than lead. Spend good money for good shot and know your shooting, not the shot, is breaking or missing the targets. You must eliminate as many variables as you can. The serious shooters will be using the best shot. So should you to remain on equal ground. The best shot to buy? Buy new shells. You generally can't get any better than that. The manufactures of shells don't play games with shot quality. They do it right. It cost more than reloading, but the quality is higher, much higher, as all components are new and engineered to match.

161. How should I deal with wind-blown targets?
The best you can. There are some tricks, though. Hold a lower gun, down on the house or a foot or a few inches below your normal high gun hold. Lower your eye focus, too. I hold the gun down on the house, and for my eye I pick a point midway between the traphouse and the center field post. I'll actually be focusing my eye on the ground on a blade of grass. When the target emerges my eye locks on to it right away and I can see the target depressed not wanting to rise. If the target flies high like a rocket I'll see that too right away. It's important to shoot where the target is, not where you believe it should be. High POI guns will tend to overshoot depressed targets so the swing must be extra smooth to the target. By slowing down the swing slightly, overshooting is greatly diminished, also, even if the wind is blowing the target hard it's still not traveling faster than you believe it is. Swing ultra smooth! Extra eye-locking to the target is required. More than you thought you could ever muster. That's how much energy is required to score high in the wind. It's very exhausting. I still score high 90's even in the wind, but not all of the time. Some targets are just so wild and unruly I can't even get close to them. You have to start thinking immediately that you are no longer shooting trap, but shooting ABT or Sporting Clays. If you think trap, you'll pull the trigger out of a timing habit and the bird is not even anywhere close. If you shoot an extremely tight zone, breaking the targets 20 feet from the traphouse, wind won't be too much of a problem, but not everyone can do that! Wind is the most challenging shooting. It's hard on everyone. For me it is the most fun. I love to look at the low scores on the scoreboard. It's a healthy humbling experience for everyone.

162. How does a shooter look at a target?
You don't look at it; you penetrate it! This is why visual fixation exercises work so well, but in addition to the act of fixation, it triggers intense mental concentration, establishing a perfect link between the eye and brain so eye / hand coordination can be realized. This visual fix must be maintained on the moving target. The eye tends to jitter or freeze and so will the muzzle. Practice allowing the eye to flow very smoothly with the target. It's a muscle skill to be learned. The eye too must be trained. I watch targets before I shoot to warm-up the eye muscles and I do this when visualizing. There are eye-exercise drawings in this book to help you establish smooth eye muscle control. When shooting targets: prior to calling, pre-focus the eye(s) then call so the eye will lock-on to the target. The target will now appear slower and brighter. Now, focus in on the edge of the target you want.

163. Primary reasons for missing targets?
Many reasons, but here's a few major ones. Head-lifting due to feeling no cheek pressure . Becoming too cautious after missing a target and tempo or timing is altered. Weak call developing slow pulls. Pushing the muzzle to the target in place of body English. not paying attention. Improper eye focus and hold. Shooting without an attitude, equating to laziness and loss of concentration. excessive confidence reduces fear of missing and the shooter's guard is let down. Not being ready for the target. Not feeling the game. Failure to incorporate a precision mind-set when shooting. Emotional intrusions and thinking. Low expectations and expecting to miss a target. Improper gun fit. Flaws in the setup. Not truly seeing the target's flight path angle, and too much more to list here.

164. Sometimes I don't feel right and then I shoot poorly. What can I do?
Nothing but the best you can do for the day. Moods determine performance. The better shooters have learned how to push past the mood barrier, but even they have their share of off days. No one breaks hundreds straight persistently. Moods are often determined on what we do the previous day. Sometimes it's the food we eat or simply lack of sleep. Job and family pressures do take a toll. It happens to everyone. For many shooters drinking a wee bit too much alcohol during the Calcutta bidding event ruins the following day's mood. Wining and dining women all night long certainly does not help!

165. I often feel like quitting trapshooting, especially after a huge failure.
Stress and disappointment weaken the spirit and will. It is perfectly normal to feel dejected and incompetent after shooting a low score. You have to look at your past successes to put reality back into your mind-set. If failure is your only recent memory perhaps it is time to see a coach to save you from the slump. The better shooter you become, the more susceptible you will be to minor

inconsistencies and flaws in technique. The more fine-tuned you are, the harder you must try to be precise in all you do. It's okay to quit shooting for a spell to rejuvenate the spirit and rest the mind.

Tip: Be patient, seek advice and instruction if you wish to excel in the clay target sports. It is a complex game.

166. It seems trapshooting was easy, then the game became harder. Why is this?
Knowledge increases complications. The game is easy to the uninformed, but once you fully understand the physics taking place out there -- trap settings, target angles and speed, wind, timing, etc. -- the game can be broken down into a science. Learning the technicals is tough enough, adapting your shooting to match variable conditions is a royal challenge. With experience the game becomes easier, but you must still work hard to break every target. The game becomes difficult because as you progress you discover yourself. You learn what affects your shooting for good or bad: moods, foods, sensitivity, irritants, attitude, etc. Not only must you control the gun, but dominion of mind and health takes a high seat in the arena to win events. Who said it was easy?

167. I punch good scores in the high 90's but one, two, three or four targets still escape. Why?
Not paying attention is the prime reason for an accomplished shooter. For others it is a formula set deep into the psyche to expect to miss a target or two or more. Perfect scores happen less often than imperfect scores. This builds a habit, an expectation to miss a few targets. Nervous stress upsets ability and it's hard to control for most of us when a perfect score is near. Tiny errors in the setup or technique often show their true complexion as skill and scores increase. Weekend shooters will always have a tough time in comparison to someone on tour shooting multi-day events for months on end whose body acclimates to the repetition. For the weekend shooter, what is upset the most is timing, smooth swing, vision skill and endurance. It's hard to be consistent if you're not consistently shooting. The last factor, we are not machines so missing targets will be with us for a long time to come.

168. Nervousness. It comes upon me with a vengeance and I can't shoot a good score.
Experience dispels severe nervousness, but for some shooters it always remains a monster in the mind, striking without warning, often for no particular reason other than fearing missing the targets due to nerves. It's called anxiety or panic attacks and some shooters are cursed with it, never knowing when it will surface. For most, it happens on the first trap then dissipates thereafter to perfect calmness, but the damage is already done, dropping targets on trap one, ruining any chance of a good score. To face reality, I know shooters who must take a mild sedative to calm down. Medicine is not a preference, but it can help stabilize the mind to the point of breaking the trigger mechanism that induces anxiety until sedatives are no longer needed, or used only on rare occasion. I've had shooters tell me, *"If it were not for medication I would have to quit the sport." "Trapshooting is exciting... it scares the heck out of me!"* Some people have sensitive nervous systems and must seek assistance. If you go this route, use moderation. When tension rises, find a reason to smile. It's an icebreaker. It's hard to be agitated when happy.

169. I become angry when I miss a target and then I miss more.
Reverse your direction of frustration. Instead of being irate at the lost target, be furious when firing. Take out your revenge on the next target not the one that slips beyond reach and control. You can't change the fate of a lost target, but you can prevent another loss from occurring. Be calmly aggressive. Focus anger into your vision, sort of like a mean cat's stare before it pounces.

170. I try so hard to hit targets and they still evade me. Why?
You may be trying too hard. Shooting is primarily a vision skill more than muscle dexterity. Eye / hand coordination comprises eye / mind coordination. Inner aggression is the key to solid hits, not combative moves to the target. The war is won by pure will power with smooth moves. When you try too hard to smack targets, you'll discover smoothness is lost producing random snapping of the muzzle to the target. Try channeling all your energy into seeing the target then looking at it with all your powers of awareness then trust your swing mechanics to get you there. Think precision and you'll smooth out. The harder you try to smoke targets with brute force body moves, tension, stiffness, stress and anxiety increases. Think of the muzzle gliding to the target, not forced or pushed. To control body moves you must think of them first so your mind can obtain and retain the instruction. Practice visualization.

171. There must be an easier way to raise scores. What is the secret?
Most shooters rely totally on eye / hand coordination, call for the target and hope for the best. But trapshooting truly has a formula, a science not only of mind but of physics. You can engineer the game because the angles are known variables. Zone shooters have studied these angles and the timing factors then have adapted their shooting technique to the dynamics of the game. Once you know where you want to break targets, all you need do is work on your timing to ensure you arrive at the target intersection point within the zone. It's spot shooting instead of tracking and riding a target. The bad news is it is an advanced shooting method that is not easy to learn and requires many months and likely years to shoot the zone accurately. The key is seeing the target quickly, more quickly than most trapshooters can perceive. See Fig. 36 through 45, 71 and 73 for illustrations. It's not snapshooting where the target is taken at random at accelerated pace. Zone shooting is controlled. The danger to this technique is the susceptible errors of

slow and fast pulls. Things are happening very quickly here and an errant pull will devastate the setup, causing the target to escape the zone. By practicing zone shooting you will train your eye to lock-on to the target faster. This will help any shooter increase scores despite the technique he uses. Swing to the target is not always the problem, it's the eyes and how they see the target that is the key. To raise scores, practice visual skills so you can acquire the target quickly and focus hard on it when you do look at the target, but don't forget to also see it's angulation in relation to the barrel. That is a prime reason targets are lost. The swing was okay, the eye fixed squarely on the target, but the true angle was not discerned. You can see a target yet still miss clean because the moment you see the proper sight picture the target's angle has evolved and changed when you pulled the trigger. Shoot where the target is, not where you think it should be. Keep experimenting until you discover the best means to smoke the targets. Study the game. It's not just calling and chasing down targets. It's much more than that.

172. Why should I shoot a high point of impact gun?
Numerous reasons. Some to consider: the target is rising so the shot can rise and catch the target by applying automatic lead. At 40-yards the shot will drop about 3 to 5 inches, so you need to compensate for it and a high POI does just that. Those are the two big reasons, but there are more benefits which "*Trap Shooting Secrets*" reveals such as using canting to apply even more lead, shaping the shot trajectory for centering target hits, enhancing timing, sight picture, etc.

173. I can't seem to learn how to shoot quickly. What can I do?
The better shooters shoot fast and it is to your advantage to do so. When you try to speed up you are likely pushing the muzzle to the target faster. Now you have a gun totally out of control and you are snap shooting. The trick is not how fast you move the muzzle it's how quickly you see the target! The sooner you see the target, the faster your gun's muzzle will move without any conscious thought or effort on your part. It just happens. To shoot fast, you don't swing harder. In fact, fast shooting still retains a smooth controlled swing as long as the eye truly locks-on tightly to the target. Eye hold is the key. See Fig. 45. This does not mean your eye must be on the edge of the traphouse. On the contrary, the eye is held higher above the traphouse. This may seem contradictory but it's where your eye can see a clean streak-free target that determines how quickly you can move to it. This gives more speed without swinging harder. Even if you hold a low gun, try raising your eye focus way above the traphouse near where you plan to break the target and see your speed increase. Don't think of swinging fast, just think of seeing the target quickly and you'll speed up and still retain accuracy with explosive target impacts. That is the first step. The next step is to alter your footing, stance, gun grip, etc., to better adapt to the faster form. You may need to employ a moving gun technique, the forward stab or bow with a canted gun method, or both, to get the muzzle to the target faster with less body movement complications. Efficiency of body moves is important. Wasted movement gives rise to mistakes. It is very difficult to shoot fast and retain accurate precision and consistency without employing a means of body English. Fail to do so and you'll likely resort to pushing the muzzle randomly, resulting in a ton of missed targets. For shooters using only their arm to direct the gun, they should use the upper body pivoting by the hips, even at the 27 yard line, as this will be more forgiving with truer consistency and fewer misshots.

174. I don't feel I can ever break a good score. It's been so long since I have.
Trap is a brain game. Perhaps you don't feel entitled to break all the targets. You've developed a losing mind-set due to a succession of losses. Raw desire to excel has eroded. Competitive nature and attitude is lacking. This mental clutter has created inconsistencies. You expect to lose or score poorly based on past performance. You must learn to lift your spirit and begin to believe you can smash the targets, one by one. Often shooters beat up on themselves when they shoot a poor score when they should be kinder. Everyone is tired of being told to keep a positive attitude, but it is important so negative thinking will not adopt firm roots. The powers of suggestion are a confounded mystery to give you a superior level of activity. Step aside and get out of your own way and scores will likely increase. Information is everywhere on how to shoot well, but insight is all too rare. The secret to high scores is knowing you can. As others shoot aggressively, shoot wisely with intensive accuracy with easy power in the swing. Never think of score results, focus only of destroying the targets. It's a one-target game! Believe in yourself.

175. A pattern board will tell me what my shot cloud is doing?
Nope. It only gives you an approximate idea of what it could do if you were shooting a straightaway target that has reached its crest of flight. In other words, a target not in lateral motion. Also, the shot does not arrive all at the same time, though very close to it. The pattern board is 2-dimensional (height & width) and not moving, but the shotstring is 4-dimensional, moving fast and the target is moving fast, too. We all keep forgetting the time factor and the third dimension which are never revealed on a pattern plate... and those two missing elements are the most important and we can't see them, because no one has taken high-speed photography of these elements at 40-yard distances. And even if they did, your barrel may behave unlike the film version. Use the pattern plate to establish a hot core and set point of impact and then see how the targets break. If you can dustball them, you've got a workable real world solution. If the breaks are chippy and you're using a large 30" pattern, targets will slip through and so will your scores.

176. If the shot string is 8 foot long, then I have a lot of room for error in my aim.
Oh no you don't! You may be pumping out 460 pellets but they all essentially arrive at the same time, in milliseconds. Not really enough to rely on for errors in aim, no matter how large your 30" pattern may be. To prove this to yourself, shoot at a lake of water and you'll see the pellets all arrive in one big splash. So another lesson to be learned? You can follow-through as fast as you normally swing to trap targets with your barrel and still that splash will only be one big thud, not a long spattering of pellets racing across the water. Any arc perceived will be negligent anyway on trap targets. You still have to be on the money when shooting trap or you'll miss. Try it at 35 yards and see for yourself. Another lesson? Well, if you think you can follow-through the target hoping you can stretch the shot string like a rubber band ahead of the target, hoping the tail end of the string will rip the target, go back and look at the splash. You can't bend the shotstring at the back fence from a swing alone as you would be swinging too hard and fast. Recall that real world conditions always prevail over theory. Remember this, the entire shot charge exits the barrel in the wad and the wad can't be bent, and, the shot charge arrives in milliseconds. There is only one *true* reason why follow-through is taught. It's not for elongating the shot string, but to stop you from stopping the swing of your barrel and shooting behind the target! You are shooting a bullet made up of 460 #8 pellets. That's reality. So, you had better learn how to aim... precisely. You are in effect, shooting a bullet at the target and that's how you should be thinking when shooting at trap targets.

177. Other writers and shooters say to anticipate the hard angles. You don't. Why?
We basically mean the same thing but use different wording. Other writers/shooters use the word, *anticipate*. That means to *expect* the extreme angle target. I take it a small step beyond that by saying not to anticipate/expect, but to setup for the shot and never anticipate any specific angle. This is so there will be no surprises. If the extreme angle arises, you're setup to hit it. Anticipating anything in trapshooting will always induce a pulse of adrenaline or fear when the expected does not occur. Then shooters panic and make fast moves to the target. Fast moves will only cause you to make mistakes and miss. Just setup and move to the target with a controlled swing using the hips to pivot. Be prepared but be smooth. Remember, it's a target just like any other. Stop making these extreme angle targets into mountains. Nothing special about them. Convince yourself of this and you're way ahead of the game.

178. You say to use the hips to pivot. What about the shoulders?
Yes. Shoulders are used to pivot a swing, but I don't like to tell shooters "swing with the shoulders" because they will tend to take it literally and only swing the shoulders. The main pivot is the hips to move the upper body. The shoulders do move and generally comes naturally. But if the hips are frozen stiff, the shoulders won't work right anyway.

179. Sometimes I just fall apart and forget how to shoot. Why?
The answer is simple, though not encouraging. You don't know how to shoot precisely. Confusion sets in when targets are missed, often not knowing why then the sight picture is lost and the bottom falls out of the game. It's a mental lapse that happens to everyone especially when learning new techniques. It happens to everyone who shoots a trap that is not set properly, even the pros, but they have the good sense not to shoot the defective trap as is. Most shooters perform erratically because they have not identified the zone where they plan to dispatch the targets, plus, have not perfected their timing, including experiencing lazy-eye syndrome. Once these factors are missing, confusion spirals and targets are lost. You have to know what you are doing out there. Pay attention! Be aggressive! Stay tuned! Poor shooting lingers on for days until you recognize what is causing the problem. Fatigue is the #1 cause of forgetting how to shoot, the mind just shuts down. But if you truly know your zone, timing and eye hold points you'll score respectably or at least better than many even when you are ill. Shooting is a groove, a feel and a mind-set. Trapshooting is a difficult sport and its elusive nature drives us back again and again to the challenge as though it were an addiction. To master the game one must master one's self. Writing a diary of when you shot well, how it felt, where you broke the targets, eye hold point, level of aggression, etc., will solidify in your mind how to reset the mood and form you know you need to have to shoot well. To pull out, you must make the effort to discover the defect. Sometimes there is simply no answer to give. A bad day is simply a bad day. Every major athlete has off days where perfection is as distant as the moon. These down days can be minimized with experience. Nobody is perfectly perfect. I have my days I can't shoot anything, mind goes blank and can't find the fire and actually forget how to shoot the targets. When I have a severe down day, it's usually pretty embarrassing. An 89 in a handicap event is simply horrible and means I'm one sick puppy on that day. Usually because I did something stupid like eat some heavy food the night before and I'm ill on the day of the shoot and can't hit a thing. It's all my fault.

180. Tell me some secrets to high scores.
It doesn't take a stroke of genius to hit targets, but it certainly requires diligence to smoke them all. Top shooters proclaim they don't attend registered shoots for fun, they shoot because they have a job to do; that job is to win the events. It's serious business, so, attitude ranks high for performance. There is no random pointing when they shoot, it's all precision shooting. They know where to break the targets and how to break them. When you understand target trajectory angles and timing you'll develop accuracy. Professionals have the temperament of controlled fury clawing their way up target by target. They have developed fine focus visual reference points before calling for the target. The best advice is to formulate a technical plan on how to break targets on each station

then stick with the plan. Timing plays an immense role as to where the target will be broken (shooting a zone). Many shooters need to advance from chasing targets to dispatching them in controlled areas. Once this is discovered and performed repeatedly "muscle memory" sets in and consistency increases. It's hard to be consistent if you inconsistently break targets all over the place, some close, some far away. When you do this, the degree of difficulty increases.

181. Why should I keep buying books and magazines when I don't seem to get better scores?
You probably already know the fundamentals of stance, swing, grip, hold points, etc., and all the things you should mimic from renowned shooters. But without learning how to put your own signature of confidence and focus on your own game you will be consistently inconsistent. It's not what you learn or how you learn, but what you applied. Deeper knowledge still requires reading along with doing. The two cannot be separated. Books and magazine articles keep you from going stale, confer ideas and impressions to spark the fire within. When the intake of knowledge ceases, performance often decreases. Keep learning. When you think you know it all and stop learning the mind will also stop, opening the door to the slump department. I've spoken to pros who have shot for a living for over thirty years, and they too are still learning the game. Get the idea? There is so much information in *Trap Shooting Secrets* and *Precision Shooting - The Trapshooter's Bible* that it will take you years to decipher all the information in these two books alone. When you run into a problem you will find the solution in these technical books.

182. On timing, how fast should I shoot a target?
As soon as the eye has solidly acquired the target. Timing is related to eye and gun hold, but don't forget to pull the trigger only when the bird / bead relationship is dead-on. Practice this trigger control often. It requires a great deal of discipline to learn and apply. If you're snapping or tracking targets and missing, your eye hold and / or gun hold point is wrong, or you were not truly ready for the target when you called for it. The zone you use must be comfortable and reliably break the targets for you. As time and experience allow, you will shoot a tad quicker. The pros can break targets way too fast, and they know it. Often, they have to remind themselves to slow down a bit. So when you see them shooting quick, they are actually shooting slow. Imagine that!

183. How much lead should be placed on a target?
Two-foot lead at 16 yards, 4 foot at 27 yards. But what does that mean to the shooter? Nothing. Lead is simply placing the sight bead ahead of the target so as to allow time for the shot to arrive. It's a sight picture measured in inches from the shooter's point of view or target diameters. Depends on your point of impact adjustment settings. If POI is set high 80/20 or more, the sight bead may be on the leading edge of the target or a couple inches ahead of the target if POI is set low. This also depends on your timing. If you shoot fast, less lead is required and if POI is high there may be no perceived lead at all. Just stick the bead on the target and pull the trigger. Getting the gun and your timing set up to do that is time consuming and a trick of the trade. The result is well worth the effort. The goal is to set up the gun's POI and adjust your timing and technique so you can put the bead on the target to break it… even if it takes you years of practice to get to this point.

184. How to deal with discontent?
Trapshooting should be renamed; frustration. Discouragement and defeat is part of the game, inseparable, and afflicts all. Take a break, feel sorry for yourself if that helps, shake it off and push on to a brighter day. It's only a game. You'll live if you lose to win again tomorrow. Don't be a grouch. Be happy you're able to even attend the shoot. Life is too short to be miserable. Enjoy life. Be thankful you are not a pro shooter. Everyone expects them to win, and they put money on these pros to win. When they don't win, the pros have to live with that weight. Be thankful you don't write magazine articles or coach people on trapshooting because everyone expects you to "know it all" and therefore "do it all" and when you don't measure up you'll get tons of criticism. So, you see, you really don't have any real reason to feel discontent after all. Be happy!

185. Is the shotstring really over 9' long?
Yes, the shotstring is 7 to 9 feet long or longer, but in truth: at 40-yards, the entire pattern all arrives to the target at the same time, within milliseconds. This means, in essence, you are shooting a two-dimensional "bullet" at the target (height & width). So what? Well, it's important to develop precision shooting. Your subconscious mind may believe the string is elongated and will trick you into thinking you have room for error, when in reality you don't. Let me correct myself. The shotstring is four-dimensional; it has height, width, length, and time factors. This makes playing around with the pattern board a waste of your time, except to set point of impact and discover the hot-core area of the pattern. Counting pellets in the 30" annular ring is frivolous, trying to spread out the pattern to fill that large circle. Only the core is reliable and it needs to be dense. Still doubt it? Then why do the pros use full chokes? It's the dense inner 25" core they are working with, not a 30" pattern. We are not shooting large pheasants or ducks. We are shooting a very small edge-on targets flying at dashing speeds. Too many people crossover these lines between hunting and target shooting. Both are different species and require alternative adjustments. A pro can use a 30" pattern because s/he 'shoots the core' anyway, that's how good their aim is!

186. You mention that 7 ½ lead shot arrives faster to the target than #8 shot. How much faster?
Not much at 40-yards distance. Fact is, 7 ½ shot may get there about a tenth of second faster, if that. Without delving into mathematical formulas, it will make about a 2" actual reduction in leading the target. The 7 ½ shot hits harder with a tighter cloud of shot and those are the main benefits, not so much for its speed.

187. Sometimes I just become totally flabbergasted with all the knowledge I have to learn. What can I do?
Welcome to the zany club. Everyone belongs to that club at one time or another. Fact is, we often return to it. Trapshooting is not an easy sport, but it's very easy to slip into an emotional straightjacket. The problem is impatience and trying to absorb way too much instruction in too short of time. Just learn one thing at a time. As the years pass, it will all come to you without having to think about it, it just happens on a subconscious level. This is not to say the more you shoot, the better you will be. There are many poor shooters who have been shooting for 20+ years. Learn the techniques one-by-one and you'll see improvements.

188. How do I handle season burnout?
It is difficult to maintain an elevated level of excitement, especially after you've been shooting a number of years. This causes lethargy to set in and scores dive. It's just something you have to work out for yourself to get that exhilarating feeling back again. Maybe cutting back on a few shoots will give you that needed rest. What you *don't* want to do is find diversion in playing another sport as this will only cause you more frustration in the end. You simply have to do something different to divert the mind away from anything challenging so it can rest.

189. Will I ever shoot scores like the pros do?
Yes and no. Yes, if you put in the dedication, time and money the pros put in, you could be shooting in their caliber. No, if you don't. The pros shoot on a higher level -- it's their job! Most are sponsored by major industry in one way or another to promote ammunition or what have you. They shoot and shoot and shoot and shoot and shoot, year-after-year. Like an alcoholic in a brewery. Get the message? These guys and gals are operating on an advanced plane weekend warriors can never achieve. Ultimately, you'll have to hit the road, play the circuit, pound the pavement to get that polished. Not many of us can do that. If you can, then you will be a professional trapshooter. All it takes is time, dedication and money like all things in life. If you can't, you shouldn't care. Your scores can rise up there and beat the pros, too. It happens all the time. You don't always see the same pro winning all the shoots. They miss targets, too, just not as many, but they do have off days and no one can keep breaking every target no matter how great they are. I don't see many 1,000 straight long-run handicap scores, do you? Everybody misses targets. We all have good and bad days, even bad weeks. It's all part of being human.

190. What can I do to stop stabbing at targets?
Easy. First, stabbing at targets is an amateur method of shooting. It's simply jumping at the target by *pushing the muzzle* with the forearm in a snappy or jerky manner. Lots of shooters do it. Here's how to stop it. Apply a millisecond delay into your timing scheme. When you call for the target and the target dashes from the traphouse, most shooters are already moving the gun to chase it. Just intentionally hold the gun still until you really see the target cleanly as it passes by your barrel. This smidgen of delay tends to create an unhurried phase of relaxation and confidence to smoothly attack the target. I've seen pros use this technique. It's a very tiny delay, unnoticed to the untrained observer, but now that you know it exists, watch the pros and you'll see this micro-delay. If you hold a low gun on the house, just delay until the target has passed the streak stage, which it will do naturally as the target will enter your centralized vision if you have properly refocused your eye(s) up from the traphouse. It's really easy once you know these little tricks. If you eye hold is up away from the house looking into the zone of interception (where you plan to acquire and break the target) the millisecond delay is already built into the scheme. This is just one example of why you need to use proper eye hold and pre-focus prior to calling for the target.

191. I'd like to have more confidence in myself. Any suggested readings?
Yes. Read *Science of Mind Magazine* P.O. Box 75127, Los Angeles, CA 90075 (800) 421-9600. It's heavy stuff, but it's absolutely effective. I found a copy going to a shoot and it's changed my life ten-fold. But first, you should buy this book, *"How to Change Your Life"* by Earnest Holmes. You can order it from the above address or from our web site book section. The book will open your mind up quite a bit into the concepts prior to subscribing to the magazine. I guarantee it will change your life for the better. It's very powerful reading. I wouldn't pass up reading this book. Order it now! It will teach you how to believe in yourself with 100% conviction to make good things happen in your life. Of course, the principles apply to trapshooting, too.

192. Some of the techniques you mention just don't feel right. Why?
Every new experience feels *strange* and uncomfortable. Every shooter who takes lessons from a shooting coach gets all bent out of shape trying to undo bad habits and form. After a time, this new form *feels* just fine. The important thing to remember is you can

make alterations to any form to fit your *style* of shooting so it feels just right for you. Nothing is chiseled in stone. It's the theory and technique learned that's really important. How you execute the form is your privilege to make it adapt to you. Feel better now?

Tip: It may feel wrong until it becomes right. Such is the way to perfection. Improper technique always feels right simply because it is habitual. If you keep missing targets, obviously, something is wrong with what you perceive as being right.

193. If the shot pattern is filling the 30" circle then the pattern is perfect?

A wide-open pattern is a recipe for missed targets. What you want is a hot-core with a decent distribution of pellets in the annular ring. It's the 25" pattern that builds reliability. If you attempt to fill the 30" circle you will hit some targets and miss many others wondering, "*How did I miss that?*" It's a hit & miss problem. So pattern for the 25" making it as dense as you possibly can. The annular ring up to 28 inches will then fill in okay. It's just a matter of reversing your thinking. If you pattern for 30" the reliable hot-core weakens. You don't really see this weakening on the pattern board because; the shotstring is elongated, and it doesn't arrive at the same time on a fast-crossing edge-on target, so what looks great in the two-dimension pattern board actually refuses to hammer targets reliably time after time. Remember, if you can't smokeball each target you have a serious problem out there. Chips and flakes score a dead target, but you are shooting on pure luck and you will miss more targets than you deserve due to pattern-core failure and failing to use precise aim. About 90 to 95% of all shooters are using the *wrong* choke and getting overly wide patterns and poor scores to show for it! Why do you think the pros dustball each target? It's not that 30" pattern it's the 25" hot-core they are using. This is one of trapshooting's biggest secrets, *revealed.*

194. Okay? How do I make a dense 25" pattern?

Full choke at long yardage automatically does the trick, in most cases. For some guns you may have to tighten a bit more. Mid-yardage use a light-full choke. At 16-yard line use an improved modified or light-full choke. The 8 or 7 ½ shot both work fine, but use competition grade hard lead shot with 5% antimony. Now accuracy must increase to hit the targets, but this is the point... when you do put that bead on the target it *will* smoke. Good Glory, you don't want to hit targets due to an unreliable wide-open hit 'n miss pattern do you? Keep patterning down from 30" to 28" and you'll see the hot-core will appear too hot, it's not... it's just right. You'll see when you do hit the target, it will burn into a ball of smoke. When you misaim, it will chip or dust. Now you can concentrate on learning precision back-sighting and you will soon be breaking targets from skill, not luck. Now your proficiency level rises and wins accumulate. Huge 30" patterns will keep your scores in the mud because you're not learning precision shooting and you lose that all-important reliability of target breaks factor.

195. I tried the 25" pattern and I'm missing too many targets. Now what?

That is to be expected and it is good news! Now you can see *why* shooting has been so hit 'n' miss over the years. You never had the opportunity to learn precise shooting. Now you're on the right track. When you miss a target you want to miss because of some error you made, not due to pattern failure. If you keep shooting a huge 30" pattern you'll never really know what is actually going on or going wrong. You miss and can't seem to figure out why because the pattern is so monstrous and spread out it turns into a massive cycle of guesswork. Now, by shooting that 25" hot-core pattern you can find and resolve your shooting deficiencies. Of course, your scores will drop for a time, but when you get precision shooting down, you're going to be a mean machine out there. Some shooters are so shy they won't tighten their chokes for fear of missing targets and other shooters will rib them, beat them at the Sunday afternoon practice sessions. Don't get caught up into this trap. Be willing to take a temporary reduction in your scores to learn precision.

196. I can't afford to try things that will destroy all I've learned. I'm worried about this 25" pattern stuff.

You can't go wrong. You can't make a mistake here. Why? Because at any time you just can't seem to get it down you can go back to your 30" pattern and nothing is lost. One thing that will happen is your score average will increase even with the 30" pattern because you have momentarily stepped into the arena of precision shooting. If you aim is off a bit, you'll likely bust the target. Once you try it, you won't want to return to the 30" pattern, you'll be spoiled. You may get discouraged and give up for awhile but you'll be back. Remember I said to practice with an extra-full choke in the "*Trap Shooting Secrets*" so you could learn precision? It sure did work, didn't it? You bet it did. Believe you are shooting a bullet at the target, not a pattern, and sloppy shooting vaporizes if you have a hot-core pattern to shoot with. If you insist on staying with your 30" pattern, conforming to conventional wisdom, expect your scores to remain conventional. You just can't fill a 30" pattern properly, you don't have enough pellets to do the job. It's reality. The laws of physics and ballistics work against you on the 30" pattern. Try as you may, you'll never gain reliability without that 25" hot-core and 28" annular fill. A two-inch reduction makes all the difference in the world.

197. I use a modified choke on the 16s and short handicap and I break targets. Why should I change?

Because missing the targets is likely due to the weak pattern. Also, you are not learning precision shooting. You are relying on a huge pattern to get you close to the target, not *on* the target. You'll keep missing targets due to pattern failure, mistiming and poor aim. There is no reliability factor in a huge 30" pattern where all the pellets are evenly distributed. Believe me, it's too wide. It's like shooting a cylinder choke at a 35-yard target, the spread is so large at the target nothing can break the target with *repeatable* reliability. You'll break the target sometimes and not other times. If you stay with a wide choke, you will run into major problems as you get punched back in yardage and at the 27-yard line you'll have to learn how to shoot all over again to win. It's a heavy penalty many shooters on the back line pay. Start learning precision shooting now.

198. Give me a hot tip how to build precision into my shooting at the lowest cost?
Slam a quality extra-full choke into your gun and get to work. The pattern will be so tight you'll have to center the target to break it. Now that's the secret to becoming a precision shooter! Now you can really discover the gun and eye holds, zone and timing, required to break targets repetitiously and with authority. Then when competition arrives, switch to your full choke. Now, when your aim is off just a smidgen, you'll still burn the target. Another alternative is to use 1 oz. or even 7/8 oz. loads matching the *same* speed as the 1 1/8 oz. load you normally shoot. You can see how precise you'll have to be to break the target. It's simple, it works.

199. I know shooters who are using 1 oz. loads in handicap and doing quite well.
Here's the problem. Even if you use a full choke the *effective* core and annular ring pattern is about 12% smaller than the other shooters using 1 1/8 lead shot. That is a huge sacrifice to pay for obtaining higher velocity. And, let's not forget there are less pellets working against you too. Don't even play this game if you want to win tournament trapshoots. The odds are already stacked *against* you. You must stand on equal ground with your competition. Handicap shooters who use 1 oz. loads are only covering up their inadequacy to shoot the 1 1/8 oz. load. They are having *serious* timing, zone, point of impact and target lead problems. Instead of resolving the puzzle, they find the 1 oz. load as the lazy method to compensate. It's all an illusion. They shoot well, but do they win? Very, very, few do. The 1 oz. load is quick and capable, with a smaller effective pattern as a tradeoff. Now, if the rules change and everyone has to shoot 1 oz. loads, then that's okay, we are all back on equal ground.

200. You stress the importance of the setup. Can you explain why it is so important?
Piece of cake. Ever go to the drag races? Ever talk to the pros in the pits? I have. They tell me that when their tractor trailer rigs pull in off the road the setup begins when they setup the shop area. If this setup is not properly performed the race is lost even before the nitro engine is first started. The setup sets the pace and tone of the race and the efficiency of the crew to work as a team. The same is true with trapshooting. The setup really begins the night before you arrive for the shoot. The setup on station prior to mounting the gun is critical. Mess up the setup here and the shoot is already lost before you even fire at the first target. Precision shooters know the importance of the setup routine. Just ask any professional trapshooter about the setup and you'll get the picture. So, start concentrating on your setup. If you don't have one, then develop one. To just walk out on the line and call for the target is not going to place you at the top of the score sheet -- maybe once in awhile, but not consistently, you can be certain of that. Some of the best shooters have a slow setup, less than 6-seconds from gun mount to firing, but it's slower than the amateur and others who don't shoot very well. Setup also takes into consideration breathing properly and using correct posture and call intonation.

201. A positive attitude doesn't work. Why is that?
It works to a small degree to be positive but it's based too much on a wish. Everyone wishes to win, strives to win, but as I've said before in "*Trap Shooting Secrets,*" beware of emotions as they often lead us astray. It's okay to anchor positive emotions but it has to be welded with skill. If the skills are patented, the emotion will no longer be necessary. Get the idea? Your thoughts have power. More power than you may realize. Emotions are thoughts that can be put into action, but what action? To feel good or to break the target? You can feel good and miss. It happens all the time. Just wishing or being upbeat won't break targets. A burning desire will. That is not a wispy emotion, but a strong conviction within. It's an aggressiveness that is not expressed with thoughts of being happy, winning or losing. It's a very controlled state of mind which triggers intense concentration. When you concentrate properly, emotions are thrown out the window along with thought. The next time you win a shoot you'll see what I'm talking about. Learn to recognize this energy force and use it. It can be mentally rehearsed once you've experienced it.

202. I sometimes jerk my arm when I pull the trigger. Why?
A few things can cause it, like being out of time with your inner time clock, knowing you should have pulled the trigger but the sight picture was nowhere near the target. You may be squeezing and not pulling (slapping) the trigger firmly. Trigger may have a hang-up where the sear is notched or worn, or whatever. If you have trigger problems? Take up the question with a pro trapshooter. They will set you straight, fast. You have a trigger flinch. Most all shooters have one. Flinching is too complex to explain here. Read *Trap Shooting Secrets*. The book has a lot of advice on curing a flinch, many forms of flinching, too.

203. I shoot the practice trap and do fine then bomb in the tournament. Why?
The practice trap is throwing soft targets (slow and high) and the main tournament traps are set fast and shallow. When traps are set for competition, some clubs forget to set the practice traps! It has happened that some clubs will actually do this on purpose to give

their members (who are aware of the altered settings) the winning edge. It's cheating shooters. When you hit the practice trap you begin to implant sight pictures and a feel for the targets. Then when you shoot the main event suddenly those sight pictures don't work because the targets are not behaving properly. So, you have to be aware of not being *preconditioned* to the practice trap. That's why I say you should walk the traps you are assigned to shoot so you can see the target behavior and settings along with the backgrounds, eddy currents, target speed and spin, station offsets, etc. There are a few clubs in the Pacific Northwest who are notorious at not setting up the practice traps to equal standards of the tournament traps. I saw it happen in a state shoot and droves of people pulled out of the shoot. Not because of the practice trap, though that did setup the shooters to fail, but the tournament targets were all thrown *hard-fast* and *flat* as razorblades. Guess who won the shoot? The guy who set the traps! This happens.

204. So, there is cheating?
When there is big money there will always be someone who will try to rig something to throw everyone off. It can be done on purpose or it can be by sheer mistake. The truth of the matter is, local club member always have an edge. They have a little bit more inside knowledge of who is doing the pulling, what traps are worn out or set improperly in the house and what traps have the worst background interference, difficult lighting conditions, changes in wind patterns, damp targets, etc. These homeboy shooters can tilt the odds in their favor by selecting the best traps and time of day to shoot. A good tip? See where the professionals are shooting and try, if you can, to shoot those same traps at the same time of day. Pros are tough to follow, but they usually know all these inside tricks. Just being aware of these things will open your mind and that alone will help you to compensate for these anomalies. Experience is the best teacher but only if you are receptive to learning and adapting. Some pros will not shoot specific clubs for just some of these reasons. We do live in an imperfect world. So again, it's a good thing to walk your traps so you'll know just what you face before you step on line to shoot. That will give you the edge without cheating anyone.

205. Do you favor one-eyed shooting over two-eyed?
No. Two-eyed shooting is just great, so is one-eye. Each has merits, but the one-eyed had one major disadvantage. You have to practice a bit more to prevent not looking back at the sight bead and risk freezing your muzzle swing when trigger is pulled. You really have to learn how to back-sight no matter how many eyes you use... it's mandatory. Back-sighting is not looking back at the sight, it's "seeing" the sight bead approaching the target. It's the sight picture seen clearly. Just like you see in the mirror practice session. See *"Seeing the Sight Picture"* subheading on how to do it.

206. I lose hope when I miss a target. What can I do?
Forget it. You can't change the past, only the present. Way too many shooters worry about the lost target when they should be thinking about breaking the next target. I know, I've suffered from this, too. You have to apply extra effort to forgive yourself, forget the past, and move on into the next target. Easy to say, hard to do. Shooting is hard work. It really is hard to break a high score. You always have to have that inner burning desire to win on each target. The moment you apply a half-effort letting your guard down, the target will slip away. Learn to apply "faith" and you won't need "hope."

207. I shoot behind the target. What can I do?
Shoot ahead of the target. Just get your gun swing moving and let the muzzle pass through the target after the trigger is pulled. But, follow-through is not necessary in trapshooting if you know how to get that bead on the target and have the discipline not to stop the muzzle swing until the trigger is pulled and the shot is fired. A fast swing will apply more lead, but you can lose accuracy, too. A slower swing is better, then concentrate on pulling that trigger when the sight picture is just right.

208. I shoot over the target. What can I do?
Shoot under the target. Shoot quicker. Aim at the bottom of the target. Adjust point of impact. Adjust the zone with gun and eye holds. Fix your stance and swing geometry because that's usually the major culprit. Swing by the hips, never push the muzzle around with your hand/arm. If your gun doesn't fit it'll happen all too often, and if you're lifting or turning your head when the target emerges, well, stop doing that.

209. I know shooters who will never shoot #8 shot. What's the reason why?
Smart shooters, take lessons from them! They likely already know the following: 7 ½ hard shot retains tight patterns and impact energy. But they may know that various gun clubs use differing brands of targets, which some are harder to break than others. Also, the targets may be damp, absorbing moisture over a period of time, cold targets, traps that have worn rubber on throw-arm preventing fast spin on targets (centrifugal force breaks targets, not just the shot hits), dense air conditions impeding shot energy, wind, rain, etc. Pretty involved stuff trapshooting is, isn't it? Long yardage shooters know 7 ½ hard lead shot will work for them, not against them under most variable conditions.

210. What sort of a call should I use?
Use creative thinking to find the right call for you. The call you are used to using is very likely the wrong call. Rule #1 is to keep an open mind and be willing to experiment. When you observe shooters, listen to their call routine and see if you could develop a better call for that shooter. You'll likely see muzzle-dancing, heaving of the chest, eyes squinting, all sorts of nasty things. Are you doing any of the same? Any call can be a good call as long as it does not disrupt eye focus, gun or eye hold or concentration. Vowels such as A, E, I, O U are really nice. A staccato call verses monotone call? Pick one or the other, but never an intermediate call because it generates a *perception* of slow or fast pulls even when the pull is good. How you call will determine many things; eye pickup of the target, zone, timing, feel, and much more. Just yelling, "*Pull*" ain't gonna cut it. Your call must have an ulterior purpose more than just asking for the target to be released. It's all part of the setup. Best advice? See how the pros call and try to work that into your technique. I know a shooter in Oregon that calls, "*Heyyyy*." It's a great call. He thinks I'm teasing him when I compliment that call. It's really a perfect tone and I can't do it. It makes me jealous to hear that call. I've had trouble finding the "perfect" call. It's really not easy to find. Another great shooter from Washington calls with a, "*Yeah*." Just like the Beatles and he breaks targets real nice, too. How you call is very important. It may only be to get the target out of the house, but there is an emotional link, that's why some shooters move the muzzle when they call, or pull the trigger when the call tone fades and miss. Finding that call is the magic.

211. What sort of method are you teaching?
I'm not teaching methods, just exploring individual talents and presenting the knowledge in understandable form. I suppose you could say it's a method, and one day it may very well be categorized as such, but for now I consider it a compilation of thoughts and wisdom on the game of trapshooting as I've learned from personal experience, research, observing and interviewing professionals. That includes the many interviews I've had with top guns over the years. Canting the gun; Moving Gun and the Bow Technique, are methods I am truly sold on because they work so well. To teach the method I'll have to shoot a combination video film and instructional guidebook, which I may do in the future. Books still convey more technical information than a video as data and illustrations are hard to beat when learning. Textbooks have never gone out of style.

212. How do I adjust POI using only my stock?
It's easy. If POI is too low, raise the stock. If too high, lower the stock. This applies to both the left or right-handed shooter. If POI is to the left and you're a right-handed shooter? Apply cast-on to the comb/stock. Shoots to the right? Apply cast-off. If you're left-handed shooter? Just do the opposite. Now, before making any permanent adjustments, you can apply foam, sheet rubber or duct tape to the comb to make some of your measurement tests such as adjusting cast on and raising the comb height. Cast-off and lowering the comb / stock requires cutting or shimming the stock if these features are not adjustable on your gun. See a stock fitter.

213. I don't understand options. That's why I don't play them. Any help here?
The money options in handicap shooting is where dollars can be earned to pay for your shooting and then some. You should read, "*Trap Options*" manual. You can order it from Scattergun Press, 4919 Westview Drive, Austin, TX 78731 (512)-419-9345. It'll tell you everything you need to know.

214. What is the proper mentality when shooting -- wrapped up in one sentence?
There is only one target in the entire event, only the one you are shooting at.

215. What new things would you like to see presented in trapshooting?
My wish list? Are you sure you want to know? Okay, here goes. I wish the trophies were of higher caliber. Perhaps golden calves should be presented or maybe a real live girl. Win a wife for life! I think if guys knew they could win a wife they might shoot better! And more women would come to the shoots! Three ounces of #6 depleted-uranium shot powered with 5-drams of powder would make a great handicap load. Change the rules! Disqualify all the good shooters. Instead of doubles, shoot triple-trap where you have to quickly insert the third shell to hit the third target. Exploding targets that sound like 4th of July aerial bombs when hit. That way nobody can cheat. Large 8" diameter targets so the pros can shoot them better. Laser guns like they use in the movies for night shooting. Voice-activated traps would eliminate fast and slow pulls. We need to introduce the sport to the masses to gain more shooters. There's a couple generations passing us by who are not taking up the sport. This responsibility should be shared with the major arms and component manufactures to assist the grassroots shooters.

216. What time of day is best for handicap shooting?
Midday, generally. Each location is unique. This is so you can see as much of the face on the target as possible.

217. Any more advice?
It always helps to say a prayer. I know many pros who do this. There is power in it. Then believe and act accordingly.

218. What can I do to expand the sport of trapshooting?
Tell people you are a trapshooter. Invite them to join you on a shoot or a practice round at the local club. Word of mouth is powerful and it's likely that's how you stepped into the sport. Trapshooting is a hidden sport. On a worldwide basis, it's a sport reserved for the rich and famous. Every elite resort hotel in the world offers trapshooting as a recreation. From Saudi Arabia to Europe the rich play the game and that tradition has been going on for many decades. In America, the interest in golf has sideswiped trapshooting, but we can all do our part to promote the sport. Promotion is really needed at all levels. My trapshooting books are one way of raising interest in the sport. The ATA and PITA and USA Shooting offer bumper stickers, T-shirts, etc. Buy them because it enhances awareness and makes people ask what it's all about. It's your chance to promote the sport and make new friends. It's not the environmental issues that will kill the sport, it's the lack of shooters. We need to do more to promote the sport. I believe we will. I see the ATA already moving in that direction with their Internet presence and other outreach programs. The PITA should follow along. But it's the grass roots, me and you, individuals that will make the ATA and PITA stronger, or break them. Just keep inviting people you meet to come on out and try the sport. That's all it takes. Tell them they can win money and prizes and interest levels rise with perky ears. Good news spreads like wildfire.

219. I'm fed up! I've tried everything, and I still miss targets. Why?
I could get into serious trouble telling you this, but… okay, I'll take a chance, here it is. It's Boney! (pronounced: bone-eee, like a bony skeleton). A mystical alligator-like creature with levitation abilities -- thought by paleontologist to be extinct - who lurks in trapfields hungry for intact targets. It could be female, but we just don't know. You must *sacrifice* many targets and *money* to obtain Boney's favor. Though *never* truly satisfied, each time Boney returns, he (she?) will give you a break, letting you off the hook as Boney lurks about seeking to devour some other shooter's targets. Every professional trapshooter knows Boney, but has sworn not to talk about it for fear of retaliation by Boney himself ("him" being figurative with no disrespect for Boney intended). So there you have it. It's likely not the answer you wanted to hear, but as a fellow trapshooter I am bound to tell you the truth, no matter how much it may hurt. Like the mysteries of the universe, we still just don't understand all there is to trapshooting. Boney is taking a few of your targets. He has a right to do so. Let Boney have his/her fill. By George, you don't want Boney to starve to death do you?

220. So, it's a waste of time to pattern a shotgun for trapshooting?
This question comes up often. No, you should use a pattern board to check point of impact, then use the pattern board as a guide to tighten up the inner core of the pattern, the first 25 inches should be tight. When you do tighten the inner core, the annular ring will weaken… 26 to 30 inch area. You trade off a hit 'n' miss 30" pattern for a 25" reliable target-chewing pattern. If you try to fill a 30" pattern so as pellets will be evenly distributed, good luck. It's virtually impossible to do so and have any area of reliability, except for a 12" hot-core and that's too small to hit targets. The bigger the pattern, the more holes will exist in the "real world" not on the pattern board. The board may look great, but you can forget about reliability. Keep in mind I'm talking handicap shooting, not 16 yards. A 30" pattern is fine for singles and double trap, generally speaking. Tighten the pattern if you shoot from 20 up to 27 yards, or more if the rules one day change and 30 yard line is introduced.

221. A lot of shooters pattern for 30" so that makes everybody wrong?
You said it. It's true. People keep forgetting the shot string is four-dimensional: height, width, length, and time. They also forget the target too is four-dimensional and this deems the stationary pattern board very outdated and unreliable. The pattern board is two dimensional (height & width) and reveals no length (depth) or time (movement). What hits the pattern board is not what you are *really* getting out there at the target. A perfect pattern is loaded with holes you'll never see because all the shot does not arrive at the same time on a *crossing* target at 40+ m.p.h. Since most trap targets are traversing angles, a perfect 30" pattern is simply too wide and loose for reliable breaks in handicap shooting. It's only reliable on a straight target reaching it's peak of flight. You'll smoke it hard with a 30" pattern, but you'll end up missing or chipping too many of the angle targets. Sooner or later you'll realize the truth of this, and the sooner the better, because your scores are likely crying for reliability, too. You don't test a pattern's reliability as to how it hits a straightaway target. You test it on the hard and other angles. Keep choking down until you see that 25" hot-core pattern. The annular ring will fill in. Remember, all patterns have hot cores. You can't get rid of it. Even a cylinder choke has a hot core at 5 yards. It's ballistics physics. With a 25" hot-core, you'll still have a 28" pattern and some flyers in the 30" area.

222. I tried a 25" hot-core pattern and my scores dropped. Why?
Because now you don't have a huge sloppy pattern out there breaking targets with lucky hits. With hot cores you must be accurate. At this point, you must now learn precision shooting. Once precision is established the targets will break with a very high degree of reliability. When you miss targets you don't want to miss by a wide margin. If you use a modified or improved modified choke at the 20-yard line, you are going to break a lot of targets. Your scores will be good and you'll win shoots. Then, when you get to the back-fence area the ball of wax will meltdown and you're going to be burned. Why? Because you earned your way back on luck alone, not precision. Now you have to use precise aiming to get the shot onto the target and that wide 30" pattern is going to murder your scores if you don't shrink it down. Too many targets will slip through because there is no *reliable* hot core to break the target

consistently. If you don't learn precise shooting methods and you continue to use the 30" pattern it will always be your demise. You'll be "on" the target and the pattern won't break your target. You'll keep thinking you missed when you really didn't miss at all!

223. Explain why canting a shotgun can be beneficial?
Canting on high point of impact guns can shape the shot angle to intersect the target at increased right angles. Canting gets you to the target *faster* with less swing. But you have to know what you are doing to use it correctly and it's a real tough tactic to learn. Canting is discouraged by many instructors with beginning shooters because it can cause the shoulders to dip and muzzle to rise over the top of the target. The mind knows how to shoot but the body doesn't. Canting, believe it or not, is a natural form of shooting. That's why beginners do it. They look at the target and the target is bending in an arc. The subconscious mind sees it and mimics this arc. The cant is in fact a correct method, but since it is a difficult maneuver it's not for everyone. You don't have to cant a shotgun for trapshooting so that's why instructors can say, "*Don't cant that gun.*" And I do agree with them. But for those who want to build *extraordinary* precision and break targets close in, you're not going to make the job easy trying to swing at them with the traditional trapshooting moves. If you watch the sporting clays shooters, they cant the muzzle to get there quicker and line up the shot for the dead-on hit.

You have to know how to *bow* smoothly from the hips and how to turn the upper body properly to cant a trap shotgun so you won't shoot over the tops of targets. Some trapshooting pros, not all, intentionally cant the muzzle. Everyone does to a small degree and does not even know it. If your eye is truly on the target, the target bends in the arc shape and your gun is going to follow that arc whether you realize it or not. Canting is simply putting *more* cant, intentionally, on the aim when back-sighting to get that dead-on hit faster than swinging. Canting with the bow technique makes for a very lively and maneuverable gun to *correct* sight pictures numerous times before pulling the trigger. It's deadly accurate. Most trapshooters only see one sight picture and pull the trigger because the swing is following a straight line and it's difficult to make course changes with the gun once the swing is committed. With canting, you could make 3 to 4 fast sight picture adjustments and break the target faster than people who only use the traditional swing technique. You can literally dance the sight bead in a figure-8' around the target then put the bead on it and smoke it. That's how much speed and control you have over the gun. But with this control comes a high level of responsibility because you have to back sight and you must manage the gun. Most shooters are not going to put in the time and effort to learn this technique. I explain it for those who want take that next step.

224. Nobody seems to have the answers to flinching. Where do I go for help?
There are no flinch courses, but talking to professional trapshooters can help you because they've been there, done that. *Trap Shooting Secrets* gets into the flinching subject, big-time, with real solutions you can try today, not just talking about flinching. There are many flinches. Sometimes it's "trigger freeze" where you can't pull the trigger. Other times it's like being hit by a bolt of lightening and the entire body spasms. Others simply close their eyes or violently push or jerk the gun. It usually occurs when you "perceive" the target is escaping your zone. Instant fear in the subconscious is set up and bang! The flinch. For most it's excessive trigger sensitivity and combined forces of recoil expectation double-acting on the mind. The brain rebels when it has too many things to do at one time. It hates sensitivity, especially pulling triggers. The release trigger works, but it's not the *real* cure for a flinch. Recoil reduction is not the *real* cure. It's all in the timing of the shot, shooting the proper zone and "yanking" the trigger, not squeezing it off. There is much more as it is an involved subject. It *can* be cured! I've cured mine and other shooters' and it didn't cost them a dime and they did it in *one day.* Amazing, but true it is. It's all laid out in *Trap Shooting Secrets.* I've met shooters who were going to quit the sport due to flinching and my techniques have saved them. I'm sure they will help you.

225. How come other shooters don't flinch?
Everybody flinches. It doesn't start happening until you've shot over 10,000 rounds, usually. For some it begins after many years of shooting. It just arrives from nowhere. "*What the heck is going on here?*" Then it gets worse and worse as time progresses as you try to find that magic cure. Nine out of ten times it's simply a derivative of an improper technique that is now surfacing after years of shooting the wrong way. For some, they shoot the right way and still a flinch can arrive. Writers keep telling shooters, "*It's recoil, recoil, recoil. It's the anticipation of the big-bang!*" It's not recoil or the bang that triggers the flinch, those are only secondary reactions. This is deep stuff here. It's in the subconscious mind, that's why it's so hard to make it go away for those who don't know it's real *cause.* A flinch is your mind *screaming* out to you to stop shooting like you're doing. "*Stop it. I've had enough!*" Then the mind triggers nerves to explode to get your attention. Is it anticipation of the bang and recoil? Nope. It's that little trigger finger of yours causing this entire mess along with your *timing* of the shot. If you're shooting out of time with your "natural time clock" you're begging for a flinch and when the flinch arrives you'll feed it with fire if you don't change your style of shooting. The insidiously vicious circle becomes worse as you try to resolve the flinch with recoil pads, low-power loads, release triggers, etc. That's not where the flinch came from. This is why flinching occurs at a point when you are really getting to be a good shooter, your mind is telling you to shoot differently than you are now. "*It's time to change. It's time to do it right. I've shot your way for 10+ years, now do it my way. I'll show you a better way.*" And it will be better, too. Sensitivity increases as your skill rises.

226. Can a flinch be cured by using dummy-loads?
It's the worse thing you can do, putting a few dead-shells in a box not knowing which is dead or live. Then when the gun doesn't fire, you'll flinch. This is not a flinch… it's a surprise! Everyone will flinch this way, because something went wrong, not right. We expect the gun to fire and make a bang. When it doesn't, you'll stiffen up and jerk the gun wildly. Not the same kind of flinch when shooting normally, not at all. It may feel the same to a degree, but it's not. Don't ever do this because it will train the subconscious mind to flinch! It's torture to the mind and nervous system. The trapshooter's flinch arrives *before* the gun fires.

227. The release trigger will cure a flinch. Shooters have told me so. What do you think?
Shooters mistakenly believe the flinch occurs due to anticipation of the recoil and noise. It seems that way because it always occurs just before recoil is about to happen. But it's the eyes and the trigger finger causing the flinch. Something is "not right" to the eyes seeing the target and when you try to pull the trigger, whamo! The flinch hits hard. The brain is so used to recoil and the bang, it's not becoming sensitized to that, it's becoming sensitized to you shooting improperly. It's really very simple. Go ahead, shoot low-power loads. The flinch will return. Now, recoil does play a small part, often because of *belief* it is recoil creating the flinch. That's why you'll see improvement at first. The brain gets fooled for awhile only to wake up and make you flinch again. That's why you will still flinch with a release trigger. It will help at first, but it's not the *real* cure. Some shooters shoot correctly and get a flinch and the release trigger does the trick, but for many flinchers it's going to take more than just that. It requires a new, and better, method of shooting targets.

228. What is the underlying reason why we all shoot over the targets?
Geometry. You could have a perfectly horizontal swing like tracking a floor/ceiling line as we are told to do to insure the muzzle does not rise. This is correct, we don't want the muzzle to rise, we want it to drop! That's right, the muzzle should be descending a very small degree because the targets are falling. I know this sounds strange because we are shooting rising targets, but are we? From post three all seem to rise like rockets, but posts one and five the extreme angles are falling. They don't rise straight up. They start off at an angle and gravity goes to work on them immediately and begins to pull them down, flying on a bent arc. So when you swing to the target, pull the trigger, the target is diving and you shot over the top. That's why you have to keep your eye on the bottom leading edge of the target. If you're looking at the entire target your eye will not see this drop, it will inform you the target is traveling straight and rising when it certainly is not. It's an optical illusion. Another thing to remember is you can't get to those hard angle targets as fast as you can with targets on post 2,3, and 4. Gravity and the arc is stronger. The insidious thing is, you can't see these arcs with the eye nailed down along the gun's rib unless you use the bow technique which most shooters are not going to do because it's a beast to learn. So for all you shooters out there, you have to at least know this phenomena exists. And now that you know why you will shoot over the top, you just track the bottom leading edge of the target and the correction is made *automatically*. You don't have to consciously drop the muzzle because your eye is looking at the right area of the target, so when you pull the trigger you are compensating for the gravitational suppression. Remember, all targets travel in arcs, so you are shooting a circle not a straight line. Now consider that many shooters don't have a flat swing so when they do swing the muzzle rises, and the target is dropping you can see how self-defeating this can be, both moving in opposite directions of each other. No wonder they shoot over the top of the target! Flatten out your swing and keep the muzzle *below* the target. These are little secrets the pros have learned over decades of shooting.

229. Tell me more about target arcing.
Trap Shooting Secrets exposes these arcs. Probably 99.5% of shooters believe the trap targets are traveling straight lines. If you casually just watch targets they all look like they are rising on straight railroad tracks. But the hard angles do look a little different don't they? They don't rise up on sharp angles, they travel fast and sideways. Then after you discover that these targets are bending downward you examine all the other targets on posts 2, 3, and 4. *"My goodness, they are all bending! Nothing is straight here at all!"* So if you shoot with your eyes only, with no back-sighting, the target will not be where you thought it was when the shot arrives and you miss all too often. Sure you hit a lot of targets and get a decent score, but those missed targets are always there to keep you out of the winning circle. By shooting off the end of the muzzle, it focuses your eye deeper on the target so a more precise sight picture develops. The sight picture is now so tight you don't care about arcing targets because you are dead-on that target and that's why the pros dustball each target. This is a simplistic explanation, but you'll understand the concept once you practice it. Stand at the 20 to 27 yard line, extend your arm with a ruler in hand and set it a bit off the traphouse and you'll see the targets flying up and bend hitting the ruler at differing points. You'll see them bend prominently. The trick is to develop a sense of these bending targets and when you miss ask yourself what you can do to compensate for these bending targets. **Example:** For targets on all posts that are traveling fairly straight, you'll have to shoot to the left or right of the targets, never right at the target or it will not be there when the shot arrives, due to the bending away of the target on the arc flight path. You probably need to start learning to look at the bottom of the targets, not the leading edge or the middle leading edge. You have to find your own formula, *where* you look at the target will give you that advantage to truly see the target where it will be when the shot arrives. Just by learning to look at specific

areas of a target begins to train the eye to focus intensely to see the target with greater detail. Then natural eye/hand coordination brings the muzzle to a much more accurate place to be. The aim/point scheme becomes more precise instead of, "Well, that's close. I'll pull the trigger now." Now you are learning deep-sighting techniques. Most shooters are using shallow-sighting and at most everyone is posting unimpressive scores.

230. How come I've never heard of all these shooting tricks before?
The reason you don't hear of all these neat tricks is because few people knew they existed and those that knew did not know how to communicate the phenomena or didn't want to. Some pros are not going to give away their secrets that took them a lifetime to learn. They paid their dues and it cost them a fortune to be where they are today. Can you blame them? But I found very few pros who would not talk. They want to share, but believe it or not I've found many to be actually shy and I found that quite amazing in itself. Shy? Yes. I had to drag the answers out of them like pulling chickens' teeth. They felt awkward and embarrassed because many didn't know how to explain technical aspects of the sport. At first I thought the shallow answers they gave were to brush me off, but I've learned that many pros simply can not teach or explain why they shoot so well and they don't want to get a reputation of giving bad advice. How can a singer explain why they sing so well? How can an artist explain why s/he can paint so fabulously? Get the picture? They don't know why. It's just that they see things differently than other people. Their subconscious mind has picked up on things we ordinary mortals just don't see at all.

Now, when I began studying trapshooting with an engineers' point of view, I was astonished to learn that shooters were never talking about target arcs, zones and how to adjust them for trap misalignments, gun and eye hold points, etc. It was like none of this mattered and was deemed unimportant to the masses. But when I spoke to professionals a lot of them looked at me with wide eyes, *"You know? That is exactly what is going on out there and I couldn't find the words to even describe it. What took me years to learn I couldn't put into words."* I received answers like this too: *"I don't know why I shoot so well, I just do."* I studied the subject on a very deep level and discovered the underlying factors that have remained hidden from the eyes of many shooters. It was no easy task and everything had to be verified. Trapshooting is a very subjective sport, it's not something you can simply draw on paper and say, *"Here it is. Now go out and do it."* Everyone shoots differently and it's a tough nut to crack, but everyone seems to make the *same* mistakes. This fact led me to dig into why everyone falls into the same pit. From there, common ground was found and exposing the defects became clearer. In essence, I've discovered new knowledge and that is why you haven't seen these tips and tricks before in print or videotapes. I have also struggled to the best of my ability to take this new knowledge and try to communicate it so it makes sense and can be assimilated.

231. Why did you write *Trap Shooting Secrets* and *Precision Shooting*?
It all happened by accident. I couldn't find any real "technical books" on trapshooting. In engineering we have plenty, but trapshooting? No such animal existed. There were books and videotapes that *talked* about trapshooting, and some did give a few basic instructions, but I still walked away not learning much of anything. I didn't know how to apply the instructions. Other shooters experienced the same. I'm not condemning others' efforts, it's just that trying to make a video or writing about trapshooting is a very daunting endeavor. You should try it sometime to see how tough it really is. I've learned something from ever book, every video and you should do the same, for knowledge is the key to this game. I wasn't satisfied and I wanted the "inside scoop" the true source of the principles of trapshooting and there I stood, alone one day at the gun club *"There are no technical books on trapshooting!"* I felt it was unfair. Every sport has a technical manual: golf, rifle shooting, pistol shooting, silhouette, table pool, tennis, etc. We trapshooters were left out by the major publishers deeming trapshooting was not worthy. We had to learn by listening to the advice of well-meaning unprofessional shooters. Some were lucky to have the money to hire good coaches and attend clinics. Not everyone can do this due to location difficulties and finances. I was frustrated that no one had written a book that gives exploratory advice, step-by-step practice tips to find the answers to shooting defects, etc. I started with making little notes for myself and studying why targets are missed, etc. I spoke with as many good shooters as I could, picked their brains, asked the right questions, etc. And that's how it happened, all by accident.

232. What made you believe your books would make a difference in the sport?
As a writer, I decided it was time trapshooting had some textbooks because learning the sport is tremendously fatiguing for the novice and even worse for those who love the game and can't reach proficiency. I've seen the misery out there. New shooters quitting because they can't compete with the better shooters getting whipped at the meat shoots, etc. It's so embarrassing many new shooters simply walk away from the sport. How many new shooters arrived at your gun club in the past year and did not return? Then I see the accomplished shooters in eternal slumps. They love the game so much and they keep trying to practice and they just have lost the fire within. They go to a registered shoot with a defeated attitude, knowing they are going to lose, believing they are in a slump and maybe one day they will come out of it... but they never do. Then you don't see them practicing every weekend, then they miss a registered shoot here and there, then you don't see them anymore at all. When I saw these things it affected me deeply, "Is that going to happen to me? After all these years of shooting and the money I've invested in this and I'm going to hit a dead

end?" There had to be a solution and when I searched I found none to exist. Even coaching doesn't always work because the shooter ultimately has to find the problem within himself. Some coaches didn't even know targets arc, or how to adjust timing and zones. They just couldn't teach that deep knowledge because they didn't have it themselves. I believe if you have the inside knowledge my books will give you, and you have a coach to help you put it together, that will be a dynamite package. But you need a coach with an *open mind* and coaches are so individualistic personalities, some are so rigid they will not let you experiment, as it is deemed a deviation from acceptable form. Like being taught that canting a shotgun is an abomination, but the pros have been canting their guns all along as if it were invisible. Crazy isn't it? It's invisible because the cant is slight and hard to see.

233. You are turning conventional wisdom of trapshooting on its head. How can you do that?

It's not easy. When I began discovering the many misconceptions of the game that traditional wisdom upheld, I became more than a bit scared to tell you the truth. It's like the world is wrong but you're right, and then you discover, "Yeah, the world *is* wrong." It's like Thomas Edison and Albert Einstein, two great thinkers who discovered new things. They didn't invent anything, they just discovered what already existed. I'm not Edison or Einstein, but I used their frame of mind, the way they think to find the solutions to problems: daring to challenge the status quo. Now when you think of it, both Edison and Einstein used "experimentation" and "analysis" to come up with new discoveries. A new way of doing things comes from experiments, and most great inventions came from accidents in the course of seeking the answer to something else, from synthetic rubber to C-4 explosives. I stumbled upon a few shooting realities by accident, too, so I'm saying I am not hyper-intelligent. Trapshooting has always been a secret and that's what the problem is for many shooters... they don't know the secrets. All I've done is pry out the invisible aspects of the game, the fine subtleties that have gone unnoticed. I've created nothing, only exposed what is.

Now, conventional wisdom says use a soft eye focus. Okay, try it and it will get you nowhere. I say use a hard intense focus. What happens? You start seeing targets brighter and in slow motion. Now you can shoot fast as the pros and hammer the targets. Now why do the pros say use a soft-focus? Because they hard-focus and don't even realize it! To them it's a soft focus because their vision skills are elevated from the average person from seeing and acquiring so many targets in centralized vision. Coaches will tell you to swing muzzle straight horizontally, but we know if you do that you will shoot over the top of targets if you don't keep the muzzle under the target. Trapshooters believe they have to shoot faster at the back fence and we now know you have to shoot slower. Targets bend away and nobody was teaching how to compensate for it. Not once have I ever read to make sure your shoes are not worn out, so I see shooters with worn heels and when they swing they lose balance and the muzzle geometry is upset and they keep missing angle targets. Amazing? It is. Everyone says to mount the gun and bring it to your cheek, but nobody tells you to feel the cheek pressure and steer the gun with your cheek to stop head-lifting, yet watch the pros and they steer that gun with their cheek. It's buried and they get to the target so easily because the cheek is an "element" in the swing dynamic. The list goes on. This is what happens when you open your mind to "experimentation." Each shooter will discover new knowledge about their shooting skills.

234. Why is it my average rises then drops like a rock?

Primarily setup errors creeping in, but worse yet is the failure to manage concentration. You can't keep a high level of concentration throughout the entire season if you are too intense all of the time. Burnout affects everyone. Sometimes something simple has changed; a gun setting has moved, stance changed, swing changed, eye and gun holds, changing to improper shoes, using a new shooting vest, switching shells, chokes, lazy eye syndrome. Something changed physically or mentally. Find out what it was (easy to say than do). Sometimes it's an instantaneous slump that attacks the shooter and feeds on itself with excessive worry and concern. Take a break then return with a new frame of mind. If it happens again? Get back to the practice trap and go over each setup routine diligently. Slow down your shooting! Somewhere along the line you speeded up and exceeded your ability to break targets reliably. Often the club you shoot can ruin your average. The target flight angles, trap settings, backgrounds, target composition, target spin, eddy currents, and optical illusions can all have negative effects until you learn to compensate for the anomalies. Be aware of streak-shooting where you perform in streaks. After you hit 10 targets you drop one, then hit eight and drop one. This too can become a mental habit that is performed by the unconscious mind. To manage it is to be aware of it, and that alone reverses the groove. Look at your score sheets and you'll see a pattern. A bit sophisticated, but a pattern will eventually emerge over the season and you'll recognize it. Even the posts and months that are causing the misses are revealed. Biorhythms can also play a role in poor or good performance. Read a book about it. Maybe it will apply to you. I believe we all have certain days in the month that we are up or down and these patterns are quite regular and predictable. Charting moods on a calendar does the trick.

235. So experimentation is the key to obtaining the inside secrets to trapshooting?

Yes. It unlocks the door from mediocre to an explosion of new ideas. And that breaks a shooter out of a slump. There is more than one way to break a target. The way you have habitually been doing it is likely the wrong way. Experimentation will find the right way for you. The problem is there are too many frigid shooters. They actually *fear* deviating from anything. They shoot targets only one way and can't seem to find another way because when they try, scores immediately drop, they lose interest then go back to shooting wrong again. There is an ironic joke, "To be a good trapshooter you must have no brain." Trapshooters have a reputation of being frozen in stone because we are told again and again to be robotic so consistency can develop. That is fine, but being robotic closes the mind, and when that happens you're in trouble if you're rehearsing improper technique. Pros will tell you they are still learning how to shoot targets. That's incredible when you think about that as some have shot professionally for 40+ years and are members of the Hall of Fame! That should tell you something about experimentation... the pros experiment. Not during competition in the sense we would do at practice, but they know how to break the target six different ways while we only know how to do it one way or maybe two if we are that fortunate. We are creatures of habit. You will never find perfection if you don't look for it. You won't even know perfection exists if you don't experiment to find it within yourself. Perhaps 90% of shooters are in slumps, really. They are not getting better, they arrive at and stay on a plateau. True progress is not taking place because of fear of deviations to try new things, reluctance to believe there really is a better way to break a target, and not knowing how to experiment.

236. I tried experimentation and it ruined my scores. My average went way down. It doesn't work.

Everybody desires instant results, looking for shortcuts, striving for the magic charm to boost their scores. It could be a new gun, a recoil pad, different vest, muzzle weight, barrel work, etc. Looking in all the wrong places for the magic bullet is within you. When you experiment, you are going to see a drop in scores. Every shooter would gladly accept a temporary reduction in score for an increased average later. Some techniques will give you instant results, like: eye and gun holds and eye-pre-focus that I teach, but I'm talking of going even further than that... discovering the inner-self. But you can't do that until you resolve yourself to breaking out onto new ground to discover the real potential that lies within. It all begins with keeping an open mind, being receptive to discover new ways of breaking targets. That's what true practice is, experimenting. Rehearsing is a form of practice that polishes what is learned after you have imbedded the chosen technique. People confuse the two but they are both very different. Are you practicing or rehearsing? A word of caution, don't experiment with too many things all at one time. Once confusion sets in it serves no purpose. Like eye and gun holds, try them but just a few at a time on the targets or post that are giving you the most trouble. Evolve slowly without extreme deviations. One step at a time, just like shooting one target at a time. Don't push yourself too hard. Learn to relax and learn patience and experimentation will work for you. All you are seeking is new knowledge, a new way to do a better job. Isn't that what all new inventions do?

237. I spoke with pros and they never revealed many of the things you do. How is that?

It is true pros know how to shoot targets with extreme precision, but not all really understand or know why they perform at such high levels of precision. They have learned from years of experience. This is why most all top guns will tell you, *"Practice, practice, practice."* Yes, if you shoot 25,000 targets a year you are going to learn through sheer trial and error and that will teach the subconscious mind a thing or two by beating it into submission to obey. But practice doesn't work for everyone, only the few, because practice in itself can be self-defeating for many, many, shooters as they practice the same old mistakes over and over again and never learn anything new. When you ask pros questions you have to be very precise in the form of your question or you will receive a very simple explanation. So if you have not heard pros speak of things you read in my books it's because you didn't ask. Now that you know a few of the inner secrets of the game and you ask the pros, they will verify much of what is here, based on their own personal knowledge of how the game works from their perceptive. Quite a few pros I spoke with never knew targets bend. I found that a bit shocking. I've seen pros cant their guns and not admit they are doing it saying, *"It's a mistake to do that"* yet they go on line and the muzzle is canting. Go figure! I say, "I saw you cant the muzzle on those hard rights." Then I get that sheepish look, *"Since you mentioned canting I wanted to see if I was or not and I suppose I do a little bit."* That's what I'm saying, "If you're eye is truly on the target and the target arcs then you will cant the gun." "Yeah, but the targets don't arc." Moments later... "Oh, gee whiz they do don't they?" So, don't be surprised to learn that the pros don't come right out and say, *"Well, you're missing the targets because your eye hold is improper for the zone and you're gun hold is causing horizontal cross-firing against the target's flight path."* They are not going to talk to you like that because they don't have the communication skills to give you a technical answer. But if you ask, "If I drop my gun hold will this help me to acquire the target better?" Answer: "Yes, you will see the target sooner and give your gun an advantage to follow-through to the target." So, communicating with top guns isn't always a simple matter. Those snappy answers you normally get from them are the best they can give you for the simple and broad question you likely asked. Be more creative and precise in your question and they will give you a better explanation. Another thing, most pros shoot for a living, not teach for a living. Those that do teach are more communicative than those who don't.

238. This new information seems foreign to me. It's hard to believe anything new could be correct. Why is that?

The information you are reading is new knowledge about the technical aspects of the sport, on a deeper level. All the traditional advice has been hashed and rehashed over and over again: basic gun swing, 30" patterns, mental motivation, recoil flinching, etc., etc., and it's getting quite boring and uninformative. Where are all the new discoveries? Gosh, even cars are evolving with new technology but trapshooting just sits still? Golf is evolving with new swing techniques, new clubs, new ways to identify the target (that hole in the ground) and trapshooting just lies dormant? I suppose I'm just waking up the establishment that we need to start using our imaginations and search deeper into the reasons why things are the way they are. We need real solutions to the problems shooters face. Someone has to start the process. Writers need to stop fearing being wrong when trying to correct a wrong. If we dig deeper for the truth we will see a flood of eye-opening insights to the game we never thought of before. I think we all are experiencing a slump. We have come to believe traditional wisdom works for everyone when it doesn't, that there is nothing new, all the shooting forms have been discovered and there is no way of branching out. Our minds have been injected with Novocaine. We need to start believing in our own abilities to discover new ways to break targets. Through the experimentation process of trying new things, applying new information gained, you perceive new inclinations leading to invention. This creative imagination born from invention suddenly opens your mind to a flood of new ideas. It's really great for shooters who are in slumps. Just reading my books has opened up your mind to re-think the way targets are shot. That's great. It's a first step to getting where you want to go with trapshooting. The old information is good, too, so don't totally abandon it, we want to incorporate the old with the new. Now to determine if the new information you discover is correct is to try it and see if it makes sense. Edison failed thousands of times before he found the right filament for the light bulb, but it was worth the effort wasn't it? Yes, some of the information you develop may not work for you, but you may, by being creative, take a segment or idea from it and apply it to your style of shooting. That's the point... to be creative, to explore new territory so you can find that shooting secret hidden within you that is going to break you out of that slump and rise past your current abilities. I think we are just beginning to uncover trapshooting's secrets.

239. Tell me more about optical illusions. I'm not sure they exist, but sometimes I miss knowing I was on the target.
Blame holes in the pattern. That's what everyone else does. Yes it is true holes will take out a good score on straight-trending targets but unlikely on angle targets. You better believe there are optical illusion out there because there are many of them. The basic illusion is there is no such thing as straightaway targets, they don't exist. We already know that. Another illusion is so predominate yet so hidden. We are taught to use eye/hand coordination and we don't do it. How's that? Shooters are pushing the gun to the target instead of swinging to it... a ton of shooters do it out of hard-core habit believing they are not doing it. That's how ingrained that habit has become. So, they shoot via hand/eye coordination. The direct opposite of what they should be doing! And they know better! How does that happen? You call, target exits, your eye doesn't truly lock on the target so it looks fast, you don't move your body to swing so the hand pushes. The hand is now taking over control from the eye. A short stabbing motion occurs and it's hit or miss shooting. The entire setup was wrong. If you don't swing you will *push*, and when you push you'll shove the gun away from your eye and miss when you should have hit the target. It doesn't take much misalignment to miss. So get that swing back into your form. The long-yardage shooters are the worst offenders and they need more help in this area than all. Another illusion: you shoot at a target but you miss clean, but you were right on it. The target was not where you thought it was. Yes, you saw it, but it moved. Again, your eye was only seeing the target not *looking* at it, so your eye/hand coordination was fine going after a target that was once upon a time there. This is caused by improper eye focus upsetting timing, and swinging too fast to the target. Slow down! All the targets will appear as optical illusions if you shoot beyond your abilities. Try snap/spot shooting trap targets and you'll see these illusions. Busy backgrounds make targets appear faster than they really are. Not wearing blinders produces double imaging on the retina from reflection. Improper head alignment can produce distortion in prescription glasses if the eye is not aligned with the central focal area of the glasses. The testing I've performed reveals that shooters misperceive the target's location, often perceiving the target as true and straight and shoot over and/or behind the actual location. Visual skills are lacking and following the target with jerky eye motions is a huge source of these optical illusions. If your eye hold and eye pre-focus is improper or nonexistent you'll be seeing ghost targets your entire shooting career.

240. I'm trying to put the swing back into my form, but I'm having a tough time of it in long-handicap. Now what?
You are trying something new. When you do that your focus becomes temporarily sidetracked. You are becoming swing-oriented instead of target-oriented. It's a temporary diversion. You'll get over it after you've burned about 2,000 shells. To speed the process, practice at home by closing your eyes and swing the gun smoothly. Make sure you feel the gun and the swing. Get into the *feel* of things and the job gets easier and remains repeatable. Once you get the hang of it, learn to divert your thought-sense of the swing out of mind and start *flowing* to the target. Don't get deeply involved with mechanics and forget how to play the game. Realize that no two pros swing alike due to body weight, height, flexibility, arm length, etc., so you have to find what works best for you, but you have to swing, not push. Okay? Go to a tournament and study the pros' swings. It's subtle, but really watch them with an Eagle's eye. Watch how the gun hold allows them to *swing* onto the target's flight path. It's fast, but it's smooth. Observe how they cross over to the target if they use a high gun hold. How many feet from the house does the target fly before their muzzle moves? Observe foot position and stance. How does it complement each post? Do they stay in the gun after it is fired? How long? If are still having problems, your gun may be too heavy or too light. Try adjusting where you place your hand on the forearm. Extended will slow the swing, withdrawing will speed up the swing. Change your foot position and stance to get rid of the wobbles in your swing. Stability and balance are critical to a good setup. Weight must be balanced flatly on the feet, not to the toe or heel. Make sure shoes are not worn out making you tilt or rock in the swing. If you body is moving around ever so slightly during the swing being out of balance, you can forget about accurate eye/hand coordination being of any use to you.

241. How can I become a better trapshooter?
Easy. Open your mind to learn new things, to absorb new information, to ask yourself why you are missing targets and strive to resolve the problem. Too many shooters accept a missed target as just a missed target and shake their heads in disgust when they should be kicking themselves with the "Why?" questions. More often than not the answer is, *"I don't know,"* but the question serves a purpose of enlightenment -- to be aware of the deeper reasons for missing a target. Awareness then becomes a valuable tool to seek answers on a deeper level. Curiosity is sparked and suddenly you are examining the game with a fine tooth comb, seeing target angle, speed, brightness, etc., whereas you never saw these things before. You become a *technician*, not just a shooter on line calling for targets and letting the body do whatever it wants to do to break targets. Once you open that door of awareness and step inside, you'll begin to see the mistakes. Once errors are recognized and seen, you are well on your way to correcting them and that leads you to be a better shooter. He who knows what he is doing usually wins.

242. I'm in a slump. I've tried all I know to escape. Any advice?
A slump is a temporary stagnation in scores, a plateau one reaches and believes there is no possibility of escape due to past results. There is much more to it, but begin focusing not on the errors to correct, but focus on how well you do hit the targets you do smash. Knowing what you do right is better than knowing what you do wrong. Believe in yourself. A loss of confidence in yourself is damaging and many shooters suffer from it. Believe you are coming out of the slump and you will come out of it. Certainly you must not ignore errors in setup... for it is here where slumps are born and destroyed. Have faith. Believe you are not in a slump even when you are in the midst of it. That's what faith is, believing in what you don't already have. The power of your mind, your thoughts, must be turned around from the low to the high, from the bad to good, negative to positive. It's not a struggle, it is a simple faith, just believe you can hit the targets and you will! Then believe it again and again until you do believe. You make it happen by sheer thought power. Mind over matter. Trapshooting is a mental game. It's all in the mind. When you make these internalized changes you will see external results! Keep learning, for slumps arise when the learning process falls stale. Since trap is a boring, repetitive sport, the mind will shutdown if it is not stimulated and serious errors and mistakes will creep in.

243. What sort of attitude makes for a good trapshooter?
A burning desire to win. That comes after you gain proficiency in your shooting, though you must still force your thinking along those lines as it won't come naturally. You must have a kick-butt attitude toward the target, a controlled inner-focused aggression to destroy the target. It's a full-bore attack, but performed smoothly and with precise precision. It's a war. It's insulting to miss a target. Humiliation. Don't get mad, get even. If you don't have that tinge of adrenaline and excitement, then you won't find the fire to burn the targets. Don't go out on the trapfield with a lackadaisical mind-set, *"Well, I'll see what happens."* Just say, *"I'm going to use all my attention to focus and break each target, one-by-one, one at a time."* And really mean it when you say it! If you give it your best, your scores will be best. Expect to win, dare to believe. Stop feeling defeated and scared when you start your first trap. Be cool. Feel in control. Everyone has a trapshooter they admire. Visualize your icon on the line, then mimic that person. Feel professional. Believe me, this works.

244. Best shotshell?
I can't tell you. If I did, I'd have to kill you. It's top secret (just kidding). All of the manufacturers' shells today are top performers, but each barrel demands its own brand of shell. What brand worked for you in your last gun may not be ideal for the gun you are shooting now. It's a bloody buggery concocting glorious shame, the British say. Americans say, it's all a bunch of bull, we can put men on the moon but can't make a shell for my gun; but that's reality. You can retain brand loyalty with proper choking and point of impact adjustments. Amazingly, many trapshooters do not pattern their guns properly or adjust POI to work for their advantage. The pros shoot all sorts of differing shells produced by ammo makers worldwide. A lot of engineering work goes into these shells and I've found that once you determine the POI shift they all perform very well. Pattern boards will show discrepancies from shell-to-shell, but patterns are limited in dimension which is not an accurate measuring tool for performance. Now just make sure you are using a handicap load for handicap shooting. Some make the simple error of using a singles load. There are reasons why the manufactures make handicap loads and it's not a sales gimmick. The design is engineered, so don't goof around in this area.

245. If shooters are not patterning properly, how should I pattern my gun?
I'll condense the answer. Keep choking to pattern for a hot 25" core. The annular ring will fill automatically to 28" and you'll raise reliability of the pattern. Adjust your point of impact until you can put the bead on the target, or with as little lead as you can, to the zone you are shooting. That's as simple as it gets. Many shooters have adjusted their style to conform to the gun rather than have the gun perform to themselves. Reason being, POI is tedious to adjust if there is no adjustable rib, laziness and not knowing how to do it. How often have you heard shooters say, *"What is your point of impact setting?" "Maybe you should raise it? Lower it?"* Ask a pro and he'll spit out his POI in a blink of the eye. They know its importance.

246. What shooting defects do you see at most competitive shoots?
Broad question. Shooting a gun with an improper POI is commonplace. There is a huge deficiency of education in the trapshooting sports. Everyone knows they must have a gun that fits, but how many shooters' guns truly fit them? Not many. A great number of shooters are shooting guns that don't fit. Gun mounting? Where do they learn such awkward things? Stance? Who taught them to break the rules and shoot out of balance? Everyone thinks they are shooting properly, and the majority really need a coaching session to get rid of the silly things that are causing them to shoot poorly. Many are so self-defeating that they could be outrageously excellent shooters but the gun mount, stance, swing defects or gun hold is all wrong and working totally against the shooter. If I had twenty minutes with such shooters they would see scores leap upward. It's really upsetting to see a shooter missing targets due to a simple defect in the setup.

247. Give me a technique to resolve nervousness.
Nerves can't be resolved, only managed. There is a method that undeniably works, which you should be doing anyway and that is using intense eye pre-focus prior to calling for the target. The method I use, that has helped others, is to pre-focus on a blade of grass or very intensely at tiny flying chips from other shooters smashing the targets. This mental diversion does work as you become "too busy" to be nervous. You may feel some jitters, but they are not as intense. It is a lifesaver for those who experience panic attacks, for it will keep you in the game, functioning at high levels. You can even use trigger words like *"I'm too busy to be nervous"* but concentrated visual focus on an object will ultimately manage nerves. With practice, it only gets better.

248. Is there a difference between coaching and taking shooting lessons?
Night and day! Lessons are a long general process of learning the basics of shotgun shooting and conforming to traditional rules, concepts and ideals. It's a school environment. Coaching is highly individualistic where the coach works with your style of shooting and incorporates specific knowledge to make it more effective. A good coach will keep discovering why you miss targets and find the solution so you can break them easily, building confidence and a winning attitude. If you plan to be a professional shooter, you should find a competent coach who really cares about you and can put in the time necessary to develop and polish your natural skills. Traditional shooting concepts are not totally the ruling factor, but the style of shooting rules over tradition if the technique applied works for the shooter. Coaching is an advanced form of instruction. It's beyond the novice stage.

249. When I try new shooting techniques I fall apart. What am I doing wrong?
Nothing. Your scores should fall apart. The biggest mistake shooters make is trying something new to see if it will break more targets right away. They go to the practice trap and if it won't break 25 then it doesn't work. It doesn't work that way. New shooting techniques will not always give instant gratification. But they should make sense, to a degree, but not always. A coach tells you to do something and you balk because it feels uncomfortable. That's how trying a new technique should feel, uncomfortable. I've always said, *"If it feels too good, it's probably the wrong technique for you."* That's because so many shooters are in a habit of shooting improperly. That error prone form they use feels great but it's wrong. When trying technique, something inside of you should *click, "This doesn't feel right, but it sort of makes sense when I think about it. I'll try to make this work."*

250. Name one trapshooting book you recommend all trapshooters read?
I'd like to recommend my books, but I assume you want me to recommend another writer/shooter and since you limit me to one book I would say every trapshooter, at this time of printing, must read *"Trapshooting is a Game of Opposites."* Keep your eye out for new books, new videotapes, etc. Knowledge is power, it really is in trapshooting. You can purchase this book on our web site.

251. These shooting tips are great ideas but they won't work for me.
Yes they will! Effort supersedes talent. You can learn trapshooting. Natural talent is nice to have but it can be learned. Remember this, the professional trapshooters you see today often shot worse scores than you would believe when they first started shooting. They just refused to give up and took on the attitude of progressing to higher levels over time. You will do just fine. Certainly you too will also have to endure the terrible scores the pros once endured, but you will break out of it in due time. Be aware that other activities may be interfering with your shooting such as golf or another sport. Concentrate on shooting and your shooting will reward you. If you diversify your attention to other activities in your life scores will reflect that. And for goodness sake, **keep this book in your car** so you can refer to it when you need it. It's not going to do you any good whatsoever if it's collecting dust on your bookshelf. Write a reminder note right now to bring the book with you on your next registered shoot and keep the book in the car. Read it when you need help, that's what the book is for!

252. The #1 best advice in a nutshell?
Have your gun fitted and insure it still fits because body dimensions change over time. Be smooth in all you do and feel it. Believe in yourself. Realize the target is broken long before you pull the trigger, often even before you shoulder the gun. The setup is crucial. Shoot with authority. Frank Little essentially says, *"Look at the target, don't just see it, look at it."* Dan Orlick told me,

"Stop blaming the gun. It's a precision instrument, put it in a vice, pull the trigger and it'll hit the bullseye each and every time. It's *you* that needs to change." He was right. Whatever increases accuracy? Do it. Take dead aim and shoot with a plan. As Daro Handy so simply, yet wisely proclaims with a friendly grin, *"Put the bead on the target!"* Talk to professionals, ask questions, take lessons, give it your best shot, always. Be willing to learn; open your mind to try new methods of shooting targets. Dull boredom ruins good shooters. Have faith in yourself. Dare to believe. Expect miracles; they do happen.

Tip: Talk to professional shooters, read all you can about the sport, then apply what you have learned.

DOUBLE TRAP - QUESTIONS & ANSWERS
"You can't score what you don't see."

Here are answers to commonly asked questions pertaining to double rise/double trap. Numbering sequence continues from prior *Questions & Answers* chapter.

253. I have deteriorated from Double-A to a low A-class. Any advice?
Doubles is double the trouble and twice the fun. It's an entirely different technique than single barrel targets. It is possible you have fallen into a few traps here, as many shooters do. Don't use the same stance and shooting techniques as you do with single target trap, revamp your mindset strongly this is a 'different' game and setup accordingly. Readjust your gun and eye hold, timing and swing velocity to compensate. Often, it's just a mindset thing that ruins the entire setup. Double trap usually follows single target events and this is where you become programmed to shoot the targets the same way. Don't be so cautious, you must be a bit reckless on the first straightaway target so you can get to the second-angled target quicker. If you are having big problems with a slump? It's time to slow down the targets for practice so you can get back into the swing of things. You should also lock the trap so you can focus in on the target angles that are giving you trouble. Make sure your gun is still fitting and you are not lifting your head, unknowingly. Snug down your cheek to the comb and really 'feel' the cheek and heel of the gun pressure, all the way to the targets. There are many things that can go wrong in double trap; overswinging muzzle to target, laziness, improper eye and gun hold points, using the same stance on each post, gun fit changed, eyeglasses need updated prescription, wrong shooting glasses lens color, muzzle dipping on call, being too aggressive or too tense, erratic trigger pulls, etc. These are major killers for scores. Slow down, back up, evaluate everything you do and most of all, stop thinking you are in a slump. Just relax more and put the sight bead on the targets. Get your foot stance in the proper position on each post, as each must be slightly different, 1-inch foot position adjustment on average, from post to post. If you don't adjust foot position you will 'wind-up' your upper body and this will throw the gun off the target line in the swing. There are no other technical books on double trap shooting. Frank Little videotapes are sold by Shotgun Sports Magazine.

254. I struggle to hit the second target. What can I do?
Assuming your second target is the angled target; 1) review the illustrations in this book for tips related to timing, eye control and stance. 2) Stop rushing the shot, on that target. Set up properly and you will find it easier. You may want to try using the "V-dip" method gun swing, so you can get on the target's exact flight path. See Fig. 88 and 98. You will find the solution here in this book and in the DT section in *Trap Shooting Secrets*.

255. Everybody I know shoots the straight target first. Why?
There are advantages and, of course, disadvantages taking the straight target first. Most high gun hold shooters will take the straight target first, since the gun is already held high over the traphouse, but the prime reason is theoretical; the straight target should be shot first as it can be spot-shooted quickly which allows time to swing to the distancing second-angled target. However, the angle target is always the hardest to hit, and more so with increasing distance from the trap, so taking the angled target first is also a viable method. In reality, it's all personal preference, as there are no hard rules on target priority. Most shooters simply copy everybody else. There are top-gun shooters who have won Olympic medals by not taking the traditional straight target first method.

256. How can I shoot double targets fast as the pros?
By slowing down! Speed is a killer on DT and ABT trapshooting and most shooters try to shoot fast, which results in unsmooth moves to the targets. Speed is developed from technique, not from knee-jerk actions or reacting quickly. Review the DT illustrations in this book, incorporate the tips and you will be setting up properly. Once you learn how to set up the eye and gun holds, and other tips herein, you will begin to hit the targets with more ease. As a result, your speed naturally increases with little conscious effort on your part. Since the targets are not going to escape the zone, you don't feel rushed. Your moves simply flow to each target and it all happens so quickly. Slow down, first get the hold points and swing established for each post then speed will come automatically. Most shooters need to slow down anyway. Pros keep reminding themselves to slow down ! See Fig. 87.

257. Why do I shoot double trap terribly, but single-target trap I score okay?
DT is a different game than single-target trap. The shooter's distance from the trap is similar to DTL and ATA 16-yard trap and some respects Olympic trap, but that's where the similarities end. Beyond yardage, DT is totally different and you need to make adjustments to compensate; gun, chokes, ammo, stance, set up, timing, eye & gun holds, swing. It's all different than single target trap. Casually watching the pros shoot, you may not see much of a difference, but if you observe very closely you will see tiny alterations in the way they shoot DT versus single-target. These minute adjustments make a huge difference between posting a high or a low score. The first step in learning DT is to recognize the game is different and to begin applying a new set up routine specifically for this game.

258. Should I use my single barrel autoloader trap gun for DT?
No. The gun only has one POI setting and that will be a disadvantage. Using a semiauto, you can't use the higher POI bottom barrel to catch the fast rising straightaway with absolute reliability because you don't have the barrel to do it! Most single barrel shotguns are too long to swing, which allows the targets to gain distance, making it harder to hit them. The O&U is more lively to swing, more due to balance than weight, and the gun is specifically designed for DT (including DTL, Single Barrel, UT and Olympic trap). Certainly you can use a single barrel gun for DT, DTL, ABT, UT or OT, but technically you are using the wrong equipment for the game. The autoloader's single barrel will experience temperature acceleration, so be aware to cool the barrel after each shot with a damp towel or you'll risk missing targets due to barrel warping that changes the POI. The POI will usually rise when barrel is hot, but it can shift in any direction to give you a nasty surprise. The situation worsens in a short squad or shootoff situation.

259. I miss the straight target, then the angle, then visa versa. It's frustrating. What can I do to stop this?
This is a case of shooting by instinct and not with a plan. Many shooters simply step on the line and say, *"Well, let's see what happens today."* It's all a set up problem in most cases. The shooter is not prepared to see the targets and has no proven plan of action to attack the targets. Each post, and each target, requires a specific formula to execute the plan. The moment you try to use what worked on post #1 on post #4 will cause you to drop a target. When you think about this more, you will see it is the cause of why you are occilating; missing the straight sometimes, then sometimes missing the angle targets. Set up a formula for each post. You may have to adjust your stance slightly from post-to-post, eye and gun holds, etc.

260. Should I use different ammo shot size or stay with one size?
Choice is yours. The beginner should take maximum advantage of the situation by using more pellets for the first straightaway target, such as #8 ½'s. Don't use #9's as they are dusty weak and may not break the target reliably. Use #8 shot for the second target. As you get better, you may then switch to #8 and $7 ½ shot respectively. Many pros do not fool around with altering shot sizes and most will use 7 ½ shot on both targets. Why? Because their aim is down pat and they want the "shot insurance" knowing the shot will break the target with utmost reliability. Best all around is #8 shot for both barrels.

261. What choke sizes should I use in DT?
There is no need to use X-full or full-chokes in DT trap. A good all-around size is 5/8 (improved modified) or light-full for both barrels. However, you can maximize your advantage by using a ½ (modified) choke for the first straightaway target. You will get a much wider pattern spread, but you will lose the hot-core reliability of a tighter choke. For the beginner, it's a good tradeoff. The pro relies on precision aim, not pattern size advantage. There really is no hard rule on choke sizes for DT as many top-gun shooters use just about anything available on the market -- as long as it works. But the general rule is as stated above; 5/8 choke for both shots is just about ideal. Some pros use a full choke for the second-angle shot. Here's the run down on choke sizes: ¼ = improved cylinder. 3/8 =Light Modified. ½ =modified. 5/8 = improved modified. ¾ = light full. Full & extra-full have no fraction value. See question 273. Best all around is improved modified for both barrels, but whatever works for you is best.

262. What ammo is the best I can use for DT?
Any name brand ammo. The key factor to determine is; which of these name brands works best in your gun? Shooters make the mistake of falling in love with a specific brand of single-target ammo, then use the same ammo for their double-gun. This may not be correct, as the ammo might not be compatible with the barrels. Best advice? Try them all, over a long period of time. You need time to find the right ammo. A pattern board does not tell the entire story. The day you try brand X may be the day you are shooting poorly, but this ammo may be the right one for your gun. If the ammo is certainly dustballing the targets and your score is rising, then you know which ammo brand is right for you.

263. How do I shoot one target that is falling and the other is rising?
First, don't shoot a trap if it requires setting. Have the trap set properly! Even when you practice, the trap must be set according to the competition rules book. Otherwise, you will destroy your set up and timing, etc. If wind or eddy currents are creating the problem there is not much you can do about it other than paying increased attention to insure the sight pictures are on the money before you pull the trigger. Try not to make too many adjustments for wind; at most a couple such as dropping the gun hold if the first straightaway target is suppressed and raising your eye hold a bit. For the high-rising second-angled target, it's a good idea to employ a bit of "V-dip" in the muzzle, so you can catch the flight line on this target, because you will need a solid followthrough shot to break it. Shooting quicker is the most haphazard method shooters gravitate to when faced with deviant-angled targets. In fact, it's often to your advantage to slow down your swing instead of speeding up. It will increase accuracy.

264. What is the best trigger combination for doubles?
Release-pull. This is not to say the standard pull trigger can't be used with great success, but the ideal trigger set up is the release-pull. The release on the first straightaway target (or angled, if you shoot this first) allows for quick shooting, with a reduced tendency to flinch-delay the shot. Pulling a trigger can move the gun, whereas a release trigger holds it steady.

265. I tend to lurch at the first target and miss. Why?
Improper set up. There is little to no vertical eye separation. See Fig. 110. This will cause lurching or rushing as the eye sees the targets moving too fast and you react accordingly, often hastily. Raise your eye hold so you are not staring down along the gun's rib. If your gun hold is improper, the target exits clearly off line with the gun and a moment of panic sets in to make the adjustment to swing the muzzle back to the flight line. Again, rushing takes place and usually results in pushing the muzzle, abandoning the swing.

266. I fail to hit the second target. Why?
If you miss the second shot it is because there was an error in hitting the first shot -- even if you do break the first target! At some point when pulling the trigger on your first shot, the muzzle was in an improper position to swing onto the second target. Examine your first shot timing so the muzzle will be in position to initiate the swing to the second-target flight path. Crossing over is usually the problem. Also, the set up must be right from the start or errors will show up with missed targets. Swinging too fast is another culprit to be aware of; it's not speed but accuracy that counts the most. Examine your eye-switching as the eye is not transitioning smoothly or losing focus on the second target failing to lock-on. Mental perception of intense speed and distance of the second-angled target escaping will trigger a hasty swing and trigger-pull response. Your stance could be off to cause you to swing off the target's line of flight. Do not let your body wind-up during the swing, as this will cause the muzzle to drift off line.

267. I can't employ the V-dip method. Now what?
Employ the straight-line swing method, but you must shoot very fast taking the first straightaway target at the half-way point of it's flight to the peak. Then swing to the second-angled target (eyes first, of course) smoothly, but quickly. Shooting must be rapid. Controlled, but rapid. You will likely need to use the "flash shooting" method. See Fig. 91.

268. When I slow down to practice, targets escape me. How can I slow down my shooting and retain accuracy?
Slowing down the target (decreasing distance thrown) is not an exercise of hitting the targets as much as it is to "smooth out" your swing with eye-switching and lock-on ability. Once you get your set up down and practice getting smooth in swing and eye-flow, then you will understand the reason for slowing down the targets. When you return to normal fast targets you'll still be smooth and shoot with increased precision. Don't shoot for score when practicing. Use practice to polish the mechanics; stance, eye & gun hold points, eye focus and swing. When you concentrate and perfect the set up, scores rise automatically.

269. Must I employ the V-dip method if I shoot the right targets first? How do I find the sweet spot to shoot the targets?
No, but crossover is extreme. It will be to your advantage to employ a smidgen of muzzle-dip to catch the flight line for a reliable followthrough shot. If your set up is correct, crossover is not a problem in DT, usually, for the advanced shooter. When you first learn DT you tend to track the targets, but a day arrives when you must begin to shoot quicker. Using the same set up as you started with will not work. Things must be changed, so the eye and gun are essentially placed into position to ambush the targets. When performed properly, you will be crossing over to shoot the targets. There is a small window of opportunity to do this and still obtain followthrough shots, but the set up must be precise. Swing speed must be quick, yet controlled. To find this sweet spot, stand on post, place a ruler at arm's length, horizontally. Now look to see where both targets can be shot with ease on this horizontal line. It's usually at the ½ to ¾ of the target's rising flight, before it peaks.

270. When should the muzzle dip and by how much?
The moment your eye switches to the second target the muzzle should be dipped and ready to ride the track of the second target. The eyes must switch first and lock onto the target. You can dip the muzzle at any point after the eyes lock-on, but the sooner you can do so, the better. Don't look to see if the muzzle is dipping. Rely on feel. Peripheral vision will tell you as the muzzle approaches the target if you got it right or not. It does not take much of a dip. A quarter inch to one-half inch can get the job done. Excessive muzzle-dipping is not recommended. Letting the gun fall after recoil can give you the V-dip required.

271. I tend to miss the straight target more often. Why?
Rifling; looking tightly along the rib as you would shoot a rifle -- trying to line up the sights to the target is a major error for many shooters taking the straight target. The shooter tends to take eye focus off the target and look back at the gun's sight bead, but when this is performed, the muzzle freezes or drags and the target slips away. The gun must be moving to hit a moving target. This is why it is recommended in the set up to drop the gun hold a bit so you can vertically swing the gun up into the straight target. This prevents rifling and allows for a followthrough shot. Another major error is not holding the gun above the trap where the target will exit. This will create rushing, as the target will exit off line with the muzzle and you'll tend to chase it.

272. I miss the angled target more. Why?
Most of the time it will be from pushing the muzzle to the target instead of swinging. And more often than not, swinging the gun to the target without following its flight path (off line crossing over). Improper stance will always create a swing that will be off the target's line of flight. Adjust your stance, so when you swing the gun it will follow the flight line. The eyes must be trained to switch quickly to the second angled target and lock-on before the gun swings away from the first target. If you don't learn this, you will have trouble with the second target. There is more to it, but if you review the illustrations in this book, you will find the solution to your specific problem. You should also consider taking shooting lessons as it will save you tons of grief.

273. What is most important in shooting doubles?
Once you have your set up is established and you have developed your technique, you will find two items that must always be infused into the game. 1) Concentration -- you must be vigilant to pay attention and be ready to execute the shot. Let nothing distract you. Remain focused. 2) Rhythm -- doubles requires a special timing (speed) each shooter must develop. Keeping this rhythm allows you to shoot the targets with speed and consistency. See question 275 and 276.

274. I shoot with one-eye. Any tips I can use?
Hold the gun low, not high over the house. If you are shooting from a trench with markers, hold the gun on the trap marker and raise your eye hold point. If you shoot from a traphouse with no markers, hold your gun so the sight bead is resting on the lid of the house and raise your eye hold. One-eyed shooters tend to jerk the eye more than two-eyed shooters when flowing from one target to another, so practice smoothing your eye movement. One advantage you do have is one-eyed shooters do tend to lock-on to targets faster, but there is one thing to be aware of here. The eye focus can easily slip off the target if you delay or try to ride the target, so timing is important for you get under control, especially on the second target. Remember, the first target sets the timing.

275. Others tell me I must use a full choke on doubles. Is this true?
No. You are still standing at the sixteen-yard line close to the targets. There is no need for a full-choke for doubles. In fact, a good combination to use when learning is; **First shot**: modified (½) choke. **Second shot**: improved modified 5/8 improved modified or ¾ light-full at most. Some top-gun Olympic shooters even use a cylinder choke for the first shot! **Shot size**: You can never go wrong with 7 ½ size shot on both barrels, but you can use #8 shot with great success. If you wish to use two shot sizes, I would recommend #8 for the first shot and 7 ½ on the second shot. Basically, you will receive lots of advice in trapshooting, but your best bet is to verify the advice with actual performance, related to score improvement over a period of time. What works for others may not work for you or be compatible for your gun. **Note:** choke and shot size are only helpers, not solutions. Accuracy is of greater value.

276. I shoot with both eyes. Any tips to share?
You have heard the term "looking through the gun." Set up your first shot gun hold high above the house, where you wish to break the target. Looking through the gun, call for the target. When the target exits, it should rise under and through the gun right where you are looking. When you see the target rise past the muzzle you can shoot it with reliability. Two-eyed shooters have extra peripheral vision and can see both targets exit the house simultaneously. You should learn to train your eyes to focus on the first target, yet still be able to see the second target in peripheral vision to judge its whereabouts. This will give you an advantage, as you already know where the second target is. This makes your ability to switch over the eyes and swing to it much quicker. What you are looking for in peripheral vision is not so much distance, but elevation. Is the target high or is it low? Once you know this, it makes the job of acquiring the second target way easier.

277. I understand rhythm, but I lose it and start missing targets. Why?
Concentration can fail if you are too intense all of the time, so make sure you use the sine-wave relaxation method so your mind will find rest. Simply meaning; to shut down mental activity when you are not shooting and build it up when it is your turn to shoot. Assuming you already know this, be aware that rhythm timing in double trap has nothing to do with squad timing, so get that out of your mind. Rhythm does not have a relationship with the second target, it is with the first target! This is important to understand. The clock starts ticking the moment you fire the gun at the first target. If you begin your internal time clock at any other moment in time, rhythm will be lost and the second target is dropped.

278. Explain rhythm timing for singles and double trap. I get confused.
In single target trap, the timing is based on a count of 1, 2, 3. The clock begins on #1 when you call for the target. As you count to #2, the gun is moving to the target on the swing. On #3 the trigger is pulled. With double trap the count is 1, 2. When you pull the trigger on target #1 the clock starts to count-1. The swing transition has no count. It's supposed to happen quickly, so we don't count it. Count #2 is when you pull the trigger on the second target. It's a fast, 1, 2, count. Maintain these timing reminders in your mind and you will see an improvement in your shooting.

279. How do I break the first target quickly, without rushing?
Good question! Read question 269, again. Be absolutely ready when you call for the target. What does this mean? It means have your gun in proper position and your eyes focused ready to see the target exit, and be energized with an element of aggression to attack the first target without wavering or delay. When you are set up properly, the target is easier to hit. If you are having trouble with the first or second target, the set up is wrong. Don't be lazy, you must work hard and be aggressive to break targets. Negative thoughts, too, must be shoved aside and replaced with thoughts of confidence. Find the power within you and use it to break targets. Eye hold is powerful. As you raise the eye hold, the targets will appear to slow down. That's the best way to reduce rushing!

280. How do I break the second target quickly, without rushing?
Read question 267, 268, 270 and 271. You may be shooting too fast, so it's time to slow down and relax more. Learn to be mentally aggressive, but not to allow aggression to create tension in your muscles. Nervous system must be controlled. If you experience nervousness, you have to convince yourself you are "too busy to be nervous" so you can perform at your best. You will also find yourself rushing the shot if your eye is not locking-on to the target! Seeing the target is not looking at the target. Looking is more focused. The target appears brighter than normal and slower in movement due to the tunnel vision effect. Eye training will prevent chasing targets, which creates rushing. If your set up for the first target is wrong, you will be rushing the second target for sure. If you delay in shooting the first target? Rhythm timing is off. The second target will be escaping and you'll panic to catch it.

281. Which target should be taken first when not shooting the straightaway target first on each peg?
The answer depends on the shoulder you shoot on. If you are a left-shouldered shooter, you would shoot the right bird first on all posts, as this move is the most easiest to execute. If right-shouldered, shoot the left target on all posts first. Keep in mind on post #1 and #2, if you are left-shouldered, you will be shooting the straight target first (right target) and on post #4 & #5 you will shoot the angled-target first. If right-shouldered, the reverse sequence. The point here is in keeping your swing movements consistently matched to your timing, so there is no switching-over on target selection from post-to-post, as it would be with shooting the straight-away target first on each post. That is the prime focus of using this technique. It allows consistency of swing and eye motion. Nothing has to be changed. From post-to-post all targets are shot in the same sequenced order.

282. I don't see a straight target in double trap. Both targets are exiting the trap at an angle.
This is because you are standing off the trap line and/or observing from a distance. When you step on line, such as in the ATA arrangement that has a symmetrical curvature from post to post, you will see the straight target. On peg #3 there will be two angle targets. However, in advanced DT shooting with proper eye and gun hold, eye focus, set up strategy, swing attack angle and zone, you can shoot the targets and never see an angle. All the targets will appear as traveling in straight horizontal lines. Amazing, but true! It's your job to find this phenomenon. If you practice the tips in this book you will experience it. A future edition will cover more advanced DT shooting technique. See Fig. 33.

283. I rarely miss the first straightaway target. When I do, it's a mystery. What is causing this?
It could be a hole in the pattern and the best way to combat this is to not spot shoot the target, as this gives maximum advantage to the hole as the shotstring is not rising. Employing a vertical swing to the target the hole is destroyed. It is very hard for a hole to exist if both the shotstring is bending in flight instead of traveling in a straight line column. But holes are rare to cause missing at close range. Use heavy shot, 7 ½ on hard targets with maximum legal dram charge to break the target. Most often, it's shooter error. If the target is rising, you'll likely hit it, but if it's dropping you could miss, as vision is obstructed when the target dips below

the barrel and this will always cause head-lift. Try holding a lower gun. This will resolve both problems of pattern holes and head-lift. One more tip. Is your call volume so loud it is causing your eyes to defocus, flicker, blink? See Fig. 10.

284. Double-targets, for me, are too fast to catch them. What can I do?
Slowmotion mode shooting is a real phenomena and you need to learn how to do it. It's all explained in the book, *Trap Shooting Secrets*. Basically, lowering your gun hold, raising your eye hold and focusing strongly in a tunnel vision effect will initiate the slowmotion mode. The mind has the power to see things in slow motion; to stretch time and slow down the targets.

285. I keep shooting under the straightaway targets like a bad habit.
Raise your POI. You may also have excessive cheek pressure on the comb. Your timing may be off or you have a slow lock-time on the trigger. Or you eye is slipping off the target!

Tip: If you miss targets, you are seeing something you are not supposed to be seeing. Find out what it is and correct it.

286. I miss the angled-targets by shooting over the top. Why?
Swing dynamics is off. Look into your stance foot position to insure you are not winding up slightly on the swing that can cause the muzzle to rise. Lower you POI or stop head-lifting by feeling proper cheek pressure on the comb. You could even have a micro-flinch causing the muzzle to rise the moment you pull the trigger. Try placing a bandage on the trigger finger to reduce sensitivity so you will not be "squeezing off" the shot.

287. I close my eyes when I pull the trigger. How can I stop doing this?
A sound-activated nervous reaction flinch. You have to train your eyes to stay open, so use this very simple method. Go to a mailing supply store and buy large bubble-packing wrapping (½" size is the largest). Squeeze and pop them as you stare at an object to discover if you are blinking. When you get it under control, pop the bubblewrap a bit closer to your ear (but don't damage your hearing, of course being too close). This simple fix works. If it doesn't? Try using higher-rated decibel-blocking hearing protection to reduce noise that triggers this flinch. If when firing the gun you still blink? You have a physical shock recoil-flinch problem, so reduce the recoil. Have your gun fitted.

288. How important is setting point of impact when shooting doubles?
More important than shooting single targets! Since you are in effect spot shooting in doubles on the first target, the POI must be set high on the first straightaway target and flatter (lower) for the second-angled target. But don't forget, you can shoot one POI on both targets, it's not impossible. The point here is to adjust your POI so you can smokeball both targets. Whatever that setting may be, will be just fine, if it works, simply adjust your timing. If you are quick to shoot both targets? The POI can be the same, but you will always have an edge if you use an O&U with the first shot set for a higher POI, as the first target will always be rising faster than the second when you are shooting it.

289. What is the number one cause of missing doubles targets?
These three, equals one. Improper stance, timing rhythm and doubt.

290. Can you recommend a doubles gun I should buy?
1) See what brand the pros are using and make this your first consideration. 2) Once the brand is identified, find out if the gun compliments your frame. It's not too heavy or too light, too long or short. 3) Test the gun to insure it shoots straight, feels good and the price is right. It is always best to have the gun fitted. Ask pros what gun may be best for you. When the same recommendation keeps surfacing, it will get you close to the brand that's right for you. A professional gun fitter will nail it down.

291. Why do shooters tend to shoot poor scores in doubles?
It's the practice factor. Most shooters practice more shooting ATA single-target, DTL or Olympic trap. A little bit more practice would do wonders for the shooter. If you do practice on a practice trap, make certain target angles and speed are set exactly to the competition rules, otherwise it is counterproductive.

292. Can I shoot a 1 oz. load in doubles?
You can shoot any load, as long as it is at or below the maximum standard in the rules book. At 16-yards a 1 oz. load will work just fine, but you are still giving up many pellets that could be present to break the target. I recommend you shoot the maximum legal load in competition so you are on equal ground with your competitors. A professional shooter can reduce the load and still score extremely high because they are precision shooters. The average shooter should not copy this approach until they become more

precise in aim. If recoil and flinching is a problem, you may need a recoil reducer and perhaps the 1 oz. load. The 1 oz. load is generally faster and you may find this load to be better for your scores. Try them and see how it goes.

293. Can you give me a practice tip I can use this weekend?
Practice shooting a few rounds of doubles two-yards back from normal, at the 18-yard line or even the 20. Use an extra-full choke, too. Then, when you return to the 16-yard line with your normal chokes, you should see an improvement in your scores. This applies to all trap disciplines. A good eye hold focal point to try is focusing your eyes at the distant end of the clay target field. See if this helps you see the targets clearly. If so, then adjust your gun hold point so the target and gun meet with ease. I strongly suggest experimenting with eye and gun hold points and then chart the points on paper for each station that works best.

294. Which post is the best to start with?
If I tell you, nobody will shoot the other posts! Peg #3 is the best, #2 and #4 rank second place. Of #1 and #5, #1 is most certainly the most difficult, especially for a left-handed shooter. This applies to all trap disciplines. The target angles are mild on post #3 and this allows you to warm up the eyes and swing. Squad leading post #1 is the most trying of all. If you are accustomed to shooting other posts when starting, and you start on peg #1, you will see your score drop. It's much harder for another reason; the squad leader must also deal with disruptions, make judgement calls and set the rhythm of the squad. Shooting post #1 requires another learning curve and will take some time to master it.

295. Can I use my doubles gun for shooting single targets?
Yes. In Europe the double gun is Queen, whereas in the USA the single-barrel gun is King. If you use the O&U for single target games here's the formula. 1) For 16 to 20 yards use the lower barrel, as it has a higher POI. 2) For distances beyond, use the upper barrel, as it shoots flatter. This rule is not chiseled in stone, but it's valid.

296. Must I have natural talent to shoot doubles?
Nobody is born with a clay spoon. You can learn with practice and instruction. The shooter you see fumbling on the line today missing targets by the dozen may be the next generation's professional shooter! Ask any pro and they will tell you how poorly they shot in the beginning. If you are determined, willing to listen to professional advice and study the game, there will be no stopping you!

297. Must I use the sight beads in double trap?
You should learn to backsight the beads so you can obtain a precise bird/bead relationship when pulling the trigger. Some professional double trap shooters remove the beads and use the muzzle for the alignment. Being so close to the trap you can get away with a bit of pointing in the routine, but such is not the case with other disciplines where the targets are more distant and travelling much faster.

298. Sometimes I shoot behind the target like a habit. What can I do to stop this?
Daro Handy mentioned a secret of trapshooting for this problem, *"Remind yourself to get to the target before the gun goes off."* This is the solution for those who are pulling the trigger when the sight picture is not correct. We tend to fall into a "timing rut" pulling the trigger when we feel it should be pulled. This is okay, as it is the internal time clock within the mind telling you to shoot, but your body moves must be accelerated to be in phase with the time clock.

299. I'm serious about shooting well in doubles. Any advice to improve my scores?
Returning to the theme; ask the pros! The best advice for the money is simply asking the right questions from professional shooters. Also, if you can locate an Olympic-class shooter ask them a ton of questions, as they are really top-guns in the world facing horrific competition and they have professional ongoing coaching and instruction. Ask for our new book, *"Interviews With The Olympic Champions - Target Shooting."* Any bookstore can order one. Give them this ISBN Number: 0-916367-14-2. Our SAN Number (publisher's address locator) is: 295-852X. When published, the book may be purchased from the major clay target shooting magazines. E-mail or postal mail us and we will notify you where you can purchase the book. The advice in this book is simply too valuable to pass up! The target publishing date is 2001.

300. I keep seeing comet tails on the targets and I miss them. How can I stop missing?
Your eye is focused too low and close to the trap -- and much too low along the rib of the gun. Simply raise your eye hold so there is vertical eye/rib separation. See *Trapshooting Secrets* book Fig. 71. You should also try to focus your eyes further out into the trapfield so you will see the target more clearly. The comet tail can not be totally eliminated if your eyes are set low. You want to see the target rise out of the house with peripheral vision and allow the target to enter the focal point where your eye hold is placed. This way you will see a clear target and not miss. Keep raising your eye hold until you see no comet tails. See Fig. 35.

301. Terrible inconsistencies have risen into my doubles game. Why?
Some days we can't hit anything, so it's not a problem unless it lasts more than a few days, then it's a problem. Make sure nothing has changed with the gun. If the comb slipped, dent in barrel or loose choke, bad batch of ammo, worn shoes or shooting vest, etc. Check the little things first, then proceed to examine each phase of your set up to see if anything has changed; stance, hold points, timing, swing speed, etc. If still nothing here can be found, then examine your eyes for prescription glasses. Still nothing found wrong? Make sure when you swing the gun you are in fact, swinging -- even on the straight targets! There must be a tiny swing to the straight target and you do this by holding a lower gun hold so you are not 100% spot-shooting the target. Same with the angle targets, make sure you are not pushing the muzzle. Still nothing? It's a mini-slump. Start thinking positive again. See a coach.

302. What is the difference between flash and spot shooting?
Flash is shooting when you see the target *flash* by the barrel. Spot shooting is predetermining a hold point and ambushing the target as it passes the barrel. Essentially, they are identical -- except spot shooting requires a higher gun hold so no "flash" or "comet tail blur" is seen. Flash shooting is holding a low gun close to the trap. The best technique is still the followthrough shot, where you allow the target to rise above the muzzle and lift the gun with a tiny swing motion into the target. Spot shooting does work, too. Flash shooting is tougher to master and quite hard on the eyes and nervous system due to its lightening speed.

303. Why do I shoot doubles poorly at some gun clubs?
Big question! Here's a few reasons; 1) You may be relying on background scenes to set up your first spot-shot and the background at certain clubs is not accommodating this. 2) Trap angle is set too high or low or totally improperly set, or targets thrown are too fast or too slow, or very little face is showing on the target. Traps are not facing north and glare or poor lighting creates a problem, including optical illusion effect due to lighting and background. Every club has its own challenges to overcome. Some clubs are just too hard to score high with. The foremost rule you can use to help weed out these problems is to begin shooting with a slightly lower gun hold, so you can see what the targets are doing.

304. How can I practice double-target shooting at home?
Install snap-caps in your unloaded gun. Post two clay or simulated paper targets to a wall and practice swinging the gun to the targets. See Fig. 97, 98, 113, 114, 115 on how to do this. You can use a calendar to control trigger flinching and muzzle freeze problems. See Fig. 116. In fact, the calendar practice session is quite a powerful device despite its simplicity. At about ten feet away, hold a low gun below the calendar, call for the target. Your eyes should then randomly pick a date. Swing the gun to that number slowly and smoothly and shoot the number. Notice what happens when you pull the trigger. Does the barrel stop, shake, drift, flip? Are you experiencing a small trigger-flinch? Can you see the backsighting effect? The more you practice with the calendar the more precise of a shooter you will be, as it develops a fine sight picture and control of the gun and trigger.

305. I shoot DTL, Universal Trench and OT. Why is Double Rise so much harder for me?
Down the Line and Olympic Trap are totally different to Double Rise targets. In DTL, UT and OT you are taking two shots at one target, whereas in double trap, you have two shots, but each shot for targets traveling in variant directions! Also, your DTL or OT gun may not be set up for DT regarding choke size and point of impact and this will make DT much harder to master. Plus, you have to alter your set up and timing for the DT game. If you shoot with the same stance, same ammo, same everything as you do with DTL and OT, targets will slip by. This advice applies to ATA shooters. Read all of these questions and answers, including the reviews on the illustrations for DT shooting advice. *Trap Shooting Secrets* and *Precision Shooting* has detailed "technical shooting tips and illustrations" for double rise target shooting.

306. Any advice for shooting doubles in the wind?
Your stance and footing should be firm to anchor yourself to minimize wind pushing you around. The gun's grip on the forearm should be soft and the grip on the stock tight; to prevent muscles from tightening, as the wind tends to push the muzzle. Shoot the first target as quickly as you can, without recklessly rushing. Fast, but not too fast! Use peripheral vision to judge where the targets are going. In the wind, the second target will be the most troublesome, due to distance gained and speed reduction. This will allow the target to be buffeted by the wind to jink, drift, tilt, rise or fall. Wear blinders. This keeps wind out of the eyes to reduce watering that will blur vision. Wind-shooting often forces shooters to shoot too quickly, and when they do this, muscles tighten and the gun's smooth swing is abandoned. When this occurs, rhythm is lost and so are the targets.

307. Any gun modifications you recommend for double ttrap?
Barrel porting greatly reduces muzzle flip, so you can shoot the first target and get onto the second with less swing correction. However, check the rules book for the discipline in your country, as porting is not allowed in some regulation rule books. In ATA-DT, porting is allowed. Your gun should fit, so it will mount and shoot where you look. You may want to use a glow-sight to help

you get onto the targets quicker (see EasyHit ad in this book). Adjust point of impact to match the requirements of the game and your timing. Heavy mercury recoil-reducing devices can slow down the gun's swing, so you may want to remove it. Adjust your forearm grip closer-in towards you, so the gun will swing faster. You don't need barrels any longer than 30-32 inches in length for DT. A release-pull trigger would be a fine modification, but it's not for everyone.

308.   How do I raise eye hold and not remove my eye from the rib?
Easy. See Fig. 50. When you shoulder the gun your eye should be centered down the rib as in "A." This is accomplished by having a properly fitted gun and a precise gun mounting set up. Now, just look up, without moving your cheek away from the comb. You can look anywhere you want as long as the eye is locked to the rib from cheek pressure. Looking up or down is okay, but shifting the eye left or right to the sides of the gun can create problems. Use peripheral vision when you need to see side objects.

309.   My eyes get tired and I drop targets like mad. Help!
Close your eyes for a moment when you are reloading. This is also a good time to visualize breaking the targets. Use eye drops 30-minutes prior to shooting.

310.   I tend to flinch much more often when shooting DT. Why?
You are getting nervous and tense, rushing your shots. This will happen when your set up is not right. If your eye and gun hold points are off mark, you'll be tracking the first target instead of ambushing it. This allows the second target to escape and you rush to hit that one, too. Set up is critical. Adjust eye focus and raise eye hold to induce slow motion effect.

311.   Explain what a high or low gun hold will do?
On DT targets taking the straight-target-first method; a gun hold that is too low will force the shooter to ride too long on the first target and be late to catch the second target. A gun hold that is too high will cause the shooter to see the first target too late, and create a severe late crossover situation. In fact, so severe, an over-swing will occur where you will shoot over the top of the second target. The trick is to find that sweet spot where the first target rises up under the barrel, so you can spot shoot it, then swing over to hit the second-angled target with a straight-line swing with hardly no vertical correction. If done right, the shot will be a follow-through shot, even though crossover is taking place -- the set up and timing matches the target flight path perfectly!

312.   What will a high or low eye hold do?
Taking the straightaway-target-first method; a low eye hold that is too low creates streaking comet tails and this causes the eyes to flicker or defocus. Obviously, a flickering eye is a searching eye and has not yet locked-on to the target, and may never do so to any degree. You want the target to meet the eye, not the eye searching for the target. If the eye hold is too high, you lose the angle of interception. The target to barrel relationship must be close, not distant. So it is with the eye. The target should rise under the barrel and very close in the zone (exactly where you are looking) to shoot the target. If the eye hold is too high, you'll lose this angle of attack, along with time, as you'll see the target too late. If the eye hold and gun hold are not synchronized in harmony with each other you can't shoot DT targets with precise speed. Find the eye and gun hold points on each post and you'll be amazed at how well you will be shooting!

313.   What is your opinion of mixing shells when shooting?
It's okay if you can adapt to the potential of inserting the wrong shell in the wrong barrel. Doing this can really mess up your concentration. I believe it is best to use the same shells in both barrels, but using, say for example; a 1 oz. #8 ½ shot with 2 ¾-dram charge for the first shot, and a # 7 ½ 3-dram load for the second shot has benefits. The first shot has more pellets, less recoil muzzle flip, and can get you to the second target quicker. The second shot is fast and hits hard. I suggest to practice using the shell combination in reverse once in awhile, so when the day comes you do accidentally insert the wrong shell in the wrong barrel you will still be able to remain confident to hit the targets.

314.   Exactly how does the eye slip off of the target?
Our eyes do not like being focused on any object for extended periods of time. Tracking a target too long will cause the eye to slip off the target, if you have not practiced eye exercises to keep the eye locked-on the target. If the eye loses focus, it will freeze the eyeball, allowing the target to slip away. Practice eye prefocus and locking-on to the target so you can shoot it quickly. Eye prefocus, eye hold, and gun hold. All three help you to get to the target faster and with increased precision. When used, the eye will not slip off the target, unless fatigue develops.

315.   How should I practice spot-shooting the first target?
See questions 229 and 269 for using a ruler to locate ideal target break points. Once you discover the zone and target angle with the ruler, then modify your eye and gun hold points, along with eye focus in your practice routine, to determine the quickest and easiest

arrangement to dispatch the targets. You will find a specific gun and eye hold point that just makes the job much more efficient and easier. When you find it, write it down on a grid chart, so you can refer to it again on your next practice round. In doubles you have to set up the first shot so you can easily hit the second target, so you can't just learn to spot shoot the first target alone. Think in terms of duality when shooting double rise targets. Two targets are one. One technique breaks both targets, perfectly.

VETERAN'S TIP
"To see clearly, disturb muddy waters."

Age comes to all and when it does, everything slows down; eye motion control and body movement reaction time is affected. Many veteran shooters fail to score high because they have never truly learned the technical aspects of the game. They have shot for years from experience, but now this experience they have learned so well over a lifetime, fails them. They can't seem to get to the target like they used to. They often blame their eyes as the culprit, but this is not the prime reason why they are missing targets. They are shooting too fast, pure and simple! Go ahead and watch them shoot from the 27-yard line and you will see they are trying to break targets in the same zone as the young guns. They are shooting their own ingrained "habit" they have developed over the years with a simple zone adjustment they can not only see the targets better, they can now score up wins. Zone adjustments are explained in this book. POI adjustments are also to be employed, but are very easy to make in these situations. Set the POI flatter and begin to learn how to shoot the apex of the targets. It's a lot better than posting the scores you do now! Everything slows down. Sure, in bad weather you won't score well, but at least you know that going into the shoot. In good weather you'll be taking trophies and options. Nothing wrong with that! As age increases, adaptations must be made. Give and take becomes a way of life for the veteran clay target shotgun shooter. You can't shoot like you used to because you have changed. So it is, you must change to adapt to these changes. If you don't change, you will continue to lose and lose and lose against the younger shooters.

RECOMMENDED READING
"Knowledge is the key to success."

Here's a listing of trapshooting books. To order, contact *Shotgun Sports Magazine*; Shootin' Accessories, Ltd. P.O. Box 6810, Auburn, CA 95604 (800)-676-8920. E-mail: shotgun@shotgunsportsmagazine.com Web site: http://www.shotgunsportsmagazine.com Fax: (916)889-9106. Outside the USA call (916)-889-2220.
"Trap Shooting Secrets" - Learn the inside secrets professionals use to break high scores.
"Trapshooting is a Game of Opposites" - Help to improve scores.
"The Clay Target Handbook" - Explores trap, skeet and International trap shooting.
"Insight to Sports" - Featuring Trap - Help to improve scores.
"Gun Digest Book of Trap & Skeet Shooting" Help to improve scores.
"Mental Training for the Shotgun Sports" - Learn concentration and improve scores.
"Finding the Extra Target" - Help to improve scores.
"The Little Trapshooting Book" - Help to improve scores.
Many books are listed on our web site and in the pages of *Shotgun Sports* and *Clay Shooting* magazine. Other magazines such as, *Sporting Clays, PULL, Trap & Field, SKEET* also have excellent books to read. Study this game and you will see your scores rise! See the free trial issue offers in this book.

Before you consider any barrel work, read Tom Roster's *"Shotgun Barrel Alteration Manual."* You can order from: Tom Roster, 1190 Lynnewood Blvd., Klamath Falls, OR 97601. It costs approx. only $13 delivered. The 75 page book covers useful vs. useless alterations and subjects involving chamber and forcing cone lengthening, backboring, polishing, porting, choke work, screw-in chokes, barrel length considerations, choke dimensions and configurations for best patterns with all shot types. What a trapshooter needs to know!

CHAPTER 13

"Until we see the 13th floor in high-rise buildings and elevators stop... we'll just skip to 14."

CHAPTER 14

DOUBLE-RISE DOUBLE TRAP TIPS
"What you believe will be."

DOUBLE TRAP - FLASH SHOOTING
Shooting the flash. Have you heard of this before? This is simply setting up your gun's muzzle at a predetermined point over the traphouse, setting up for the straightaway target (customarily the first target shot per post). Once you set up, hunker down to the comb, call, and the moment you see the "flash" of the target pass the barrel, pull the trigger and switch your eyes to the second target. Some shooters prefer to shoot the moment they see the "blur" of the target exit the trap. Both work but it depends on your gun's point of impact along with your nervous system reaction time as to which technique is better.

DOUBLE TRAP - SPOTTING THE FIRST TARGET
You have heard to set up for target #1 straightaway to locate a distant object and hold the gun at that point and wait for the target to reach this area. There are two problems with this. 1) The background scenery can change from trap to trap, and club-to-club, so it is unreliable. 2) Using this method is often too slow and too late. If you are looking straight out into the trap field, the target will have to rise, and you'll have to wait for it to rise too high before you shoot it. This allows target #2 to speed away into eternity. Sure, it works; you'll hit target #1 but you'll keep hit 'n' missing on target #2. A better way is to know your traps! Know where the target is exiting the trap and hold on imaginary points relative to the trap (use the traphouse markers if they exist). This way you can hold the gun a tad lower and maintain consistency from trap to trap, club to club.

DOUBLE TRAP - POI
The pro trapshooter knows how important point of impact is and more so with doubles. If you are shooting an autoloader at double targets you are at a disadvantage, because you only have one POI. The Over & Under gun has the advantage of the bottom barrel, shooting a high POI to grab the fast rising #1 target, and the lower POI on the upper barrel shoots flatter to hit the shallow flight angle of the #2 target. Is your doubles gun shooting properly? It must comply with the above barrel setting pertaining to POI. Pattern check to insure the lower barrel is higher in POI than the upper barrel. Are you shooting your first shot with the lower barrel?

DOUBLE TRAP - REACTING TO THE TARGET
You have to be aggressive and a bit reckless on the first target if you want to hit the second target! This does not mean precision is lost, it means you have to wallop that first target with internal and external aggression. Get your eyes off of that target as soon as you pull the trigger and onto the second target. But remember this tip; when you pull the trigger on target #1, your "eyes" shift, not your body, arm or the gun. You *freeze* for a millisecond. Nothing moves until your eye has locked on to target #2. Then your body will allow a smooth move to that target. If this micro-delay and eye control is not established, double trap shooters will "react" with jerky motions and end up stab-shooting, hoping to hit the targets, but many will be missed. By the way in the

USA we call shooting doubles simply "doubles" but the true term is "double rise." In the Olympic arena it is called "double trap." In England it is called "double rise."

DOUBLE TRAP - TARGET SELECTION

Did you know shooting the straightaway target first could be the reason why you are not winning double-trap events? ATA and Olympic double-trap is difficult for most shooters. Double the trouble, twice the fun! The late Frank Little, ATA Hall of Fame shooter, mentioned shooting each straight target first is not mandatory. Richard Faulds, Olympic Gold-medallist champion, shoots the right target first on each post (left-handed shooter). Just because most shooters you see are shooting the straightaway target first does not mean it is right for you to do! If you have been shooting DT for years and not winning, then it's time to consider switching to a new form and style. Yes, scores will drop drastically as you learn the new technique, but it's sure worth a try. After all, what do you have to lose? The theory of shooting the angled target first results in non-confusion. Each post is shot the same way so you don't have to think about switching-over when you get to post #4 and #5. Also, the angled target is the most difficult to hit, so get this one quickly out of the way, while you can. The straightaway target is not going anywhere but in a straight line, so you have plenty of time to shoot this second target without rushing the shot! It is also a much more relaxed method to use than shooting the straight target first, then having to hurry up to catch the second-angled target. Veteran shooters who are experiencing slower reaction time can benefit from this technique, if they are willing to learn it. Both methods work! Try shooting the right or left target first on each post and remember to "slow down" your swing-over to the second straightaway target. That's the key, slow down so you don't over-swing! Then, simply follow up on the second target's flight line. Your new swing dynamic will take on an "L" shape movement, if you do it slowly. Once you become a bit more comfortable with the technique, you will naturally speed up your shooting and the swing will take on a more "horizontal" swing-over, just as in shooting the straight-target-first method. Learning a new form is never easy, but you may discover shooting some angled targets first may give you better results. It may not work for you, but at least you'll know and you tried your best. It may just work, too!

DOUBLE TRAP - GUN HOLD

When shooting double targets, set up the first shot (normally the straightaway target) with a slightly lower gun hold over the traphouse than you normally do. See Fig. 42 through 44, 87, 107 and 108. This will allow you to get on that target sooner. At the same time, lift your eye hold a bit higher than normal, not low down along the sight plane of the gun. This will create an anti-streak zone, so as not to cause "eye flicker" from seeing a target streaking a blurred comet tail. Experiment with this subtle, yet efficient method, to capture the first target sooner. The faster you catch the first target, the less hurried you will be to catch the second target and create an ease of smoothness into the swing. Learn to control your eye movement to the target, as eye-flickering and jittering is a major cause of missing targets -- a fine method to pull the trigger at the wrong time!

DOUBLE TRAP - EYE SWITCHING

Don't wait to see if you hit the first target. Forget about it. Go for the second target the moment you pull the trigger. If you miss the first target by watching to see if you did miss, it will never bring it back and only allows the second target to escape your zone. You have to discipline yourself to do this at practice. Here's another tip: When making the transition from target #1 to target #2, learn to switch the eyes without moving the gun. Don't move the body, just the eyes. When the eyes lock-on to target #2, your body should then move to the target. Why? The eye is faster than the hand. Watch a pro shoot and you will see the gun fires at target #1, then s/he freezes, then moves. They are switching the eyes. It happens fast, but now you know one secret of getting on that second target quickly. If your eye is locked-on to a target, the body will move to it like magic, at least on the 16-yard line where you are close to the targets, such as in double trap.

EASY HIT GUN SIGHT
One of the best training aids for double trap (including single barrel targets) is the EasyHit gun sight. You can order one from our web site or from the order form herein. You will be amazed at how powerful this device can be to shooting targets. There are literally dozens of benefits; establishing gun and eye hold points, sight picture development, solves eye dominance crossover problems, trigger control, seeing the target angle clearly, etc. It's almost like cheating, that's how good the sight bead really is! It's hard to miss a target with the laser-like tiny-size dot you place on the target. If you have not tried the EasyHit shotgun sight, you certainly should as it will help you solve so many shooting problems and shoot way better scores.

VISIT OUR WEB SITE
Just type in any of these key words in the search engine; James Russell Publishing, James Russell Publishing, Shotgun, *Trap Shooting Secrets*, *Precision Shooting*, Trapshooting, Guns, Shotgun Sports. You'll find us on in the links section of many of the gun sites on the web. Our URL at this printing is: www.powernet.net/~scrnplay Web site addresses may change so use the search engines. Many good shooting tips on the site. Come visit us!

WRITING THE AUTHOR
"A friend is a friend for life."

You are always welcome to write to propound how much this book has been of value to you. I read every letter and your suggestions are taken seriously. If you have a question and require a return correspondence, please include a #10 standard business size Self-Addressed Stamped Envelope. Please be patient, as I travel a lot and sometimes my mail can't keep up. Use the mailing address listed on the title page.

WANT TO WRITE A BOOK?
If you have knowledge to share, so others may improve their lives, consider writing a book. *James Russell Publishing* generally publishes how-to books, but we are open to suggestions. Contact us and let us know what you have in mind. Visit our Web site for more details.

LAST CALL
"Great gain often comes through great loss."

Now that you have finished this book, realize that having the knowledge and applying it are two different animals. A little bit of knowledge can be a dangerous thing, and as you apply differing techniques to solve problems, you will experience setbacks just as you would if you took lessons from a shooting coach. Many shooters are not willing to push through the pain, so they resort to their old shooting form to again be stuck in a rut because it *feels* right. Then there are others who will try to improve too quickly, using too many of the techniques and mass confusion develops along with severe prolonged slumps. Patience is required along with a steady increase of knowledge. Forgetting what you have learned is also another puzzle that always surfaces in life and in competition. You can reduce this by "feeling the game." Trapshooting is hard work, so you should feel the pressure. Always be ready to learn and improve. You must have this desire to excel. Trapshooting is doing what you love and doing it well. To this end, good shooting!

CHAPTER 15

ILLUSTRATIONS

"A picture is worth a thousand words."

Illustrations begin on following pages. The illustrations have been compiled, by design, into one section of the book, rather than inserted on individual pages. This makes it easier to locate the drawings, especially when experiencing problems in competition for quick reference to locate solutions.

POOR

Fig. 1

Don't Lean Forward

Very unstable allowing excessive fluidity of motion. Feet are too widely spaced and knee extended gives rise to many pointing errors hard to correct.

Spine and weight shift out of alignment. Imbalance creates inconsistency and chaos.

BETTER

Fig. 2

Don't Crouch

Less flexibility with more control, but spine is still arched forward and crouched downward. This upsets ability to track target flight path with repeatable precision.

Range of motion decreased, yet still way off balance. Excessive flexibility in knees will destablize swing causing missed targets.

BEST

Fig. 3

Stand Up Straight

Low flexibility and correct posture allows enhanced control of the gun in trapshooting.

Spine is straight and true allowing for good balance and precise gun swing dynamics.

FREEZE !

DON'T MOVE THAT GUN !

When you call for the target be absolutely certain the gun muzzle does not move up or down. Vertical or lateral movement upsets the ability to track the target.

The only acceptable moving gun techniques are the barrel roll or forward stab or both as these movements complement body English moves to the target and assist in accelerating and reducing the degree of swing to the target.

Muzzle dipping is a bad habit and it occurs when calling for the target. **Fig. 4**

FORMULATE A PLAN OF ATTACK

Don't just call for the target and hope for the best. Establish a plan to achieve the goal. Know where you plan to break each target on each station. Know the three basic angles each station comprises and prepare for the hardest angle to emerge. Be ready when the target launches. Many lost targets are due to the shooter being taken by surprise. You can reduce this by ensuring your eyes are properly focused or fixated prior to calling, and raising your eye hold from the traphouse. See Fig. 35.

The target is dead or lost long before the trigger is pulled. Know your setup intimately and always expect to hit the target by following a specific plan of action. No great accomplishments are ever made without serious planning with the exception of accidents which does not apply in trapshooting.

Fig. 5

Aim for the center of the bulls-eye not at the bulls-eye itself. Get that sight bead on the target. You can't do it consistently unless you formulate a plan to do so.

Shooting without a plan is like building a home without a blueprint. Plan each shot prior to calling for the target.

Fig. 6 reveals a high trap. The eye will see the target quicker at less distance from the trap. If the trap is set too high, the target often gets the jump on the shooter as it appears very quickly. The comet tail is prolonged so the eye hold should be raised more than shown to maintain proper timing and visual target acquisition Trap settings are important asthey will have a direct relationship to timing and where you plan to break the target. You can tell when a trap is set too high simply... the target appears to be traveling faster than normal leaving the house.

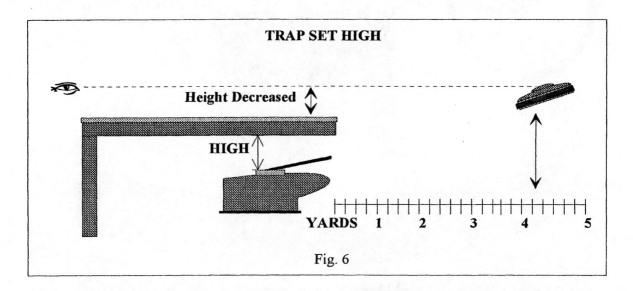

Fig. 6

Fig. 7 reveals a trap set low. The danger is obvious. The target is seen exiting the house at an increased distance. As distance increases so will the target progressively arc or bend along its flight path. You'll need to lower eye hold to maintain timing. You can determine a low trap as the target appears at distance, has less comet tail, and appears to be traveling slower leaving the house... and may appear as a razor blade due to its shallow angle.

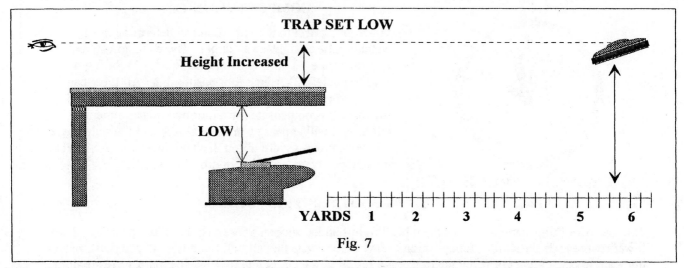

Fig. 7

Rule of thumb: If targets streak a comet tail, raise your eye hold. If small comet tails exist, lower eye hold. By adjusting eye hold you can compensate for some trap setting factors, but most important the shooter's timing is preserved regardless of when the target is first visually acquired Eye hold is arguably the most important factor in trapshooting next to gun fit. He who sees the target best is often the better shooter. Eye hold allows you to see the target and time the shot in the zone. As the eye is raised the zone actually decreases in size. Lowered, it expands. See Fig. 6

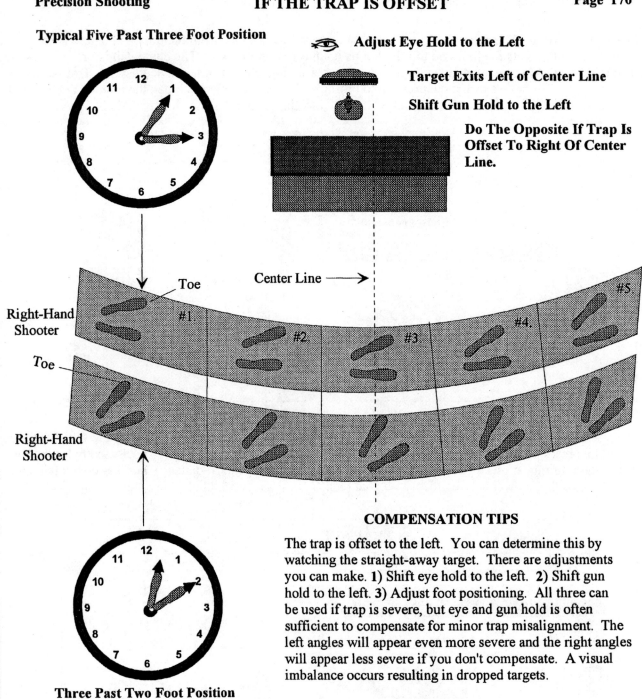

Typical Five Past Three Foot Position

Adjust Eye Hold to the Left

Target Exits Left of Center Line

Shift Gun Hold to the Left

Do The Opposite If Trap Is Offset To Right Of Center Line.

Toe

Center Line →

Right-Hand Shooter

#1. #2. #3 #4. #5

Toe

Right-Hand Shooter

Three Past Two Foot Position

COMPENSATION TIPS

The trap is offset to the left. You can determine this by watching the straight-away target. There are adjustments you can make. **1)** Shift eye hold to the left. **2)** Shift gun hold to the left. **3)** Adjust foot positioning. All three can be used if trap is severe, but eye and gun hold is often sufficient to compensate for minor trap misalignment. The left angles will appear even more severe and the right angles will appear less severe if you don't compensate. A visual imbalance occurs resulting in dropped targets.

ADJUSTING FOOT POSITION / STANCE

The top row of trap stations reveals the typical right-handed shooter's five past three foot position. The lower row reveals the shift of foot position to favor the targets that all will trend left. If you don't make a body angle adjustment you'll run the risk of not reaching the target due to "muscle memory" restriction. The swing will be extended to the left beyond normal and you'll likely not reach the target within your natural timing. Since your zone shifts to the left it is only natural to come into alignment with it so your timing and swing rhythm remains solid. If the trap is offset right, shift to the right. Left-hand shooters simply reverse the foot positioning as shown.

Fig. 8

CONTROL THE GUN

Draw a figure-8. When you do this you'll notice the gun pulls away from your cheek. Don't let it happen. Hug the gun snugly.

Fig. 9

Head-lifting and loss of gun control on swing is a serious problem for many shooters. To resolve the difficulty and insure maximum gun control, trace a "figure 8" pattern with the muzzle. Use your upper torso muscles to make the moves, not pushing with your arm. **Feel** the gun in your arms and all muscles to perform the exercise. Use your cheek to steer the gun in conjunction with your torso. This will keep your head down on the comb where it must stay when shooting. When you can do this, you'll easily keep your head snug when shooting and you'll learn the body English technique of controlling the gun.

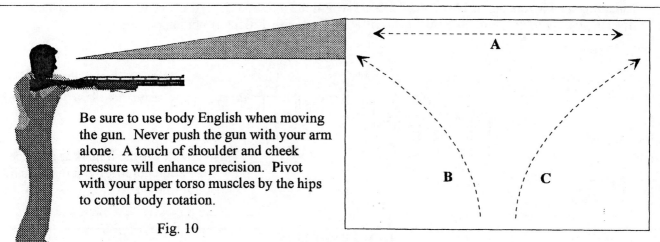

Be sure to use body English when moving the gun. Never push the gun with your arm alone. A touch of shoulder and cheek pressure will enhance precision. Pivot with your upper torso muscles by the hips to contol body rotation.

Fig. 10

To perfect and tighten the swing line, 'A' is the common approach to use, tracing the gun along a flat horizontal line such as a ceiling to wall junction. This is fine for a beginner, but once target visibility becomes obscured from lighting or background conditions the shooter will lift the head from the comb. This will also occur on breezy days as the targets rise or fall. By tracing the gun along curved lines as shown in 'B' and 'C' the shooter is better trained not only to avoid head-lift, but learns advanced gun control methods. It conditions the muscles to flow along a curve which is exactly what the targets are really doing, arcing. With your head snugly locked to the comb you will not easily see this arc due to the narrow field of view, but it still exists. Arcing targets is of less concern to a close-in zone shooter, but should never be dismissed.

1) Use body English. 2) Use cheek pressure to steer the gun. 3) Feel all movements and hug the gun.
4) Be smooth. 5) Keep eye centered along sight rib. 5) Do not let sight beads unstack, overlap or misalign.
6) Never push the gun with your hand or arm alone. 7) Pivot from the upper body torso at the hips.
8) Perform this excersise with your eyes closed to imbed the 'feel' of the swing moves. Practice this often and you'll see a rise in scores.

Applying what you learn on this page alone will increase your scores. Try it and see how hard you'll hit the targets. Force your mind to remind you to keep your head down snug to the comb and feel the cheek pressure.

MIND CONTROL

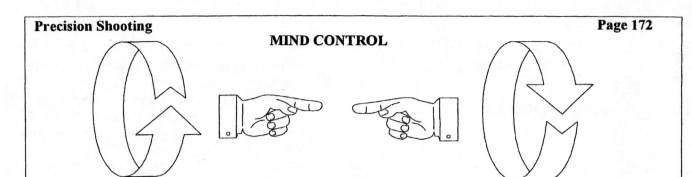

Precision shooting requires total mind control. Here's a simple, yet effect test to determine your current level of concentration. Simply rotate one finger toward you and the other finger away from you. At first it may seem to be a impossible task, but if you keep on trying periodically, you will succeed. Here we are making a communication link with the left and right side of the brain or mind. Shooting requires both will and muscle to communicate and be controlled since the opposite hand is used to swing the gun along with the opposite eye tracking the target including the trigger finger. Opposites are in play and these opposing forces must be mastered to obey the shooter's mental commands. Absolute willpower and desire is useless without control. Precision is a conscious effort to excel with the ability to execute command.

HOW TO DO IT

The trick is to focus your eyes between the tips of your fingers so both are in peripheral vision. Imagine each fingertip is rotating inside of and confined within the race of a ring. It is this visualization that makes the above easy to do. Without visual concentration it is quite difficult if not impossible.

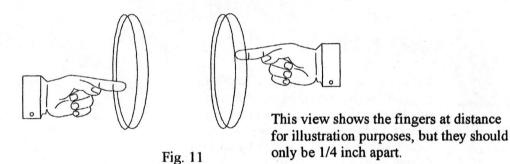

This view shows the fingers at distance for illustration purposes, but they should only be 1/4 inch apart.

Fig. 11

EYE EXERCISES

Simple easy to do eye exercises train the eye muscles to flow smoothly and remain focused. Perform this routine before you shoot and your eyes will will track the target with less effort. The eye muscles must be trained to flow since they leap and shift quickly from place to place in normal life activities. Smooth eye rotation produces a smooth accurate swing to the target.

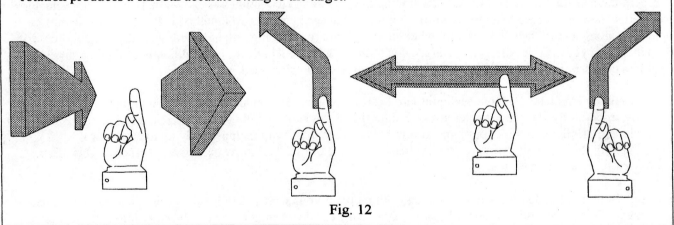

Fig. 12

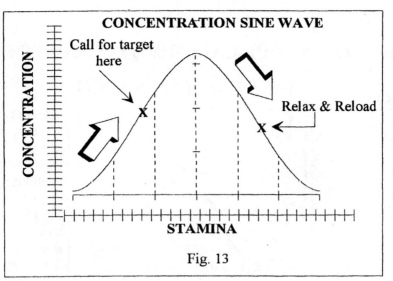

Fig. 13

Concentration and endurance is highly individualistic, unique to each shooter. Everyone, at some point of time, reaches a plateau where the body meets the wall of fatigue. It is important to recognize your ability to maintain concentration and to know how to control it. The chart to the left indicates a person's concentration that is turned on and off at will then pushed to the limit during a shootoff. This relaxation of concentration can extend the shooter's stamina and is cycled on and off when changing traps and even between shots. The chart to the far right indicates a shooter who's concentration is persistent throughout the event at which point the wall is hit early and concentration falls like a rock. Often this occurs on the last 25 targets and the perfect score is flushed down the drain. Fig. 13 reveals that concentration rises when stamina is maintained, but regardless of how much stamina you may have, concentration will still fall if it is not maintained or controlled.

The ability to turn concentration on and off is more an art than technique. It is triggered through eye fixation. When you are asked a difficult question the eyes search the ceiling or the sky for the answer. When the eye fixes onto an object, it triggers the memory portion of the brain to respond and deep concentration is ignited for a brief spell. By fixating your eyes in similar manner before calling for the target, concentration begins to rise. When you feel the concentration rising call for the target, before concentration reaches its peak. This is why it is often said, "The longer it takes to setup and call, the more prone to errors arising." On the other hand, if the setup is too rapid, concentration has not had enough time to initiate. This internal feel and timing is important to recognize and you should try to incorporate feeling the concentration rise during practice so it becomes second nature during competition shooting.

HOW TO TRIGGER AND CONTROL CONCENTRATION

1. Relax concentration the moment you unload your gun. Give your mind a rest.
2. After reloading, look into the trapfield and determine the angle targets you will receive for that post
3. Locate an object in the field you can fixate upon in line with your eye hold point.
4. Mount the gun, fixate and focus your eyes on the object you have selected.
5. When the object is in fine focus, call for the target. Concentration should have been triggered.
6. Did you _feel_ it? Try this at practice and you will.

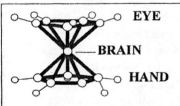

THE NEURAL NETWORK

The eye is the link to the brain that not only triggers concentration, but also controls hand / body muscles to perform given tasks. The secret to perfect eye / hand coordination is the ability to master the eye. Control the eye and trapshooting performance will certainly rise. Eye pre-focus works!

UNDERSTAND YOUR CALL ROUTINE AND TIMING

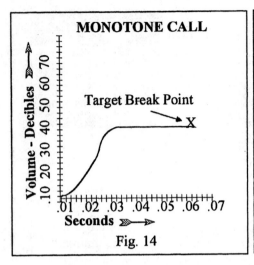

MONOTONE CALL

Target Break Point

Fig. 14

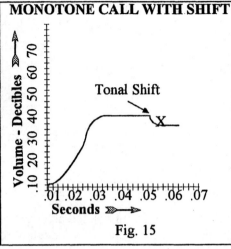

MONOTONE CALL WITH SHIFT

Tonal Shift

Fig. 15

BEWARE OF TONE SHIFT

Fig. 14 reveals a monotone call that is unchanging in duration and the trigger is pulled only when the proper bird / bead relationship exist.

Fig. 15 reveals the voice volume tone has shifted which can signal the brain to pull trigger from sheer habit. If timing is off a smidgen the tonal shift will cause a lost target.

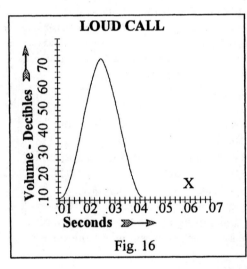

LOUD CALL

Fig. 16

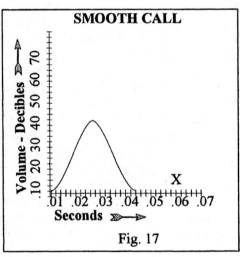

SMOOTH CALL

Fig. 17

CALL VOLUME PROBLEMS

Fig. 16 denotes a sharp loud call that can be so violent it causes muzzle dance or bounce. This ruins the ability of the shooter to locate and track the target with accuracy. Stabbing the muzzle to the target with an unsmooth swing usually results in lost targets as call is too loud and the eyes lose focus.

Fig. 17 is a better call as it is relaxing and smooth.

CALL TIMING IS CRUCIAL TO GOOD SHOOTING

How you call for the target can make a huge difference in your ability to progress. Most shooters call out of sheer habit imbedded from years of shooting, but the call can be the culprit of why targets are slipping by. There are only two types of calls: Staccatos -- a brief call, and the Monotone -- a steady call tone all the way to the target. Both are proper as long as the rules noted above are adhered to: **1)** No tonal shifts, **2)** No muzzle dance. Keep in mind a loud call can seriously upset eye focus and even cause your cheek to shift on the comb. Yet a call too soft can produce repeated slow or fast pulls, upsetting your timing -- and both produce lost targets.

HOW TO CALL FOR TARGETS

Many shooters are oblivious to the call routine and how it can upset timing. **Rule #1**. Never call for the target until the eye(s) are properly focused. **Rule #2**. Never call until you are truly ready and expect to see the target emerge... this is an easy mistake to make as it is a subtle mental preparation, but a finely tuned shooter will certainly understand its importance. **Rule #3**. The call you use must never change from target to target, trap to trap. Be aware of squad influences that may induce changes in call form, volume and duration. **Rule #4**. If your call is causing muzzle dance, head-lifting, cheek displacement, loss of eye focus, slow pulls, or upsetting your timing, then change your call routine. Experiment with many different call forms until you find the call that helps you break the most targets. Listen and observe the pros' call routines and notice how complementary they are to their shooting. The way you call for a target can make or break good scores. Be mentally aggressive when you do call!

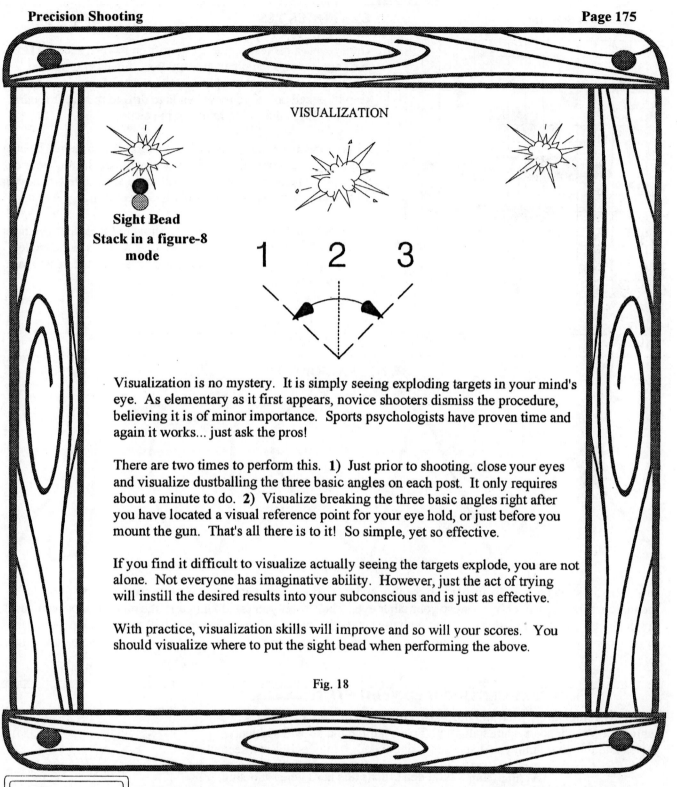

VISUALIZATION

**Sight Bead
Stack in a figure-8
mode**

1   2   3

Visualization is no mystery. It is simply seeing exploding targets in your mind's eye. As elementary as it first appears, novice shooters dismiss the procedure, believing it is of minor importance. Sports psychologists have proven time and again it works... just ask the pros!

There are two times to perform this. **1)** Just prior to shooting. close your eyes and visualize dustballing the three basic angles on each post. It only requires about a minute to do. **2)** Visualize breaking the three basic angles right after you have located a visual reference point for your eye hold, or just before you mount the gun. That's all there is to it! So simple, yet so effective.

If you find it difficult to visualize actually seeing the targets explode, you are not alone. Not everyone has imaginative ability. However, just the act of trying will instill the desired results into your subconscious and is just as effective.

With practice, visualization skills will improve and so will your scores. You should visualize where to put the sight bead when performing the above.

Fig. 18

Acts of violence often occur in a split-second of rage & frustration. Many trapshooters shoot as though they were placed in a situation where they must struggle to break the targets, using 'reactive' split-second reactions instead of formulating a precise plan of attack. It's a crime to shoot targets like this. You must premeditate each and every shot and use a precise plan to break the target. It's a formula to be discovered. Evaluate how you break targets, study the reasons why and you'll discover the ingredients for success.

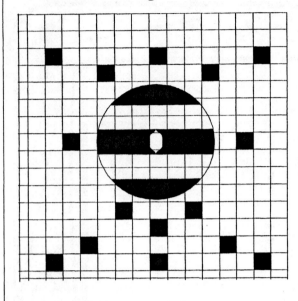

The eye has a restless tendency to drift on its own accord. Hold this page at arm's length away from you. Focus your master shooting eye in the white space in the center of the circle and keep it locked on. If your eye tends to drift to the black squares or bands, force the eye to return to the center.

As your eye is centrally focused peripheral vision should be able to allow you to count the black squares without shifting your eye from the white hole. This is difficult to do as the eye will always try to shift focus to the black squares. Keep trying!

When you've done it right, you'll see how to focus your eye prior to calling for the target. Notice how easy it is to see the angles of the square targets in relation to the center white target when your eye is centrally focused.

Fig. 19

EYE TRACKING TEST

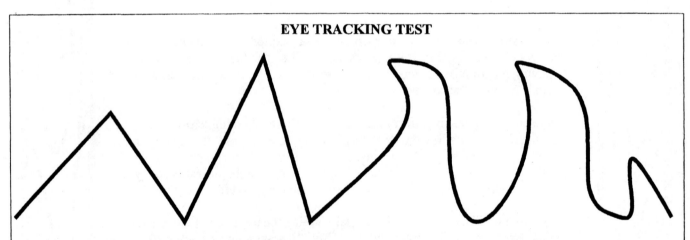

In extremely slow motion, focus hard on the line and track the eye slowly along this line from left to right. Use the master shooting eye only, so close your other eye. The slower you can do this test, the more pronounced you'll notice the eye tending to jerk its way through the maze-like shape. This eye exercise will help develop eye muscle control. Just as you had to train your arm / body muscles to swing the gun, the eye must also be trained.

Fig. 20

DEEPLY CENTRALIZED VISION TEST ⟶

Central vision is rarely used and must be learned. Stare hard at the black center dot. You'll see a white halo ring. Focus harder and all will suddenly vanish and the only thing you'll see is the central coil. It may only last a second.

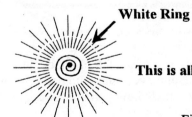

White Ring

You don't focus this hard when shooting, but it is a good eye exercise to help you see targets much better than you do now!

This is all you will see ⟶

Fig. 21   Central Coil

FILTERING INTERFERENCE

Hold this page at arm's length. First you'll see the entire drawing, then as you focus your master shooting eye on the small upper circle, your eye will float randomly from distraction. You will notice the rings fade from view the more intensely you focus and concentrate on the small circle. It may not fade away completely, but this eye training will help develop tunnel vision when looking at targets.

There is a difference between seeing the circle and looking at the circle. Looking is more intense with 100% concentration, blocking out all other interfering objects. Use one eye on this test if you prefer, then try it with both eyes open. You'll see targets much differently using these eye excersises. You'll appreciate the higher scores.

Fig. 22

EYE HOLD DETERMINES THE ZONE

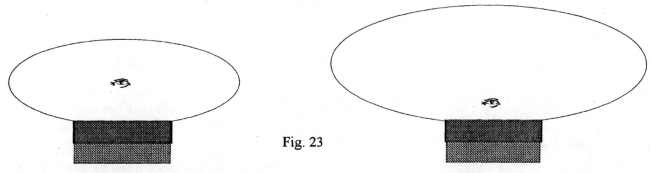

Fig. 23

Generally, if you raise your eye hold point, the zone decreases in size. Lower your eye hold and the zone will increase. The high hold is better to eliminate comet tail streaks and maintain reliable visibility of the target. So, if you hold a low gun to the house, get your eye(s) up. Don't forget that gun hold points can also shrink or expand the zone too, affecting timing. Where you hold gun and eye will determine how fast or slow you will shoot the target. This is why hold points are so important to learn, yet few shooters realize it.

If you prefocus your eye hold properly, the zone will look like this in Fig. 24. The targets rise up into the centralized focus of the eye, not peripheral vision as most shooters use to see targets. It's a tight zone. Now it becomes 90% easier to see and hit the targets when you learn to prefocus the eye(s) and fixate before calling for the target. The central portion of the eye has more photo receptors, so it not only makes perfect sense to prefocus, it works too good to ignore. Chipped targets now turn into dustballs and that's all the proof you need.

> Fig. 24
> **Learn to prefocus your eye.**
> **Where you focus will shift the zone.**

If you want to be a precision shooter, then learn these techniques and practice them. Ask the pros. They prefocus. It may be a soft focus, but in reality it's a hard focus. It's just so easy for them they believe it is a soft focus. Over time, the hard focus will become so routine it will appear to be a soft focus prior to calling for the target.

POST 3   **THREE BASIC ANGLES**

This may appear to be overly simplistic but it is surprising that many trapshooters do not take a split moment to consider the three basic angles they will receive when they call for the target. Doing so will help elliminate the 'surprise factor' which startles the shooter, often resulting in a maddening dash to the target. It is also to your benefit to never expect any target to be a true straight-away. Assume all targets are angled as they most certainly are... even those that appear straight.

Fig. 25

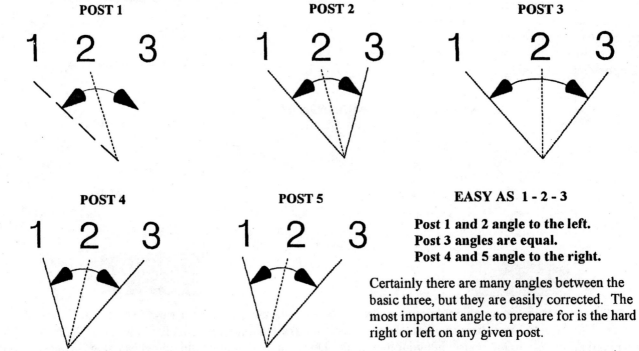

POST 1   **POST 2**   **POST 3**

POST 4   **POST 5**   **EASY AS 1 - 2 - 3**

Post 1 and 2 angle to the left.
Post 3 angles are equal.
Post 4 and 5 angle to the right.

Certainly there are many angles between the basic three, but they are easily corrected. The most important angle to prepare for is the hard right or left on any given post.

Example: The hard left on post #1 and the hard right on post #5 must be prepared for. The key is to set up for it 'Expect' but don't anticipate the hard angle, otherwise it will shock you when it doesn't emerge. Adjust your gun and eye hold to prepare for the hardest angle, look for it, but don't be overly anticipating it.

Fig. 26

It is not essential to know the exact angle in degrees as measured by a protractor or degree wheel, but it is important to know the 'expected' angles you are to receive. On your next practice session, remind yourself to perform this basic task. Every shot must be planned and if you don't visualize the target angle so as to know where you will break the target, there will be no plan.

It is also critical to know if the trap is set properly before you shoot it. Traps have a nasty habit of drifting out of adjustment and a keen eye will recognize it, an eye that knows angles. It can be to your benefit to shoot behind a squad of top-gun shooters, especially those who are perticular about target misalignments, as they will have the trap reset.

❄

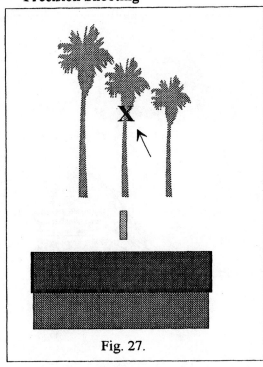

Fig. 27.

When shooting, it is often to your advantage to locate a reliable reference point to use on each station when fixating your eyes. In Fig. 27 the center tree's end branch has been selected. Try focusing your eye so the branch is highly defined. This is certainly not a soft focus when learning this technique... use a hard focus. When the branch becomes crystal clear, call for the target. The target should appear clear, bright and in slow motion. Use this reference point on each station or use another point to complement your eye hold scheme. When changing posts, it is to your advantage to select a focal point and gun hold position as part of your setup.

Can you see a potential flaw in the illustration? The error is the focal point for this type of background is too high. The target will tend to blend in with the trees. Lower the focal point so you will shoot the target before the tree branches.

Keep in mind, that where you hold your eye is the likely spot the target will be broken. The zone increases in size as the eye is lowered closer to the traphouse. A slightly compressed zone is most always better (higher eye & lower gun hold). It's not reliable to use background objects for reference points, as in Fig.27, but is shown to assist the novice shooter to begin learning eye hold points.

Fig. 28 is an example of the different backgrounds you will encounter. The 'X' marks a small wheat flower where you can fixate your eyes. You can use any of the objects shown depending on your eye hold plan. Fixating keeps your eye from focusing on the background when the target emerges. If background scenery is a problem for you, then try this technique.

Not all shooters will agree to the eye fixation method, as they prefer a soft eye focus over a hard focus. You should try both methods to find a happy median focal range that is best for you. The importance of using this technique is to establish your eye focus so you'll know what works for you. For most shooters, fixation will increase target visibility and scores.

Seeing the target is critical to trapshooting, looking at the target is ever more so. By fixing a sharp eye focus on na object prior to calling for the target, the centralized vision section of the eye is turned on. When the target enters this central focus, the target will appear much larger, slower and brightly lit, even on overcast days. This alone is worth pursuing, as any fine shooter will recognize the importance of enhancing target visibility.

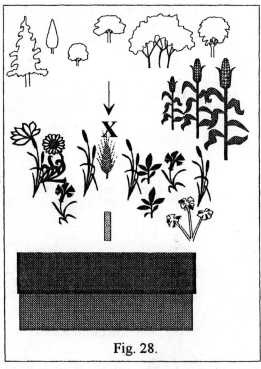

Fig. 28.

Eye pre-focus or fixation is the key to seeing targets in slow-motion. Try it... it works! When you shoot well, it is all so easy because your eyes are locking on to the target quickly and that is why the swing flows smoothly. It's a feeling summarized by "I just can't seem to miss." Those good days do occur and when it happens again you will be able to recognize the principles in this book are actually being employed. And once you realize what is taking place, you can then recall it to apply the technique again and again. Shooting now becomes not a lucky chance, but a skilled technique. This is the arena where professionals reside. Welcome aboard!

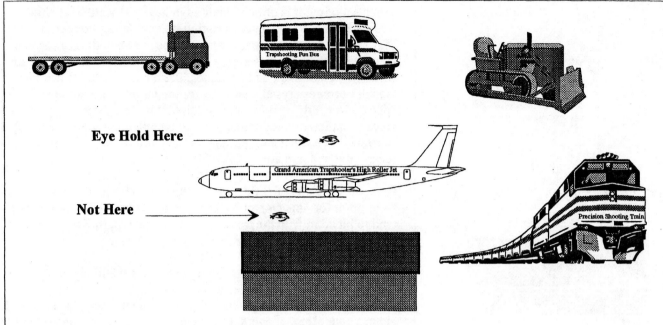

Fig. 29

Shooting with moving background objects can be a challenge. The trick to ignore the distraction is to see the distraction! If you place your eye hold at a point where you will not see the moving objects, it causes trouble. The eye will become confused and flicker when the target emerges. It is best to place your eye near the moving objects, focus, then call. Now that the eye is aware of the movements, the target can be tracked with little effort. Concentration is awareness of your surroundings yet at the same time focus on the job at hand.

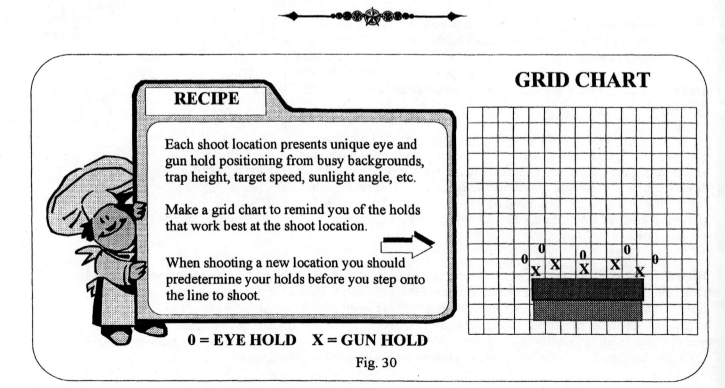

GRID CHART

RECIPE

Each shoot location presents unique eye and gun hold positioning from busy backgrounds, trap height, target speed, sunlight angle, etc.

Make a grid chart to remind you of the holds that work best at the shoot location.

When shooting a new location you should predetermine your holds before you step onto the line to shoot.

0 = EYE HOLD   X = GUN HOLD

Fig. 30

ZONE SHOOTING BUILDS PRECISION AND CONSISTENCY

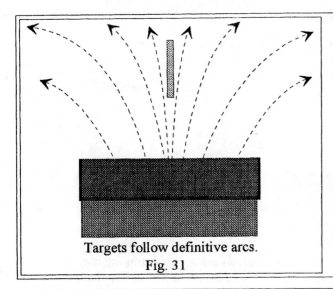

Targets follow definitive arcs.
Fig. 31

Place a pencil dot exactly where you wish to break the target. Doing this will certainly implant precision into your mind by determining the zone. This simple test triggers your subconscious mind to acquire the target and fire the gun at the precise point you have selected.

It is imperative to know when and where you plan to break the targets. Without such a plan, you'll end up perpetually being surprised by target exit and you'll likely ride the target to eventual disaster. It's a common error. The longer you wait to break a target, the more severe the trajectory arc becomes, giving rise to errors in aim.

Consistency Requires Consistency

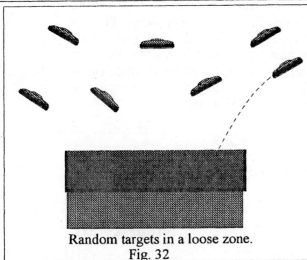

Random targets in a loose zone.
Fig. 32

Place a pencil dot exactly where you must put the sight bead to "smoke" the target with your gun. Don't assume or guess. Determine this with actual practice sessions. Doing this will implant precision accuracy into your mind by determining the required sight picture.

If you are shooting from instinct alone, you may not know where you put the sight bead. You'll need to "rifle shoot" a few targets to make the determination. Precision demands precise aim and to do this you need to know exactly where to point the gun to dustball the targets dead-on. Once learned, you can then resort to your pointing routine. When targets are giving you trouble on specific stations, resort to this test to solve the aiming problem. Try it at your next practice session.

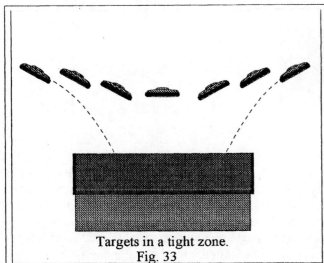

Targets in a tight zone.
Fig. 33

This is an example of a "zone" where all the targets are shot within a defined area of space and time. The hard angles naturally are extended as they travel faster horizontally. This is the picture you should be seeing in your mind's-eye before you call for the target! Now indicate a pencil dot where you would place the sight bead to dispatch each target.

Zone shooting is, at first, quite difficult to learn and it requires a tremendous amount of practice over a period of many years to learn with proficiency, but there is no better time to learn than right now! Discover your zone and strive to make all necessary adjustments to your eye / gun hold points, stance, and timing to shoot the zone. The goal is not distance but true consistency of breaking targets in the same place and time all of the time. You'll get faster as experience develops.

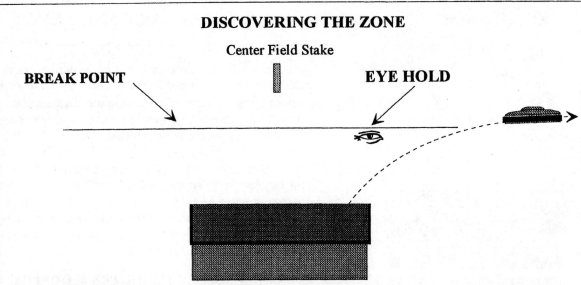

To determine the ideal timing, a starting reference point is required. Here we are using the hard right-angle target to determine the zone where **ALL** the targets should be broken. The breaking zone is just prior to the target's apex (flight trajectory). By mentally drawing a line across the trap the zone is revelealed. From this line you can now develop the timing required and rapid eye / target acquisition required to dispatch the targets repeatedly within the parameters of the zone. Note also, the eye hold is focused near the point where you plan to break the target, yet allowing the eye hold to acquire quarter-angle and straighter targets. Shift the eye hold closer to where the most difficult angle target is expected. Experiment to find the break point and eye hold points that work best for you. This is only a starting guideline to use.

Fig. 34

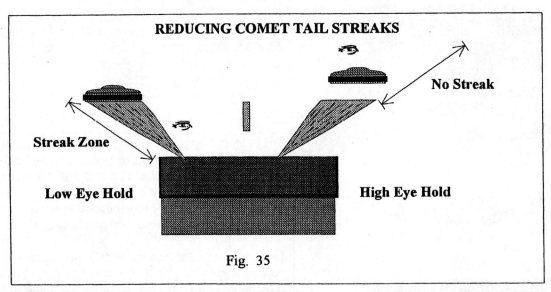

Fig. 35

The problem with a low eye hold is that the eye cannot accurately see the target cleanly. They eye is trying to focus on a streaking comet tail which has no definition and must play 'catch-up' to the target. This rapid eye movement is seldom smooth, disrupting fluid eye / hand coordination as the shooter pushes and jerks the muzzle to the target. Simply raising your eye hold removes the eye from the streak zone where it can lock-on to a well-defined target. Smoothness of the swing is reinstated, better target visibility and target angle recognition is enhanced. Also, your timing increases as eye fixation is increased despite increased eye distance from the traphouse.

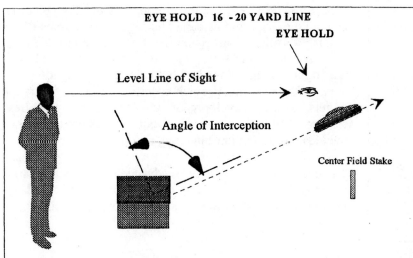

EYE HOLD 16 - 20 YARD LINE

EYE HOLD

Level Line of Sight

Angle of Interception

Center Field Stake

Contrary to traditional wisdom, the higher you hold your eye above the traphouse, the faster you will aquire the target and break it. From 16 to 20 yard line, hold your eye level as you stand. This means your eye is looking way above the gun rib out into space where you plan to break the target.

Fig. 36

One of the bigger reasons targets are missed is improper placement -- eye hold point. If you look too close to the trap, the fast flying target will streak a comet tail, creating a shock to the eye trying to focus upon a very impossible task. By raising the eye hold, peripheral vision will acquire the target.

When the target enters the angle of interception zone (when the target meets the eye hold point) the target will appear clean and whole, as in slow motion since the eye is prefocused at this point. This will allow you to dispatch the target quicker.

Proper eye hold also allows you to see the target angulation better. All targets traverse in curved trajectories, not in straight lines. Don't forget that.

What you percieve as being a straight target is often a slight quarter angle 'bending away' from your sight bead. The higher you hold your eye, the clearer the angle will appear, allowing you to center your hits accurately. Do experiment with eye hold points. Some shooters can shoot steaking targets pulling the trigger as soon as they see the 'flash' but this is clearly 'snap shooting' and not recommended except when shooting double trap.

Here at the longer yardage distances, the eye hold can be lowered to maintain the proper angle of interception. This angle is a 'zone' where the target meets the eye. You want the target to come to the eye instead of the eye chasing the target. This is important! You also want to break the target in a specific zone. To find this eye hold and timing will require experimentation on your part as no one formula exists, it's an internalized means of feeling when to break the target. Each shooter has his / her own timing to discover. It is often faster than you are shooting now.

Still, in Fig. 37 the eye hold is still quite high, not down on the traphouse as you would think would be better. Target acqution is the key to solid hits so let the target rise into your centralized vision.

Another important factor is to not move the muzzle, period, until the target has entered the zone of interception. You'll know because the target will appear bright and clear as it enters this zone.

Try raising your eye hold, even as far as you possibly can just so you can see and understand the theory. This one simple technique can increase your scores. After all, trapshooting is a game of vision. He who sees the target best often wins!

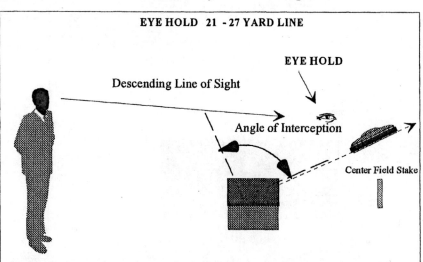

EYE HOLD 21 - 27 YARD LINE

EYE HOLD

Descending Line of Sight

Angle of Interception

Center Field Stake

Since physical distance to trap has increased, the eye hold can be lowered to maintain the angle of interception. Distance increases visibility of the target exiting the trap despite the target appearing smaller in size. There is less comet tail effecs so the eye can be lowered, which will increase target aquisition.

Fig. 37

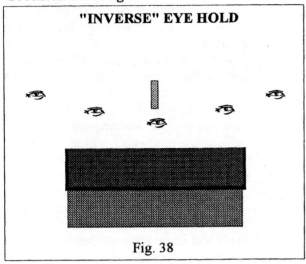

"INVERSE" EYE HOLD

Fig. 38

Where you hold your eye determines how quickly you can acquire the target and calculate its angularity. Eye hold points are critical to precision shooting and you should pay close attention to where you place your eye before calling for the target. In Fig. 38 the "V" hold diminishes target streak effects yet favors quick acquisition of Post #3 straight targets. You can develop your own formula that works best for you. This will require much experimentation to discover the ideal holds, but once learned, accuracy increases.

The eye hold positions may be adjusted up or down as target speed varies from trap to trap or geographic locations. Lower the hold if targets fail to rise, as in tailwind situations.

The "M" hold in Fig. 39 favors the hard left and right angles on Post #1 and Post #5 and the straighter targets on Post #3. Post #2 and #4 the eye is raised to allow peripheral vision to acquire the target. This method helps to set up the eye and mind to prepare for the most difficult angles. Here you will be well prepared as the eye hold "triggers" the fleeting subconscious mind to pay attention to the tough angles that will likely arrive upon call. This eye hold helps reduce the "surprise factor," allowing you to dispatch the target within or near the ideal zone you have selected. As you can see, the variations on eye hold patterns are imaginative and you can tailor the configuration to match your unique vision requirements. These examples are good starting points to begin your search for the ideal eye hold.

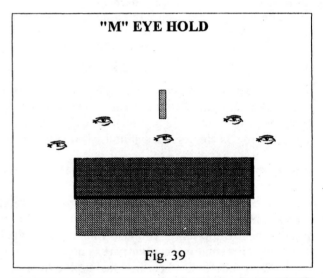

"M" EYE HOLD

Fig. 39

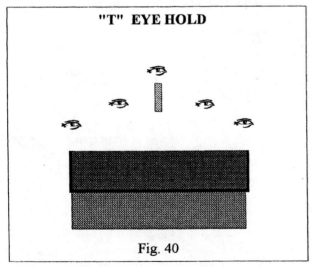

"T" EYE HOLD

Fig. 40

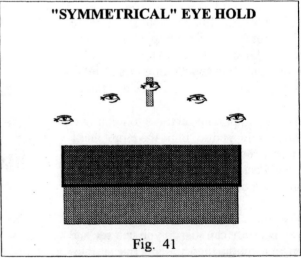

"SYMMETRICAL" EYE HOLD

Fig. 41

Fig. 40 and Fig. 41 are more variations on the theme. These tend to favor peripheral vision target acquisition. The "Symmetrical" hold should be tried first as many shooters' eyes need to be fine-tuned to use the closer focus required in the alternative techniques. If you experience problems, raise the eye hold higher than you see in the illustrations until you minimize the target's comet tail streaking effects. Eye hold height changes with handicap distance. You have to experiment to find the eye and gun hold points that work best for you.

"M" EYE HOLD & GUN HOLD

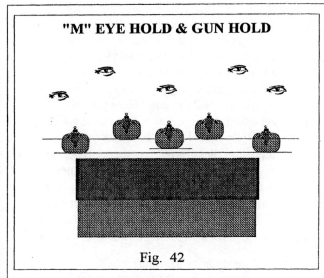

Fig. 42

The gun hold point can coincide with the eye hold point. The height of the gun over the house in relation to the eye hold elevation has the advantage of maintaining consistent timing of the shot while taking full advantage of visually acquiring the target and its angle as soon as possible.

The gun and eye holds shown conform to stations 1 through 5 respectively. Note the various heights shown. These can be adjusted to any configuration you deem works best for you. The important point of these illustrations is to spark your creativity to determine where you should hold your eye and gun prior to calling for the target. You will find the pattern that best works for you, and you alone. No one hold can be deemed perfect for every shooter.

INVERSE "M" EYE & GUN HOLD

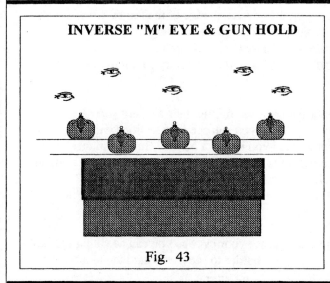

Fig. 43

Here in Fig. 43 the gun hold is inverse to eye hold; whereas, the gun is moved closer to the eye hold on the hard angle targets and moved slightly away from straighter targets. at stations #1 and #5 the gun is moved higher to reduce the time and swing angle to catch the hard left and right birds. You may want to maintain the lower height, but offset the gun to the far extreme of the eye hold to reduce the swing and to prevent shooting over the top of the targets.

The eye and gun hold points determine speed and accuracy. The better shooter you become, speed often increases, but with a penalty. These hold points help fine-tune your visual abilities to get onto the target quickly and maintain a tight zone.

"COMMON" EYE HOLD & GUN HOLD

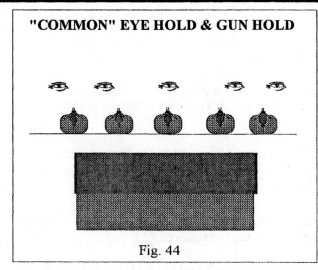

Fig. 44

Is this how you are holding the gun and your eyes? If so, you can see the technique is simplistic in nature. It does work, but fails to take full advantage of fine-tuning the unique and specific target speed and angles on each post. What almost always results is failing to break targets in the same place time and time again. It is almost impossible to shoot a zone using this "common" approach without finding yourself stabbing at the targets, and you'll develop a bad habit of shooting over the targets, especially the hard angles. This basic hold is fine for a beginner, not so for the advanced shooter. We need to get eye and gun in the maximum position of advantage. This requires that each station have its own gun and eye hold point. Why? So you can maintain timing and better see "intersections."

SEEING THE INTERSECTION

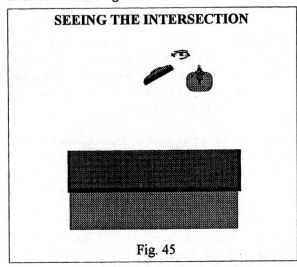

Fig. 45

The great secret to trapshooting is not chasing down targets, riding them out into the horizon. When you were learning trapshooting, you developed the habit of tracking targets. Eventually, you must outgrow this novice form and learn to see "intersections." The first step to learn this technique is to get your eyes up far away from the traphouse and the gun. Here you will not see the target exit the house, but only when it arrives and passes by your gun muzzle. At this point you will see the target angle and the intersection shot & target will collide. Your eyes are focused higher into an elevated zone so you can concentrate on recognizing these critical intersections. Once you recognize them, you can resort to a lower eye hold. Fig. 45 is an example. This is exactly what you should see. Not a streaking target to chase, but a clear snapshot in which you simply head off the target at the pass. Be careful not to miss the intersection by jumping too far ahead of the target. When you "spot" shoot targets like this, the tendency is always to exceed the required lead. The reason is your mind is no longer on the swing but on the advanced edge of the target, where it will be... not so much as where it is! This problem is compounded with distance. The further the target is, the more shooting ahead and behind become frustrating. But if you "spot the zone," shooting the intersection in a tight zone, you are well on your way to high levels of proficiency. But it is not easy to learn, though it can be fun by the sheer challenge to excel.

Remember to keep your eye hold when you call for the target higher than normal, normal being where you likely hold your eye knowing the "common" eye hold method. By raising your eye hold, you can see intersections with clarity and spot point the gun to the target. The faster you shoot, the less advance lead you need. You may find the intersection diminishing in time where the muzzle / sight bead simply locks on tightly to the target when your timing increases, but the intersection still exists, more in your mind than physical reality. It is often referred to as "maintained lead" where lead or forward allowance is applied instinctively ahead of the target, shooting where the target will be, not where it is.

When you practice next, think of these intersections and give them a try. Work your eyes so you can see them appear, for in the split second moment you pull the trigger you'll see them. They are harder to see in the hard angle targets, but you will see them with much practice. ———————o◇o———————

Most trapshooters use the 'Follow Through' method of shooting. Some spot shoot intersections using 'Maintained Lead' while others use the 'Pull Away' method, yet still others use all three methods, or combine the techniques depending on which post they are shooting from. Here's a brief explanation.

MAINTAINED LEAD: The muzzle is swung to the intersection as in Fig. 45. A definite path of tracking the target is not used. Similar to 'Spot Shooting' but with more visual precision on target. It's good for trapshooting, but not on straight-trending targets. Use Follow Through on straight targets.

SPOT SHOOTING: No lead on target. Used on shooting first target on double trap. Muzzle is placed where target will break and when the shooter sees the "flash" as the target exits, the trigger is pulled. Not reliable for trapshooting due to unknown angles. Some shooters integrate spot, pull-away and intersection methods for certain targets.

PULL-AWAY: The sight bead is placed on the target and muzzle suddenly pulled away, ahead of the target for lead. Very effective on hard-left and right angles in trapshooting. A two-stage swing is employed.

FOLLOW THROUGH: a.k.a. "swing through." Muzzle tracks target's flight path and swings through the target to apply lead with one smooth motion. Most trapshooters employ this sole technique with great success.

ATTACKING THE HARD ANGLES

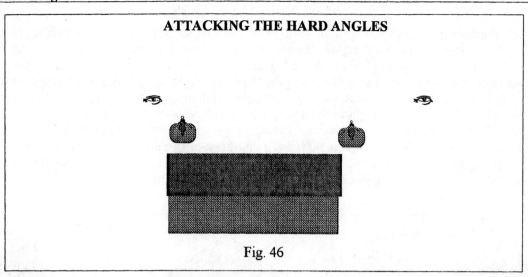

Fig. 46

Fig. 46 on Post #1 is a relatively common and a feasible eye / gun hold to prestage for the hard left target. Post #5 reveals an extreme eye / gun hold. The gun is held off the house and the eye shifted far to the right. The advantage of doing this offsetting is to acquire the hard angle target faster and have the gun in an ideal position to swing quickly. The disadvantage is obvious, the gun is off track for the straight-away target, but if you are diligent to take the straight target with patience the method works.

ATTACKING THE HARD ANGLES

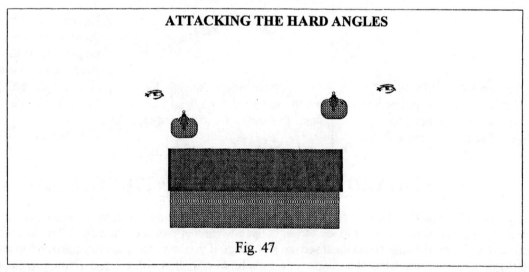

Fig. 47

By holding the gun higher as shown in Fig. 47 on Post #5 and the eye in line with the zone where you plan to break the target, you'll have less tendency to swing over the target and miss by shooting over the top. Over the top missing is caused by holding a gun too low, and when you swing to a rising target the tendency of the muzzle to continue rising from momentum at the point of intersection is relentless. If you find any of the eye / gun hold techniques advantageous remember they can be used on both Post #1 and #5. One more very important point... this entire book can become quite useless **immediately** if your gun does not fit you, as you can never implement the techniques if the gun does not shoot where you look. Nothing can help a shooter with an improperly fitted gun! And it sure won't work if you're lifting your head. Keep your cheek buried into the comb! If your gun hold is slightly lower than your eye hold, that alone will keep your head down because you will not strain to see the target pass by the barrel. Eye and gun holds are very important, and if you don't use the method you'll never be a consistent winner.

SEEING THE GHOST

You'll hear it time and again not to use the sight beads when shooting shotguns. If you talk with the pros, you'll discover they do use them. Now, who's right? The answer is obvious and the reasoning is sound... use the sight beads! It's called "back-sighting" not "rifle-sighting." There is a big difference. We know it as "sight picture." Confusion sets in as the shooter must keep his eye on the target and by doing so obliterates the sight bead. The key is to learn to do both; full central vision on the target, partial central vision on the sight bead. If performed properly the sight bead will be bright and clear approaching the target, yet not so well-defined as to distract. If you shoot keeping 100% of your vision on the target, you are making a huge mistake and precision will be lost. Why? Because the bird /bead relationship is the fuse that triggers the brain to signal the trigger finger. The next time you miss a target I'll bet you didn't see the bird/bead relationship and pulled the trigger at the wrong time, especially those random firings when you know you shouldn't have fired, but did anyway.

Fig. 48

 Upper Sight Bead **Lower Sight Bead** **Rib** **A** When mounting the gun you should see the beads stacked. The rib will appear wide.	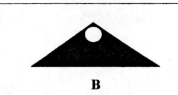 **B** Focus your eyes so the bottom bead dissolves from view as much as possible.	 **C** The rib will tend to shrink in size and from view.

 D Looking out into the field for the target before you call, you should not be hard-focusing on the sight rib, but you should see the sight bead clearly and in focus.	 **E** When you see target, the sight bead is now in tight view, though still as a ghost. The sights are used on shotguns!	**USE THE SIGHTS** **Learn to simultaneously focus your eyes on the target and at the same time see the ghost-like sight bead. This is the key to accurate shooting.** **No sights = low scores!**

LOOKING HARD AND THINKING OF THE TARGET

You know you must look <u>hard</u> at the target to make dead-center hits and shoot top scores, but looking at the target is not enough in itself. You must also look to see the sight bead when it approaches the target. Practice the above steps A-B-C-D and E because you must see the sight bead if you wish to break targets, develop precise timing and trigger control. Never pull the trigger unless the bird/bead relationship exists. Now you can focus your eye attention to the target and the bead, and this alone will improve your handicap scores immensely.

You've heard it said, "Focus harder." Now you know what it means. It's the ability to see the target and the sight bead come into proper alignment. Concentration is the execution of channeling all your visual and mental energy to perform the above procedure. Thinking is often bad news to trapshooters, but you must think of the bird / bead relationship, otherwise you will miss a target or two. When you think of this you will see the target better when it emerges from the traphouse. Try thinking of this and see that it works! Just the thought alone triggers the subconscious mind to energize eye focus and helps you block every other thought out of your mind.

If you are not thinking of the bird/bead relationship, chances are you are thinking of the wrong things at the wrong time and likely worried and concerned about something else. Sound familiar? Think and you shall see!

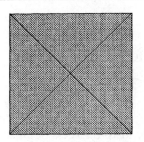

DEEP EYE FOCUS

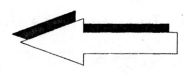

This is what many trapshoters see when they call for the target, a flat field of view.

This is what you should see! A deep tunnel-like effect that prefocuses the eye into the field.

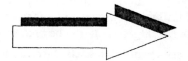

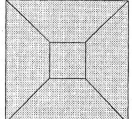

When you prefocus your eyes (or eye for one-eyed shooters) and the eye is held close to where you plan to break the target, many things happen to increase target annihilation **1)** The eye is ready to see the target enter its field of view -- which is highly centralized - and no comet tail is produced to throw off eye / hand coordination. **2)** The target is acquired quicker so timing increases and is more consistent. **3)** The gun won't move when the target emerges from the traphouse, only when the eye has acquired the target will the swing begin. **4)** A smooth swing is produced. **5)** Target / muzzle intersection is clearly defined. **6)** Target angulation is easily recognized and minor swing corrections are only needed to obtain the proper sight picture when pulling the trigger. **7)** Flinching is greatly reduced since the target appears in slow motion and there is less pressure on the shooter to chase or ride the target. To bring about these benefits, prefocus your eyes and raise the eye hold point away from the traphouse.

Fig. 49

EXACT EYE ALIGNMENT   **EXCESSIVE EYE SHIFT**

**NEVER
UNDERESTIMATE THE
IMPORTANCE OF EYE HOLD AS
IT DETERMINES
PRECISE SHOOTING !**

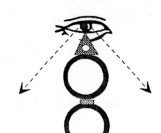

A   B

There is more to eye hold than meets the eye. Here we can see eye alignment must be dead center. This is accomplished with a properly fitted gun, solid gun mount and firm cheek pressure at all times. Shifting the eyeball up or down to solidify a eye hold causes no problem with eye / rib alignment. However, excessive eye shifting in relation to gun hold can be damaging, causing a separation of the eye / gun relationship. This is a subtle shooting tip not known to novice shooters. If the eye hold is too far away from the gun hold, the gun can't be brought into alignment smoothly or fast enough to reliably break the target. If the eye hold is too close to the gun, the eye will 'jerk' causing the hand to 'stab' at the target. Snap shooting begins and smoothness is lost. Find the proper eye-to-gun hold distance through trial and error, then incorporate it into your form. Be aware of this smidgen of advice as it is a substantial flaw why targets slip by accomplished shooters. Try to keep the eye and gun holds as close as possible yet distant enough to ensure solid timing and swing rhythm.

Fig. 50

THE GOAL IS TO PUT THE BEAD ON THE TARGET

This is more difficult than you think! You can't put the bead on the target if you apply lead to targets because the sight bead is pushed through the target and ahead of it. But you can shoot targets without any lead and you can put the bead dead-on the target. How? The answer is within POI, eye and gun hold, timing and zone.

1. **First select a zone. A realistic location where you plan to break all of the targets - Fig. 51.**

2. **Maximize eye and gun hold to accomplish the goal - Fig. 52.**

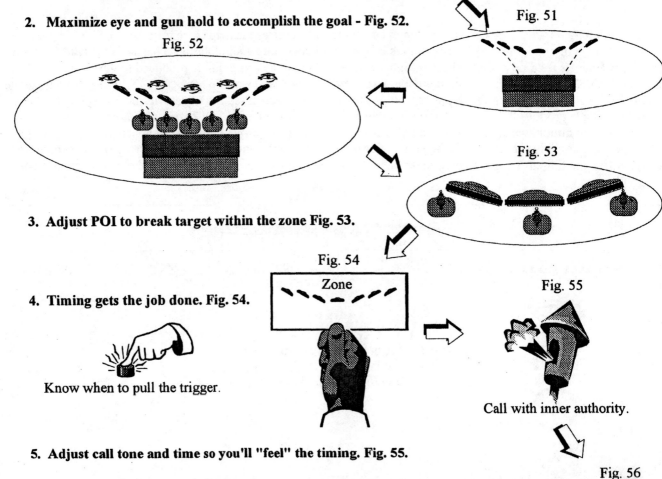

3. **Adjust POI to break target within the zone Fig. 53.**

4. **Timing gets the job done. Fig. 54.**

Know when to pull the trigger.

Call with inner authority.

5. **Adjust call tone and time so you'll "feel" the timing. Fig. 55.**

6. **Only you can apply the formula . Fig. 56.**

So there is a plan to break targets with absolute reliability. Anyone can break targets, but to do so with precision and consistency a formula must be learned and applied. The pros know precisely what they are doing because they have these formulas locked away in their minds. They do not shoot with luck. Everything they do, everything, has a purpose blended into technique. Observe the pro when s/he shoots and you will recognize the secrets now that you know them. Never just put a gun up, call, and hope for the best. Many have shot this way for tens of years and still can't win events consistently, especially the long-yardage shooters. It's time to learn precision shooting and get that plan into motion.

First, a properly fitted gun is imperitive to insure the eye lines up perfectly centered along the rib. Once this is accomplished Point of Impact is the second critical phase towards good trapshooting... the gun must shoot where you look! If it doesn't you'll always have inconsistent scores and many a troubling days. To be successful in this sport you must, without exception, insure the two criteria above are performed.

Point of Impact is where the center of the pattern of pellets land in a 30" circle measured at 40 yards on a pattern board. Here's how to measure POI. In reality we don't want a 30" pattern but we'll use this familiar formula.

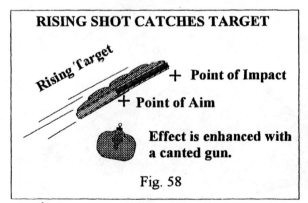

Center
Core

Aim Point

Patern Board
30" Circle

Fig. 57

DETERMINING POINT OF IMPACT

1. Draw 30" circle on pattern sheet with a 3" center bull's-eye.
2. Fire at the aim point. Use a solid bench rest.
3. Measure the center of pattern in relation to the aim point.
4. If center pattern is dead-on the gun shoots flat. 50/50 POI.
5. Each 3" of pattern rise from aim point, POI is 10%.

FORMULA

1 If you divide the diameter of 30" circle by 10 it equals 3".
2 3" = 10% of the 30" circle. If the gun shoots 9" high above the center aim point divide 9" by 3" = 3.
3 Multiply 3 x 10% = 30%.
4 Add 30% to the flat shooting 50% standard = 80%.
5 This gun' s POI is 80/20.

WHAT DOES IT MEAN ?

80/20 means 80% of the pattern is above the center aim point as shown in Fig. 57 above.

HOW MUCH POI SHOULD I HAVE ?

As a general rule 80/20 is very efficient for edge-on rising targets as is found in the trapshooting diciplines. It is not an absolute. Each shooter may prefer alternative settings depending on their timing.

If the POI is higher than where I look, then the gun is not shooting where I look, right?

Yes and no. The targets are rising fast and by the time you pull the trigger the target is long gone. But with a high POI the gun will shoot where you did look and the shotstring will rise and catch the target where is is now.

MANY SHOOTERS DO NOT EVEN KNOW WHERE THEIR GUNS SHOOT !

RISING SHOT CATCHES TARGET

Rising Target

+ Point of Impact

+ Point of Aim

Effect is enhanced with a canted gun.

Fig. 58

A high POI can come in handy shooting singles, as target speed is faster and the shooter's timing can remain the same as when shooting handicap targets. However, a high POI is critical to successfully shoot handicap targets... the further back you are punched the more POI you'll need, or you'll have to shoot faster to compensate which is not a good idea. It is better to make POI adjustments and allow the gun to work for you rather than you working harder, altering timing and sight pictures everytime you earn yardage. In most cases, 80/20 POI will work very efficiently at all yardage posts. Future POI adjustments are rarely needed once set.

BE WISE. MAKE THE ADJUSTMENTS !

Adjusting POI and timing is a delicate balancing act and will likely consume considerable practice sessions and adjustments to get it right. Most shooters will not proceed with making the necessary adjustments to match POI and timing parameters, which is why most shooters don't shoot well. If the gun fails to fit and shoot where you look, a lifetime of practice will do little good in the long run.

DETERMINING EYE HOLD POINT

**Use A Reliable Reference Point.
This Is An Excellent Method To Use.**

On each station use the 'thumbs-up' method shown above to determine your eye hold. You'll want
to use this when shooting traps with distracting airport or freeway backgrounds. Here, the eye hold is
at the junction between the second and third finger, a good starting point for rising targets. Shooting
suppressed targets you may want to lower eye hold. The general rule: raise eye hold on rising targets,
lower eye hold on suppressed targets.

Fig. 59

LOCATE A FIXATION POINT

A ridge on a background mountain is located to
fix eyes upon when shooting. Any object will
work: a tree, fence post, flower, stone, etc.

Keep in mind you must develop your own
form of eye holds and each post you shoot
may require a different hold. The hold
also changes when targets are set fast, slow,
high or low. In time you will develop your
own formulas unique to your shooting style.

Where you place your eye determines where
and when you will break the target. It has a
major effect on timing, so practice developing eye
holds along with gun hold points so you can shoot in
a consistent zone.

Fig. 60

 **T**RAPSHOOTING IS FORMULA

 **W**ITH 97% SKILL
&
3% LUCK.

You must learn the theory and rules and it's here
in this book and the *Trap Shooting Secrets* book.

Fig. 61

#1. Keeping your eye on the target is crucial or else the muzzle stops cold,
but there is more. You must keep your eye on the correct target zone, too!

Leading Edge   **Top**   **Leading Edge**
Middle →
Bottom

#2.
Deep tunnel vision on the
target develops high
precision with dead-on
target hits.

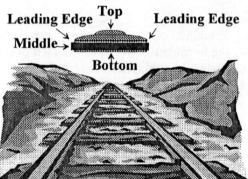

#3.
Timing is everything!
Develop a zone where all
targets are broken in the
same place and time, but do
it precisely, not randomly.

#4. 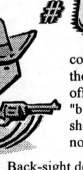 Quickdrawing doesn't work all of the time. To break targets
consistently every time, you will need to use the gun sights when mounting
the gun and at the moment of pulling the trigger without taking your eye
off the target or looking back at the sights. The proper terminology is
"back-sighting" where a smidgen of back-sight is always visible to the
shooter to place the bead on the target. It is not rifle shooting and it is
not pure instinctive shooting with the eyes only! It is a blend of both forms.

Back-sight does not mean the center or rear sight bead. Once the beads are stacked
they become one in the shooter's peripheral vision. Back-sighting is seeing the ghost.

Fig. 62

SLOW & FAST PULLS

These most insidious enemies upset timing and visual acquisition of the target and disrupt the shooter's nervous system, sending a shockwave to the eyes searching for the target that either does not exist or appears suddenly. Chasing down a fast pull or sustaining a gun mount waiting for the target causes flinching, head-lifting unsmooth and inaccurate moves, resulting in a lost target. Everyone knows this, yet still, they continue to shoot these defective and damaging pulls with disastrous scores to show for their efforts. Ask yourself, "How many targets did I turn down?" It is rare to have perfect pulls during an event and if you find yourself not turning down bad pulls and missing targets, it's time to pay more attention to intricate timing details so you can pick up those lost targets to turn a higher score.

Fig. 63

TROUBLE HITTING HARD RIGHTS AND LEFTS ?

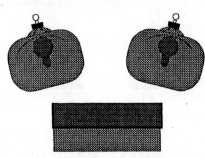

Try precanting the gun before calling for the target. This will prevent shooting over the top of the targets and advance lead from point of impact rise and predispose the gun to tackle the hard angle when it emerges and keep your head down on the comb.

Keep in mind, when missing these extreme angle targets you are likely to shoot over the top and occasionally shoot behind.

Everyone has a problem with specific posts and angles. The key is to know how to break the targets, not just shoot at them from instinct alone. There is a formula to break each target. Learn how to center hit each target and lock the formula away in your mind, then apply the formula by reminding yourself of it before you call for a target. This is part of concentration, to have a plan of attack. Missed targets are often caused by forgetting how to shoot it. When you set up a plan of action you'll instantly remember how to smokeball it when the target leaves the house.

Fig. 64

It is important to see the target the moment it leaves the house. This does not mean your eye must be focused on the very edge of the traphouse or looking over the side of the barrel. You can adjust your gun hold so your eye remains behind the sights, yet with peripheral vision, still see the top of the traphouse. Keeping your eye as close as possible in line with the gun's rib sight plane will eliminate slop and slag time to get to the target and keep the eye / rib relationship in check during the swing. It is okay for the eye to deviate from the rib and sight beads, to a degree, but the closer your eye's field of view remains in line with the sights and you can still see the top of the traphouse, the higher your scores will be. Catch-22, a vertical eye lift from the rib will increase target visibility

WHAT YOU SHOULD SEE WHEN LOOKING DOWN THE RIB

Eye and gun holds can be tricky to learn so be patient with yourself and keep experimenting until you find the holds that work best for you. There is no one formula that works for all. Try not to make the process too complicated or think too much about the holds when shooting in competition. Do your thinking and experimentation at the practice range.

FIELD OF VIEW

Remember, eye and gun holds often change from station to station so you'll need to work out a formula and write it down for future reference to use at practice and at registered shoots. Eventually the process becomes second nature, but you should always see a bit of backsight; otherwise, you are shooting with your eyes only. The sight bead on the target determines "when" to pull the trigger

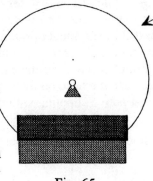

Fig. 65

TRAPS FOLLOWING LAYS OF THE LAND

Fig. 66

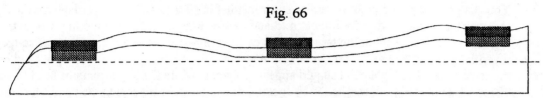

The lay of the land is often not graded when installing traps and at many clubs you'll find misalignments both
vertically and horizontally which cause problems for the shooter creating busy backgrounds to gun and eye
hold and swing geometry alteration. Undulating surfaces often develop eddy currents so it is important to shoot
a tight zone before the wind alters the target's flight path. Take all things into consideration. If you are shooting
"not so good" at certain gun clubs, you may find the solutions here on this page.

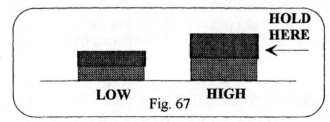

Fig. 67

Traps come in varying heights which can be puzzling at times as to where you should hold the gun. The low
house doesn't create as much problem as a high house, for the house may be so high as to disrupt the shooter's
swing geometry, especially those who hold a low gun on the far edge of the house. It is best to lower the gun
hold to your normal hold position as shown in arrow above. If you don't change your gun hold by pointing the
muzzle at the usual edge of the traphouse, timing and swing geometry will be upset, resulting in not seeing the
target properly leave the house and unsmooth moves to the target. Shooters who hold a high gun may also
need to lower their hold point. Keep in mind eye hold may also need to be adjusted. Develop a plan of action
when confronted with high and low houses. You can hold over the house just as you normally would. Each
shooter must determine his/her own plan of attack. There are things you can do to compensate so try them.

HORIZONTAL MISALIGNMENT

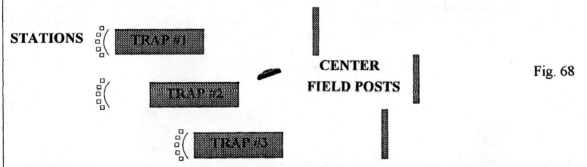

Fig. 68

Horizontal trap misalignment can upset a shooter's timing due to speed and distance to target when it emerges
from the house. Traps #1 and #3 are okay, assuming the distances from stations to the traphouse and from the
traphouse to the center field stake are correct. Trap #2 is a problem. The distance from the stations to the trap
are excessive, along with the distance from the traphouse to the center stake. This will have the same effect as
being punched yardage and will also result in faster targets. Though this illustration is exaggerated, you can see
shooting Trap #2 will likely upset your scores. There are three things you can do. **1)** Don't shoot the trap. **2)**
Apply a tad more lead to the targets when shooting them. **3)** Lower your gun and eye holds. Be aware of these
irregularities and compensate for them. When the first target exits, you should know from experience that
"something" is wrong. Don't say, "Oh, well" and keep on shooting blindly. You must compensate or face
the penalty. It's the little trapshooting secrets learned that pay the highest dividends in wins.

Fig. 69

YOU DON'T JUST POINT A SHOTGUN AT TARGETS

You can get away with pointing out of sheer instinct in singles and short-yardage handicap, but you won't get away with it for long at mid-and long-yardage, you'll drop too many targets. Then again, you don't rifle shoot the targets. This causes confusion among many shooters so they revert to "point shooting." Train your vision so you can see the target and the sight bead both at the same time. The sight bead should appear as a ghost while the target remains bright in central vision. This is easily accomplished by looking down the sight rib seeing the beads then lifting your eye up a tad away from the muzzle before you call for the target. In the lower peripheral portion of your vision you should still see the sight beads stacked. This is called "backsighting" and you need to use it when shooting trap targets. The moment the target emerges, the eye will follow the target leaving the muzzle and sights behind, then as the swing accelerates you should see the ghostly sight bead align with the target. At that moment the trigger is pulled and a proper bird / bead relationship exist. The tighter the zone you shoot the less lag time you will experience - and if you're really fast - the muzzle will never lag out of view keeping your vision perfectly aligned along the rib sight plane. Just reading about all these techniques in this book will not help you. The subject matter is complex and each shooter is unique. You must try the techniques to understand them and find the combination that works best for you.   Fig. 70

| More Eye / Hand Coordination Required | **PROPERLY ACQUIRING THE TARGET ONE - EYE SHOOTER** | Less Eye / Hand Coodination Needed |

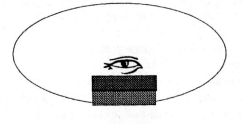

Fig. 71

A

Fig. 'A' reveals the eye hold is too low on the house. Lower peripheral vision extends below the traphouse which will create long comet tails and a fuzzy fast flying target. The shooter will likely produce a stab-like swing from nervous system shock.

B

Fig. 'B' denotes the eye hold is higher so peripheral vision can properly acquire the target, seeing little to no comet trail. When target is seen it is often bright and slower in motion, producing a clear concise target.

TWO - EYE SHOOTER
RIGHT MASTER EYE

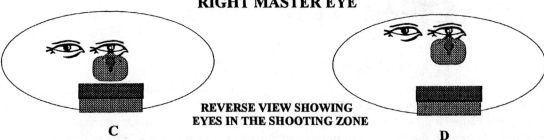

REVERSE VIEW SHOWING EYES IN THE SHOOTING ZONE

C

Fig. 'C' the gun is held too low allowing the shooter to see the target leave the house with both eyes. This leads to eye cross-over, focus shifting that averts the master eye from centering on the target.

D

Fig. 'D' the hold is higher so the master eye can't see the target leave the house. This is correct. The left eye sees the target leave, then the master eye locked behind the sight plane takes over.

In reality, a two-eye shooter is still only shooting with one eye and the sight picture appears identical to what the one-eye shooter sees when firing. The one-eye shooter normally holds a low gun and requires increased gun movement. Two-eye shooters require less swing. This is the only true difference between the techniques.

EYE FOCUSING

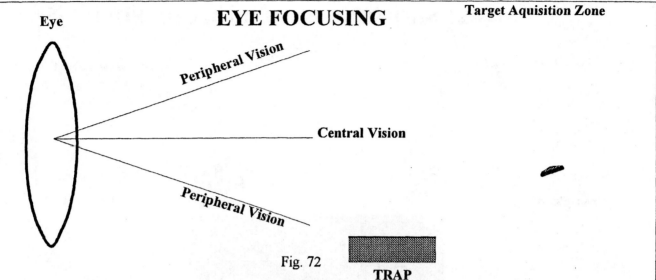

Eye

Target Aquisition Zone

Peripheral Vision

Central Vision

Peripheral Vision

Fig. 72

TRAP

The above illustration denotes the field of view where peripheral vision first picks up the target. The target then enters the highly focused core of central vision. No eye movement is required as the target enters the visual zone. If the eye "searches" for the target the muzzle will, too. This is why developing a still eye hold is crucial. When you are shooting great you'll notice the eye flows so smoothly to the target with ease. Get the idea? You have prefocused your eyes prior to calling for the target and you didn't even know it.

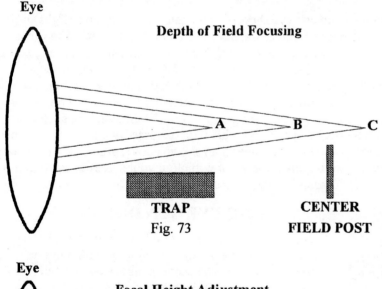

Eye

Depth of Field Focusing

A   B   C

TRAP

Fig. 73

CENTER
FIELD POST

For the eye to pick up the target you must develop an eye prefocus point. Some shooters focus at point 'A' whereas 'B' may be much better. 'C' is also a technique used focusing on a distant object. Regardless of where you prefocus at distance you will always see the target immediately leave the house with peripheral vision. But the closer the eye focus is to the trap? Problems develop: rapid eye movement, eye fatigue, comet tails, snapping at targets, timing problems develop. Find the focal zone that works smoothest for you. It will take time to find it. Maybe as long as a year or two to really discover it, and each post and trap layout may require alterations. It's really not easy to be a precision shooter.

....

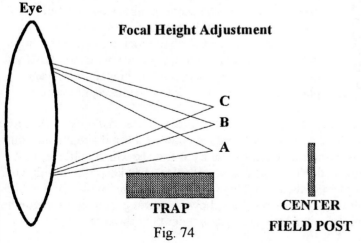

Eye

Focal Height Adjustment

C

B

A

TRAP

Fig. 74

CENTER
FIELD POST

But there is more. The eye focal point can also be adjusted up or down, left and right. Here the formula becomes even more tricky to find due to the increased variables. Then you have the gun hold to deal with on top of all this. It becomes complex and confusing. These are advanced trapshooting techniques. So, if you want to break 'em like the pros, you need to learn these little secrets. Be patient. You will find the focusing zones and the perfect timing to match. It won't happen overnight.

ONE-EYE SHOOTING WITH HIGH GUN HOLD

Three Basic Target Angles   **Three Basic Target Angles**

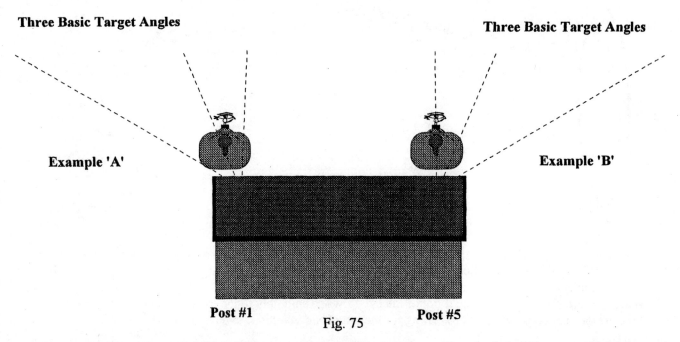

Example 'A'   Example 'B'

Post #1   Post #5

Fig. 75

There are advantages to holding a higher gun for the one-eye shooter. The gun is held just so a slight air gap is between the gun and traphouse, or gun just touching the top of traphouse so no air gap is seen. The eye is sighted directly in line with the rib at point of call. The gun hold in example 'A' is shifted between the straight-away and quarter angle. Example 'B' the hold is favoring the straight-away. Try both methods to see what works best for you. 1) You enhance swing geometry with less vertical swing and suppress shooting over the top of the targets. 2) Easy to identify fast and slow pulls. 3) Helps maintain a tight zone. 4) You see less comet tail streak reducing the tendency to jump and stab at the targets. A slight disabling of not seeing the target immediately leave the house, but the benefits often outweigh this with increased accuracy. 5) The hard left and right targets become easier to hit. Now, raise the eye higher than shown above, prefocus, and the targets will appear in slow-motion. When you learn to see targets travel in slow-motion your scores rise and trap shooting becomes quite a bit easier. You're not "chasing" targets anymore.

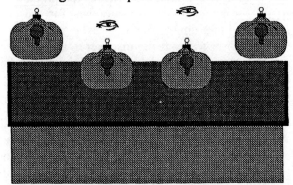

ONE-EYE GUN HOLDS

You can try this scheme of holding high on the ends and lower on the middle. Or you can hold high on all posts. Note: The center guns are not held all the way down to the traphouse roof. Why? Because you don't want your central vision looking where the target will only streak, throwing your eye out of focus. If you hold low, keep your eye hold up higher. You want peripheral vision to see the target leave, not central.

The purpose of shifting eye and gun holds is to reduce swing movements, obtain better visibility of the target, and increase timing. When experimenting with hold points, don't confuse yourself, keep it simple, and shift gradually in small increments. There is nothing complicated here. Just try it and see which hold makes it easier to hit the targets. You'll need to practice it a bit, so don't expect instant miracles. Just keep fine-tuning your holds until it seems easier than how you broke them in the past. Then write down the holds so you don't forget and practice them. After a good score, write down what you felt, saw, how you swung, note eye and gun hold everything you can possibly think of. The pros did when learning. No wonder they shoot so well.

Fig. 76

TRAPHOUSE SIZE ALTERS GUN HOLD POINTS
Fig. 77

   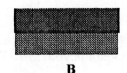   

A   **B**   **C**   **D**

Just when you thought it was safe to use your perfected gun hold on all traphouses suddenly targets are mysteriously lost.

E

Take a second look at the traphouse you are shooting and determine if your gun and eye hold will need to be adjusted.

Traphouse 'A' is short; 'B' is normal; 'C' is wide; 'D' is short and tall; 'E' is low and wide. There are two things to consider when determining your eye and gun hold points. **#1.** Are the targets exiting within the confines of the traphouse roof line? Or are they exiting to the left or right below the roof near the sidewalls? **#2** Will your eye and gun be placed too high or too low to upset swing geometry, balance and timing?

When in doubt, begin with your normal eye / gun hold. If you shoot low-gun then keep the gun on the far edge of the house. High-gun shooters keep the gun at the horizon level or slightly lower. Watch the targets carefully. If you feel it is a struggle to hit the targets then small adjustments should be made gradually. If your eye is not picking up the targets as it should be then again a minute eye / gun hold adjustment is required. Do not make drastic deviations as then your concentration will be side-tracked thinking about the house and holds instead of the targets, especially when you lose a target.

Examples: Trap 'A' and 'D' the gun and eye hold may need to be held off the house on post #1 and #5. Trap 'C' the holds will be shifted inward toward the center of the traphouse. 'D' the holds should be lowered for a low-gun shooter and raised for the high-gun shooter. 'E' the holds should be raised for low-gun shooter above the roof of the traphouse if swing dynamics become extremely awkward and troublesome. High-gun shooter can lower the hold a smidgen. Be aware of the feel of the timing. The best hold point is when the eye picks up the target quickly and the swing dynamics feel as close to normal as possible and the shooting zone is established.

 It is advantageous to write down your proven gun hold methods when encountering problematic traphouses for reference. Just as all good shooters keep a diary of what they did right, so should you. This comes in mighty handy after the winter layoff and will help you get back into the groove very quickly come springtime. If you think you will remember, remember that you will forget !

WHY ARE EYE & GUN HOLDS SO IMPORTANT ?

Each sentence you read, your brain takes a mini-vacation when it hits the end of the line. Each time your eye shifts focus the brain resets itself and there is a lapse of cognitive abilities. If the eye hold is too low, the target comet tail will force the eye to shift focus and direction numerous times and a jerky unsmooth swing will develop. The eye and gun hold designs an environment where the eye will shift focus the least to reduce visual shut down. By keeping your eye fixed steady and true, near or in the break zone, the central vision portion of the eye will not shift so you can see the target in peripheral vision exiting the house allowing the target to enter your centralized vision sector. Less eye movement = immediate target pick up and greater accuracy. The gun hold is adjusted so you can see the target leave the house and maintain "muscle memory" when executing the swing. If the hold is changed to the point it feels awkward to swing, the geometry has been upset. The size of the traphouse can affect your eye and gun holds, affecting visual target acquisition, swing geometry, and timing. Shoot a tall or low house and you'll see how it affects your ability to break targets, then formulate a written eye / gun hold plan to tackle these traphouses in the future. Keep in mind target speed and backgrounds may also affect the hold points. Trapshooting is not easy. It only becomes easier once you learn the inside secrets. Learning is the hard part. Make it a fun-filled adventure.

TIMING THE SHOT

Being at the right place at the right time is what timing is all about.

Timing is a complex subject and highly individualistic to each shooter. It's something you need to discover for yourself. When you do, it will be like finding a gold mine.

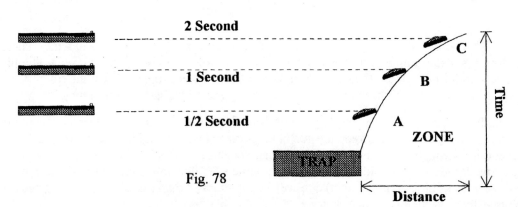

Fig. 78

Timing is a "feel" for when the target should break within the 'zone.' Zone 'A' is tight and close-in to the traphouse with target broken at 1/2 second. Zone 'B' is midway from trap to the target's maximum angle of arc. A good place to break targets if you can't shoot zone 'A'. Zone 'C' breaks the target in two seconds from when the target left the house. That's too long for reliable hits.

As you can see, distance increases as time is delayed. Which target zone would be more susceptible to wind and eddy currents? Zone 'C' will cause you trouble in the long run, so tighten up the zone to 'A' or 'B'. This is easily said, though difficult to do. Everything must change. Gun hold, eye hold, call tone and duration development, speed of swing, including foot and body stance. No easy feat.

Sometimes, you'll have to be flexible and shoot two of the zones due to mood swings and energy. If you are tired, shooting zone 'A' will only cause a disaster as your body reflexes won't be in tune for the required speed. So, shoot zone 'B' but never shoot all three zones... it won't work as the sight pictures and timing variations are too extreme, giving rise to many lost targets due to human error.

Timing is only half the story. When you try to shoot fast you'll notice many missed targets develop. The timing may be right, but the sight picture is wrong. The trick is to blend these two elements and only pull the trigger when the sight picture is right. If it is not right, the odds are very high you got a slow pull. When shooting zones, you'll know when the pull is bad based on your call timing. If the target is not out of the house at the "specific point of no return" you must learn to turn it down. If it exits on a fast pull, turn it down. Target exit must match call timing. You know when the target should exit. Don't you?

Inside of you, there is a time clock that tells when to shoot. This is important and it's great to have it, but without the sight picture you will pull the trigger based on time alone. What does this mean? It means you have to use the gun sights to align the bird / bead relationship, otherwise you are shooting with your eyes only. And there is swing timing to deal with on top of all this. I didn't say it was easy.

Fig. 79

BEWARE OF SQUAD TIMING

The rhythm of the squad can upset your setup, more so if the pace is fast. It forces you to hurry-up-and-shoot. When you feel this pressure you will likely do just that and lose targets. Maintain your own timing. You are generally allowed 10 seconds after the prior shooter has shot. Trim your setup to a comfortable 6 seconds from gun mount to time of call and retain this timing regardless of the squad is shooting slow or fast. Play your own game!

There are other influences you should be aware of that lie more on the subconscious level. **#1** Seeing other shooters' on the squad miss targets will give subtle internal instructions to your subconscious mind to miss the target. This is why you have seen everyone on the squad miss a target once one is missed like a chain-reaction. Watch them hit the ground and break then mentally. Tell yourself these lost targets are indeed dead, especially when the shooter before you misses a target. You must break this string of unbroken targets. Once you understand what is happening here it is easy to not be influenced by squad missed targets, but you must apply this extra effort or else you fall victim to the squad's influence.

#2 Where the squad members are breaking the targets will have a powerful influence upon your timing, often upsetting it. If targets are lost the squad will tend to slow down breaking targets with caution allowing the targets to escape the zone. You may find yourself doing the same... don't slow down! Keep breaking your targets in the zone. Be aware even the score caller can yell "*Lost*" so loud as to influence your mind to believe you too will lose a target!

#3 Distractions will unlock concentration. The situation becomes ever worse when you try to block them out of your mind. Usually, you can't and then the emotion of anger or disgust settles in only to ruin your own scores. This includes a bad puller to a sloppy squad shooter who has nothing better to do but to use poor reloads and fumble with gun jams and setting up so slowly it upsets the squad rhythm dramatically. Some shooters will do this intentionally so they turn in the highest score on the squad whereby eliminating some of the competition It's an old trick. For this reason many shooters build their own squads, especially the pros. But you need not rely on squad building once you learn not to allow distractions to upset you, for distractions will always exist. Perfect concentration is being "aware" of all around you, yet remain focused to the job at hand... breaking the target!

#4 Some shooters use psychological warfare to upset your day and your scores. They may or may not be squad members. Beware of subtle comments that can ruin your score even before you pick up your gun and step on the line. Here's a few: *"Jonny Hotshot just broke a 99 in handicap." "Trap three has a horrid background and windy to boot." "The puller on trap two is incredibly incompetent and doing it on purpose, too!"* You get the idea. These comments are often made by "mood destroyers" hoping you will succumb to bad fortune, sometimes unintentional. The game of trapshooting is 90% mind control, so beware of conversations that create mood alterations.

"There's only one way to beat a stronger and better opponent..use precision!"

The better trapshooters fully understand the complexities of the game. They realize there is a science to achievment. While each has arrived though individualized means the common thread still remains, *"Eliminate mistakes or they'll eliminate you!"*

Seeing the target is not enough. It is imperitive to also have a plan of action to complement good vision!

Good vision is important and quality shooting glasses with raised frames so as not to obstruct view are recommended. When you feel you are in a slump the first thing to check is your eyes. But the best eyes and the best glasses in the world will not help a shooter who fails to apply proper eye hold and fixation. You don't need crystal clear vision when you shoot precisely and have a well-grounded plan to break the targets. But you'll need sharp vision if you don't apply proper form and technique. Good vision alone is of no use without a reliable proven plan of action to break the target.

HANDICAP CHAMP

Frustration is the trapshooter's worst opponent.

The best way to handle discouragement is to recall the moments of past victory. You will have off days in which you'll swear you have forgotten how to shoot! This is normal and the harder you try to break free from the oppression of poor shooting the worse the score tumbles. Experience, over time, will enable you to quickly recognize the error to minimize the damage. However, perpetual frustration is a valid signal that something terrible is wrong in the setup and execution of the shot. The cause is often minor but overlooked or unrecognized. A total reevaluation is in order which you may want to consider employing the services of a shooting coach.

Winning always comes by surprise. You win by losing. Lose more; win more. It's all part and parcel of the game. A good attitude is a good remedy!

TIME IS OF THE ESSENSE

Timing is everything! This is not often discussed by trapshooters yet they win or lose depending on how well they timed the shots.

Observe the pros and you'll see just how precise their timing is. Every target is exploded within a time zone.

Professionals often shoot a tight zone which requires precise timing. They were not born with this talent, but they did strive hard to reach the goal. Practice your timing often. During practice, at least one trap session should be solely dedicated to "snap-shooting" the target as close to the house as possible. It's a long slow process, but your timing will increase as the years stroll onward. Like all things, difficulties lessen with determination and acclimation. The sooner you can break the target the better shooter you will be.

TRAPSHOOTING EXPENSE FORM

DATE									
	SUN	MON	TUE	WED	THUR	FRI	SAT	SUN	TOTAL
CITY FROM									
GUN CLUB TO									
BREAKFAST									
LUNCH									
DINNER									
TOTAL										A.
AIR/ CAR										B.
PRACTIC TRAP										C.
TAXI / BUS									
TIPS									
MILEAGE									
OTHER									
SUBTOTAL										D.
HOTEL										E.

AMMUNITION		F.
OTHER EXPENSES (Vehicle / Gun Repair, etc.)		G.
TOTAL SHOOTER EXPENSES = (A+B+C+D+E+F+G) ⇨		

TOURNAMENT ENTRY FEES

ATA / PITA									
EVENT FEE									
OPTIONS									
OTHER:									
SUBTOTAL										H.

TOTAL EXPENSES = (A+B+C+D+E+F+G+H) ⇨		I.

EXPLANATIONS

Remarks / Other Explanations: _____ .
Vehicle Odometer Miles; Start _____ . End _____ .

PROFIT / LOSS

SHOOTER _____ TOTAL WINNINGS ⇨ $ _____ J.
TAX S.O.C. #_____ TOTAL EXPENSES (From Line I) ⇨ $ _____ K.
PROFIT / LOSS (Subtract line K from J) ⇨ $ _____ L.

RIDING THE TRACK TO THE TARGET

Three Basic Target Angles

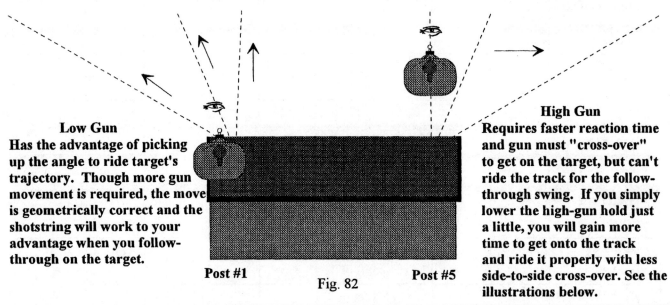

Low Gun
Has the advantage of picking up the angle to ride target's trajectory. Though more gun movement is required, the move is geometrically correct and the shotstring will work to your advantage when you follow-through on the target.

High Gun
Requires faster reaction time and gun must "cross-over" to get on the target, but can't ride the track for the follow-through swing. If you simply lower the high-gun hold just a little, you will gain more time to get onto the track and ride it properly with less side-to-side cross-over. See the illustrations below.

Post #1   Post #5

Fig. 82

HIGH GUN MOVES SIDEWAYS

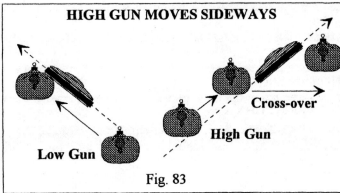

Cross-over

High Gun

Low Gun

Fig. 83

You can see the disadvantage of the high gun hold if you "cross-over." Many shooters do this, thinking a horizontal swing is all that's required, but it's a huge mistake. Now you have to be "dead-on" the target as the shotstring is flying at a right-angle. No wonder you're missing targets! Lower your gun hold, so you "can" ride the target's track. If your gun is held straight out at eye-level, it's too high! You lose time and ability to followthrough on the target flight path. See Fig.85. You'll flinch less & won't rush the target!

GEOMETRY WORKS AGAINST YOU

High gun hold is too high. Look at the cross-over required to catch the target's track. Very inaccurate means to hit targets. Don't do this.

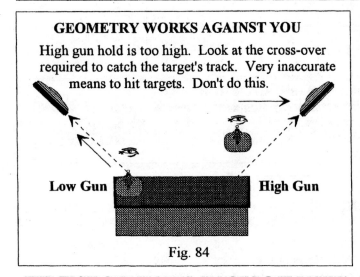

Low Gun   High Gun

Fig. 84

GEOMETRY WORKS FOR YOU

Drop gun muzzle angle and now you can ride the track. You still have a high hold. No major change in technique is needed. You just don't have to cross-over.

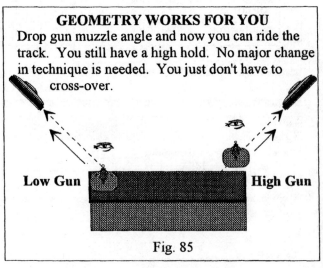

Low Gun   High Gun

Fig. 85

THE HIGH GUN WORKS, IF YOU DO IT RIGHT! MOST SHOOTERS DON'T FIND THE TRACK.

 # DOUBLE TRAP TIPS
DOUBLE TROUBLE -TWICE THE FUN!

TAKING THE FIRST SHOT

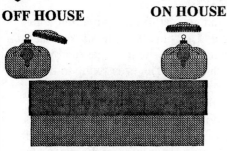

OFF HOUSE   **ON HOUSE**

Fig. 86

You <u>can</u> hold the gun off the house to take out the first target, but only if you shoot the angle target first. Hold the gun on the house when shooting the straight target first. Most shooters prefer the later, but some Olympic double-trap pros always shoot the angle target first. You may want to try it to see how it works for you. The point is, you get the hard target out of the way first, so you have 'plenty of time' to swing and hit the straight-away target. You need to be a bit reckless when shooting straight target, but less so when shooting the angle target first, as time is no longer critical as when shooting the angle target first.

GUN & EYE HOLD

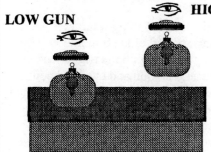

LOW GUN   **HIGH GUN**

Fig. 87

Time is very critical when shooting doubles. By holding a lower gun, even just 1" lower than normal, you can see the target sooner and shoot it quicker. The lower you hold the gun, the faster you can shoot, but keep your eye hold up high! This will prevent seeing a strong comet-tail streak and allow you to better see the bird/bead sight picture for an accurate first shot hit. Hold the gun where you 'know' the target will exit, so when you see the "flash" of the target you can pull the trigger quickly and get the eye moving immediately over to the second target. Get the eye moving, not the gun. The gun will follow the eye, but you must work on moving the eyes quickly and smoothly.

V-DIP SWING

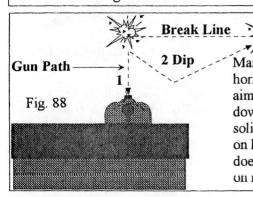

Break Line   **3 On Track**

2 Dip

Gun Path

1

Fig. 88

Many shooters attempt to cross-over the gun from left-to-right in a straight horizontal line to catch the second target, but this can create many errors in aim and missed second-angled targets. By simply dipping the gun one inch downward you can catch the true track of the target and rise up into it for a solid follow-through hit. The targets will still be broken as shown quite close on line, once your speed is perfected. The straight-line cross-over technique does work, but the V-dip method can be a lifesaver for those who just keep on missing those nasty second-angled targets. Veteran shooters will benefit.

EYE CONTROL

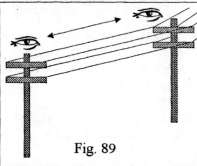

Fig. 89

This exercise is so simple it defies reason, but it works well. You have to learn how to switch your eyes from one target to the other very quickly and with dead-on focus. Try switching your eyes from one telephone pole to another--real telephone poles, that is. Doing this, you will begin to get the feel of controlling the speed of your eyes to locate and lock-on to targets. Now, remember to switch your eyes to the target without moving your gun. The eyes must switch first, lock-on, then the gun follows as the eye continues to track the target.

If you begin hitting the second targets, and then find yourself dropping the first targets, it's because you are rushing or getting too nervous to hit the first target. Be ready, but relaxed. Know that you do have plenty of time to hit the distancing second target if you practice moving your eyes away from the first target the moment you pull the trigger. Do not wait to see the target explode or sail away unburned, get the eyes moving and be smooth about it.

DOUBLE TRAP TIPS

DOUBLE TROUBLE -TWICE THE FUN!

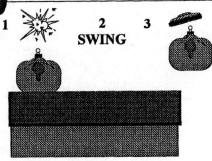

Fig. 90

1-2-3 TIMING

Number 1 time count begins not when you call for the target but when you pull the trigger on the first target. Don't make the mistake of starting the count when you call or it will force you to shoot too fast and you will drop too many targets being in a rush-mode. The eyes swing to the target on count #2 and the gun is allowed to follow naturally. Do not swing when your eyes are still looking for the second target! This timing sequence allows you to catch the second-angle target with little to no lead in the sight picture. Shoot the first straight-away target then 'glide' smoothly over to the second-angle target. Be precise on the second target.

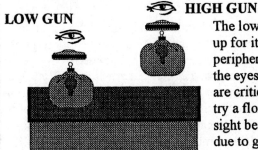

Fig. 91

FLASH SHOOTING

The low-gun need not rise by much to catch the first straight target if you set up for it properly, knowing where it will exit the lid of the trap house. Use peripheral vision to see the "flash" of the target then pull the trigger and get the eyes away quickly to the second-angle target. Gun and eye hold points are critical here to establish the timing and accuracy of the shot. You should try a florescent gun sight as they work great on double targets, since white sight beads tend to blend with the scene causing missed targets, and fade due to gun and target speed. See the advertisement in this book. Timing is way less important than accuracy, yet accuracy creates proper timing.

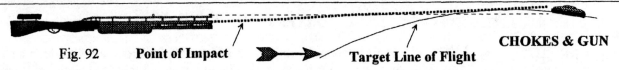

Fig. 92   **Point of Impact**   **Target Line of Flight**

CHOKES & GUN

Pro trapshooters know how important point of impact is, and more so with doubles. If you are shooting an autoloader at double targets, you are at a disadvantage because you only have one POI. The Over & Under gun certainly has an advantage of the lower barrel shooting a high POI to grab the fast-rising straight-away and the lower POI in the upper barrel shoots flatter to hit the shallow angled target. Is your doubles gun shooting properly? It must comply with the above barrel setting pertaining to POI. Pattern check to insure the lower barrel is higher in POI than the upper barrel. Are you taking your first shot with the lower barrel?

TECHNIQUE

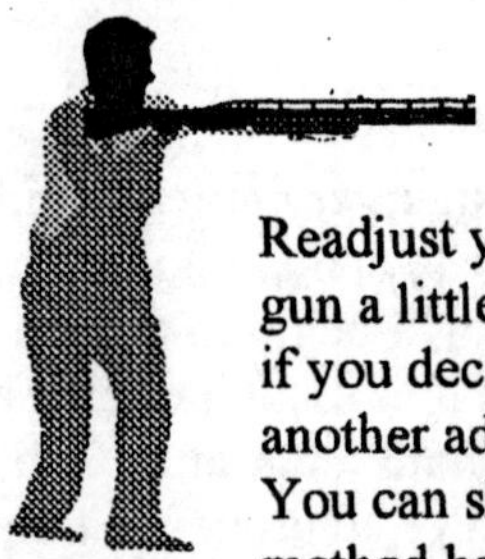

Don't use the same stance and shooting techniques as you do with single target trap. Revamp your mindset strongly that this is a 'different' game and set up accordingly. Readjust your gun and eye hold and timing and swing velocity to compensate. You can lean into the gun a little bit more in doubles than you should in singles as shown in the illustration at left. Also, if you decide to shoot the angle target first, do so on all posts -- do not switch-over. That is another advantage, since there is no confusion of which target should be shot first from post to post. You can shoot the straight or the angle target first, it is a personal preference, not a rule. Each method has advantages. Try both to see which one works best for you.

Fig. 93

If your double-rise (double-trap) scores are falling or not rising at all, it's time to change things. Doubles usually are shot after shooting single target events. You may fall into the habit of shooting the same way; same stance, same eye & gun holds, same timing, etc., when shooting double-trap. It's an entirely different game with its own set of rules. Change your technique. Take lessons to make the learning experience easier and more enjoyable.

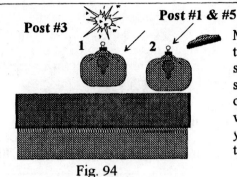

Post #3   Post #1 & #5

Fig. 94

HIGH-GUN HOLD TIP

Many shooters make this common error when shooting wide-angled targets; they hold the gun lower to the top of the trap house as shown in #2, at left. Hold the gun a bit higher and you'll be hitting more straight targets on post #3. When you are on post #1 and #5, do the opposite; hold the gun closer to the trap house. You would think it would be best to hold further away, due to the fast-angle targets, but if you hold too far away, you'll miss the target's line of flight too many times. Here's the rule:

Shallow Targets -- Hold Away. Wider Targets -- Hold Close.

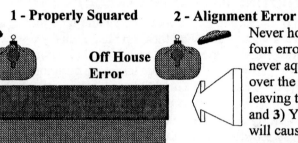

1 - Properly Squared   2 - Alignment Error

Off House
Error

Fig. 95

HIGH-GUN HOLD TIP

Never hold the gun off the house as shown in #2. You can see four errors here. 1) You will tend to hold the gun too high and never aquire the target's true flight path causing you too shoot over the top of the target, and 2) You will see the target late leaving the house, as the target will pass in front of the gun, and 3) You will see a blurry target with a horrific comet tail that will cause the eyes to lose focus. 4) You will rush the target with an unsmooth swing. Hold points are important! Number one is correct as the gun is square to the house and target.

GUN FIT TIPS

Fig. 96

If the gun's stock is too short it will increase recoil and the gun may swing too fast. If the stock is too long it will obstruct the swing. Both will create mounting errors and missed targets. Right-hand shoters with right master eye will need 'cast off' on the stock, cast on for left-handed shooters. Add more cast if you have wide shoulders. Keep in mind, the less cast you apply the better, more is not always best, but some casting will need to be done. Drop the comb so the eye floats at the proper height above the muzzle, this is critical. Unload gun, mount and look in mirror. The sight should sit at the bottom of your eye's pupil. The butt of the gun, when mounted, should contact the shoulder fully. If the butt or toe contacts first, fix this problem or it will cause you many lost targets. It is very important to see a stock fitter to make personal adjustments to gun fit. Doing it yourself usually does not work well at all.

SHOOTING THE WALL

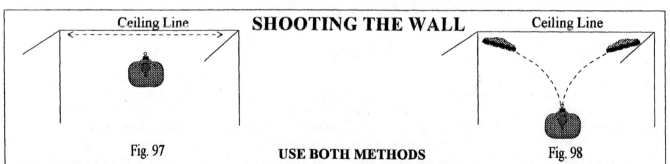

Ceiling Line   Ceiling Line

Fig. 97   **USE BOTH METHODS**   Fig. 98

When first learning to swing a shotgun to a target many instructors will tell you to mount the unloaded gun in a room and practice swinging along the top ceiling line. This is okay to begin with as in Fig. 97 but don't stop there. Practice following curved lines to the imaginary targets to increase gun control and learn advanced methods of tracking flying targets. Targets in flight are rising and arcing. Following a straight line, as in Fig. 97 gives you no practice lifting the gun upward to the rising target. Fig.98 illustrates a realistic practice method. You can apply string with tape to the wall in curved arcs and follow them to a paper target as shown in Fig. 98. Both methods solve different swing problems. Use both to resolve swing difficulties.

DOUBLE RISE TIP

Be careful not to swing the gun on a straight horizontal line as shown in #1 after breaking the first straight target. You can see the second angle target (#2) is rising, so the gun must rise ever so slightly even if your shoot timing is quite fast. Many shooters miss the second angle target by failing to compensate for this target rise. After shooting the straight target, dip the muzzle down just a tad and you can see how easy it will be to catch the proper line to target #2. See Fig. 84, 85, 88.

Fig. 98

'Double Rise' is the same as the ATA 'Double Trap' game in America. It is the doubles game played in the Olympics, along with Olympic Trap and Olympic Skeet.

Fig. 99 **TAIL CHIPPING - SHOOTING BEHIND THE TARGET**

If you find yourself chipping the tail end of the target, this is what you should look into as to the cause: **1)** Trigger setting is too tight or worn out defective allowing lock time to be mushy or slow. **2)** Trigger flinching may be the cause, as the trigger is set too light causing finger to spasm. **3)** Swing speed is too slow failing to keep up with the target. **4)** Eye flitter will cause eye to disengage target, so be smooth with the eyes when tracking target, do not rush or stab at the target, stay smooth. **5)** Gun hold too high causing shooter to see the target too late. Lower the gun hold an inch or two. **6)** Eye hold is too high seeing the target too late. Do lower eye hold point so you can see the target clearly and quickly when it exits the trap house. **7)** Comb cast is set wrong. **8)** Rib, choke or barrel is bent. **9)** Ammo velocity too slow. **10)** Slow or fast pull. **11)** Not being ready when you call for the target. **12)** Read *Trap Shooting Secrets* to resolve these problems.

Fig. 100 **SHOOTING OVER THE TARGET**

If you are shooting over the top of the target check these parameters: **1)** Head lifting. Apply proper cheek pressure at all times during the swing and when you pull the trigger. **2)** Point of impact set too high or comb height not correct. **3)** Not seeing the sight picture. Try using a fine-dot florescent gun sight to find sight pictures. See *Easy Hit* gun sight ad in this book or on our web site to order one. **4)** Gun does not fit, eye not properly aligned to rib. **5)** Eye freezing prior to pulling trigger can create a lurching motion to swing, similar to a flinch in effect, creating a stabbing motion to the swing. **6)** Shooting target too quickly can create a zone problem with a high point of impact gun. Shoot the target where you know your POI will break it. **7)** You could be shooting under the target, not over, so make sure opinions of others do not mislead you here. **8)** Swing is too fast, raise gun hold a bit more.

EYE CONTROL

Trigger control begins with eye control for it is the eyes that launch the trigger. The sight picture is King of the hill here. Once your sight picture is nailed down for each post and for each angled target, which is easy to do over a short period of time, we wonder why we miss targets. Once the gun is fitted, stance, choke, ammo and swing dynamics is ironed out, beyond this, it's all in the eyes! Learn to control your eye focusing and eye movements. Learn about eye prefocus technique, eye flitter. Looking too hard can tighten eye muscles. Looking too softly will create a lazy swing and a poor sight picture. Most of us move our eyes fast from place to place in this fast-pace world we live in. Practice moving the eyes slowly so the view flows seemlessly like a movie without any jittering or stalling. Apply this technique to flying targets. You can watch targets and practice these eye flowing techniques anytime, especially before you shoot a tournament event. Do this and you will certainly hit more targets dead-on and improve your game.

Fig. 101

MIND CONTROL

Be careful to check your thoughts. They are creative and will produce exactly what you believe will happen. If you entertain thoughts of doubt, lack of ability, poor performance, missing targets, etc., guess what will happen? You will perform as you feared. There comes a time each shooter must step over the line from amateur to professional. It begins with a thought, a vision, a determination to make it happen. Maybe you don't want to be a pro, but you can think like one to raise your shooting performance to higher levels. Believe in yourself as being a good shooter and wipe out all negative thoughts to the contrary. Cancel them with positive statements, positive thoughts. You will begin to see great improvement in your scores. This prophesy fulfills itself the more you practice mind control.

Fig. 102

TOP AND BOTTOM TARGET BREAKS   Fig. 103

Fig. 13-7

1 When you find yourself breaking the target from the top as showen in #1, check for these errors: Head-lift, swing dynamic and stance error causing muzzle rise, choke pattern too open creating aiming inconsistencies, gun hold point too high seeing target late leaving the house and not catching the true flight line of the target. Point of impact set too high, ammo not matched for gun, rushing.

2 When you find yourself breaking the target from the bottom as shown in #2, check for these errors: Cheek to comb pressure too intense, timing error, shooting too fast, point of impact not matching zone and shooting flat, eye misaligned on rib; should be centered. Some shooters need to have eye set a tad off center from rib. Ammo velocity too slow lacking power to sustain straight flight of shot.

---

1 - Straight Target   **2 - Angled Target**

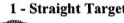  

DOUBLE TRAP - GUN HOLD

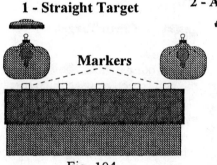

Markers

Fig. 104

When shooting double-rise targets it is important to set your gun hold exactly where the straight-away target exits the house so the target can rise up into your muzzle's line of sight. If the house has no markers, such as in ATA trap, implant them into your mind and set up from these points. This way you do not need to use any background objects as aiming reference points. This applies when taking the straight target first. Taking the angled target first, set up for the angle, offset gun from the marker, just a little.

DOUBLE TRAP TIPS

CHOKES: There are no absolute rules. Some Olympic DT shooters use a full choke on each barrel of the double gun, while some use more open chokes, even cylinder chokes, for the first shot on double trap. Choke is only half the story, the ammo you use is of prime consideration. Custom made chokes to perfect the pattern is the winner's edge. Use the proper ammo for your gun. Experimentation is required. Many top-gun shooters use an improved-modifed or light-full choke for the first shot and, use a full or extra-full choke for the second shot.

SHOT SIZE: Some Olympic DT shooters will use #8 shot for the first target and 7 1/2 for the second. Some use 7 1/2 for both barrel shots. Experimentation required.

ANGLE SELECTION: Most shooters take the straight target first, especially in ATA trapshooting, but a few top-guns always take the angled target first on each post, to avoid confusion from switching target selection on posts 4 and 5. If you do prefer to use this method, and are right-handed, always take the left bird first on all posts. If your are left-handed, shoot the right bird. If your double rise scores are just flat and will not rise, then consider taking lessons or switch technique. You won't know if it is right for you if you never try!

Fig. 105

SWING SPEED CONTROL

Low Gun

High Gun

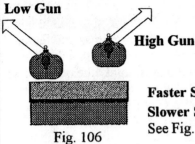

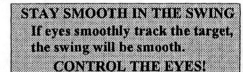

STAY SMOOTH IN THE SWING
If eyes smoothly track the target,
the swing will be smooth.
CONTROL THE EYES!

Faster Swing: Lower the gun hold, raise eye hold to increase swing speed.
Slower Swing: Raise the gun hold, lower eye hold to decrease swing speed.
See Fig. 23, 24, 38, 76, 77 for gun and eye hold advice.

Fig. 106

FINDING THE TARGET - <u>LOW-GUN</u> SHOOTER

Comet Tail & Blurred Target

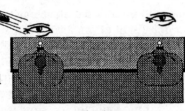

Clean Target

Holding the gun low is fine, but
holding the eye too low, as shown, will
produce a blurred target with long comet
tails. This will cause eye-flitter and ruin
a smooth move to the target. In fact, it will
be very difficult to pick up the true flight
line of the target creating an erratic swing.

Fig. 107

By simply raising your eye hold, you
can elliminate the comet tails. The
target will appear to travel slower.
You won't be tempted to rush the shot.
You'll see the target clearly and be in
control to aquire the flight line.

FINDING THE TARGET - <u>HIGH-GUN</u> SHOOTER   Fig. 108

Comet Tail & Blurred Target

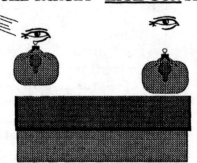

Clean Target

High gun shooters tend to hold the eye
too close to the gun's rib. This will cause
a blurred target image with strong comet
tail effects. The eye will flitter seeking
the target, creating a stabbing motion to
the swing. The target flight path is often
lost and the target missed.

Raise your eye hold above the rib of
the gun so you can see the target with
clarity. Experiment to find the proper
eye seperation for each post. Once
found, your scores and consistency
will increase. Lower gun hold a bit.

Wrong - Shooter Looking Down

BACK-SIGHTING

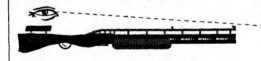

Here the eye focus is solid, but is too tight
on the gun's sight bead. The eye hold is
too low. This will create a tendency to
look backward to the gun sight, causing
muzzle to freeze, missing the target. Bird
and bead alignment is hard to see. The eye
is out of phase with the gun.

Fig. 109

Here the central eye focus is solid on the target. Peripheral vision
(top & bottom lines) are narrow and close to the target and can still see the gun's sight bead.

Correct

There is less tendency to look back at the sight, so the
gun will swing without interruption. Train your
eye so it can see both the target and the sight at the
same time, all of the time. The eye's central focus
will be strong on the target constantly, while peripheral vision takes in the entire picture seeing target speed, angle,
flight deviations, etc. Notice the eye hold is high and not looking downward or straight along the rib, but is raised
upward. A very powerful shooting technique.

Fig. 110

20 REMINDERS TO IMPROVE YOUR GAME
Use This List Before You Shoot In A Competitive Event

1 Be Positive - Do not think negetive. Expect to win. You will shoot better even if you don't win.

2 Firm Stance - Remind yourself to stand on line with a firm, yet flexible shooting stance.

3 Solid Gun Mount - Shoulder the gun firmly and make sure to feel heel and cheek pressure.

4 Gun & Eye Hold - Know where to hold gun and eye before you call for the target.

5 Authority - Call for the target with internal power and authority. Do not move gun or eyes.

6 Look For Target - Expect to see target. Do not react hastily. Respond smoothly.

7 Aggression - Swing with energy, but do not push the muzzle. Do not be lazy. Go get it!

8 Eye Tracking - Keep eye nailed down solidly on the target. Don't let your eyes slip off the target.

9 Sight Picture - See sight picture before you pull trigger. Let the eyes trigger the trigger, not timing.

10 Rest - Wind down adrenelin after you shoot. Turn up concentration when it is your turn to shoot.

 KEEP YOUR HEAD DOWN!

Fig. 112

1 Be a bit reckless on the first straight-away target. Set up eye and gun hold so you can shoot quickly.

2 Move eyes smoothly, yet quickly to the second angled-target. Don't wait to see if first target is broken.

3 Employ a method to insure you can take the second angled-target with a followthrough swing.

4 Do Not swing the gun to the target until the eyes have locked-on to the target.

5 Be Smooth in your swing to the second angled-target. If eyes are tracking smoothly, so will the gun.

6 Insure your eye and sight picture tells you when to pull the trigger, not timing.

7 Make Sure you do not shoot behind the target. Get your eyes on the leading edge of the target.

8 IF you are shooting over or under the target, adjust stance and gun hold, so swing dynamics will be correct.

9 Be Confident even if you miss a target or two. Maintain positive mind pressure at all times.

10 Missing targets? Slow down and smooth out! You are shooting too fast and reckless. Relax.

DOUBLE TRAP

SHOOTING THE WALL - PRACTICE (unloaded gun)

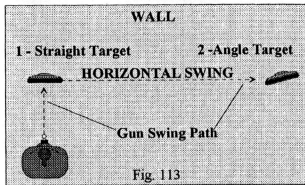

Fig. 113

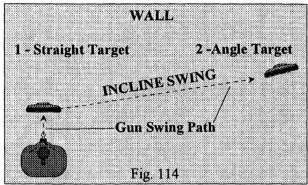

Fig. 114

Fig. 113 reveals a low gun hold for the first straightaway target. The muzzle must rise upward to take the shot, then swing on a straight horizontal line to the second-angled target. Use this to practice swinging the gun rapidly from target-to-target. Fig. 114 reveals a higher gun hold where you can spot or flash shoot the first straight target, then swing upward on an inclined angle to the second-angled target. Use this method to practice swinging the gun slowly, so you can learn to aquire the angle and track the target.

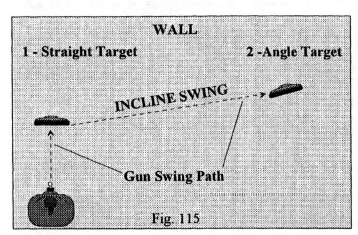

Fig. 115

Fig. 115 reveals a combination of the above; a low gun hold against a rising second-angled target. Use this practice technique to develop a swing to the first straightaway target and, to swing to the second target. You'll need this lesson when the targets are subjected to wind. You may employ the three examples given here to incorporate into your technique. As you can see, there are some variations here you can use as a plan, as part of your formula of shooting double-rise targets. The point here is to see the variations and then try them to see what works best for you.

SHOOT THE CALENDAR (unloaded gun) 10-Foot Distance

Fig.116 reveals a little known secret to manage flinching and developing precise trigger and eye control. Start with a gun hold below the calendar, call for target and swing slowly to a number, pull the trigger. Notice when you do pull the trigger how the gun lurches or even stops cold! This method will fine-tune your nervous system, develop eye focus and lock-on control.

Try to smooth out all jittering movement. Over time, you will! Hold the gun with forearm grip closer or further away to find the smoothest swing.

Also see Fig. 104 and 105

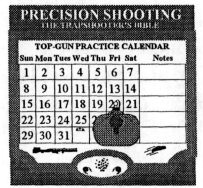

Fig. 116

NOTES

"FREE TRIAL OFFER"

Clay Shooting Magazine

Send For Your
FREE ISSUE

Of The Best All-Around Shotgunning Magazine!

- **Sporting Clays Action**
- **Trapshooting How-To's**
- **Skeet Shooting**
- **Shotshell Reloading**
- **Shotgun Patterning**
- **Shotshell Evaluation**
- **Waterfowl/Upland Hunting**

SECOND PLACE IS ONLY THE <u>FIRST</u> LOSER!

You shoot to win, that's why you compet and why you love trapshooting, but it sure isn't fun losing. Fact is, it can be quite depressing to see your name scratched from the option pay-out list making everyone else a tad bit richer.

Okay, you had a bad day. But how many more *bad days* are still to come? Wouldn't you like to turn that situation around and insure you take home *your* share of purse money and prizes?

Trap Shooting Secrets will help you do just that by polishing you into a finely-tuned competitor, increasing your scores, and hammering those targets that now slip into the horizon.

You're a good shooter -- you wouldn't be reading this if you weren't -- but too many targets slipped away today, just like yesterday, last month... and last year too. Something is wrong, and you can't seem to identify the problem to resolve the difficulty. The same mistakes keep repeating themselves and targets are *"Lost."*

SEEING TARGET ANGLES
A simple test verifying targets do not travel in straight lines, but indeed do traverse definitive arcs.

Targets 'bend' away causing many low scores.
Fig. 3-3

WHY DID YOU MISS THOSE TARGETS?

Not by mistake, but through miscalculation of target angle and the target *bending* away from shotstring. Problem is, you'll keep on missing targets like a <u>bad habit</u>! Sound familiar? Once you understand target angularity and behavior... it'll be hard to miss! Why? *Trap Shooting Secrets* will tighten-up your sight picture to a micron. You'll be shooting with fine-tuned accurate precision, smokeballing targets dead-on. And if you do miss, you'll likely rip a piece off the target so you won't be hearing *"Lost"* ringing in your ears. Figure 3-3 reveals a hidden secret of how targets *bend*. Did targets bend away from you today? They sure did, but do you know how to hit them?

You will as Trap Shooting Secrets shows you how easy it really can be to hit *more* targets *consistently*!

KNOWING WHERE TO LOOK AT A TARGET IS CRITICAL FOR HIGH SCORES!

If you're just looking at a target and chasing it down with the muzzle you will *always* keep missing. Hit 'n' miss days will never end. There are 4 specific zones and you must know *when* to use each 'zone', *how* to see the zone in the sight picture, and *why* reading the zone is so important for proper target/shotstring alignment. Precision shooting requires precise aim!

Left Leading Edge   Right Leading Edge
Top
Middle→
Bottom

Where would you point at a quarter-left target?

Nevada residents add 7 1/2% sales tax **YOU CAN RAISE YOUR SCORES !**   Dealer Inquiries Welcome

Everyone drops a target now and then, even professionals do, but maybe you're dropping too many, which is keeping you out of the money. One thing *Trap Shooting Secrets* will do for you is develop precision shooting, especially in handicap events, because this book is focused on mid/long yardage shooting. The bottom line is your scores will increase when you <u>stop missing</u> those flying beasts that slip and slide far into the horizon all too often. Those are the 'hard' targets and you'll learn how to not let them escape. Ask for a copy of *Trapshooting Secrets* at any major bookstore or write to: James Russell, 780 Diogene Drive, Reno, NV 98512 Send $34.95 + $4 Shipping.

"SHOOTING IS FUN... ESPECIALLY WHEN YOU WIN!" ORDER YOUR COPY... TODAY!

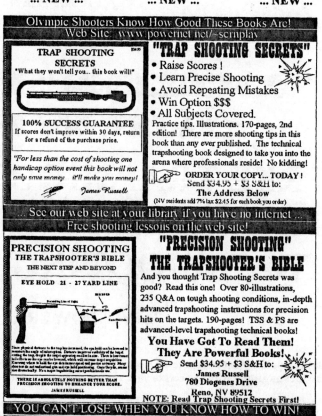

TESTIMONIAL EDORSEMENTS

DARO HANDY
Top Gun Hall of Fame Shooter

There is a lot of constructive information in Trap Shooting Secrets and Precision Shooting - The Trapshooter's Bible. The concepts in these two books are strongly presented, understandable and easily applied. If you would like to step into the world where professional trapshooter's reside, these books can reveal valuable technical information to improve your shooting. And, in conjunction with a qualified shooting instructor, these two books should give the trapshooter a high measure of success. *Daro Handy.*

LUCA SCRIBANI ROSSI
Olympic Medallist - Twice World Champion

I strongly recommend shotgun competition shooters to read both, Trap Shooting Secrets, and Precision Shooting The Trapshooter's Bible. If you read these books you simply can 't go wrong. Just follow the steps outlined and you'll leap ahead in the rankings of any competition you'll attend. That's my recommendation.
Luca Scribani Rossi.

PHIL KINER
ATA All-American Shooter

I have reviewed both of James Russell's new trapshooting books and I have found them to be full of useful trapshooting tips. These books will be an excellent edition to every trapshooter's library. *Phil Kiner.*

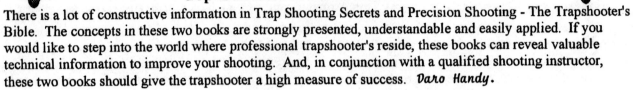

DOZEN'S MORE ON OUR WEB SITE !

FREE TRAPSHOOTING LESSONS ON THE WEB SITE --HUNDREDS OF TRAP SHOOTING TIPS AND ADVICE

WWW.POWERNET.NET/~SCRNPLAY

No computer or Internet access? No problem. Go to your public library or college and they will connect you. Many trap shooting articles await you with answers to your shooting questions, how to select a trap gun, product reviews and much more!.

<u>Note</u>: If the web site address fails to work, use a search engine and type in the word; trapshooting and look for JR Publishing or James Russell Publishing. We are linked on most all the major trapshooting site link pages. You'll find us!

NEW PRODUCTS

EASY HIT SHOTGUN SIGHT

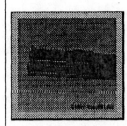

Put the laser red dot on the target and the job is done! Unlike other fiber optic shotgun sights, only Easy Hit's 2.5 m.m. small size ruby red dot is easily seen, but will not distract or pull your eye away from the target! Instantly learn why you hit or missed a target. The sight picture is that crisp and clean with high-resolution. You'll save money on practice fees, ammo and shoot higher consistant scores. It's the 1-minute miracle shotgun shooters must have! Once you try this sight you'll be amazed at just how fast your scores will rise. You will see the sight picture perfectly for dead-center target hits. If it flies, this gun sight will dustball it! Made of high-quality aircraft aluminum. Easy to install and use. You truly will be satisfied once you see how good this gun sight really works!

LSR OLYMPIC GRADE SHOOTING GLASSES

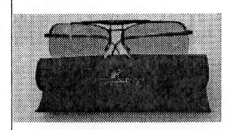

Superior quality for all sporting disciplines. Comes with three lenses, frames and hard case all for only $100. Lens colors: purple, rose and clear. Frames are bridge adjustable to center the lens when shooting. Flexible cable temples for comfort and secure grip. Absolutely designed for clay target shooting and are used by Olympic professionals. Prescription lenses also available at extra cost, ask for a prescription form and we'll mail it to you. These are professional shooting glasses. When you are ready to see targets with true clarity, order these fine shooting glasses today! After all, you can't hit what you can't see!

MPRO-7 GUN CLEAN & LUBE

The best cleaner & lube you can buy. No odors or fumes! Extremely powerful for gun cleaning and the lube is simply quite unbelievable -- even a tight gun will glide smoothly! Used by the military on all cannon and machine guns, missiles, etc. It truly is the ultimate. Lasts much longer than other products by far. Try it!

CHAMPIONSHIP TRAPSHOOTING

Now on cassette tape! Shoot with consistency. Stop forgetting what you have learned in the Trap Shooting Secrets book. Imbed the techniques into your mind. Reduce nervousness and increase concentration and your scores! Phase-1 is a two-tape set.

ORDER FORM

Item   Quantity

Easy Hit Gun Sight $38 _____
MPro-7 Gun Cleaner $19.95 _____
MPro-7 Gun Oil: $10 _____
LSR Olympic Shooting Glasses $100_____
Championship Trapshooting Phase-1 $34.95 _____

Add $4 shipping/handling (or Priority rate $6) per item ordered. Nevada Residents add 7.25% sales tax.

Your Name:_____
Address:_____
City:_____
State/Prov:_____
ZIP/Postal Code:_____
Phone:_____
Special Instructions:_____

MAIL TO:

**JAMES RUSSELL
780 DIOGENES DRIVE
RENO, NV 89512**

You can also order from our company address as listed on the title page.

Nevada Residents add 7 1/4% sales tax. Allow 3 to 4 weeks shipping. Add $6 per item for faster Priority Mail service. Phone: 775-348-8711 No Credit Card Orders - Mail in orders only. Photocopy this page if you wish, then fill in and mail your order. Or visit our web site: www.powernet.net/~scrnplay and print the order form directly.

Printed in the USA by

MORRIS PUBLISHING

3212 East Highway 30 • Kearney, NE 68847 • 1-800-650-7888

Printed in the United Kingdom
by Lightning Source UK Ltd.
9853400001B/25